GLOBAL ENVIRONMENTAL POLITICS

GLOBAL ENVIRONMENTAL POLITICS

THE TRANSFORMATIVE ROLE OF EMERGING ECONOMIES

JOHANNES URPELAINEN

Columbia University Press
New York

Columbia University Press
Publishers Since 1893
New York   Chichester, West Sussex
cup.columbia.edu
Copyright © 2022 Columbia University Press

Library of Congress Cataloging-in-Publication Data
Names: Urpelainen, Johannes, author.
Title: Global environmental politics : the transformative role of emerging
economies / Johannes Urpelainen.
Description: New York : Columbia University Press, [2022] |
Includes bibliographical references and index.
Identifiers: LCCN 2021051820 (print) | LCCN 2021051821 (ebook) |
ISBN 9780231200769 (hardback) | ISBN 9780231200776 (trade paperback) |
ISBN 9780231553773 (ebook)
Subjects: LCSH: Environmental policy—International cooperation. |
Economic development. | Energy policy. | Climatic changes.
Classification: LCC GE170 .U75 2022 (print) | LCC GE170 (ebook) |
DDC 333.72—dc23/eng/20220118
LC record available at https://lccn.loc.gov/2021051820
LC ebook record available at https://lccn.loc.gov/2021051821

Cover design: Milenda Nan Ok Lee
Cover photo: Paulose NK / Shutterstock.com

CONTENTS

ABBREVIATIONS

BASIC	Brazil, South Africa, India, China
CBD	Convention on Biological Diversity
CCD	Convention to Combat Desertification
CCM	Chama Cha Mapinduzi
CDM	Clean Development Mechanism
CERs	certified emission reductions
CFC	chlorofluorocarbon
CITES	Convention on International Trade in Endangered Species
COP	Conference of Parties
CORSIA	Carbon Offsetting and Reduction Scheme for International Aviation
CTE	Committee on Trade and Environment
DETER	Detection of Deforestation in Real Time
EPA	Environmental Protection Agency
EPL	environmental protection law
FSC	Forest Stewardship Council
GDP	gross domestic product
GEF	Global Environment Facility
GMOs	genetically modified organisms
HFC	hydrofluorocarbon
IAS	Indian Administrative Service

ICAO	International Civil Aviation Organization
IFF	Intergovernmental Forum on Forests
INDC	Intended Nationally Determined Contribution
IPCC	Intergovernmental Panel on Climate Change
IPF	Intergovernmental Panel on Forests
LRTAP	Convention on Long-Range Transboundary Air Pollution
MARPOL	International Convention for the Prevention of Pollution from Ships
MDGs	Millennium Development Goals
NIEO	New International Economic Order
NGOs	nongovernmental organizations
OECD	Organisation for Economic Co-operation and Development
OPEC	Organization of the Petroleum Exporting Countries
PIC	prior informed consent
REACH	Registration, Evaluation, Authorisation, and Restriction of Chemicals
REDD	reducing emissions from deforestation and forest degradation
SDGs	Sustainable Development Goals
UNCED	United Nations Conference on Environment and Development
UNCTAD	United Nations Conference on Trade and Development
UNEP	United Nations Environment Programme
UNFCCC	United Nations Framework Convention on Climate Change
UNFF	United Nations Forum on Forests
WTO	World Trade Organization

GLOBAL ENVIRONMENTAL POLITICS

INTRODUCTION

I n December 2009 world leaders gathered in Copenhagen to form a global climate treaty. At the negotiations, any lingering doubts about China's importance to the politics of climate change disappeared. One of the more troubling features of the summit was that the final text, the Copenhagen Accord, did not even mention a shared global ambition for emissions reductions. When journalists gathered to ask Lars-Erik Liljelund, the Swedish climate ambassador, why the goal of an 80 percent global emission reduction by 2050 had disappeared, he said: "China don't like numbers."[1]

Since the Copenhagen summit, however, China's position on global warming has changed markedly. In September 2015 Presidents Barack Obama and Xi Jinping announced a U.S.-China Joint Presidential Statement on Climate Change, outlining a "common vision for the Paris climate agreement" supported by domestic policy announcements, and even new commitments on climate change.[2] China has also received a lot of positive attention for its massive investments in renewable electricity generation. In 2019, the year before the COVID-19 pandemic, renewable power generation capacity grew by 9.5 percent to 750 gigawatts.[3] And in October 2020 China announced that it aspires to become carbon neutral by 2060.

While the world observes China's new policies with a curious combination of admiration, awe, envy, and skepticism, the future and fate of the global climate are increasingly being decided elsewhere. According to the International Energy Agency's *India Energy Outlook* (2021), for example, current policies would leave India's energy demand in 2040 about 70 percent above the year 2019, despite the economic hardship caused by COVID-19 in 2020–2021.[4] Based on these numbers, India is to play a pivotal role in the future of the global climate. While China has already completed its industrial transformation, India is still at the early stages of the process. India's massive and growing population, which will soon be larger than China's, also guarantees that sustained economic growth will translate into large increases in the demand for energy and natural resources. These increases, in turn, will have massive effects on the global environment. India will play a decisive role in shaping planetary conditions, depending on whether it meets its energy and resource demands through sustainable (e.g., wind and solar power) or unsustainable (e.g., coal) means.

And it's not just India. In 2019 over a billion people lived in sub-Saharan Africa.[5] The consumption of energy and natural resources per capita remains low in this region, but it will skyrocket unless these countries fail to achieve their aspirations of economic development. If India reaches a high level of economic development in the next three decades, then sub-Saharan Africa will be the next economic frontier. Each such transition means that billions of people consume much more energy and many more resources today. Unless these countries manage to replace coal with cleaner alternatives, such as renewables like wind and solar power, the consequences for the global climate are serious. In global environmental politics, the twenty-first century is the century of previously poor countries that are undergoing an economic transformation and thus enjoy rapid economic growth—the century of emerging economies.

Climate change is not the only way in which emerging economies are shaping the future of life on planet Earth. Consider the rampant deforestation from the world's ravenous hunger for palm oil—the world's most popular vegetable oil, used not only in cooking and foodstuffs but also in products such as shampoo. The production of palm oil in Malaysia and Indonesia is a major driver of rainforest destruction,[6] and environmental groups frequently complain about the unsustainable land use practices of the industry.[7] By 2016 India had already become the second largest consumer of palm oil, with an annual consumption of 10.3 million tons—behind only Indonesia (11.7 million tons).[8]

Or, take mercury. When the international community finished the negotiations on the Minamata Convention on Mercury in October 2013, it had to grapple with the fact that 40 percent of global mercury emissions came from East and Southeast Asia, while sub-Saharan Africa was responsible for 16 percent, Latin America for 13 percent, and South Asia for 8 percent.[9] In fact, emissions from North America and Europe, though historically important, were almost negligible in the global picture by that time. Again, economic activity in emerging economies and least developed countries currently generates a lion's share of the global problem. The geographic distribution of mercury emissions reflects the corresponding distributions of industrial and natural resource extraction activity, and these activities are increasingly concentrated outside the industrialized West and East Asia.

The common thread running across these seemingly unrelated cases is the combination of explosive economic and population growth. The global population grew from four to seven billion between 1974 and 2012, and most of this growth was found in initially poor Asian countries. Driven by China's phenomenal economic growth after the economic reforms in 1978, the world's real GDP per capita increased from U.S. $3,729 to $7,614 between 1978 and 2008.[10] At the same time, China's GDP per capita increased eightfold and India's fourfold. Africa saw a 50 percent growth in real GDP per capita between 1970 and 2008.

To see how momentous this ongoing shift is, consider that by 2030, there will be 700 million more air conditioners in the world.[11] Because cooling is very energy-intensive, Americans today use 5 percent of their electricity for air conditioning—and Americans consume a lot of electricity per capita when compared to most countries. As countries around the world install close to a billion new air conditioners, global electricity demand in the residential sector is bound to grow rapidly, even after adjusting for efficiency improvements. If this electricity demand is met by clean sources, such as renewable electricity, then the impact on the global environment may be limited. But if the electricity demand is met by fossil fuels, the world is in for a dramatic expansion of carbon dioxide emissions.

All this goes to show that we now live in a world of emerging economies, and this structural shift in international political economy puts immense pressure on the global environment. Regions such as South Asia and sub-Saharan Africa will soon be the main engines of global economic growth. Populations in these areas demand energy and natural resources for industrial activity, services, and household conveniences. As governments strive to meet these demands, the potential for resource depletion and pollution grows. These countries now have more "power to destroy" than ever before,[12] and they can threaten other countries with environmental deterioration. In 2019 China's greenhouse gas emissions exceeded those of all OECD countries taken together, while India's emissions exceeded those of the European Union.[13]

In the past, the global South—or the "Third World," as these countries were called during and after the Cold War—played a different role.[14] In the twentieth century the economic importance of countries outside the capitalist West and the socialist Soviet bloc was negligible, with the exception of natural resources such as oil, natural gas, fisheries, and rainforests. Back then, these emerging economies did not yet consume enough energy and resources to shape global environmental outcomes across the board. They had power to destroy, and therefore a major role to play in debates such as population control, deforestation, and fisheries. But they were marginalized in other negotiations, such as ozone depletion and climate change, because their energy and resource consumption was still quite limited.

The ongoing transformation of the world economy shapes global environmental politics, and this book offers an analytical framework and an empirical assessment of global environmental politics in a world of emerging economies. In this world, the number of countries pivotal to avoiding global environmental destruction is higher than ever before. These countries' growing energy and resource consumption means they have the power to destroy, yet they are also very different from the industrialized nations. For one, their governments' environmental concern mostly remains relatively weak, despite growing ecological mobilization. More important, their institutional capacity to formulate effective environmental and energy policy is constrained.

This interaction among (1) growing power to destroy through energy and resource consumption, (2) still relatively weak environmental preferences, and (3) a lack of institutional capacity is key to understanding the transformation of global environmental politics.

GLOBAL ENVIRONMENTAL POLITICS: A PRIMER

When, why, and how can governments of the world cooperate to mitigate global environmental deterioration? Environmental problems are *international* when an activity within one country harms ecosystems and people in other countries. They become *global* when environmentally destructive activity harms many countries across the world.[15] Put simply, global environmental politics is the messy business of trying to control such global, cross-country environmental destruction. Because the source and victim of the destruction do not fall under one sovereign jurisdiction, international negotiations between governments are often required to mitigate the problem. Coming to an agreement is difficult for many reasons, but two of them are fundamental.

One is distributional conflict: governments that contribute significantly to the problem but suffer only little from it want to avoid regulations, while countries that suffer heavily from the problem but do not contribute to it prefer strict regulations.[16] Governments' preferences for different negotiation outcomes vary widely, and finding a mutually acceptable compromise—a package that enough governments can accept for a treaty to form—is the cornerstone of "environmental diplomacy."[17] As any negotiator knows, the finding of such a compromise is not a simple process of aggregating preferences. Governments negotiate treaties under domestic constraints,[18] strategically misrepresent their preferences to gain concessions,[19] and make decisions under institutional rules that may complicate bargaining.[20]

The other main problem is enforcement: in the "anarchic" international system,[21] there is no world government that can force parties to an agreement to comply with it—or, as Barrett[22] would add, even remain parties to it. International environmental cooperation requires that members of a treaty adjust their behavior (policies, programs, and so on) in a way that benefits *others*. Every member of a treaty facing such requirements faces the temptation to free ride by contributing a little less than it should, in the hope that it can benefit from the contributions of others without paying the cost. In a well-organized domestic society, legally binding contracts can often minimize such temptations because willful defections result in a punishment, such as a fine. In international relations, however, contracts—treaties, really—are difficult to enforce: "There is no common government to enforce rules, and by the standards of domestic society, international institutions are weak. Cheating and deception are endemic."[23]

Given the combination of distributional conflict and enforcement, any useful government-centric model of global environmental politics must consider both the negotiation and implementation of treaties. It is a general feature of international cooperation that governments first bargain over the terms of the contract and then proceed to implement the treaty if the bargaining succeeds.[24] The expectation of enforcement shapes the bargaining interactions, and the bargaining outcome sets the stage for enforcement and compliance. These problems and their interaction are clearly seen in global environmental politics, as governments bargain over burden-sharing and then try to enforce compliance with the treaty.

Today, the most famous and widely discussed global environmental problem is climate change. While I do not want to reduce the diverse field of global environmental politics into one problem, climate change nicely illustrates the basic themes of distributional conflict and enforcement. The basic premise is simple: economic activity, from deforestation to burning coal for electricity generation, generates greenhouse gases that warm the planet and thus generate problems such as sea-level rise and extreme weather events. The geographic location of emissions sources is irrelevant, however, as greenhouse gases spread into the entire atmosphere and affect everyone, from Iceland to Chile to Myanmar. When the government of a country decides to invest in coal—the most carbon-intensive fossil fuel—it understands that others bear much of the environmental cost. American households do not pay the price when floods caused by climate change threaten livelihoods in Bangladesh.

Given this "problem structure,"[25] distributional conflict and enforcement problems ensue. Some countries, such as the United States, generate a lot of greenhouse gas emissions. Others, such as Mali, generate virtually none. Some countries, such as Bangladesh, face near-existential threats from climate change. Others, such as Canada, are much less vulnerable and may even gain from a little warming because of enhanced agricultural productivity. Yet others, such as Saudi Arabia, are economically almost completely dependent on exports of fossil fuels. Their economic systems cannot survive without fundamental changes if large countries move away from fossil fuels. When the governments of these different countries negotiate, they have very different preferences for outcomes: they are more worried about emissions reductions than they are worried about climate change itself. Government preferences, in turn, reflect domestic distributional conflict between interest groups.[26]

Enforcement remains an equally severe problem. Even if these governments can agree on a treaty, implementing it will be difficult. If a large country such as Russia fails to achieve its emissions targets, who dares to punish it? If a large country such as the United States fails to ratify the agreement, who can coax it to join? International scholars have long argued that the difficulty of enforcing contracts, commitments, and pacts is maximized between countries because there is no government with a Weberian monopoly of violence to punish defectors and violators.[27] From the perspective of international relations, then, global environmental problems are among the hardest to solve. They require countries to refrain from unilateral policies that benefit them, and only because these policies harm ecosystems and people in other countries. Even worse, the group of other countries often covers the entire globe, creating maximal incentives to free ride.

Global environmental problems can also be grouped under two primary categories: pollution and resource depletion.[28] When economic activity within a country produces pollutants that travel to other countries in the atmosphere, the first country's policies and decisions are of concern to other countries. Climate change is one such problem; others include ozone depletion, sulphur emissions, and mercury emissions. Of these four examples, climate change and ozone depletion are the quintessential global problems because the effects of pollution do not depend at all on the location of the source. While the vulnerability of ecosystems and societies to climate change and ozone depletion depends to a large extent on their location, the harmful environmental phenomenon itself is truly global: there is only one atmosphere, only one ozone layer. In contrast, sulphur emissions and mercury emissions are more localized in that the source of the pollutant determines the range of the pollution.[29]

The other category of environmental problems is resource depletion. Many natural resources are "commons" in that they are nobody's private or sovereign property.[30] Such resources create problems because individual businesses and governments have incentives to overuse them. For example, oceanic fisheries have collapsed because the fishing fleets of the world use advanced technologies to catch so many fish that the stock cannot renew itself. Similarly, although forest resources are in some sense national because they fall under a sovereign jurisdiction, they furnish many benefits to people in other countries as well, and thus governments clear too much forest for economic purposes. Although many of the early concerns about resource scarcity focused on nonrenewable resources, such as fossil fuels or minerals,[31] these fears have proven largely unfounded thanks to the abundance of key nonrenewable resources. As companies have explored for resources or developed substitutes for them, they have been able to postpone conditions of scarcity.

Today, concerns about depletion instead relate to renewable resources, such as groundwater, fisheries, rainforests, and habitat in general. These resources have proven to be fragile and vulnerable to exploitation, and as the numbers and economic activity of humans continue to expand, the consumption of such resources increases. New problems continue to appear, including the threat of widespread plastic pollution to the oceans. Recent assessments suggest that many renewable resources are under severe stress and present a much more imminent threat to human well-being than the scarcity of nonrenewable resources does.[32]

Another way to classify global environmental problems is to distinguish between "green" and "brown" problems.[33] Green problems are traditional environmental problems that threaten ecosystems, species, and, in the long run, human societies. They include issues such as climate change, ozone depletion, deforestation, and habitat destruction. Brown problems, in turn, are environmental issues that have a direct, immediate, and localized effect on human beings. Examples include soil erosion, groundwater depletion, and the pollution of rivers. In 1971 a group of intellectuals from the global South authored the so-called Founex report and explained the environmental foes of the Third World:

> However, the major environmental problems of developing countries are essentially of a different kind. They are predominantly problems that reflect the poverty and very lack of development of their societies. They are problems, in other words, of both rural and urban poverty. In both the towns and in the countryside, not merely the "quality of life," but life

itself is endangered by poor water, housing, sanitation and nutrition, by sickness and disease and by natural disasters. These are problems, no less than those of industrial pollution, that clamour for attention in the context of the concern with human environment. They are problems which affect the greater mass of mankind.[34]

The brown-green distinction has generated a spirited, and often acrimonious, debate among scholars and practitioners. Industrialized countries have by and large solved their brown problems with domestic policy, and so their environmentally aware populations tend to emphasize green problems. But in emerging countries, brown problems are often more salient and immediate, as they harm the lives and livelihoods of poor people.[35] Thus an important cleavage in global environmental politics concerns the relative importance of brown versus green issues.[36]

The common thread running through global environmental problems is the need for *global cooperation*.[37] According to Keohane, "cooperation" occurs when actors adjust their behaviors to achieve a collectively desirable outcome, as compared to the baseline of what individually rational choices would produce.[38] The key element of this definition is that each actor changes its behavior to the benefit of others, and everyone benefits— possibly to different degrees—from this collection of adjustments. Keohane is careful, however, to avoid conflating cooperation with "harmony," a situation in which individually rational behaviors are collectively desirable because there is no conflict of interest. Cooperation is necessary exactly because individually rational behaviors generate bad outcomes. In the case of global environmental politics, these bad outcomes are environmental deterioration—be it pollution or resource loss—and its negative effects on nature and human societies.[39]

Unfortunately, cooperation is hard. Because actors promise to change their behavior to the benefit of others, they face the temptation to break their promises and thus avoid costly adjustments. Achieving cooperation requires solving distributional conflicts about who gets what and who pays for it,[40] enforcing commitments through mechanisms such as "tit for tat" reciprocity,[41] and monitoring behavior and outcomes.[42]

If cooperation is hard, North-South cooperation—between industrialized and emerging countries—has proven that much harder. Ever since the first global summit on the environment in Stockholm in 1972, emerging countries have expressed numerous concerns about the possible negative effects of multilateral environmental cooperation on their ability to develop economically.[43] When the prime minister of India, Indira Gandhi, gave her speech on the environment to the United Nations community in Stockholm on June 14, 1972, she highlighted the difficulties that the world's poor countries face at a time when industrialized countries have exploited the poor for economic purposes:[44]

> The stirrings of demands for the political rights of citizens, and the economic rights of the toiler came after considerable advance had been made. The riches and the labour of the colonized countries played no small part in the industrialization and prosperity of the West. Now, as we struggle to create a better life for our people, it is in vastly different circumstances, for obviously in today's eagle-eyed watchfulness we cannot indulge in such practices even for a worthwhile purpose.

She then drew the conclusion—one that has become a common thread running through North-South environmental politics over the past four decades:

> On the one hand the rich look askance at our continuing poverty—on the other, they warn us against their own methods. We do not wish to impoverish the environment any further and yet we cannot for a moment forget the grim poverty of large numbers of people. Are not poverty and need the greatest polluters? For instance, unless we are in a position to provide employment and purchasing power for the daily necessities of the tribal people and those who live in or around our jungles, we cannot prevent them from combing the forest for food and livelihood; from poaching and from despoiling the vegetation. When they themselves feel deprived, how can we urge the preservation of animals? How can we speak to those who live in villages and in slums about keeping the oceans, the rivers and the air clean when their own lives are contaminated at the source? The environment cannot be improved in conditions of poverty. Nor can poverty be eradicated without the use of science and technology.

Today, Indira Gandhi's words are more important than ever, for global environmental politics is increasingly about the preferences and choices of the world's poor majority. The days of economic gloom and doom in Asia, Africa, and Latin America are long gone. The powerful combination of population growth and economic dynamism ensures that the rate of global environmental deterioration is now in the hands of governments that rule poor but growing countries. This change in international political economy is moving global environmental politics into new directions, and this volume deals with the nature, origins, and consequences of these changes.

THE TRANSFORMATION OF GLOBAL ENVIRONMENTAL POLITICS

This book aims to understand and explain how key trends in the world economy and international relations shape global environmental politics in the twenty-first century. I aim for a robust analytical framework that captures the most important drivers of change. These are the number of relevant governments, their preferences regarding environmental outcomes, their structural power, and their institutional (i.e., implementation) capacity. None of the drivers is new to the literature, but scholars have yet to put these pieces together. The ultimate goal of the analytical exercise is to understand and assess the value of global environmental cooperation relative to a business-as-usual scenario.[45]

My analytical framework is old-fashioned in that it emphasizes the behavior of *governments*. Nonstate actors, ranging from private businesses to foundations and environmental groups, play an important role in global environmental governance today. They monitor state behavior,[46] exercise private authority,[47] and lobby for policies in national capitals and international summits alike.[48] And yet the fact remains that governments alone can enact and implement policies that set real constraints on environmental destruction. No other authority has the ability to formulate the policies needed to stop environmental destruction, and there is no change to this fundamental reality on the horizon. The most important decisions at the global level remain in the hands of sovereign governments, as they alone negotiate and implement treaties that move countries from the unsustainable business as usual toward better outcomes through reduced environmental deterioration.

Where I depart from classical accounts of global environmental politics is my emphasis on governments instead of states. In the past, scholarship on global environmental politics often assumed that states are unitary actors.[49] While this approach is parsimonious and focuses on some very important issues of cooperation, such as the difficulty of collective action, it is not at all suitable for an analysis of drivers of change. As I will show, the most important changes and developments underway in global environmental politics stem from deeper transformations in the world economy. Governments are the most important actors shaping and responding to these transformations, but they do so in an environment populated by business, political opposition, civil society, and public opinion.

Let's now look at the four drivers of change. The combination of global economic and population growth has significantly increased the number of relevant players in many environmental negotiations of global import. Many emerging countries have controlled important natural resources and large populations from the early years of global environmental politics, but they have only become important producers and consumers of goods and services over time. The basic driver of the growing number of players in the system is the combination of population and economic growth that I have already used to motivate this research. As large populations in emerging countries grow wealthy, they generate environmental impacts through increased industrial activity, consumption of energy, consumption of natural resources, and waste.

The total impact of a society on the environment is but the product of population size and per capita impact, which in turn consists of the product of technology and affluence.[50] Population growth and technology continue to change, but the transformation of global environmental politics ultimately stems from the increased affluence in emerging economies. While concerns about "overpopulation" have a long history, they are misplaced unless they consider differences in per capita consumption. The real environmental challenge is a large, affluent population using inefficient, polluting technology.

These changes add to "power to destroy"[51] in emerging economies. A government can be said to have lots of power to destroy when its population and economy can, without environmental safeguards, cause substantial deterioration in the quality of the local environment. Countries with large and wealthy populations tend to have more power to destroy than small countries trapped in poverty, given that the potential environmental impact of a country is essentially the size of the population multiplied by per capita pollution and resource depletion.[52] Given the importance of the power to destroy in global environmental politics, rapid economic growth in emerging economies makes their governments more important players in global environmental negotiations than was the case in the past.

Although the product of population size and per capita resource destruction is mechanically a correct representation of a society's environmental footprint, this product also shapes global environmental politics by shaping the relative bargaining power of different governments. When a government oversees and controls a large and growing population that promises to consume more and more resources over time, it can threaten to cause global environmental degradation simply by doing nothing—by failing to implement environmental and energy policies. This threat, in turn, allows the government to demand concessions, such as financial contributions or transfers of clean technology, from other governments. Depending on the responses of other governments, such power to destroy could not only have distributional consequences—how the pie will be divided—but also change the extent and impact of environmental cooperation.

The newly powerful governments differ in two important ways from the pivotal players of the previous century. The first is that their environmental preferences remain relatively weak. This is quite understandable and justified, given the necessity of economic growth to alleviate poverty, build infrastructure, and create jobs. Emerging economies still have lower per capita emissions than industrialized countries, and their historical responsibility for environmental destruction is limited because their economic growth started only recently. Their large populations do not enjoy the luxurious lifestyles that are common in the industrialized world.

Although emerging economies hold the power to destroy the global environment, their relatively low level of economic development means that economic growth remains an overriding priority for them. If governments of major industrialized countries have sometimes opposed environmental cooperation, such opposition has often reflected domestic political or institutional constraints, as in the case of the United States not ratifying multilateral treaties that would not pass the Senate or that would require major changes in domestic legislation. In contrast, pivotal emerging economies share a commitment to economic growth, and while they are sensitive to environmental problems, such sensitivity is still new and mostly reflects practical concerns about public health and resource security.

The second way newly powerful countries differ from previous ones is the lack of institutional capacity, which I define as "an inability to actually implement" the policies needed to minimize environmental deterioration.[53] The important word here is "actually," as the lack of institutional capacity need not mean the government wants to reduce pollution, cut waste, or sustain renewable resources. A lack of institutional capacity prevents governments from solving their environmental problems, or perhaps complying with environmental treaties, when they simply cannot do the job of protecting the environment. A simple example of this problem is the difficulty of enforcing air pollution regulations when the environmental ministry does not have the resources to hire competent and honest inspectors to visit factories and measure their pollution output. Sometimes there are simply not enough inspectors to credibly threaten factory owners with penalties for noncompliance; other times, the problem is that the state pays so little that the inspectors are willing to look the other way for a bribe.

The major economies of the twentieth century, in North America and Western Europe, had the administrative capacity to enact and implement effective policies. Their governments had, over centuries, built an administrative state that is able not just to enact but actually to implement sophisticated policies, such as markets for emissions trading. Today's emerging powers, however, are often growing without having built such institutional capacity. The lack of a long history of state building means that the implementation of the complex policies required to protect the environment is challenging. This challenge is compounded by the rapidly changing socioeconomic profile of these societies, as well as the prioritization of capacity building in areas related to national security or economic growth. Industrialized countries have built up their environmental governance systems for decades, whereas such pursuits are very recent for most emerging economies.

The key implication of these changes is the growing importance of capacity constraints as an obstacle to global environmental cooperation.

In the past, the prospect of environmental deterioration came from countries with relatively high levels of institutional capacity, but this relationship is now broken. Already today, global environmental politics revolves around ways to enhance institutional capacity at the regional and national levels. This need to invest in capacity is not a simple technical issue, however, because the lack of capacity has complex implications for domestic politics, international bargaining, and enforcement of treaty commitments in the global environmental realm. I thus propose that debates on external support for institutional capacity will play an increasingly important role in global environmental politics of the twenty-first century.

The ideal comparison for understanding the role of institutional capacity is between China and India. Over the past decades, both emerging economies have grown rapidly and asserted themselves as the two pivotal players in global environmental politics. As I venture to show below, however, their patterns of growth, domestic environmental policy, and global environmental positions could not be more different. China's growth has been fueled by impressive gains in institutional capacity over time, and as a result the Chinese government has also been able to mitigate the environmental damage caused by the country's breakneck economic expansion and unprecedented poverty alleviation. At the same time, India's economic growth has occurred in spite of stringent and persistent limitations of institutional capacity. Consequently, the Delhi government has been, compared to its counterpart in Beijing, much less effective in securing high rates of economic growth while mitigating the environmental impact.

Because most remaining emerging economies of the world are much closer to the Indian realities than to the Chinese ones, institutional capacity is emerging as a key policy issue. When emerging economies grow despite limited institutional capacity, the environmental impact of their economic expansion is severe. Institutional capacity would allow these governments to control their growth trajectories, minimize negative externalities, and plan for the run. China's impressive gains in environmental protection show the benefits of investment in institutional capacity, but realizing these benefits is a major challenge to the growing emerging economies, as decades of experience with governing economic development show.[54]

This problem is particularly severe in negotiations on economy-wide issues, such as the use of fossil fuels or land. The main exception to this general rule is that when treaty negotiations focus on a specific substance or a narrow sector, a conventional approach with rigid, uniform rules remains viable because the narrow focus of the treaty circumvents the more difficult political conflicts surrounding the negotiations. The playbook of the twentieth century, which saw lots of success in issues ranging from ozone depletion to marine oil spills, remains relevant to specific issues, such as stopping the use of specific environmentally destructive substances. However, it has become obsolete for the challenge of minimizing the total environmental impact of population growth and economic expansion in emerging economies. Old wine in new bottles will not be enough to save the planet, because the most important environmental pressures stem from a growing demand for energy and natural resources. There is no silver bullet that can break the strong link between energy use, resource consumption, and environmental deterioration. Cleaner products help in some cases, and improved energy or resource efficiency can

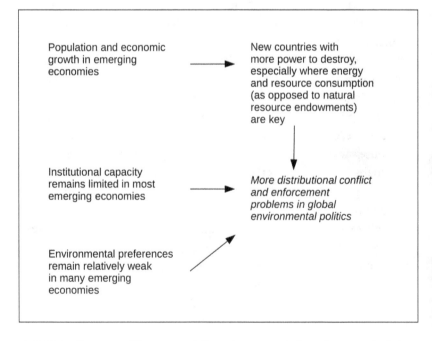

FIGURE 0.1 Summary of the argument. Emerging economies' growing power to destroy complicates global environmental cooperation, and this effect is amplified by weak environmental preferences and limited institutional capacity.

make a big difference in many sectors, but any such solution is partial at best because most sectors remain unaffected.

The main argument is summarized in figure 0.1. Rapid population and economic growth in emerging economies contributes to an expansion of energy and resource consumption, which increases the number of countries with the power to destroy in different global environmental negotiations. Institutional capacity, however, grows at a slower pace than the economy while environmental preferences remain weak. This *interaction* between (1) a growing power to destroy, (2) mostly weak environmental preferences, and (3) constrained institutional capacity drives the transformation of global environmental politics. The interaction raises new barriers to global environmental cooperation.

PROTECTING THE PLANET IN A WORLD OF EMERGING ECONOMIES

The argument just outlined has important implications for the study of global environmental politics. Toward the end of the twentieth century, the study of global environmental politics began to shift from a traditional state-centric mode toward the study of nonstate governance.[55] The twenty-first century, however, presents a host of new challenges, and the most pressing research questions in the field now focus on the political economy of energy and environmental policy in emerging economies. The future of global environmental politics depends, first and foremost, on the national policies that the governments of a growing number of emerging economies formulate.

These developments highlight energy as the single most important driver of environmental deterioration in today's world. The most important environmental consequence of the growth of emerging economies has been the rapid increase in demand for energy. Recent economic studies suggest that the global explosion of energy use is likely to continue in the future, as billions seek the convenience and productivity that abundant amounts of modern energy can afford.[56] The disruption caused by climate change mostly stems from the burning of fossil fuels, and energy is also the most important source of air pollution globally.[57] The centrality of energy is significant because it cuts across virtually all sectors of society. Both the consumption and production of energy have huge potential to contribute to global environmental deterioration, and almost any kind of economic expansion results in higher demand for energy, thus necessitating more consumption and production. Emerging economies now become pivotal to a wide range of environmental problems, and not just those focused on their natural resources.

As we shall see, traditional approaches to global environmental negotiations have continued to achieve at least some degree of success when addressing narrow sectoral problems, such as hydrofluorocarbons, aviation, or mercury pollution, but they have mostly failed when addressing more fundamental problems, such as deforestation or carbon dioxide emissions. Given that energy is relevant to virtually every global environmental problem today, this state of affairs presents a challenge for the future of environmental governance. Future success in global environmental politics requires recognizing the limits of narrow sectoral approaches and focusing instead on cross-cutting efforts to conserve energy through efficiency and to promote the displacement of dirtier fossil fuels, especially coal, with clean and sustainable sources of energy.

Although the ongoing explosion in global energy use raises environmental concerns, it is a necessary consequence of human development on a planet with over seven billion—and counting—inhabitants. Until the early years of the twentieth century, the benefits of modern energy access were limited to a small number of people living in advanced industrialized countries. The continuation of such a state of affairs would be normatively troubling, as life without modern energy is by necessity inconvenient and precarious. The challenge for practitioners in the field of global environmental politics, then, is not to prevent the global energy explosion, but to control it with policies that promote conservation and to capitalize on the opportunity to invest in clean energy infrastructure instead of fuels such as coal.

Despite these threats and challenges, the future of global environmental politics also suggests significant opportunities. In cases such as the Paris agreement on climate change, we already see negotiators moving away from rigid, top-down treaties toward solutions that put more emphasis on national sovereignty and allow governments to first formulate, and then collectively "ratchet up" over time, their national commitments.[58]

These approaches are well-suited to the new realities of global environmental politics in the twenty-first century, as they recognize the challenges that preference diversity among a large number of players with limited institutional capacity present. On the one hand, access to environmental clubs allows proponents of environmental protection to tailor "accession deals" to encourage emerging economies to adopt progressive environmental policies in exchange for concrete economic gains from membership,[59] such as improved trade cooperation or access to new technology and financing. On the other hand, clubs that emphasize the specific needs and challenges of emerging economies offer a flexible, expedient solution to the problem of global environmental cooperation when the group of relevant governments is large, is heterogeneous, and lacks both a strong preference and the institutional capacity for ambitious domestic environmental policy.

The growing power of emerging economies highlights the importance of heavy investment in capacity building. As emerging economies increasingly face pressing environmental challenges that compromise their societal stability and ability to pursue economic growth, it is in their direct interest to formulate effective policies to govern energy and the environment. Such policies, however, require investment in institutional development, and here industrialized countries have an opportunity to lay the foundation for more effective global environmental governance in the future by supporting capacity-building efforts in emerging economies. If such efforts are made early enough, the next generation of emerging economies may avoid policy traps such as dysfunctional, unenforceable pollution regulations or energy subsidies that contribute to wasteful consumption. Adequate institutional capacity would enable emerging economies to take full advantage of new clean technologies such as solar power, electric vehicles, and advanced biofuels.

In supporting emerging economies in the development of their national environmental policies, it is important to focus on the relevant governments' own policy priorities. In twenty-first-century global environmental politics, externally imposed agendas are going to fail in all likelihood, given the growing structural power of emerging economies. Because economic growth is necessary for poverty alleviation in emerging countries, their governments also have a strong moral case for focusing on economic development. Wealthy countries simply are in no position to criticize their poorer counterparts for using energy and natural resources to pursue growth. In practice, recognizing this shift in the balance of power means that addressing local environmental issues and sustainable human development should become an increasingly important priority. Even though leaders of industrialized countries, nongovernmental organizations, and international organizations face the temptation to focus on big global problems, such as climate change mitigation, a smart strategy also entices emerging economies to engage in global environmental politics by supporting the development of national institutions and the formulation of policies to address pressing local concerns.

This strategy not only secures the participation of emerging economies but also generates spillovers, as growing institutional capacity enables more effective action on global environmental issues in the future—even if they are not a priority for the government just yet. Additionally, addressing local environmental deterioration may have direct positive effects. Protecting forest resources or reducing urban air pollution can, for example, contribute to climate change mitigation. Perhaps even more directly, renewable energy can contribute to energy security and enhance energy access while also decarbonizing the power sector.[60]

Global environmental cooperation would thus benefit investments in institutional capacity, even if the initial focus of such investments were on the domestic environmental challenges of emerging economies. Investments in institutional capacity both make global environmental cooperation attractive to emerging economies and create the foundation for effective global action in the future. Over time, emerging economies will continue to find global environmental commitments both less costly and more appealing.

CHAPTERS OF THE BOOK

This book deals with an enormously complicated global challenge. In chapter 1 I propose a theory that can illuminate the past, present, and future of global environmental politics. The biggest question for the field of global environmental politics today is how the changing nature of international political economy affects the international community's ability to halt global environmental destruction, and answering this question depends on getting two things right. The first concerns the nature of the fundamental obstacles to environmental cooperation. The second concerns changes in the size of these obstacles under different international political economies. I thus combine ideas and insights from those bodies of literature that answer the two questions to develop my original argument. In doing so, I explain how changes in the structural power, preferences, and institutional capacity of a growing number of pivotal countries change the nature and outcomes of global environmental politics.

The bulk of the book is focused on presenting and assessing empirical evidence. Chapters 2–3 do so at the global level, focusing on the logic of international negotiations. The first of these two chapters presents a stylized view of conventional global environmental politics in the twentieth century, after the Second World War, based on how I have come to understand it. I characterize both the broad patterns of twentieth-century global environmental politics and the underlying international political economy. I then apply my theory to explain the patterns of global environmental politics with the international political economy of the time. Faithful to my emphasis on North-South politics, I put particular emphasis on the role, positions, and achievements of what used to be called the Third World—countries outside the capitalist West and the socialist East.

In chapter 3 I summarize, evaluate, and explain changes in the core nature of global environmental politics between the late twentieth and early twenty-first centuries. I emphasize both continuity and change: the more things change, the more they stay the same. In other words, my analysis is based on the premise that the basic *system* of global environmental politics has not changed, but its parameter values have undergone a major transformation. We now live in a world of emerging economies, and the countries that used to belong to the Third World are more important for global environmental politics than ever. And yet the basic model of twentieth-century global environmental politics can explain these changes, provided we consider the change in power to destroy and how it interacts with weak environmental preferences and limited institutional capacity.

Chapter 4 focuses on the trajectories of three specific environmental regimes: climate change, biodiversity loss, and chemicals. By focusing on specific cases, I demonstrate how my analytical framework can illuminate developments in three important global environmental regimes. I show that in each case, the rise of the emerging powers has changed the logic of multilateral bargaining and treaty formation. Climate change negotiations are increasingly about finding constructive solutions to the problem of supplying emerging economies with clean energy to power their economic growth. Efforts to combat biodiversity loss can no longer be neatly separated from the pressure that economic growth puts on habitations across continents. Progress in controlling the production, consumption, and trade of hazardous chemicals cannot be disentangled from finding alternatives that fit the needs of countries such as China and India.

Next I look at the role and experiences of different emerging economies. Although I emphasize the growing number of countries that shape global environmental futures, there is no way I can avoid discussing China and India. These two giants are today's leading emerging powers. China is on the verge of becoming a service economy. India could become the world's next economic powerhouse, as China's growth inevitably slows due to decreasing returns to scale. Chapter 5 is dedicated to surveying China and India in global environmental politics.

The next batch of countries joining the game are other major emerging economies. In chapter 6 I survey the economic prospects, environmental situation, and negotiation positions of four countries: Vietnam, the Philippines, Indonesia, and Nigeria. While the survey is admittedly cursory, it adds comparative insight into how changes in international political economy can have deep impacts on the economics, politics, and diplomacy of the next wave of emerging economies. All four countries already have a lot of power to destroy in combination with a relatively weak environmental preference and, to different degrees, lacking institutional capacity. I also explore the case of Brazil, which has exceptional power to destroy thanks to its sovereign power over most of the Amazonian rainforest. While Brazil is not a recently emerging economy, it provides an illustration of the challenges of global environmental cooperation on natural resources controlled by one country. A cursory review of Brazil's environmental policies and participation in global environmental negotiations offers insights into why North-South cooperation on natural resources has been fraught with difficulty from the very beginning.

Because my argument is inherently forward-looking, in chapter 6 I also look at more recently emerging economies—countries that have seen economic dynamism only during the first two decades of the twenty-first century. For this survey, I focus on Bangladesh, Myanmar, Ethiopia, and Tanzania. While all these countries are still some distance from holding enough power to destroy to be a significant presence in global environmental negotiations, I show that they are moving in this direction and formulate expectations about their trajectories over the coming decades. Here my analysis is necessarily somewhat speculative, as I am considering the future.

The concluding chapter leaves me with the opportunity to reflect on the argument and discuss its broader significance. Besides reiterating my key assumptions, hypotheses, and the empirical record of global environmental politics in a succinct form, I discuss the need for a reorientation of the study of global environmental politics toward the political economy of policy formulation in emerging economies and expand on the policy implications discussed in the previous chapter. I conclude with a more general discussion of the future of global environmental politics on a crowded planet, with billions in the global South finally escaping abject poverty.

The key point is, in fact, a simple one: global environmental politics in the twenty-first century is ultimately about enabling the entire human civilization—and not the wealthy minority—to survive, thrive, and prosper.

1

INTERNATIONAL POLITICAL ECONOMY AND GLOBAL ENVIRONMENTAL POLITICS

My goal here is to capture the *effects of changes in international political economy on global environmental politics*. I propose a short list of key drivers and explain how fundamental changes in one of these drivers—structural power—affect the logic and outcomes of international environmental negotiations. This assumes that the other drivers, environmental preferences and institutional capacity, mostly remain weak and change slowly at best. In particular, I consider the interactive effects of these drivers on individual bargaining outcomes (i.e., whose preferences shape cooperation) as well as the likelihood and depth of cooperation (i.e., how often and to what extent cooperation addresses global environmental problems).

I focus on political economy drivers because the ongoing transformation of global environmental politics cannot be attributed to the internal logic of the negotiations. "Super wicked" issues such as climate change certainly create new challenges for global environmental politics,[1] but the most important difficulties stem from nonenvironmental changes in international political economy. Instead of only emphasizing the difficulties of environmental cooperation, such as the tragedy of the commons, I consider how the problem structure varies depending on the broader characteristics of the international political economy underneath.

The two strands of literature that inform my account are strategic institutionalism and political economy.[2] Compared to existing approaches, my argument puts more emphasis on how changes in political economy produce changes in cooperation. I integrate insights from both traditions into a synthetic theory of the relationship between international political economy and global environmental politics. Key to understanding the evolution of global environmental politics is thus to bring these arguments together. Institutionalist approaches are important because they focus on the fundamental problem at hand. They allow clear definitions of why environmental cooperation is needed and how different factors either enable or inhibit achieving cooperative outcomes that benefit the key players. Political economy analysis can breathe life into the abstract, stylized models that institutionalists have constructed. By considering concrete drivers of environmental performance, such as power to destroy and institutional capacity, we can tailor institutional considerations to understand the changing reality of global environmental politics.

To summarize, I argue that growing energy and resource consumption in emerging economies has contributed to a rapid expansion of their power to destroy. This growing power, in turn, has increased the number of relevant players in many areas of global environmental cooperation. Because many of these players still have relatively weak environmental preferences and limited institutional capacity to implement policies, global environmental cooperation has become increasingly difficult, and outcomes have moved closer to the preferences of emerging economies. This is particularly true for those global environmental issues for which consumption patterns, as opposed to natural resource endowments, are central.

TWO APPROACHES TO GLOBAL ENVIRONMENTAL POLITICS

The strategic institutionalist approach is all about understanding and creating incentives for global collective action.[3] For Mitchell, this approach is an effort to explain "why humans harm the natural environment, why some of these harms emerge on the international scene, why negotiations sometimes succeed and sometimes fail, and why some international environmental treaties alter behavior and others do not."[4]

In this literature, the common underlying assumption is that a group of countries face a joint problem. Each country harms others by polluting, and the governments of these countries must decide on designing, joining, and implementing an agreement to reduce pollution. However, collective action to reduce pollution is easier said than done. Each government faces the temptation to keep polluting too much because the cost of abating such pollution is *domestic* while the benefits of abatement are *international*. If a government considers the abatement cost to be ten dollars per ton of pollution and the environmental benefits are worth fifty dollars per ton, the government has an economic incentive to act only if it captures more than one-fifth of the total benefit. Environmental agreements help governments overcome this problem when they condition pollution abatement on reciprocity: each government agrees to abate pollution, provided other governments also abate. If a government stops abating, then others retaliate.

Some of the early works, most notably Barrett, focused on demonstrating how difficult the problem is: even if countries could enforce the agreement, they could not prevent countries from refusing to participate.[5] In other words, a "self-enforcing agreement"—one that does not require policing by a world government—has few members. To understand this argument, suppose the members of an agreement can somehow credibly commit to collectively optimal pollution abatement. If a hypothetical agreement has many members, then any one of them could leave the agreement and still count on the remaining members to keep abating pollution among themselves. In the end, however, this calculus leads to many governments leaving the agreement so that only a small membership is left to act to reduce pollution.[6] As Barrett puts it, international environmental agreements "cannot increase global net benefits substantially when the number of countries that share the resource is very large."[7]

More recent works, in contrast, have focused on the potential of institutional designs to alleviate such problems. This approach begins by recognizing the strategic problems raised in early work as valid and then examining if changes to the institutional design of treaties could deal with these strategic problems. This line of research does not investigate the politics of making changes in institutional design but instead conducts thought experiments on the *consequences* of changes in institutional design. Mitchell and Keilbach, for example, examine the ability of issue linkages and side payments to achieve cooperation in upstream-downstream situations. If an upstream country causes a pollution problem and a downstream country suffers from it, then the downstream country must either coerce or bribe the upstream country to mitigate the pollution. Thus Mitchell and Keilbach infer that in the absence of a clear power asymmetry in favor of the downstream country, an effective agreement would have to feature side payments from the downstream to the upstream country. In contrast, if the downstream country has more structural power, then such side payments are not necessary for reducing pollution: "Downstream states that are stronger than the perpetrators may employ such positive linkage but also can use negative linkage to coerce perpetrators into mitigating an externality and can do so without the aid of an institution."[8]

Other, related work has focused on monitoring arrangements,[9] the role of clean technology,[10] domestic enforcement of commitments,[11] the role of scientists and others in epistemic communities,[12] and the special case of climate change.[13] The shared premise of these works is that variation in the nature of an agreement or other factors, such as domestic politics, explains variation in the ultimate outcome—improved environmental quality.

The political economy approaches offer a very different perspective, as they focus on explaining global environmental politics with the features of international political economy. In these approaches, the nature and outcomes of global environmental politics are explained with underlying political and economic structures. As Clapp and Dauvergne explain in their overview of the political economy of the global environment, "how polities and societies allocate financial, human, and natural resources directly influences how we manage local, national, and ultimately global environments."[14] In other words, political economy approaches ground the analysis of environmental outcomes in broader politics and economics. While the strategic institutionalist approach focuses on bargaining and enforcement themselves, the political economy approach looks at the role of the broader social, economic, and political setting.

Scholars of political economy have emphasized the role of factors such as economic growth, capitalism, and technology. In a global economy, the combination of increasing productivity and a growing population has broad environmental effects. These effects are not straightforward, however, as increased economic activity contributes to environmental destruction, but wealth also allows societies to invest in environmental protection.[15] In a similar vein, international trade can have complex countervailing effects on the environment. Trade not only enables economic expansion but may also trigger "race to the bottom" dynamics as governments respond to competitive pressures by relaxing environmental regulations,[16] yet scholars have also noted that trade channels allow forerunner governments to spread their stringent environmental standards, such as automobile emission standards, to trigger a "race to the top."[17]

By investigating these questions, political economy approaches can generate insights into whether capitalist economic growth can be environmentally sustainable, whether trade liberalization is a threat to the global environment, and how international economic institutions should handle environmental issues. Some works even adopt an integrated approach, proposing that a short list of key changes can best account for changes in global environmental politics. For my analysis, studies focusing on the North-South political economy of global environmental politics are of particular importance. These studies pay attention to the different preferences, ideologies, and worldviews of governments from the traditional industrialized countries and the rest of the world. When global environmental politics grew in prominence and multilateral negotiations began in earnest for the United Nations Conference on the Human Environment in Stockholm in 1972, North-South conflicts were also high on the global politics agenda.[18]

At the time, the Third World coalition looked for an alternative to the ideological camps led by the United States and the Soviet Union. In 1964 the southern coalition had established the G77 by issuing the Joint Declaration of the Seventy-Seven Countries at the United Nations Conference on Trade and Development (UNCTAD).[19] The recent decolonization of a vast number of poor countries had raised questions about fundamental issues in the world economy, and in the 1970s the developing countries campaigned—in the end, without success—for a New International Economic Order (NIEO) through the UNCTAD, calling for measures such the regulation of multilateral corporations, respect for national sovereignty, cooperation (i.e., cartels) among primary commodity producers, and guaranteed prices for trade in raw materials.[20] The North-South environmental politics of the time understandably reflected many of the themes of the broader North-South "structural conflict" over the rules, principles, and norms governing the international economic order.[21]

Indeed, the importance of this cleavage never escaped scholars. Rowland wrote a fine case study of the Stockholm conference, showing that developing countries were deeply suspicious of the environmental endeavor in the beginning.[22] Egged on by domestic environmentalists and public opinion, governments of industrialized countries flew to Stockholm to signal their commitment and to lay the foundation for global environmental cooperation. The view of the rest of the world was very different, however, as governments worried about "pulling the ladder" constraints on their ability to achieve economic development.[23] In his review of developing country positions in global environmental negotiations, Najam explains that "developing countries came to Stockholm quite reluctantly and after much cajoling by the conference secretary general, Maurice Strong. They questioned the need for such a conference and viewed it not just as a distraction but as a threat to their interests. . . . What is most important to recall is that they were contesting not the conference as much as its very purpose—that is, the importance of environmental issues as a global priority."[24]

In other words, the global South made its first appearance in global environmental negotiations as an adversary ready for combat. The two camps, South and North, disagreed on the importance of different issues, as "the developed countries wanted to address ozone depletion, global warming, acid rain, and deforestation, whereas the developing countries were more interested in examining the relationship between developed countries' economic policies and developing countries' sluggish economic growth. Leaders of developing countries insisted that environmental protection alone was not enough: therefore, any agreement about global environmental issues must also include measures of economic development."[25]

Work in this line of research has since then grown and emphasized the robust political unity,[26] evolving positions,[27] and specific challenges of poorer countries,[28] including racial and class-based inequities,[29] in global environmental negotiations. It has also recognized that the growth of emerging economies has failed to force the industrialized countries' hand,[30] and that there are now signs of fragmentation among the developing country bloc.[31] The literature has also shown that the BASIC countries

(Brazil, South Africa, India, China), a key group of emerging economies, have continued to insist on developing country status in responsibility for climate change but have also collectively distinguished themselves from smaller countries.[32]

These two approaches—strategic institutionalism and political economy—are neither competing with nor unrelated to each other. Strategic institutional analysis is ultimately not about variation in empirical outcomes. It is instead motivated by the urge to understand the nature of political obstacles to international environmental cooperation, and then to use this understanding to take steps toward solving the problem. Political economy approaches also seek to understand the deep and central features of global environmental politics. But the focus shifts away from strategic considerations of sovereign governments to a broader analysis of how contemporary international political economy contributes to global environmental deterioration, and how changes to that structure could contribute to a more sustainable global society. In this book, my goal is to combine insights from both approaches.

KEY ASSUMPTIONS

The four drivers I consider are (1) governments' structural power, (2) their policy preferences, (3) their institutional capacity, and (4) the number of different players in the global system. Together, the four variables constitute my analytical model of global environmental politics. Given that my general argument is about the appearance of emerging economies as key players in global environmental politics because of their growing power to destroy, the thought experiment I conduct boils down to explaining the effect of adding new governments on bargaining and cooperation, considering that the players are heterogeneous in their preferences and institutional capacity.

First, I focus on structural power. While power is a difficult concept to define or measure,[33] by *structural power* I simply refer to the different resources, opportunities, and vulnerabilities available to a country in global environmental negotiations. This definition encompasses a variety of assets. Most of them are straightforward and concrete, such as financial resources or access to advanced technology. Others, such as preexisting political and economic alliances, are less tangible.

In the case of global environmental politics, the most important source of power is the power to destroy.[34] Power to destroy draws on the idea that total environmental impact is the product of population, affluence, and technology.[35] The concept adds particular weight on the future, however, as preventing future impacts is often easier than reducing present impacts. For example, if a country has already built a huge fleet of coal-fired power plants, the opportunity cost of shutting these plants down is high. In contrast, if the country is only planning to build such coal-fired power plants in the future, the opportunity cost is lower because no capital is wasted on building plants that will be shut down before the end of their technical lifespan.

When negotiating with other governments, a government can expect concessions and favorable outcomes if it can credibly threaten to cause environmental destruction in the absence of a favorable deal. The easiest way to achieve such credibility is when the government can cause environmental degradation simply by not enacting policies to protect the environment, as business as usual is enough to destroy the environment. A government that has authority over key policies, programs, and practices that may or may not constrain environmental harm caused by expanding economic activity is pivotal for achieving success in international environmental cooperation.[36]

For a government to have power to destroy, it must have access to resources that could potentially contribute to environmental destruction. Economic power may come from growth in consumption. For example, if demand for electricity grows rapidly because of industrialization, the government can threaten others with a construction spree of coal-fired power plants. The alternative is growth in production. If global demand for timber increases, a country with rich rainforest resources can threaten others with deforestation.

In practice, different governments draw their power to destroy from multiple sources. The two most important are natural resource endowments and consumption. Natural resource endowments, such as rainforest or fisheries, change only slowly. Some countries, such as Brazil and

Indonesia, have always had such endowments. Those endowments are shrinking over time, but the change is slow. Consumption, on the other hand, depends on the size, wealth, and technology of the population. The transformation of global environmental politics is driven by growing potential for consumption in emerging economies.

The importance of power to destroy is best seen in cases of capital-intensive economic activities. Davis and Socolow examine the case of coal-fired power plants and suggest that the construction of such plants in China, India, and other economies could lock these countries into the use of coal for decades to come.[37] In such cases, the future demand of electricity combined with plans to build coal-fired power plants would add to these countries' power to destroy. As long as a country such as India has coal-fired power plants in the pipeline, other countries have reason to be concerned about their future use.[38]

Economic power to destroy is not enough, however, as the government must be able to credibly threaten other governments with environmental destruction. Even if a country could build a huge number of coal power plants or clear vast tracts of rainforest in principle, such a threat is not credible when other governments know that there is not much to gain from such destruction. In conventional bargaining models, such as the Nash bargaining model,[39] players secure better outcomes when their losses from a failure to seal a deal are small. In the case of global environmental politics, economic gains from using cheap energy and natural resources at the expense of pollution and depletion increase the value of a negotiation failure and thus give governments the power to destroy.[40]

Governments can also be characterized in terms of their "power to protect."[41] Countries with thriving economies and financial or technological resources can have a positive impact on global environmental outcomes if they choose to use those resources to abate pollution, conserve resources, and reduce waste. Thus while rapid population and economic growth typically increase power to destroy, they also contribute to greater power to protect. A good example of this dynamic could be the choice between power generation sources: the ability to invest in coal-fired power generation represents the power to destroy, while the ability to support clean technology innovation represents the power to protect.

In practice, however, the growth in power to destroy is more significant than the growth in power to protect for emerging economies. When energy and resource consumption grows across the board, the power to destroy increases almost mechanically, in a linear fashion. The power to protect, on the other hand, grows only under specific circumstances, such as the availability of clean technology, rapid growth of environmental awareness, and—as we shall see later—improvements in institutional capacity. To understand global environmental politics in the twenty-first century in a world of emerging economies, understanding the growing power to destroy is more fundamental than understanding the uncertain and contingent growth of the power to protect.

By preferences, I refer to each government's ordering of different combinations of policies, and thus the outcomes they produce, in terms of their desirability. These combinations comprise not only the government's own policies but also the policies of other governments. I do not restrict my attention to environmental policies: any "issue linkages,"[42] such as side payments, are part of these orderings. I include outcomes in the definition to ensure that the reactions of other actors, such as businesses and civil society groups, are considered. For simplicity, I assume that each government has a consistent preference ordering. In making this assumption, I abstract away from considerations such as bureaucratic politics.[43]

The governments are assumed to be self-interested. Their preference orderings reflect both ideological preferences, such as when India's first prime minister, Jawaharlal Nehru, had a firm belief in the virtues of central planning, and considerations of political survival.[44] Political survival is particularly important because, unlike specific ideologies, it is a shared concern for all governments. Political survival is also the mechanism through which interest groups, ecological activists, and public opinion can shape governments' policies and negotiation positions.

Preferences are multidimensional, but empirical evidence highlights the continued importance of political cleavages between governments of industrialized and growing economies over economy-environment trade-offs. Although these cleavages are complicated, the fact remains that governments of emerging countries consider the pursuit of economic growth their primary objective, even if such growth is achieved at the expense of environmental sustainability.[45] Industrialized countries also value economic growth, of course, but their populations exhibit greater willingness to pay for environmental quality.[46] In any case, environmental protection is not a binding constraint for the growth of a service-oriented economy: even if the public is at best weakly interested in environmental issues, economic growth in a service-oriented economy is not very sensitive to environmental protection compared to, say, a commodity-exporting or heavily industrialized economy.[47]

The classical approach to understanding these differences and their changing nature is the "environmental Kuznets curve."[48]

In this theory, economic development initially results in rapid increases in pollution, as industrialization increases the scale of economic activity and the onus of growth lies with relatively "dirty" industries. Over time, however, access to clean technology, a move toward a service economy, and environmental policies reflecting popular demand allow the economy to reduce pollution. Recent country trajectories that illustrate this development include Japan's and South Korea's phenomenal rise from agricultural production to heavy industry and then to services and innovation. In each case, their pollution levels first increased rapidly but then returned to low levels as new technology, environmental policies, and a shift away from heavy industry started to have an impact.

Recent research, however, shows that the story is quite a bit more complex than that. For Dasgupta et al., governance plays a critical role in mitigating the environmental impacts of growth.[49] Aklin explores the Kuznets curve in an open-economy setting and notes that it appears to be less relevant in the case of carbon dioxide, an invisible global pollutant with few local negative effects, than for sulphur dioxide and other local pollutants.[50] As Carson notes his review of the literature, the data do not support a simple relationship between income and environmental equality: "More plausible explanations for the observed data revolve around good government, effective regulation, and diffusion of technological change. These factors tend to be related in a diffuse manner with higher income and suggest it is likely, but not inevitable, that a society will choose to reduce pollution levels as it becomes wealthier."[51]

Indeed, besides economic development, different countries' preferences over environmental outcomes—and willingness to pay for improvements—depend on a wide variety of factors. In their classic discussion of countries' positions in environmental negotiations, Sprinz and Vaahtoranta emphasize the balance of costs and benefits of environmental action as the key criterion: countries that face high abatement costs and expect minimal gains from environmental protection are less likely to act than countries with low abatement costs and large expected gains.[52] The gains from environmental protection depend on the extent to which the environmental problem at hand threatens economic activity, public health, quality of life, and other assets that both the public and the elites value. Abatement costs, in turn, depend on factors such as the availability of mitigation technology and the structure of the economy. In the case of climate change, for example, the decreasing cost of renewable power generation—a low-carbon source of electricity—has created interest in renewable policies around the world. Countries that depend heavily on fossil fuels and have few clean alternatives to them, however, continue to resist climate mitigation because their costs remain high.

The fundamental economic logic of costs and benefits is modified by political considerations. In their research on corporate preferences for environmental policy, Oye and Maxwell note that big business sometimes supports environmental policies that deter newcomers from entering the market or impose high costs on competitors.[53] When ozone depletion was widely recognized as a threat by the mid-1980s, major chemical corporations supported regulations that would drive chlorofluorocarbon (CFC) producers out of business and create profitable opportunities for technological innovation for the majors. Similarly, although many environmentalists oppose nuclear power, the nuclear industry has always had a positive view of climate mitigation because nuclear power is a low-carbon energy source.

This research demonstrates that emerging economies need not be trapped in a low-performance equilibrium. Over time, changes in economic structure, public opinion, technology, and policy can bring emerging economies closer to a path of sustainable development. As I will show, the empirical record reveals considerable heterogeneity among emerging economies. Some of them have begun to develop stronger environmental preferences while others have not. On balance, though, emerging economies have a long way to go.

Historical experiences also shape preferences in a powerful manner. In global environmental politics, poorer countries initially approached cooperation with profound suspicion based on a long history of colonial and imperial exploitation.[54] Although these attitudes have softened over time, inequity remains a pertinent concern. Race and class continue to determine access to environmental protection and the burden of pollution, both in domestic politics and globally.[55] To date, these experiences reduce emerging economies' interest in environmental agendas dominated by industrialized countries.

For industrialized countries, the key challenge lies in their willingness to spend money on other countries. Although industrialized countries have higher levels of environmental awareness than emerging economies, their populations tend to oppose resource transfers to other countries.[56] Even populations with high levels of environmental awareness tend to oppose the notion of supporting other countries' pollution abatement and instead prefer to spend the money at home. The problem is worse at times of populism when political leaders campaign on nationalism and argue against international cooperation. This home bias, we shall see, raises important barriers to global environmental cooperation as it complicates the strategy of using side payments to encourage action in emerging and least developed countries.

The most important part of my argument is the role of institutional capacity. By institutional capacity, I refer to a government's ability to implement the policies it has enacted and wants to see carried out. According to Grindle and Hilderbrand, capacity refers to "the ability to perform appropriate tasks effectively, efficiently and sustainably."[57] Effectiveness means achieving the goal; efficiency refers to doing so with at a low cost; and sustainability means that the achievement lasts over time. Grindle and Hilderbrand go on to argue that institutional capacity has five important dimensions: the general action environment, the institutional context, the network of relevant actors, organizational structures, and the quality of human resources.[58] Institutional capacity is thus not a simple question of budgets or training but instead depends on a wide range of constraints and opportunities for effective, efficient, and sustainable policy.[59]

These complexities notwithstanding, institutional capacity captures the government's ability to shape society, provided the government has a political interest in doing so. As VanDeveer and Dabelko note, "Issues associated with state inability (or incapacity) to meet international commitments—and how to build such capacity—are ubiquitous in both the theory and practice of international environmental cooperation. . . . One might ask what environmental benefits international agreements are likely to have if the parties lack the ability to comply."[60] In this telling, institutional capacity is a binding constraint on the ability of environmental treaties to alter behavior. If governments are simply unable to implement the policies that would reduce environmental harm, then issues of willful noncompliance lose their importance.[61]

Measuring institutional capacity in a systematic fashion is even more difficult than measuring the other components of my model. In their analysis of institutional capacity for energy-related climate policy, for example, Hughes and Urpelainen examine the presence and characteristics of sectoral institutions, such as environmental ministries.[62] Here, institutional capacity depends on *sectoral* preparedness to implement different policies to meet the government's substantive policy goals. In a more comprehensive approach to global environmental politics, however, it is important to consider the capacity of the bureaucracy more broadly. For example, the ability to make effective social policy can be essential for dealing with the negative effects of environmental policies on poor and vulnerable communities.[63]

Studies of policy responses to the 1970s oil crises and climate policy in the energy sector show that institutional capacity goes a long way toward explaining variation in how governments of industrialized countries choose policy options, though not always in a straightforward fashion.[64] Variation in responses to the oil shocks in industrialized countries, for example, can be explained with the state's ability to enact and implement different types of policies. While the French government—a "state as producer"—chose to increase its direct control of the energy sector, the United States—a "state as facilitator"—only reduced price controls.[65] In the Hughes and Urpelainen model, institutional capacity similarly determines whether democratic governments are likely to use regulatory instruments, instead of simpler subsidies, to reduce carbon emissions in the energy sector, and evidence from country case studies supports the hypothesis.[66]

In the case of industrialized countries, the notion of institutional capacity is nuanced because *all* industrialized countries have achieved a reasonably high level of capacity. They can create law and order, collect taxes, invest in infrastructure, and provide social security and healthcare for their citizens. The variations seen in the studies mentioned are nuanced and often sectoral in nature. In contrast, the assumption of sufficient institutional capacity is clearly misleading when we study emerging countries as a lack of institutional capacity has always been a key problem for them.[67] In many cases, their limited capacity to prevent crime and violence, collect taxes, and construct infrastructure for economic activity reduces opportunities for economic development. Such problems are all the more serious in the case of national environmental policies and the implementation of treaties, because these policies are a relatively new consideration for the governments of emerging countries.

This book is not an inquiry into the origins of institutional capacity, but the literature on comparative politics offers several useful insights into why some countries tend to have stronger institutions than others. One approach emphasizes fundamental geographic factors, such as population density and terrain.[68] In this telling, high population densities and territories that make transportation easy help states gain control of the population and build basic infrastructure for governance.

Another approach emphasizes the deep historical roots of culture, noting that building institutional capacity requires extended periods of time—perhaps centuries, or even millennia—and areas with long histories of state-building tend to perform better than more recent entrants.[69] Many emerging countries suffocated under the yoke of colonialism for centuries, losing valuable time to build their own institutions. From a more recent perspective, scholarship has also investigated the incentives of politicians to invest in state capacity, noting that creating a powerful and capable bureaucracy can constrain a ruler's power.[70] The key point here is that the lack of institutional capacity is not specific to energy and environment, but rather an overarching constraint and challenge for many emerging and developing economies that have not inherited homegrown Weberian bureaucracies. The lack of institutional capacity, therefore, cannot be attributed to a lack of interest in sustainable development. It is a pervasive problem that cuts across different sectors of the economy and society.

Unfortunately, the problem of institutional capacity cannot be easily solved by simply copying the institutional structures of industrialized countries. As Andrews, Pritchett, and Woolcock note, such "institutional isomorphism"—the tendency to replicate formats that have proven successful elsewhere—is unlikely to solve the problem of institutional capacity.[71] Institutional forms that perform well in the peaceful, prosperous, and organized Swedish society may achieve nothing in unstable and violent Afghanistan. What is worse, the mimicry of "best practices" in industrialized countries may even be counterproductive, as scarce resources are dedicated to constructing administrative systems that do not fit the needs of the local context. As Ostrom, Janssen, and Anderies have noted in their work on local institutional solutions to the problem of the tragedy of the commons, the breathtaking diversity of conditions on the ground means that the quest for a panacea—in other words, a global best practice—is futile.[72]

In the case of environmental policy, it is certainly true that Western institutions are proliferating across borders. Aklin and Urpelainen report quantitative evidence of the proliferation of environmental ministries across the world, while a volume edited by Weidner and Jänicke shows that Western environmental institutions and policies are slowly finding their way to postcommunist and even emerging countries.[73] The ability of these institutions to thwart environmental degradation, however, remains in doubt. While Aklin and Urpelainen find that pollution levels decrease upon the establishment of an environmental ministry, they only compare countries with and without ministries—a low standard of performance, as countries that still have no environmental ministry whatsoever tend to suffer from a wide range of governance problems. Weidner and Jänicke, in turn, do not even attempt to link environmental institutionalization and pollution or resource depletion outcomes.

To drive home this essential point, consider a few examples. The first is the difficulty of controlling groundwater depletion in India. As Shah notes in his overview of groundwater management in South Asia, India's groundwater resources are disappearing at an alarming rate because of excessive extraction with electric pumps for irrigation from ever-deeper wells.[74] While the "green revolution" brought high-yield plant varieties to India and thus enabled massive gains in agricultural productivity,[75] it also greatly increased demand for irrigation. As Narayanamoorthy notes in his discussion of "India's groundwater boom," 14 percent of India's groundwater blocks "are classified as over-exploited" across India, with 90 percent of such blocks concentrated in six states only.[76]

In this situation, many Indian states offer farmers heavily subsidized electricity, even though the low cost of electricity is a key reason for the rapid decline of groundwater levels. While replacing subsidized electricity with direct cash transfers would allow farmers to maintain their income levels and avert the tragedy of the commons of ground water depletion, Indian policy makers have not found a practical solution to the problem of achieving such a policy change. And, as Victor notes, it is much easier for policy makers to regulate prices than to develop a credible, effective system that allows cash transfers and prevents abuse.[77] The lack of institutional capacity raises obstacles to policy changes that would benefit large swaths of the Indian population in the long run.

Even environmental policy in a middle-income country, such as Brazil, is restricted by a lack of institutional capacity. Until recent advances in satellite monitoring, for example, the Brazilian federal and state governments faced major difficulties in even detecting deforestation.[78] According to Nepstad et al., for example, it was only in 2004 that the Brazilian government launched a satellite system, Detection of Deforestation in Real Time (DETER), capable of monitoring deforestation events on a short notice.[79] To the extent that deforestation is detected, the enforcement of policies against deforestation at the municipal level has always been an issue for the poor Amazonian municipalities. As Cisneros, Hargrave, and Kis-Katos note, corruption at the municipal level is associated with more rapid deforestation in the Brazilian Amazon.[80]

Trade in endangered species and hazardous waste offers yet another illustration. Although agreements such as the 1973 Convention on International Trade in Endangered Species of Wild Fauna and Flora (CITES) created a legislative framework for preventing the exploitation of endangered species for economic gain,[81] stopping the hunting and trading of such species in poor countries has proven to be an enormous challenge. In a comprehensive review of the enforcement of CITES, Reeve finds that noncompliance is often related to lacking institutional capacity at the national level. For example, "A key institutional weakness at the national level is the lack of specialized wildlife law enforcement units in all but the few parties where they have been established voluntarily. Among the scientific and management institutions that exist, there is enormous variation in capacity, funding and competence from party to party."[82] Because the prevention of illegal trade in endangered species requires either the stopping of poaching or effective control at customs, national institutional capacity clearly plays a critical role in the enforcement of this global environmental treaty.

In a similar vein, the Basel Convention on the Control of Transboundary Movements of Hazardous Wastes and their Disposal (1989) both addresses and raises issues of capacity building.[83] As illegal traders import hazardous waste into developing countries, these countries lack the capacity to enforce rules against dumping, and hence there is a need for a multilateral treaty.[84] At the same time, implementing the provisions of the treaty to stop dumping requires institutional capacity, and the treaty puts a lot of emphasis on capacity building for waste-importing nations. Indeed, Marcoux and Urpelainen find that weak regulatory capacity is a strong predictor of the ratification of the Basel Convention among developing countries, whereas the subsequent Ban Amendment, which would specifically prohibit trade in hazardous waste, has received little support among developing countries.[85]

When some countries lack the capacity to control their environmental externalities, the role of their governments in negotiations changes. They are no longer at the bargaining table to make demands and promises in the sense that conventional negotiation theory would have it. Instead, they are there to highlight their power to destroy and inability to stop the destruction without financial and technical assistance from other countries. This feature of North-South negotiations is essential to understanding the direction of global environmental politics today.

In the long run, institutional capacity and power to destroy go hand in hand, as institutions play a key role in generating economic growth.[86] In the short to medium run, however, improvements in institutional capacity may lag behind economic growth. International commodity prices, demographic changes, foreign direct investment, public investment, development aid, and global economic booms can allow countries to grow despite institutional deficiencies. What is more, countries often generate growth from solving specific institutional problems, such as excessive licensing requirements in pre-1991 India, without improving their capacity for energy and environmental policy. Thus it would be a mistake to expect institutional capacity to automatically follow economic growth in the short run. It certainly seems unlikely that a country could become a full-fledged innovation economy without robust institutions, but a country need not be an innovation leader to have power to destroy. Quite the contrary, countries that can generate industrial growth but perform poorly in advanced technology, such as China at the turn of the millennium or the Soviet Union at its peak, had tremendous power to destroy despite fundamental institutional weaknesses.

If anything, the importance of institutional capacity is amplified by domestic politics. When institutional capacity is low, governments can use this as an excuse for inaction.[87] A government with limited institutional capacity can choose not to invest in environmental protection and then attribute bad environmental outcomes to problems in implementation. The lack of institutional capacity thus becomes linked to both preferences and structural power, as governments can use their lacking capacity to hide their true preferences.

This relationship, in turn, can amplify the effects of structural power on negotiation outcomes. A government with lots of structural power is particularly dangerous when it has little institutional capacity, as the failure to stop environmental deterioration cannot be unambiguously attributed to the government's preferences and behavior.[88]

Finally, the number of players in the game is a systemic feature. This number can be defined as the count of governments that have enough power to destroy to shape outcomes of negotiations. Although there are today about two hundred sovereign countries in the international system, the reality is that most of them are at most marginally relevant in international environmental negotiations. Only countries with large and/or rapidly expanding economies, high willingness to pay for environmental protection, or control of special resources such as rainforests or fisheries can expect to play a key role in negotiations. In some cases, such as climate negotiations, governments of countries that are particularly vulnerable—say, low-lying islands threatened by sea level rise—are also potential candidates.[89]

The exact measurement of the number of players is difficult, but a rough estimate can be easily derived for any given issue that is being negotiated. The first step is to rank countries in terms of their power to destroy. Any government from a country that has enough power to destroy to materially influence environmental outcomes is included in the set of players for the game. Among the remaining countries, one must then investigate whether they have other relevant resources. The most important among these is the ability to offer side payments or issue linkages. The government of a country without the power to destroy but with financial resources or structural importance in other areas could thus play an important role. For example, if a Scandinavian country has a high willingness to pay for rainforest conservation, its government can qualify as an important player in the game in spite of its lack of any rainforest whatsoever.

To illustrate this notion, let us consider the case of ozone depletion, where we can create a rough count of players at any given time by looking at a few economic fundamentals. Negotiations to address ozone depletion began in the late 1970s and were mostly a transatlantic affair, with 85 percent of the chlorohydrofluorocarbon market controlled by the United States and members of the European Community.[90] Besides these two camps, several major developing countries, notably China and India, later came to play a minor role because of their *future potential* for ozone depletion.[91] Other players, such as the Soviet Union and Japan, did not play an important role in the negotiations by this logic. As Hoffmann puts it, "Ozone depletion did not have to become a problem requiring universal participation."[92] Thus we can say that the number of players in these negotiations was small, especially if we consider the European Community as one player.[93]

A POLITICAL ECONOMY OF GLOBAL ENVIRONMENTAL POLITICS

Equipped with these assumptions, I will now discuss the relationship between international political economy and global environmental politics. In particular, I derive predictions about the effects of changes in structural power, and thus the number of players, on environmental policies, agreements, and outcomes. The most important predictions are interactive in that they concern the impact of emerging economies' growing power to destroy under conditions of relatively weak environmental preferences and limited institutional capacity.

The basic logic of the argument is illustrated in figure 1.1. In the figure, the rectangles are countries. The size of a rectangle indicates a country's power to destroy, whereas the color indicates the environmental preferences, with darker shades indicating more pro-environmental attitudes. Finally, the numbers within the rectangles indicate each country's

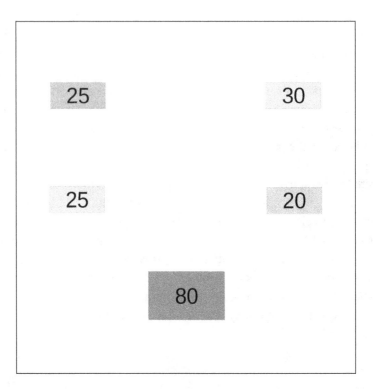

FIGURE 1.1 Basic components of the argument. The size of each rectangle indicates a country's power to destroy; the depth of the color indicates the strength of proenvironmental preference; the number inside each rectangle indicates institutional capacity.

institutional capacity on a 0–100 scale, with higher values indicating more capacity.

The values of my four variables can thus be easily read from such a graphic for any given global environmental issue at any given time. The number of rectangles reveals the number of players that can be considered pivotal to negotiation outcomes, while their relative sizes show the distribution of relative bargaining power. The colors and numbers inside the rectangles, in turn, show the distribution of preferences and institutional capacity. The constellation of these four factors constitutes my analytical model for both the twentieth and the twenty-first centuries.

To begin with, structural power determines the extent to which preferences translate into preferred negotiation outcomes, as countries with lots of structural power secure outcomes close their preferences. If a country's policies are pivotal for realizing good environmental outcomes, it can expect a lot of concessions and effort from other countries. If this government considers global environmental outcomes important, it can offer sizable concessions in exchange for comparable efforts of other governments. If the government is not very interested in environmental outcomes, it can instead focus on side payments and issue linkages. In any case, structural power is a key ingredient in the formula that generates answers to the central question of politics: Who gets what?

Now consider preferences. Roughly speaking, negotiations can be understood as interactions between governments with different environmental preferences. Governments with strong environmental preferences are in the negotiations to secure a deal, and they are looking for ways to coax their less interested counterparts to join the effort. On the other hand, governments with weak environmental preferences are primarily interested in avoiding costly commitments and securing side payments for their efforts. The strength of a country's environmental preference thus depends on the balance of costs and benefits from increasing the ambition of environmental protection, as aggregated and weighted by the country's political institutions, under an international environmental treaty. Countries with strong environmental preferences are willing to pay a relatively high cost for ambitious outcomes, countries with weak environmental preferences oppose any move to increase the ambition unless the accompanying cost is low.

Although there is considerable variation across the specific preferences of different countries, in the end a government's bargaining position depends, first and foremost, on whether they are willing to offer concessions—whether effort, issue linkage, or side payment—in exchange for the environmental effort of other governments. From this perspective, the distributive outcomes of global environmental negotiations can be characterized as a set of environmental commitments made by the parties and a set of accompanying transfers (issue linkages or side payments that typically benefit those parties with weak environmental preferences).[94]

Finally, variation in institutional capacity adds another complication to the system. If a government has little institutional capacity, the dynamics of both bargaining and enforcement change. At the bargaining stage, the lack of institutional capacity means that the country can request assistance from others and thus put a burden on countries with strong environmental preferences. Such a request is potentially appealing and difficult for donors to reject, as it appears to reflect a certain helplessness, instead of simple greed or material self-interest.

At the enforcement stage, the lack of institutional capacity can be expected to complicate enforcement, and indirectly participation. Unless governments find ways to solve problems of institutional capacity, the risk of (unintended) noncompliance increases. In international relations, Chayes and Chayes consider such lack of capacity—as opposed to willful defection—to be a central factor in explaining noncompliance.[95] Even if governments are interested in meeting their treaty obligations and understand that a failure to comply could threaten the future of the treaty, including attractive side payments and issue linkages, the lack of institutional capacity may prevent them from implementing the policies to bring about the desired outcome.

ADDING NEW PLAYERS WITH DIFFERENT CHARACTERISTICS

Based on these considerations, we can now consider the effects of adding new players with different characteristics into the system. Recall that new players are added when their structural power reaches a level that makes them important in the negotiations. In the case of emerging economies, the growth in structural power typically takes the form of growth in power to destroy.

At the systemic level, the number of players shapes both individual and collective outcomes. As the number of players increases, the dimensionality of possible deals grows. Even if we retain the one-dimensional approach to environmental preferences, the number of possible deals with different degrees of burden-sharing changes. Equally important, the difficulty of enticing participation and enforcing implementation grows larger and larger. When more countries play an important role in negotiations, fewer of them are individually pivotal. Thus individual countries have incentives to avoid costly individual actions and let others carry the burden. And when everyone does so, the environmental problem at hand remains unresolved.

There is, however, a critical difference in expanding the number of players by adding governments with weak versus strong environmental preferences. When governments with weak preferences are added, the difficulty of securing deals increases, and both participation and enforcement become more complicated. As noted, governments with weak environmental preferences are not terribly interested in collective environmental outcomes, so adding them to the system puts more and more pressure on governments with strong environmental preferences to offer side payments and lucrative issue linkages. Because even governments with strong environmental preferences not only face competing demands and domestic constraints but also have an incentive to downplay their willingness to offer concessions for environmental promises for bargaining reasons, the number of governments with weak environmental preferences is closely linked to the difficulty of negotiations.

When countries with strong preferences are added, however, the effects on negotiation outcomes are by no means obvious. On the one hand, complexity in negotiations does increase, and the usual collective action problems related to participation and enforcement become more difficult. Even a country with strong environmental preferences has an incentive to free ride when dealing with global environmental problems and the associated transboundary externalities. At the same time, countries with strong preferences are willing and able to dedicate resources to secure the participation and compliance of countries with weak preferences. As the number of countries with strong preferences increases, their collective ability to make concessions to governments with weaker environmental preferences grows—of course, subject to the inherent difficulty of collective action in making concessions to others, as each potential donor wants others to foot a larger share of the bill.

Another essential consideration is the modifying effect of institutional capacity. When new players are added, their institutional capacity plays an important role in shaping national policy, negotiation outcomes, and environmental policy. Governments with lots of institutional capacity can, if they so wish, deal with their environmental problems through effective policy. They can also implement their treaty commitments.

A government with a lot of power to destroy but no institutional capacity, on the other hand, is a cause for concern. Such a government may fail to prevent environmental destruction out of sheer incompetence or lack of resources. A lack of institutional capacity can even make the threat underpinning a country's power to destroy credible as a matter of course. A country without institutional capacity cannot act effectively to prevent destruction, and thus the power to destroy will likely translate into destruction unless other countries or external actors step in to help with mitigation and abatement. This external support, in turn, contributes to the country's bargaining power. Weak institutional capacity can help a country secure concession from others, as the lack of capacity motivates external support and resource transfer.

In a proposal for engaging developing countries with climate governance, Victor proposed "climate accession deals" that address the interplay of preferences, institutional capacity, and power to destroy. As he explains,

> Those nations, so far, have been nearly universal in their refusal to make credible commitments to reduce growth in their emissions of greenhouse gases for two reasons. First, most put a higher priority on economic growth far above distant, global environmental goods. Even those that have signaled their intention to slow the rise in their emissions have offered policies that differ little from what they would have done anyway to promote economic growth. Second, the governments of the largest and most rapidly developing countries—such as China and India—actually have little administrative ability to control emissions in many sectors of their economy. Even if they adopted policies to control emissions it is not clear that firms and local governments would actually follow.[96]

Recognizing the dual problem of diverging interests and lack of capacity, he proposes that industrialized countries offer emerging economies contracts that condition various benefits, such as technology or finance, on programs and policies proposed by the emerging economies themselves. By doing so, governments of industrialized countries can simultaneously be sensitive to the challenges faced by emerging economies and yet create concrete incentives for action. While emerging economies have increasingly embraced low-carbon solutions like renewable energy, they continue to prioritize economic development over climate mitigation, noting that industrialized countries have far higher per capita emissions and have polluted the atmosphere for centuries.

The most important interactions between structural power and the other country-level variables can thus be summarized as follows:

- Low environmental preference amplifies the effects of emerging economies' growing structural power, especially power to destroy, on individual bargaining outcomes (+) and the likelihood and depth of cooperation (–).
- Low institutional capacity amplifies effects of emerging economies' growing structural power, especially power to destroy, on individual bargaining outcomes (+) and the likelihood and depth of cooperation (–).

The growth in structural power, and the resulting increase in the number of players, need not itself be critical. If the growing structural power were underpinned by strong environmental preferences and adequate institutional capacity, managing the entry of new players with power to destroy would be relatively easy. Governments would invest in environmental protection and achieve success thanks to their implementation capabilities. Instead, the key challenge lies with achieving cooperation when the increasingly powerful emerging economies are not fully committed to environmental cooperation and lack the institutional capacity to implement policies. These emerging economies hesitate to invest scarce resources in environmental protection because even if they decided to do so, they might fail to achieve their goals because of implementation failures.

Finally, we need to consider the interaction between institutional capacity and preferences. A government with strong environmental preferences and weak institutional capacity is an ideal target for side payments or assistance, as other governments can trust it to use any resources available for good purposes. Such a government is interested in environmental protection, and others can trust it to implement policies in good faith, but side payments and assistance help remove the capacity constraint.

The more difficult case is a country with weak environmental preferences and weak institutional capacity. Such a country is both unwilling and unable to protect the environment, so using side payments to secure deals is very difficult. Even if the government negotiates a deal to invest in institutional capacity in exchange for support, be it technology or technical assistance or money, the government has an incentive to accept the resources but then divert them into other uses, instead of institutional capacity building for environmental protection.

The challenge for the wealthier countries is formidable. On the one hand, we have already seen that public opinion tends to oppose resource transfers to foreign recipients regardless of their environmental merit. On the other hand, the fact that environmental preferences in many emerging economies remain weak means that (1) only large side payments would seal the deal and (2) the risk that the recipient diverts the side payments to other uses is real. For political reasons, governments hesitate to make large side payments that could be diverted. Thus the combination of domestic political constraints in industrialized countries and weak environmental preferences in emerging economies makes the use of side payments a major challenge in global environmental negotiations.

So far, I have focused on the country-level variables and their interactions. The appropriate application of this model, however, also requires considering the nature of the issue at hand. Here I draw a distinction between two archetypal cases: narrow and broad issues. In narrow issues, the environmental problem at hand originates from behavior within a specific sector, such as the use of a specific chemical or the production process of a specific industry. In broad issues, the environmental problem stems from behavior that cuts across wide swaths of the economy, such as the use of energy or demand for land clearing.

In narrow issues, negotiators can often find creative solutions to circumventing the political difficulties prompted by the rise of the emerging economies. When the problem at hand has a specific source, the behavioral adjustments required to solve the problem are limited to controlling that particular source. Even if preferences are diverse and institutional capacity limited, negotiators can have confidence in the effectiveness of simple and straightforward policies, such as banning a specific product. If some governments are concerned about the cost of such solutions, compensating them for their losses with exceptions, graduated phase-outs, or direct compensation is not very difficult.

But when the issue at hand is a broad one, the rise of emerging economies creates very difficult challenges in the negotiations. Modifying socioeconomic patterns of behavior across multiple sectors with potentially complex spillovers and general-equilibrium effects is both difficult and expensive. With diverging preferences and severe limitations of institutional capacity at the national level, finding an effective and mutually agreeable solution is hard; when the requirement of incentives and capacity for compliance is added, this difficulty is further amplified. In this sense, it can be said that the rise of emerging economies creates greater complications in negotiations to address broad rather than narrow considerations. This observation, however, does not significantly limit the importance of the analytical model, as the environmental significance of the rise of the emerging economies lies mostly with broad issues, such as energy and land use, rather than specific sectoral challenges.

SIMPLE AND COMPLEX SITUATIONS

The transformation of global environmental politics is essentially a story of the changing role of emerging economies. To understand these changes, I construct two hypothetical situations: one simple and the other complex. In the simple situation, the number of players with power to destroy is relatively small, while both their environmental preference and institutional capacity are relatively strong. In the complex situation, the number of players with power to destroy is relatively high, and many of them both have weak environmental preferences and lack institutional capacity.

In the twentieth century both problem structures were common. In negotiations on global environmental issues driven by energy and resource consumption, the situations were often simple because industrialized countries dominated the negotiations. In contrast, negotiations focused on natural resource endowments, such as rainforests, were complex because many of the key players were developing countries with weak environmental preferences and limited institutional capacity.

In the twenty-first century most global environmental negotiations now present complex situations. Emerging economies' power to destroy has grown so much that they are almost always pivotal players, regardless of whether they have natural resource endowments. Because these emerging economies' environmental preferences and institutional capacity remain relatively weak, this power to destroy produces bad outcomes in global environmental politics. Emerging economies are reluctant to invest in environmental protection, and industrialized countries fail to amass the resources required to remedy the capacity constraints of cooperation.

The two problem structures are summarized in figure 1.2. On the left is a stylized illustration of the simpler problem structure. The number of

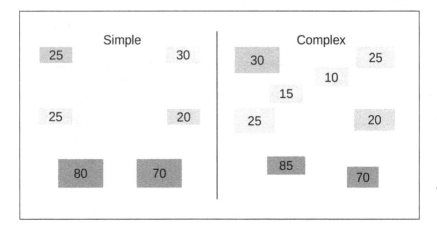

FIGURE 1.2 Comparing the simple and complex logics of global environmental politics. The key change is that new players enter the game because of the growth in their power to destroy. From left to right, the number of players increases and the power to destroy is more evenly distributed. Institutional capacity and environmental preferences are no longer highly correlated with the power to destroy.

players is relatively small, and the countries with the most power to destroy have both a relatively high environmental preference and relatively extensive institutional capacity. There are countries with only a weak preference for the environment, but these countries do not have a lot of power to destroy. Their institutional capacity is also limited, but this fact is not significant because such capacity has little relevance for the global environment in the absence of substantial power to destroy. As a result, the core logic of global environmental negotiations is that of bargaining in a small group with relatively similar environmental preferences and lots of institutional capacity for implementation and compliance. The right side of the figure illustrates a more challenging problem structure. Here the number of players has increased, and the power to destroy is more evenly distributed. Most important, the numbers of players and the power to destroy of countries with a *weak* environmental preference and a *low* institutional capacity have both increased significantly.

In these negotiations, deal-making among governments with relatively strong environmental preferences continues, but the process is complicated by the need to consider the interests of the new players. Because the

number of relevant players is now larger than in the past, achieving substantive outcomes requires more complicated deals than in the past. The
number of pivotal governments who must join and comply with a treaty
for effective environmental cooperation grows, and thus the likelihood
of success decreases. Because the new players that have entered the game
often have relatively weak environmental preferences and little institutional capacity, their aggressive demands for accommodation and limited ability to deliver on their premises further add to the difficulty of
global environmental cooperation. All else constant, then, the logic of
global environmental politics in the twenty-first century is less favorable
to cooperation than the logic of the previous century.[97]

Historically, the twentieth century saw global environmental negotiations of both types. Some issues, such as ozone depletion and transboundary air pollution, were relatively simple in that the important
governments with power to destroy were mostly from advanced industrialized nations. Others, such as deforestation, were always difficult
because developing countries controlled the key endowments, and thus
North-South politics surrounded the negotiations from the beginning.
In the twenty-first century the complex situations will be more common
than the simple ones.

The first central difference between the simple and the complex situations is the difficulty of negotiating global environmental treaties. In the
simple situation, a relatively small number of parties with relatively high
environmental preferences were, for the most part, able to find solutions
to problems such as ozone depletion. In the complex situation, the large
number of relevant parties, many of whom are represented by governments with weak preferences and limited institutional capacity, greatly
complicate such negotiations. Because of this difference, the new logic is
less conducive to success in global environmental cooperation than the
old one.

I expect these differences to manifest themselves in negotiations on
issues that require broad and deep behavioral changes, such as fossil fuels
or land use. The need for deep behavioral changes is what makes negotiating broad-based multilateral treaties among a diverse group of countries
with limited institutional capacity difficult. Simple and narrow problems,
such as banning a specific product or regulating a small sector of the industry, remain manageable because they do not create the deep distributional

conflicts that other, broader issues do. While they are not as effective as economy-wide approaches,[98] they tend to perform better in political feasibility and implementability.

THEORY MEETS DATA

My integral approach to mapping the broad contours of global environmental politics does not lend itself to conventional micro-analytical hypothesis testing or causal inference. One does not have to be a Buddhist to recognize that the world is one interconnected system, which means that we cannot define "treatment" and "control" groups for the analysis. Global environmental politics is ultimately one single phenomenon, and any analysis thereof must recognize that the subject matter is the planet as a whole. A systemic, instead of reductionist, approach is necessary for a satisfactory analysis of the causes of global environmental deterioration—and for finding solutions to the problem.

Recognizing the difficulty of systemic problems, my empirical analysis combines insights from two perspectives. The first is a dynamic systemic analysis. I examine changes in international political economy over a period of five decades and then see whether these changes generate the kinds of effects my theory predicts. This investigation can be considered a single case study with two time periods.[99] I do not have any cross-sectional variation I could exploit, so the focus is exclusively on understanding the logic of the system at the two time periods and then linking changes in the dependent and explanatory variables. Before-and-after comparisons are not the ideal scientific method, but such is the lot of a scholar of global environmental politics. There cannot be variation across units when the number of units is one. Therefore the best I can do is to triangulate my empirical findings by testing several hypotheses, providing multiple sources of evidence, rejecting alternative explanations, and exercising due caution in interpreting the findings.

I then turn to my second approach, country case studies. Given my emphasis on emerging economies, I survey their evolving positions over time and assess whether they are consistent with the predictions of my theory. Here, I face the difficult choice of choosing case studies. One approach would be to compare industrialized and all kinds of developing countries over time. Such an analysis, however, would limit my ability to explore patterns in a meaningful number of developing countries. Thus I focus on different types of developing countries, beginning with two of those that have already benefited from years of robust economic growth: China and India. I then turn to countries at the beginning stages of their emergence, and finally I examine the case of least developed countries with future potential. For each group, I look at both their past and current status and can thus see if temporal trends in their positions and policies accord with the theoretical expectations I have formulated.

When conducting the system-level analysis, I begin by discussing changes in the values of the four fundamental variables: number of players, structural power (power to destroy), environmental preferences, and institutional capacity. I amass empirical evidence for what those values were roughly in the second half of the twentieth century for different kinds of problems and then summarize how they have changed over time. Here my approach is somewhat selective. The field of global environmental politics is far too broad for me to cover all relevant issues and negotiations; yet focusing on individual issues would also move the analysis away from the goal of understanding general structural changes. Thus I rely on my own reading of the literature and knowledge of the subject matter in choosing areas of focus. I try to paint a clear, vivid picture of general trends in global environmental politics that characterize the evolution of negotiations and treaty implementation across multiple issue areas.

To give the inquiry structure, I specifically compare the trajectories of three important environmental regimes over time: climate change, biodiversity loss, and chemicals. Climate change is the most salient facet of global environmental politics today, with possibly the highest stakes and most activity at both the international and national levels. Biodiversity loss, in turn, is another major environmental issue that highlights the challenges of dealing with the tragedy of the commons at the international level. The chemicals regime, in my assessment, is one of the more dynamic and positive fields of global environmental politics and thus lends an opportunity to explain a regime with a relatively high degree of success. I define each regime broadly and look beyond multilateral treaties to issues such as the operation of multilateral development agencies, rules governing export credit, and national policies.

The following country-level analysis allows me to be more specific. As I conduct country case studies over long periods of time, I am unable to comment on the intricacies of each country's strategy in different negotiations but can offer a comprehensive and accurate picture of the broad contours of the country's preferences, structural power, institutional capacity, and policies as well as outcomes in global environmental politics. In these discussions, I emphasize changes over time and their drivers over cross-country comparisons. However, I rely heavily on the system-level analysis to situate the country case studies into the broader international political economy framework that I am using. In global environmental politics, all governments are acutely aware of the surrounding international political economy, negotiating and implementing policies under a host of domestic and international pressures.

No book on global environmental politics today can ignore China and India, so I begin my country case studies with an analysis of these two giants. There is a consensus on China's centrality in contemporary global environmental politics.[100] The country's spectacular industrial boom since the decision in 1978 to liberalize and modernize the economy has made the world's most populous country a leader in greenhouse gas emissions and the demand for fossil fuels and other natural resources. Given China's ravenous hunger for resources and the resulting capacity to pollute, it is essential to understand how its positions in negotiations have changed. What is more, China stands out among emerging economies as naturally pivotal given that its economy is much, much larger than those of other emerging economies, including India.

India, on the other hand, is only now beginning to have the kind of power to destroy that it needs to be a major player in international environmental negotiations. Although India has a history of vocal opposition to the environmental agenda of industrialized countries,[101] until recently such opposition was largely cheap talk and of symbolic importance. But today the situation is very different because of the country's bright growth prospects and rapidly growing population.[102] All eyes are on India now, so understanding its evolving role in global environmental politics is critical. India is not yet the major economy that China is, but there is every reason to believe that this will change in the future.

If my theory is useful, it should also say something about a much larger number of emerging economies that are only slightly behind China and

India in their growth. These countries are Vietnam, Philippines, Indonesia, and Nigeria. I also consider Brazil, given its critical role in deforestation, as an illustration of the persistent difficulty of global environmental cooperation on natural resources.

Because my project is future-oriented, I also investigate the situation of least developed countries with significant economic growth potential: Bangladesh, Myanmar, Ethiopia, and Tanzania. These countries have yet to play a major role in global environmental negotiations, but their large populations and rapid economic growth rates mean that they are becoming important players in their own right. By observing their recent trajectories and considering the lessons from the six other case studies— China, India, Vietnam, Philippines, Indonesia, and Nigeria—we can arrive at informed expectations about the future of global environmental politics.

With the exception of Brazil, the regional focus of my analysis is restricted to Asia and sub-Saharan Africa. Because the most important Latin American countries have already reached upper-middle-income status, they will not drive the transformation of global environmental politics in the same way that the populous nations of Asia and Africa will. The Middle Eastern countries do have significant potential for population and economic growth, but they have already established themselves as global important players thanks to their large fossil fuel endowments.

2

GLOBAL ENVIRONMENTAL POLITICS
IN THE AMERICAN CENTURY

I n 1995 the international community gathered in Berlin, capital of the
recently unified Germany, to initiate negotiations on a protocol that
would turn the United Nations Framework Convention on Climate
Change (UNFCCC) of 1992 into concrete action. Following the successful and widely applauded model of the Montreal Protocol, the negotiation outcome—the Berlin Mandate—reaffirmed the principle of "common
but differentiated responsibilities" by excusing developing country parties from any and all emission reduction targets. With the Berlin Mandate set in stone, the Kyoto Protocol in 1997 accordingly imposed no
requirements on developing countries to reduce their emissions.

The Berlin Mandate captures an important dimension of twentieth-
century global environmental politics. In 1995, only five years before the
end of the century, negotiators in industrialized countries accepted a principle that all but excluded most of the world—including all of today's
emerging economies—from climate cooperation. While such a negotiation outcome would have been preposterous in the Bali negotiations in
2007 or after them, in the early days of the climate regime it was com-
monly understood that when it came to global warming, industrialized
countries were both the problem and the solution.

Drawing inspiration from the Berlin Mandate, I describe and explain
the model of global environmental politics in the twentieth century. Having outlined my argument in the previous chapter, in this chapter I first

describe core features of global environmental politics in the American century. I briefly review the origins of modern global environmental politics, while giving its predecessors due attention. At that time, important global environmental problems stemming from energy and resource consumption were addressed in negotiations between key industrialized countries. A small number of countries with relatively, though not perfectly, similar environmental preferences and high levels of institutional capacity held the vast majority of power to destroy. These characteristics can explain why top-down, multilateral treaties achieved a relatively high level of cooperation. On the other hand, those issues that were about natural resource endowments or population growth in the Third World saw much less cooperation—fewer treaties, with lower levels of ambition—because of heterogeneous preferences and low levels of institutional capacity in a large number of relevant players.

The first environmental agreements are older than the twentieth century, but interest in global environmental politics exploded in the aftermath of the post-1945 industrial boom in Europe and the United States. As households grew wealthier and the costs of pollution became obvious, politicians faced new pressures to stop environmental destruction. It soon became clear, however, that domestic policies would not be enough. Transboundary air pollution, risks related to nuclear power, the decline of oceanic fisheries, and the environmental problems caused by population growth were all seen as global problems requiring international cooperation. These problems resulted in the negotiation and implementation of a large number of multilateral environmental treaties that, all the cynicism aside, did a reasonably good job in an imperfect world. These treaties worked fairly well when their main goal was to enable cooperation among a small number of countries with largely similar preferences and relatively high levels of institutional capacity—and less well in other circumstances.

THE EARLY YEARS

International environmental agreements date back at least to the nineteenth century. Mitchell lists the Agreement Respecting the Regulation of the Flow of Water from Lake Constance between Austria, Switzerland, and the German states of Baden, Bavaria, and Wurttemberg in 1857 as the first multilateral environmental agreement.[1] Although the data suggest that only fourteen original treaties were formulated by the year 1900, they covered a wide range of topics from plant protection to fisheries and water pollution. Their geographic focus was not limited to Europe, either, as the Convention for the Preservation of the Fur Seal and Sea Otter in the North Pacific Ocean and Bering Sea in 1897 included Japan and the United States as members, whereas an agreement in 1885 focused on the Congo River Basin.[2]

The real surge of global environmental politics, however, had to wait until the end of the Second World War. While only 32 multilateral environmental agreements were negotiated between January 1900 and the end of the Second World War in August 1945 after Japan's surrender, as many as 45 agreements were negotiated by 1959 and another 58 in the 1960s. From 1970 until 2012 another 981 agreements were negotiated. During the golden decade of global environmental cooperation, 1990–1999, 384 new agreements came into being. This large set includes such central conventions as the United Nations Framework Convention on Climate Change and Convention on Biological Diversity, both negotiated in 1992 at the United Nations Conference on Environment and Development in Rio de Janeiro, also known as the Earth Summit.

The origins of this surge in environmental cooperation can be found in growing environmental awareness, first in the United States and then in Western Europe. In the 1960s the rapid expansion of industrial production had both created a host of serious environmental problems, such as air and water pollution, and brought unprecedented wealth to the citizens of the United States and Western Europe. As Dalton notes, "The writings of conservationists took on added force because of several dramatic environmental crises that occurred in the later 1960s."[3] These crises included a variety of oil spills in the English Channel and off Santa Barbara, California; smog in Los Angeles and London; the Love Canal toxic waste disaster in Niagara Falls, New York; and countless others.

An important milestone in the development of modern environmental awareness was the publication of Rachel Carson's *Silent Spring* in 1962.[4] In this hugely popular but controversial volume with a memorable title, Carson demonstrated the dangers of excessive pesticide use for ecosystems, wildlife, and humans. Her analysis was fiercely debated in the media between her supporters and detractors, especially the chemical industry, which dismissed Carson as a "hysterical" woman. The book contributed to the emergence of an environmental awareness, first among Americans and then Europeans, and thus provoked demands for solutions to a wide range of environmental problems, including but not limited to pesticide use. By 1970 the environment had become such a popular and salient cause for Americans that on April 22 Senator Gaylord Nelson led the first Earth Day, initially as a "national teach-in on the environment."[5] Since then, Earth Day has been celebrated every year not only in the United States but across the world as an expression of public support for environmental protection and solidarity among environmentalists.

In the United States, where environmental issues began to play an increasing important role in politics, "the federal government, which frequently moves at a glacial pace in dealing with social problems, responded in the 1960s and 1970s with surprising speed to the rising concern over the deterioration of the environment."[6] Under President Richard Nixon, a Republican, the National Environmental Policy Act was enacted on January 1, 1970, and on December 2 of that year the Environmental Protection Agency (EPA) was created. Other landmark legislation to deal with environmental problems was formulated by the Nixon administration in the early 1970s, before the October 1973 oil crisis. But when energy prices shot through the roof in the United States after the Arab countries imposed an embargo in response to the Yom Kippur war with Israel in October 1973, interest in environmental issues took a back seat as the United States struggled with inflation, unemployment, and low economic growth.[7]

THE GROWING NORTH-SOUTH DIVIDE

At the global level, early efforts to protect the environment culminated in June 1972 at the United Nations Conference on the Human Environment in Stockholm, only a year after the Ramsar Convention on Wetlands. The proposal for "the convening of an international conference on the problems of human environment" came from Sweden in 1968 and was endorsed by the United Nations Economic and Social Council and General Assembly.[8] As Rowland writes, "Public pressure for action was enormous, and still intensifying. . . . Throughout most of the industrialized world, it was now unthinkable to neglect a mention of ecology."[9] Growing public awareness of the deteriorating status of the global environment, which could be seen in highly visible problems such as Los Angeles smog or, indeed, the silent spring from the pesticide-related deaths of birds, put pressure on democratic governments to develop solutions to environmental problems—or lose elections and be replaced by their greener competitors.

Already at the preparatory stage of the Stockholm conference, however, the difficulties of global environmental politics became apparent. Some members of the preparatory committee wanted to clearly separate international law and domestic policy to avoid legally binding provisions, while others emphasized the importance of a clear statement of universal principles to guide environmental policies and cooperation.[10] This conflict forebode similar conflicts, often along North-South lines. A particularly important challenge for the conveners was to dispel the then-prevalent belief among the developing nations that "developed nations were using environmental doomsday predictions as a racist device to keep the nonwhite third world at a relatively low level of development."[11] These concerns stemmed from a long and brutal history of colonialism, which left the newly sovereign countries suspicious and concerned about Western dominance in the international system.[12] For emerging countries, the entire idea of global environmental politics was suspect. The industrialized countries lecturing the world about pollution had only recently enforced colonial structures of domination, often using violence, and now their excessive consumption was the real reason for environmental degradation.

Before the Stockholm conference, developing countries rejected the need for global environmental cooperation, considering it not only a distraction but a potentially dangerous obstacle to economic development—a conspiracy of the industrialized countries to sustain inequalities in the world order. As Najam notes in his case study of the conference, the developing countries had defined their collective position—an achievement unto itself—in the aforementioned Founex report of 1971 authored by prominent Third World intellectuals.[13] In this report, the authors raised concerns about the uneasy relationship between global environmental politics, as envisioned by the industrialized world, and economic development: "The developed countries should ensure that their growing environmental concern will not hurt the continued development of the developing countries, or result in a reduction of resource transfers, or distortion of aid priorities, or adoption of more protectionist policies, or insistence on unrealistic environmental standards in the appraisal of development projects."[14]

The most important concrete outcome of the Stockholm summit was the creation of the United Nations Environment Programme (UNEP).[15] Because of the North-South conflict, developing country delegates rallied behind Kenya's call for establishing the UNEP headquarters in Nairobi, instead of the usual suspects Vienna, Geneva, or Washington, D.C.[16] The Stockholm declaration also laid out a series of twenty-six principles for multilateral environmental cooperation.[17] For North-South politics over environmental issues, principle 9 set an important precedent: "Environmental deficiencies generated by the conditions of under-development and natural disasters pose grave problems and can best be remedied by accelerated development through the transfer of substantial quantities of financial and technological assistance as a supplement to the domestic effort of the developing countries and such timely assistance as may be required." Principle 9 affirmed both the importance of economic development and industrialized countries' responsibility to support the Third World coalition in their efforts to protect the global environment.

After the Stockholm conference, governments of the world began to negotiate a host of important environmental agreements. The year 1973 saw the birth of both the International Convention for the Prevention of Pollution from Ships[18] and the Convention on International Trade in Endangered Species.[19] In 1983 the Convention on Long-Range Transboundary Air Pollution (LRTAP) was signed,[20] and in 1989 the Basel Convention on the Control of Transboundary Movements of Hazardous Wastes and Their Disposal came into being.[21]

The most important and most celebrated of the multilateral agreements of the time was the Vienna Convention for the Protection of the Ozone Layer (1985) and the associated Montreal Protocol (1987). Chlorofluorocarbon use in spray cans, refrigerators, and other appliances causes ozone depletion in the stratosphere. In turn, ozone depletion results in severe public health problems, such as skin cancer and eye cataracts. While the ozone issue had already been recognized in 1972 in Stockholm, U.S. scientists recognized the role of CFCs as a key cause in 1974, and in 1981 "UNEP formed a working group to draft a global framework convention." The resulting Vienna Convention was a framework only, but in 1987 twenty-four countries and the European Community negotiated the Montreal Protocol and agreed on a 50 percent CFC and halon reduction.[22]

The ozone regime has been extensively studied, in large part because scholars consider it a triumph of multilateral environmental diplomacy.[23] Ozone depletion is a rare environmental problem in that global progress toward solving it is unambiguously positive. As a *Science* article in June 2016 shows, for example, "healing of the Antarctic ozone layer has now begun to occur during the month of September."[24] Measures to reduce CFC use have been successful, and the chemical industry has found substitutes that do not cause ozone depletion. The Montreal Protocol is thus often held as an example of the success of multilateral cooperation on the environment. The ozone layer is recovering, and this achievement has drawn a lot of attention from researchers of global environmental politics, making the Montreal Protocol a celebrity among environmental—and other multilateral—treaties.

The next major episode of institutionalization was the United Nations Conference on Environment and Development (UNCED) held in Rio de Janeiro in 1992. At this Earth Summit, the environment-development interface was the central theme. In 1987 the World Commission on Environment and Development had published the pathbreaking *Our Common Future*, or the Brundtland Report. It was named after the lead author, Gro Harlem Brundtland, who served three times as the prime minister of Norway.[25] The report introduced the notion of sustainable development, and at the Earth Summit in 1992 developing countries and industrialized countries began bridging the gulf between them on global environmental affairs. The key achievements of the summit include Agenda 21 for local action to deal with environmental issues, the Convention on Biological Diversity, and the UNFCCC. Although Agenda 21 has since generated little action, the two framework conventions have given rise to two global environmental regimes.

The Earth Summit also produced the Declaration on Environment and Development, adopted at the summit by the participating governments.

This statement lays out a series of principles to guide international efforts to protect the environment without sacrificing economic development. Principle 7, in particular, lays out the critical notion of "common but differentiated responsibilities":

> States shall cooperate in a spirit of global partnership to conserve, protect and restore the health and integrity of the Earth's ecosystem. In view of the different contributions to global environmental degradation, States have common but differentiated responsibilities. The developed countries acknowledge the responsibility that they bear in the international pursuit to sustainable development in view of the pressures their societies place on the global environment and of the technologies and financial resources they command.[26]

This principle, which soon came to play a critical role in the politics of global climate change, is a stark reminder of how different things looked only two decades ago. At that time, it seemed perfectly reasonable to negotiators to state that industrialized countries are key to global environmental protection.

The principle also acknowledged the importance of institutional capacity. In the UNFCCC treaty text, common but differentiated responsibilities came with "respective capabilities and their social and economic conditions."[27] The aforementioned principle 7 similarly noted differences in "technologies and financial resources." As we shall see, these considerations grew in salience over time and contributed to intense North-South conflicts.

The UNFCCC gave rise to a particularly important series of negotiations. Although many scholars question the effectiveness of the United Nations climate regime,[28] no environmental agreement has received as much attention and generated as much diplomatic activity as the UNFCCC. It is the cornerstone of the global regime to address the single most salient and complicated problem that human societies have ever faced: climate change. While climate change became the central theme of global environmental politics only in the first decade of the twenty-first century, the negotiations began as early as in 1988.[29] Although the World Climate Conference of 1979 had already raised the issue, it was only at the Toronto Conference in 1988 that the Intergovernmental Panel on Climate

Change (IPCC) was formed and governments began working to adopt a multilateral convention on the issue. In 1992 the Earth Summit produced the UNFCCC, and, following its entry into force in 1994, the Conference of Parties (COP) in 1995 began the negotiations toward what was to be the Kyoto Protocol.

The Kyoto Protocol of December 1997 was the culmination of efforts to create a global treaty to deal with climate change. After much drama, the negotiators unveiled an agreement based on "targets and timetables," placing emissions reduction targets on industrialized countries. Because the targets were set relative to base-year emissions in 1990, the United States faced difficult targets while European countries, and the postcommunist world in particular, would have an easier time meeting the targets. After 1990, emissions in Great Britain collapsed thanks to Margaret Thatcher's attack on the coal industry, and Germany was given a generous allocation because the polluting industry of socialist East Germany was no longer there. All postcommunist countries would be able to *increase* their emissions because of the collapse of the socialist industrial order. The basic idea of the Kyoto Protocol, then, was that U.S. emissions reductions would allow the world to begin a process of decarbonization. Although the initial targets were mostly modest, over time other industrialized countries would also follow suit—and eventually the developing world.

North-South conflict was a major theme in climate change negotiations already in the 1990s, as the much derided Berlin Mandate of 1995 shows. In the 1995 Conference of Parties to the UNFCCC, negotiators agreed to "not introduce any new commitments for [developing country] Parties not included in Annex I."[30] This commitment excluded countries such as China and India from legally binding emissions reduction targets in the Kyoto Protocol. The commitment was made at the insistence of the developing country delegates, who pointed out that economic growth is a core priority for them and that both current and historical emissions are much smaller among developing than industrialized countries. Indeed, the guiding principles of the Berlin Mandate note that the Kyoto negotiation process would be guided by

the legitimate needs of the developing countries for the achievement of sustained economic growth and the eradication of poverty, recognizing also that all Parties have a right to, and should, promote sustainable development . . . the fact that the largest share of historical and current global emissions of greenhouse gases has originated in developed countries, that the per capita emissions in developing countries are still relatively low and that the share of global emissions originating in developing countries will grow to meet their social and development needs.[31]

For developing countries, the Berlin Mandate was essential. Because their historical experience was characterized by exploitation under colonialism and imperialism, they were deeply suspicious of industrialized countries' motives. The Berlin Mandate provided reassurance that participation in climate policy under the Kyoto Protocol would not constrain developing countries' carbon space for development.

The industrialized countries disagreed with this logic. In particular, the U.S. Senate unanimously passed a resolution—the Byrd-Hagel Resolution, S.Res.98—stating that because "the exemption for Developing Country Parties is inconsistent with the need for global action on climate change and is environmentally flawed," the United States would not join any treaty abiding by the Berlin Mandate.[32]

And join it did not. The Kyoto Protocol did enter into force in 2005 after Russia's ratification, but the United States never ratified the treaty. In a politically polarized American society, it would have been very hard to secure enough votes in the Senate, as the U.S. Constitution requires two-thirds of senators to support a treaty for it to be ratified. With the vast majority of Republicans at the time being either openly hostile to or uninterested in climate science,[33] it would have been all but impossible for the president to secure congressional support for ratifying the Kyoto Protocol. Thus the Clinton administration never sought formal ratification.

The Kyoto parties moved forward without the United States, with European aspirations of climate leadership playing a major role.[34] Although recent studies suggest that the Kyoto ratifiers did achieve their emissions targets,[35] it is hard to tell whether these countries achieved their targets *because* of the Kyoto Protocol or for other reasons, such as the financial crisis of 2008 and Europe's poor economic performance. Even if the Kyoto Protocol did play a role in reducing emissions, despite the lack of U.S. involvement and not imposing any obligations on developing countries, it was clear by the Bali conference in 2007 that there was an opening for a new approach.

The primary way in which industrialized countries did engage developing countries in climate policy from the beginning was the Clean Development Mechanism (CDM) of the Kyoto Protocol.[36] In the CDM, developers—whether public or private—can propose projects that reduce greenhouse gas emissions relative to a counterfactual baseline. Upon validation, these projects generate carbon credits that the developers sell to industrialized countries, often through financial intermediaries, for carbon offsets. While the CDM does not impose any binding constraints on developing countries' emissions, it allows them to participate in global climate cooperation on a voluntary basis, with the goal of minimizing abatement costs.

To summarize, the twentieth century ended at the unipolar moment, and global environmental politics saw an outburst of important treaties. The 1990s was the decade during which the Montreal Protocol proved to be effective; the Earth Summit produced framework conventions on climate change and biodiversity; the implementation of the Basel Convention began; the United Nations Convention to Combat Desertification (1994) was negotiated; the Rotterdam Convention on the Prior Informed Consent Procedure for Certain Hazardous Chemicals and Pesticides in International Trade (1998) was negotiated; and the negotiations for the Stockholm Convention on Persistent Organic Pollutants in 2001 began.

CORE FEATURES OF THE SYSTEM

I now analyze the core features of the system of twentieth-century global environmental politics. To explain variation in the likelihood and depth of cooperation, I first review the nature of the system and then consider separately global environmental problems that were and were not about natural resource endowments in the developing world.

Table 2.1 provides a summary of the values of the four variables of my theory. The left side shows the structure of simple systems. A low number of players, each having relatively high environmental preferences and institutional capacity, shaped the landscape of international environmental cooperation. Because there were few players, the distribution of structural power was relatively even across them and, in a sense, set the scene

TABLE 2.1 Core Features of the System in Twentieth-Century Global Environmental Politics

Variable	Value: simple situations	Value: complex situations
Number of players	Low	High
Range of environmental preferences	Medium to high	Very low to high
Range of institutional capacity	Medium to high	Very low to high
Distribution of structural power	Even	Uneven

Note: Complex situations are those in which the developing countries held important natural resource endowments and thus had the power to destroy that made them important players.

for bargaining and enforcement. In complex situations, the number of players was much higher, and both environmental preferences as well as institutional capacity varied widely.

On the right, complex situations were very different. Where developing countries had important natural resource endowments at the center of the global environmental problem, complexity replaced simplicity. Here the pivotal role of developing countries introduced a *large number of players with the power to destroy.* Think, for example, of Brazil and Indonesia threatening to cut down their rainforests. Although the global South's economic power was minimal throughout the twentieth century, in some special cases the geographic distribution of resources gave them an unusual advantage. By looking at these cases, we can better understand the importance of structural power in global environmental politics.

Let us begin the analysis with the number of players. From 1945 to the negotiations of the Kyoto Protocol or so, the irony of "global" environmental politics was that many key negotiations—the simple situations—were mostly about industrialized countries. They caused much of the environmental deterioration in the world either directly or indirectly, and they alone had the resources to purchase the participation of the members of the global South in international environmental agreements. In spite of all the hype about the difficulty of global collective action, at the time international environmental negotiations were essentially about Olsonian "small group" dynamics.[37]

During this period, industrialized countries dominated the world economy. Consider the year 1980, about a decade after the emergence of environmental issues in world politics. At that time, total world output in current dollars was worth U.S. $11,154 billion. The output of the United States alone was $2,863 billion—more than one-fourth of the total. At the time, manufacturing also remained an important component of the U.S. economy. The total economy of members of what is today the European Union was even larger, at $3,860 billion—more than one-third of the total. Together, these two economic entities produced more than 60 percent of total world output. If we then add Japan's $1,087 billion, this triangle of industrialized countries produced more than two-thirds of all output.[38]

To the extent we can set aside the European politics of the environment, it is thus fair to say that the economic activities contributing to global environmental deterioration originated to a large extent from three key players. Similar patterns can also be seen in environmental pollution. In 1980 the United States generated 4.72 trillion tons of carbon dioxide emissions, while members of the European Community generated 4.52 trillion tons. With world emissions at 19.44 trillion tons, the United States and Europe together were responsible for half of *all* carbon dioxide emissions globally.[39] In this setting, it is not hard to see why all eyes were on the industrialized countries, and the developing world played a marginal role at best.

Of these three centers of power, the United States and the European Community (or, after 1992, European Union) were much more active in global environmental politics than Japan. Across a wide range of issues, the United States and the European Community have consistently played the central roles in negotiations. On ozone depletion, it was first the United States that showed leadership, followed by the initially reluctant European Community. In climate and hazardous waste negotiations, the European Union played the leading role throughout the 1990s. Changes in domestic public opinion and interest group politics changed the relative levels of ambition between Europe and America, but third parties never threatened to replace these two giants.

Japan's role in global environmental politics has historically been relatively passive. In the early 1970s "Japan had some of the world's strongest environmental regulations, yet was also known for its strong commitment to economic development and business interests. . . . However, by 1990, Japan was no longer a clear leader."[40] While Japan's early leadership reflected the political pressure from serious pollution problems,[41] by the late 1980s "Japan's international environmental record was being harshly criticized in both journalistic and more academic reports. Japan was singled out as the world's largest importer of tropical hardwoods. It was attacked for its drift net fishing practices, whaling, and trade in endangered wildlife products. It was criticized for exporting polluting industries to Southeast Asia."[42] As a result of this criticism, Japan substantially increased its environmental aid and became more proactive in international environmental negotiations, but "until Japan's environmental NGO community matures and more environmental think tanks form, Japan is unlikely to become a leader in the development of new environmental policy ideas."[43] While Japan has become increasingly active in global environmental politics in response to external pressure, it has not risen to compete with Europe or the United States for leadership in the field.

Until its collapse, the Soviet Union played a somewhat peculiar, and usually not very constructive, role in the negotiations. Although the Soviet Union was actually a major source of pollution, the government faced only limited domestic political pressure to act. In many instances, the Soviet Union's participation in global environmental politics was but a reflection of other considerations through issue linkage. In the LRTAP, for example, the Soviet Union's concerns were related to "broader interests in East-West relations," as "Moscow continued to utilize the LRTAP process as a vehicle for portraying the members of the Soviet bloc as responsible environmentalists while prominent western states (chiefly the United States and Britain) played the role of renegades."[44] Conversely, when Soviet economic interests were under threat, Moscow simply ignored international law. In the case of commercial whaling, for example, "widespread violations conducted by the U.S.S.R. were arguably the worst example of . . . mismanagement," as the state-controlled Soviet whaling fleets ignored quota restrictions and falsified catch data submitted to the International Whaling Commission.[45]

Developing countries, in turn, played a mostly defensive role in these negotiations.[46] Consistent with Krasner's general argument about the centrality of shared internal and external vulnerabilities of the global South in world politics,[47] developing countries initially saw global environmental politics as a northern effort to prevent the Third World from escaping poverty.[48] At least until the Earth Summit in 1992, developing countries were thus reluctant to participate in global environmental negotiations. As Najam puts it, "The pre-Stockholm era was exemplified by a politics of contestation by the South; the Stockholm-to-Rio period was a period of reluctant participation as a new global compact emerged around the notion of sustainable development."[49] Unlike the industrialized countries, the developing country bloc contested the legitimacy of global environmental governance, insisting on a framework that would better accommodate their vulnerabilities and create space for economic development.

It was only at the Earth Summit that the notion of sustainable development began to thaw the ice: as "Rio provided the South with opportunities to reshape the emerging global environmental discourse . . . developing countries have attempted to do this by molding global environmental politics into the global politics of sustainable development."[50] Indeed, the summit in 1992 appears in retrospect to be a peak of global environmental cooperation. For the first, and perhaps last, time, global environmental cooperation produced a series of landmark multilateral treaties that promised a more sustainable future, with wealthier and poorer countries working together. As it turns out, this ambitious vision was difficult to implement.

Even after the Earth Summit, the participation of developing countries focused on emphasizing the principle of common but differentiated responsibilities. While Najam is correct to assert that the notion of sustainable development enabled developing country participation in post–Cold War global environmental politics, this shift did not dissolve the fundamental issue of equity. As we saw in the discussion of the Berlin Mandate, or the North-South politics of deforestation for that matter, developing countries' commitment to the ideas of historical responsibility for environmental degradation and total respect for national sovereignty remained intact. So while developing countries were more eager to participate after sustainable development rescued global environmental politics from the threat of a southern exit, their participation focused on defending their own perceived interest and preventing industrialized countries from abandoning the sustainable development focus.[51]

As I will show, the Third World coalition's relatively unified position masked two different situation structures. In many key issues, such as ozone depletion and climate change, the coalition was a marginal player because of low power to destroy. But in other issues, such as deforestation and fisheries, the developing countries did have the power to destroy and thus created complex situations.

Consider now preferences in twentieth-century global environmental politics. Given this structure of players, the constellation of preferences can be described as bimodal. One small cluster of governments of industrialized countries had relatively strong environmental preferences, though the strength of preferences varied across issues, between governments, and over time. Another, much larger cluster of governments had weaker preferences. With the exception of Japan, countries outside the industrialized transatlantic world did not see environmental concerns as a priority. Their populations did not insist on environmental quality, and resource scarcity or pollution did not (yet) threaten their economic futures. To the extent that they were actively involved, much of that involvement centered on an effort to insist on the primacy of economic development.

Variation in environmental preferences across the governments of the powerful industrialized countries and over time in turn reflected a complex set of social, economic, and political considerations. As I noted earlier, Vogel shows that the United States and Europe—the two most important players in twentieth-century environmental politics—have fluctuated in their relative interest in environmental protection.[52] In the early years of global environmental politics, the United States often led calls for multilateral environmental cooperation, with the Montreal Protocol as the crowning achievement. Later, however, a series of regulatory scandals related to food, nuclear power, and other issues strengthened the position of the "precautionary principle" in Europe. Meanwhile Americans had solved most of their environmental problems and, thanks to the majoritarian political system, had no powerful Green Party. As a result, the burden of leadership on issues such as climate change fell more on Europeans than on Americans.

Overall, though, there is no denying that the level of environmental preferences among the key industrialized countries was relatively high—if perhaps self-centered and mostly focused on their own problems. Public opinion, environmental groups, and the clean technology industry all contributed to the demand for environmental protection. A Harris survey on environmental preferences in developed countries in 1988 revealed that 92 percent of respondents believed that their government has a major responsibility to protect the environment, and a Gallup poll in 1992 showed that, among industrialized countries, 60 percent of respondents said that they were willing to sacrifice economic growth in order to protect the environment.[53] Citizens in developed countries also had specific concerns. Studies of public opinion in developed countries in the late 1980s showed that a vast majority had heard of and were concerned about climate change, although their understanding of the complexities of the issue was limited.[54] From 1960 to 1980 the number of international environmental nongovernmental organizations (NGOs) more than quadrupled, further pressuring states to protect the environment.[55]

This high level of environmental preferences reflected a variety of considerations. Most obviously, the environmental cost of rapid industrialization and rising living standards provoked a public backlash, as the popularity of Carson's *Silent Spring* readily illustrates. At the same time, the technological component of the environmental Kuznets was working its magic, with American and European companies graduating from rudimentary mass manufacturing into global innovation leaders. These changes in economic structure and technological capabilities reduced interest groups' opposition to environmental policy and ambitious environmental agreements, as abatement costs decreased and, in instances such as the ozone depletion, global environmental rules served to discriminate against low-innovation competition from China, India, and other developing countries.

Finally, the distribution of institutional capacity followed closely the distribution of structural power. A remarkable feature of twentieth-century global environmental politics was the strong association between institutional capacity, environmental preference, and structural power. Both the United States and the major European countries scored high across all three variables. As we have already seen, advanced industrialized countries in the West generated a lion's share of the world's economic activity and were accordingly responsible for almost as large a share of energy use, resource consumption, and pollution.[56] At the same time, available indicators of institutional capacity, their inherent limitations notwithstanding, also put industrialized countries at the top of the list. According to the 2015 Worldwide Governance Indicators, in 1996—the first year available in that dataset—OECD countries scored high across all six dimensions of governance: voice and accountability (88th percentile on average), political stability (83rd), government effectiveness (88th), regulatory quality (87th), rule of law (88th), and control of corruption (87th).[57] If one were to exclude Mexico and Turkey, neither of which is an advanced industrialized country, the numbers would be even more impressive.

In contrast, the developing countries had very low levels of institutional capacity. In the low-income group, the average of each of the six indicators falls below the 25th percentile; in the lower middle-income group, the average scores range from the 34th (regulatory quality) to the 41st percentile (voice and accountability). It is easy to see that there is a strong and robust association between institutional capacity and the level of economic development, debates regarding the direction of the causal arrow notwithstanding. Indeed, the Third World bloc itself recognized its lack of institutional capacity, as the following lengthy but informative passage from the Founex report of 1971 shows:

In order to formulate environmental policies, the developing countries require a lot more information and knowledge than they currently possess. We suggest therefore that one of the first priorities should be to broaden their knowledge and information in the environmental field. It would be useful if the developing countries undertake a survey of their present state of environment and the major hazards to which they are exposed. They should also undertake studies and research to define the kind of environmental problems that are likely to arise in the process of development over the course of the next two to three decades. It would also be helpful to compile all existing legislation regarding environmental control, including the regulations dealing with urban zoning, location of industries, protection of natural resources, and so on. This accumulation of information and knowledge should enable the developing countries to get a clearer perspective of their environmental problems and of the corrective action that they may require at different stages of development. Since public participation in any such efforts is vital, efforts should also be made to build the environmental concern into education curricula, and to disseminate it to the general public through media of mass information. We would like to stress once again the need for a good deal of careful research and study in this field, and the importance of avoiding hasty guidelines and action.[58]

This lack of institutional capacity can be seen by looking at very simple sectoral indicators, such as the presence of administrative agencies for environmental protection. Using data from Aklin and Urpelainen, we can see, for example, that by 1990 only 40 non-OECD countries (out of 170 in their data) had established an environmental ministry—a bureaucratic agency led by a cabinet minister.[59] By this measure, most non-OECD countries had not even created a ministry for environmental affairs. What is more, this measure probably overstates the spread of environmental ministries, as the measure in Aklin and Urpelainen captures both active environmental ministries and those that exist on paper only. Many of the so-called environmental ministries in the developing world had minimal budgets, few staff, and were led by weak ministers who had little say in cabinet talks.

These issues of lacking institutional capacity can also be seen in the implementation of environmental treaties in the developing world. The requirement for informed consent in the Basel Convention does not mean much when many developing countries are unable to monitor their coastal shores. The CITES convention depends significantly on monitoring by potential importers—that is, industrialized countries—of illegal endangered species from developing countries. In both cases, implementation hinges on the willingness of industrialized countries to comply with the treaty provisions and to assist the developing countries in treaty implementation.

To summarize, the twentieth century was characterized by a sharp North-South divide. Where the global South played an important role in the negotiations because of substantial natural resource endowments, the situation was complex. Where the global South was marginalized because the industrialized countries hold most of the power to destroy, the situation was simple. This bifurcation is essential for understanding the likelihood and depth of cooperation at the time.

EXPLAINING TWENTIETH-CENTURY GLOBAL ENVIRONMENTAL POLITICS

To what extent can we explain the key outcomes of twentieth-century global environmental politics with the constellation of variables I have discussed? In my reading, the system produced three key outcomes: First, and most important, *new treaties were created often* and, compared to what was to come in the next century, with relative ease—the likelihood and depth of cooperation were not low. Second, these outcomes failed to materialize where *developing countries and their natural resource endowments were the central focus.* Finally, governments focused heavily on *top-down environmental treaties.*

The most important feature was the constant negotiation, ratification, and implementation—however imperfect—of new agreements: the likelihood of cooperation was high. The explosion in the number of multilateral environmental agreements between the early 1970s and the late 1990s was not a simple reflection of growing global awareness about environmental issues. Instead, the mass production of global environmental agreements *can* be explained with reference to the core features of the system outlined earlier. As long as the number of core players was small and their preferences relatively consistent, creating additional agreements was not particularly challenging. In most cases, securing the support of the United States and the key European countries was more than enough to make progress in solving the problem at hand; when developing countries had specific assets, the cost of securing their support—or, alternatively, coercing them into action—was not very high.

Although the participation of developing countries was limited, they did join agreements and made meaningful policy adjustments in specific cases; and when multilateralism failed, forerunners were able to induce developing country governments to act. In the case of the Montreal Protocol, the combination of modest side payments with limited, sector-specific trade sanctions was enough to induce compliance. In the case of the Basel Convention, developing countries did not really have to do anything. In the case of hazardous chemicals, the Stockholm Convention both allowed numerous exemptions and stipulated "new and additional financial resources" for developing countries.[60]

Here it bears emphasizing that these multilateral treaties were dominated by the industrialized countries. The negotiations were driven by growing concern about the environment in industrialized countries, and they focused on issues that were of direct relevance to them, such as ozone depletion, hazardous waste, and transboundary air pollution. Although the treaties addressed the problems, they did not emphasize developing-country concerns, such as equity or common heritage. With industrialized countries in a dominant position, global environmental politics was mostly reduced to transatlantic cooperation.

This mode of participation is also important. When the number of players was high but the cost of compliance low among the less environmentally minded governments, the industrialized countries were able to use their resources to purchase participation. As long as the cost was low enough, a mutually agreeable, though not equitable, compromise was possible. The Montreal Protocol, for example, shows that although industrialized countries did formulate trade sanctions against nonparties to deter free-riding,[61] they also compensated major developing countries, notably China and India, for the cost of replacing ozone-depleting substances with modern alternatives.[62]

But when the global South held a lot of structural power because of natural resource endowments, the likelihood and depth of cooperation were low. Global efforts to stop deforestation are probably the best example of southern structural power. Because industrialized countries in the densely populated parts of Europe and North America had destroyed most of their old-growth forests centuries ago, the focus of global forest politics was on conserving the biodiversity-rich rainforests in Latin America, Southeast Asia, and Central Africa.[63] As Barrett and Bayer and Urpelainen note, such an asymmetric distribution of economic power and the assets under threat means that the negotiations are, barring draconian measures such as trade sanctions, ultimately about exchanges of side payments for conservation.[64] In such a setting, industrialized countries' economic advantage does not allow them to ignore countries such as Brazil and Indonesia, which control the key resources that other governments are trying to protect.

In the case of endangered species, developing countries played an important role because they exercised sovereign control over the key resources, but their own participation was strictly conditional on assistance from the industrialized countries. The CITES treaty, for example, prohibits trade in endangered species but does not impose binding requirements for domestic policy change and has always suffered from severe limitations of implementation capacity at the national level.[65] Although the treaty could, in principle, have formulated stringent rules on the protection of endangered species and imposed sanctions against noncompliant parties, this option was never politically feasible because it was not in the interest of the parties controlling the resources to be protected. Dickson says it best and is worth quoting at length:

> The signing of the treaty in 1973 had been preceded by a decade of debate and negotiation, chiefly among governments and conservationists from the developed world, with little influence from developing countries. In many ways CITES bears the imprint of these origins. One of the specific concerns at that time was with the effect of the luxury fur trade on the populations of big cats and the sole conservation threat addressed by the treaty is international trade. There is no recognition within the treaty that the trade in wild species might either promote conservation or have other benefits. On a wider level, this was a time of decolonisation, particularly in Africa. Many conservationists in the developed world were fearful that decolonisation would lead to a dismantling of the existing model of conservation, which was based on the creation of protected areas, from which local people were largely excluded, and bans on hunting. The establishment of trade restrictions was seen as one way of preventing the anticipated over-exploitation in the newly independent countries.[66]

CITES, then, originated from an effort to sustain colonial models of species conservation in the developing countries. But developing countries controlled the relevant resource, so industrialized countries had little ability to directly shape environmental conservation in the newly independent countries. The advocates of the colonial approach to conservation were left with trade restrictions as the only instrument available to them.

The Basel negotiations on hazardous waste offer a very different perspective: in this case, *all* victims of the environmental deterioration caused by hazardous waste were poor developing countries. In the negotiations, environmental groups from industrialized countries played a key role in advocating on behalf of the developing world, though in a rather paternalistic fashion.[67] Although some developing countries, especially from sub-Saharan Africa, advocated for a blanket ban on trade in hazardous waste, the reality is that not enough countries have ratified the Ban Amendment that would bring such a ban into force. Marcoux and Urpelainen, in turn, find that the best predictor of early ratification of the Basel Convention is limited regulatory capacity, suggesting that many developing countries were content with a focus on capacity building.[68] Overall, then, it seems that the most enthusiastic advocates of a ban were environmental groups, not governments.

The Convention to Combat Desertification (CCD) offers an interesting insight into the role of the South in global environmental politics. Led by African countries, the CCD negotiations were formally launched soon after the Earth Summit. In June 1994 the fifth negotiation session led to the adoption of the convention, which entered into force in December 1996. The CCD talks stand out in that the impetus for cooperation came almost entirely from the developing world, and African countries threatened by the expansion of the Sahel desert. The archetypal brown environmental problem, for the developed world the CCD was of little interest as "little more than a cluster of local environmental issues" along with the threat of additional calls for funding by the African countries.[69] Ratified by every country in the world except the Holy See, the CCD has few specific obligations and instead operates as a clearinghouse of data and expertise through its Committee on Science and Technology and Group of Experts. Its low level of ambition shows how power to destroy, which is mostly controlled by the developing countries threatened by desertification, does not result in positive outcomes when the industrialized countries have little interest in the problem at hand. Here the issue was not that the South opposed efforts by the North to solve a global environmental problem, but that the South called for external support to deal with largely local environmental problems, only to see the North remain uninterested and often openly hostile.

The nature of the treaties formulated on these issues reflected the complex logic of the North-South distribution of power. In stark contrast to treaties such as the Montreal Protocol on ozone depletion or the Stockholm Convention on persistent organic pollutants, the agreements on biodiversity, deforestation, and land use do not impose specific requirements on member states. Instead, they lay out guidelines and facilitate

North-South transfers. The Basel Convention on hazardous waste does not actually ban trade but only requires the provision of information and supports capacity-building exercises. CITES also focuses only on monitoring of trade and establishing a licensing system, without any restrictions on national policies of member states. These agreements, then, are remarkably shallow compared to those strongly supported by key industrialized countries.

A particular issue in which the developing countries initially had a great amount of structural power is multilateral environmental aid. The issue, of course, is not an environmental problem per se but a mechanism to mitigate environmental deterioration in the global South. At the time of the Earth Summit, the international community realized that North-South aid would play an important role in protecting the environment in the global South. In particular, donors intended to use multilateral environmental aid to combat *global* environmental problems originating from recipient countries. The idea behind organizations such as the Global Environment Facility (GEF), then, was to offer "incremental" funding to ensure that developing countries would not forgo opportunities to implement projects that generate regional or global projects.[70] The GEF, formally founded at the time of the Earth Summit, was to ensure that potential projects with substantial global or regional environmental value would not be missed because their potential host nation would not secure a large enough share of the gains. The GEF's funding was, and remains, entirely focused on projects that produce regional or global value beyond the boundaries of the host country.

Although industrialized countries control virtually *all* the money, their structural power in the GEF is actually quite limited because the organization is designed to assist developing countries in implementing projects that they would not want to implement unilaterally. No wonder, then, that the GEF relies on a double majority system that gives both the donor and recipient blocs a collective veto over all decisions. Although the industrialized country donors have bargaining power because they control the financial resource, the developing country recipients are equally powerful because they can credibly threaten to exit the system. They are, after all, not the primary advocates of global environmental protection unless their interests are represented and protected with safeguards. What is more, the GEF was quickly detached from the World Bank thanks to developing country parties' complaints about the bank's bias in favor of donors.[71] That the developing countries were able to force the donors' hand and remove the GEF from the World Bank shows how much structural power they had in this issue area. The credible threat of an exit that would cause multilateral environmental assistance to all but collapse allowed recipient countries to reduce the World Bank's influence in this issue area.

Developing countries paid a price for their political success in bargaining, however, as the total funding made available by the GEF turned out to be minuscule because of donors' dissatisfaction with the rules of the organization. As Clémençon writes, "The GEF from 1991 to 2004 has programmed $5.1 billion in grant resources and leveraged $16.8 billion in additional cofinancing."[72] Considering that the five billion in contributions is spread over a period of fourteen years, the average annual contribution is only U.S. $360 million. The GEF has 140 recipient countries, making the contribution per country rather trivial. Even the largest developing countries, which enjoy great bargaining advantages in the GEF thanks to their power to destroy,[73] have received very small contributions: "China has received the largest GEF contribution of any country, $34 million calculated as an annual average from 1991 to 2004, followed by Mexico with $13 million, India with $10 million, Brazil $7.2 million, and the Philippines $5 million."[74] This lack of support is but one example of a broader trust deficit, with developing countries criticizing the industrialized world for broken promises.[75]

The role of low institutional capacity enters the equation and requires quite some elaboration. At first sight, it might seem puzzling that a large number of countries with low institutional capacity did not create major difficulties for global environmental cooperation. If institutional capacity is as important as I maintain, why did lack thereof not prevent cooperation? How can it be that most of the world suffered from severe limitations of institutional capacity, and yet the multilateral treaty machine kept producing and implementing new conventions, protocols, and amendments in a steady stream?

The reason why low institutional capacity did not prevent North-South cooperation, when such cooperation was necessary to begin with, is the low power to destroy among the global South. The countries with low levels of institutional capacity did not have much power to destroy, so finding ways around the low level of institutional capacity was relatively easy. In the case of ozone depletion, for example, all that the governments of industrialized countries had to do was to supply a few Chinese and Indian factories in an isolated sector with technology to replace ozone-depleting substances with cleaner alternatives. Figure 2.1 displays the strong positive correlation between GDP per capita (2017 dollars) and total CFC production in 1986 (10,000 tons). The figure shows that poor countries—those with low institutional capacity—were simply not producing notable amounts of CFCs. Indeed, not a single country with a GDP per capita below U.S. $10,000 produced more than 500,000 tons of CFCs in that year. The major producers of CFCs were the same countries that possessed the institutional capacity to address the problem, and even China and India were trivial CFC producers at the time.

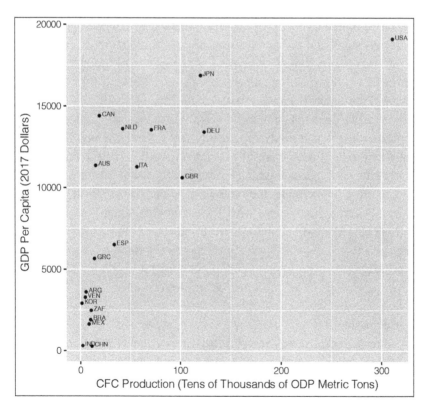

FIGURE 2.1 The relationship between GDP per capita and CFC production in nineteen major economies in 1986.

The final key feature of the system is the focus on top-down multilateral negotiations with binding targets aimed at solving global environmental problems. When the whole idea of global environmental diplomacy appeared on the international policy agenda around 1968, it created a steady stream of multilateral environmental agreements that grew more powerful until the end of the century, when treaty making quickly came to a grinding halt. Conca calls this approach to global environmental politics "legalism," as it relies heavily on international law as a solution to the problem of cooperation.[76] Multilateral treaties set general goals, often specified in framework conventions, and then enumerated a set of more precise targets or measures to achieve the general goals.

While this top-down logic of negotiations may have originated from simple mimicry of other areas of diplomacy in a pattern of "institutional isomorphism,"[77] it was also suited to the structural logic of many of the problems at hand. As long as the number of truly important players was relatively small and their preferences broadly similar, top-down cooperation was not very difficult to achieve. In the seemingly broad agreements of the time, only a small number of key players were truly important. For many of the key environmental issues of the time, including maritime pollution, ozone depletion, and initially climate change, the United Nations logic of universalism masked the reality that key negotiations focused on interactions between industrialized countries with relatively strong environmental preferences and high levels of institutional capacity.

Consider, for example, the International Convention for the Prevention of Pollution from Ships (MARPOL) of 1973. As Mitchell demonstrates in his comprehensive analysis of the evolution of the regime, over time the collective approach to solving the problem shifted from monitoring discharges at the sea to mandating pollution-control equipment, specifically segregated ballast tanks and/or crude oil washing:

> Comparing the two compliance systems shows that the equipment subregime succeeded by ensuring that actors with incentives to comply with, monitor, and enforce the treaty were provided with the practical ability and legal authority to conduct those key implementation tasks. Specifically, the regime elicited compliance when it developed integrated compliance systems that succeeded in increasing transparency, providing

for potent and credible sanctions, reducing implementation costs to governments by building on existing infrastructures, and preventing violations rather than merely deterring them.[78]

Notably, though, the "potent and credible sanctions" that play a key role in Mitchell's account were administered by three parties: "Only Germany, the United Kingdom, and the United States have detained ships often. This undoubtedly reflects a reluctance on the parts of some states to detain foreign tankers as well as the fact that most tankers were equipped appropriately in the first place."[79] It is true that the causal chain from the treaty design to compliance begins with an ingenious approach to enforcement through equipment requirements, but such enforcement would probably amount to nothing if member states did not punish violators. In fact, the other leg of the compliance regime, the withholding of insurance from tankers that fail to install pollution-control equipment, is itself but a reflection of the willingness of member states to punish violators. If such punishments were not forthcoming, insurance companies would not lose any profits from insuring noncompliant tankers.

Table 2.2 summarizes the key outcomes of the twentieth century. The table classifies some of the important environmental issues of the time as simple or complex situations. In simple situations, a relatively homogeneous group of industrialized countries played the key role in the negotiations.

TABLE 2.2 Global Environmental Politics in the Twentieth Century

Simple situations	Complex situations
Climate change, early years	Deforestation
Ozone depletion	Habitation protection
Marine oil pollution	Hazardous waste

Note: In simple situations, the likelihood and depth of cooperation were relatively high. In complex situations, the likelihood and depth of cooperation were relatively low.

The combination of relatively strong environmental preferences and high institutional capacity made cooperation easier when compared to the complex situations, where developing countries with weaker environmental preferences and limited institutional capacity played a major role. The table shows that my stylized model can account for most of the variation in outcomes, though the massive challenge of climate change shows that even simple situations can feature high levels of distributional conflict. As we shall see in the next chapter, however, these difficulties pale in comparison to those brought about by the rise of the emerging economies, with China leading the way.

3

GLOBAL ENVIRONMENTAL POLITICS
FOR A NEW CENTURY

I f the Berlin Mandate of 1995, which gave all developing countries a free pass on greenhouse gas emissions, epitomized the twentieth century in global environmental politics, then the Copenhagen summit in 2009 on climate change—the much anticipated conference that was to announce a global, legally binding climate treaty—showed how very different the next century would be. The lackluster outcome of the negotiations, the Copenhagen Accord, did nothing to constrain the growth of greenhouse gas emissions. Instead, it allowed countries to declare their own intentions. There were no restrictions, oversight, or review.

In the end, though, the Copenhagen summit—a decision to let any country do whatever it wants—paved the way to a different model of climate diplomacy. The Copenhagen Accord broke the Berlin Mandate and subjected all countries to similar, if nonbinding, rules. The negotiations introduced the idea that industrialized countries should raise U.S. $100 billion per year in public and private finance to support mitigation and adaptation in developing countries. The negotiation process was also important, as it underscored the structural power of emerging countries. At the very end of the marathon negotiations, on a Friday evening on December 18, 2009, just hours before the end of the summit, the president of the United States, Barack Obama, "burst into a meeting of Chinese, Indian and Brazilian leaders to try and reach a climate agreement."[1] At that meeting, reports the German newspaper *Der Spiegel*, "everything that was important to the Europeans was removed from the draft agreement, particularly the concrete emissions reduction targets. Later on, the Europeans—like the other diplomats from all the other powerless countries, who had been left to wait in the plenary chamber—had no choice but to rubberstamp the meager result."[2]

Only a few years earlier, the idea that a secret meeting of emerging economies would hold the keys to a climate agreement would have been all but laughable. But in Copenhagen on that Friday night, it was deadserious business. Led by China and India, a core group of emerging economies saw much to lose from concrete and legally enforceable emission reduction targets. Given their structural power and leadership position in the broader southern coalition, these countries were, for the first time, in a position to shape the outcome of a global climate summit.

In the next decade, however, China's growing economy drew the world's attention. Now we are even seeing considerable interest in India's role—with some commentators, including myself, already looking beyond India to Southeast Asia, and then to sub-Saharan Africa. Rapid economic growth in the global South has turned the tables, and pressures on the global environment mostly originate from the surge of economic activity in emerging economies. To negotiate a multilateral environmental treaty without a concentrated effort to deal with the challenges of emerging economies would simply be inconceivable today. Such a treaty would not achieve much, given that countries in the global North are not the key source of emissions growth or resource depletion.

These changes are transformative, but not in the sense that we would need a new model of global environmental politics. Changes in the international political economy have made emerging economies the pivotal players in global environmental politics, and the field is now populated by a large number of countries with lots of power to destroy, relatively weak environmental preferences, and limited institutional capacity. By adjusting the values of these variables, we can use our existing model of global environmental politics to better understand the twenty-first century.

To enable a structured comparison, the analysis follows the same logic as in the previous chapter. I begin by describing the key features of twenty-first-century environmental politics and the undercurrents of the world political economy. A combination of data, historical analysis, and literature review demonstrates that global environmental politics is in a state of paralysis, and that the freezing of environmental treaty making is linked to a profound structural transformation in the global political economy. I then turn to an analysis of the four primary variables of my model and demonstrate how these variables can make sense of the standstill of global environmental politics. Finally, I conduct an explicit comparison to the situation in the twentieth century.

Before beginning the analysis, I must warn that the argument in this chapter is necessarily more speculative than the treatment of the twentieth century in the previous chapter. We are still living in the middle of the changes described here; in a few years, some of these arguments may be less valid and predictions less successful. Such errors of prediction, however, should not discourage a forward-looking analysis. Regardless of how long we wait, there is always tomorrow, barring the end of civilization—and then it would be too late to analyze anything.

THE DECADE OF CHANGE

The late twentieth century was characterized by rapid growth in international environmental cooperation, and the first decade of the twenty-first century cut off the trend. At this time, the number of new environmental agreements collapsed rapidly, and progress on key issues, such as climate change and deforestation, came to a grinding halt. But then a combination of singular events, such as the 9/11 terrorist attacks and the growth of emerging economies with different preferences and a lot of power to destroy, changed the landscape of global environmental politics.

We can again begin the description with Mitchell's database of global environmental agreements, which I used in the previous chapter to demonstrate the growth trend in multilateral environmental cooperation. While the years 1990–1994, spurred by the Rio summit, saw a record of ninety-four new multilateral environmental agreements, treaty making continued at a respectable rate of fifty-four new multilateral agreements between 1995 and 1999 and another fifty-six between 2000 and 2004. But between 2005 and 2009 only twenty-six new agreements were formulated, and between 2010 and August 2016 only fifteen were negotiated.

A qualitative assessment of environmental treaties paints a similar picture. The Earth Summit in 1992 saw the emergence of core conventions on climate change and biodiversity. The 1990s also saw the Montreal Protocol bloom, and the negotiations on the ambitious Rotterdam and Stockholm treaties on chemicals were initiated. In the 2000s, in contrast, the only major multilateral treaties to appear were the Minamata Convention (2013) and the Paris Agreement (2015). Between the adoption of the Stockholm Convention in 2001 and the Minamata Convention in 2013, not a single major multilateral treaty was negotiated in the international community.

This rapid decline in multilateral environmental treaty making has multiple causes, and it is perhaps better to begin with some obviously important historical events before delving into the deeper issue of North-South politics. If there is a single event that sheds light on reduced multilateral environmental treaty making, it must be the terror attack against the World Trade Center in New York on September 11, 2001. Although the Bush administration enjoyed near-universal support in the aftermath of the attacks on New York and Washington, D.C., the unilateral invasion of Iraq inflicted considerable damage on the reputation of the United States: "Iraq has served as a demonstration, though largely of the opposite of what was intended. It has shown the limits of American power, and cast doubt on America's commitment to the principles espoused. The decision to go to war deeply undermined the sense of mutuality on which support for US leadership had been based. The ineffectiveness of the way the war has been fought disillusioned even many who supported it initially."[3]

It was not long until the 9/11 attacks froze global environmental politics: in 2003 only two new multilateral agreements were negotiated; in 2004 not a single agreement was negotiated. Even though the events of 9/11 probably did not cause all treaty making to freeze in global environmental politics, the turn toward American unilateralism and the end of the spirit of global cooperation in the 1990s soon showed that the cosmopolitan values of common heritage and sustainable development on Earth could not be taken for granted.

More generally, the first decade of the 2000s was not kind to multilateralism. In the multilateral trade regime, the Doha Development Round, initiated in 2001 and expected to create a major boost in agriculture and services trade, made little progress, in large part because of the stiff opposition that industrialized countries met in their negotiations with the emerging powers.[4] In the United Nations, the conflict over the potential expansion of the Security Council to include countries such as Brazil and India remained unresolved. Although the international community did see success on some issues, such as containing the damage done by the financial crisis of 2008,[5] in general it is safe to say that the 2000s have been much less multilateral than the 1990s. The multilateral system was on the defensive throughout, and the benchmark for success was now that the "system worked,"[6] instead of the much more ambitious criterion of expansion and improvement. The United States, which had already begun retreating from environmental leadership,[7] often obstructed progress under President George W. Bush's presidency.[8]

At the same time, even a brief review of global environmental challenges suggests that the secular decline of multilateralism is not enough to explain disappointing progress in multilateral environmental cooperation. Multilateral environmental cooperation did not disappear simply because multilateralism fell out of fashion or because of the mistrust and discord that followed 9/11. Instead, the growth of emerging economies created particular complications in global environmental negotiations. As we shall see, the general turmoil and hostility that was to characterize world politics in the aftermath of 9/11 came together with a more fundamental structural change—the economic, and thus political, triumph of the emerging economies.

The first environmental summit of the twenty-first century was the World Summit on Sustainable Development in Johannesburg in 2002.[9] The goal of the Johannesburg summit, held a decade after the original Earth Summit, was to review the progress of the international community in meeting the goals of the Earth Summit and to devise strategies to deal with problem areas. Compared to the Earth Summit, Johannesburg adopted a very different approach focused on partnerships. Although the theme of the meeting was again sustainable development, now the focus was not so much on new treaties, but on encouraging the private sector and civil society groups to participate in environmental governance. While the original Rio meeting was largely intergovernmental, the Johannesburg summit brought in tens of thousands of NGOs, ranging from business interests to local governments; from women's groups to youth organizations and trade unions.

Most observers agree that the concrete outcomes of the Johannesburg summit were, at least in comparison to the earlier Stockholm and Rio summits, a disappointment. As Conca notes, "Environmental concerns had been pushed so far to the margins of interstate diplomacy that many environmental activists ruefully dubbed the event 'Rio Minus Ten.'" He is, however, careful to emphasize that the summit did encourage civil society participation and thus contributed to the growth of nonstate environmental politics in an important fashion.[10] Indeed, the Johannesburg summit's emphasis on civil society can be seen in both negative and positive lights. The negative framing suggests that civil society filled the gap left by uninterested national governments; in the positive light, the entry of civil society into the sustainable development talks was an innovative step and a move in the direction.

In 2012 the international community again gathered in Rio de Janeiro for the "Rio+20" conference, with the primary goal of formulating the United Nations Sustainable Development Goals (SDGs). In contrast to the Johannesburg meeting in 2002, this time the expectations were high as environmentalists hoped to reinvigorate international environmental cooperation. Held in the aftermath of the global financial crisis, the "green economy" theme was at the center of the negotiation agenda.[11] Governments across the world found value in an agenda focused on investments in sustainable economic growth, as a way to both protect the environment and stimulate the economy after a major recession.

The opportunity to use the SDGs to set the agenda for a new wave of environmental cooperation generated great enthusiasm, given the importance of the narrower Millennium Development Goals (MDGs). The conference agenda was thus built on a three-pronged mandate: to renew and reinvigorate the global commitment to sustainable development; to update the concept of sustainability with a particular focus on the green economy in the aftermath of a global financial crisis; and to draw on these principles to formulate SDGs that would replicate the earlier success of the MDGs.

Assessing the significance of the Rio+20 conference is difficult because of the enormous scope of the summit. The SDGs are, without doubt, an important symbolic and political achievement, but it remains unclear whether they can generate any actual policy change or behavioral effects. Not only are they legally nonbinding, but they are also generic and often do not set quantitative targets or mandate specific national activities. On the one hand, it is clear that Rio+20 did not generate concrete commitments or deliver tangible outcomes. But was this ever the goal of a generic summit, twenty years after the original Rio summit? A different view emphasizes the importance of the international community's coming together and reaffirming the importance of sustainable development: "Though verbose and cautious, [the joint declaration] *The Future We Want* affirmed that the problems of today are similar to those the world faced in preceding decades but bigger and more interconnected. . . . Rio+20 brought together political capital in ways that would not have been possible without the focus of the conference."[12]

Rio+20 really was a rehashing of the original Earth Summit in 1992. Because of the rise of emerging economies, there was a clear need to reaffirm the idea of sustainable development and to breathe new life into global environmental politics with constructs such as the green economy. Although Rio+20 did not result in a concrete blueprint or action plan for saving the world, at the very least it updated the principles of the Earth Summit to reflect contemporary realities—those of a world of emerging economies. The combination of sustainable development and green growth under the SDG umbrella laid the foundation for programs, projects, and strategies that would contribute to the protection of the global environment without sacrificing economic growth or human development.

In the shadow of these mega-summits, many other things were in flux in global environmental politics. The most important of these was the governance of climate change. After the Kyoto Protocol entered into force in 2005, it was already clear that a global agreement, with some kind of commitments on all major emitters of the world, and not just OECD countries, would be necessary to halt the rapid growth of global average temperatures. At the Bali climate change conference in 2007, negotiating parties put together the Bali Road Map for a globally binding treaty. The ambitious plan was to negotiate such a treaty already in the Copenhagen conference of 2009, but this plan failed miserably: the marathon negotiations in the Bella Center produced only a weak "Copenhagen Accord"—a list of proposed emissions reductions by some of the negotiating parties.

After Copenhagen, the next deadline for a global treaty was set for the Conference of Parties in Paris in 2015. This time, the negotiations did produce an actual agreement, and one that was widely celebrated as a breakthrough. The Paris Agreement allows countries to set their own goals and encourages them to stick to those "pledges" through collective reviews every five years. The treaty further set the ambitious goal of U.S. $100 billion annually in climate finance by the 2020, along with the lofty goal of "holding the increase in global average temperature to well below 2 degrees C above pre-industrial levels."

Enthusiasm for the Paris Agreement may initially sound odd because the Paris Agreement does not, in fact, impose any binding commitments on countries. This bottom-up approach has merit, though, because enforcing any binding commitments in "international anarchy" without a world government is very difficult.[13] Unlike the Copenhagen Accord, the Paris Agreement puts reputational pressure on countries through peer review, creates an institutional framework for the continuous upgrading of targets over time, and links country commitments to the broader goal of avoiding an increase of more than two degrees Celsius in the average global temperature.

On the other hand, even the innovative Paris Agreement is in a sense at best a return to the fledgling efforts to control climate change in the early 1990s, well before the Berlin Mandate with its common but differentiated responsibilities and the Kyoto Protocol with its targets and timetables. Already at that time, countries such as Japan had proposed that the climate regime should be built on voluntary action without any legally binding obligations. Academics were still skeptical: "In the first place, the weaknesses of many existing legal regimes are too great to be ignored. The numbers of agreements may well be large but sanctions for compliance are weak. There is a marked preference for non-binding targets/guidelines which states are free to implement at whatever pace they see fit rather than the acceptance of firm and unambiguous obligations."[14] So while the Paris Agreement was met with enthusiasm—and not without reason—among advocates of climate action, it also signaled a return to the very early years of the climate regime, when governments were more honest about their opposition to binding targets and timetables. Such a turn is not surprising when virtually all the potential for emissions growth is found in emerging economies that are vocal proponents of national sovereignty and emphasize the importance of historical responsibility as a method for assigning blame for global warming.

In October 2016 the climate regime saw another step forward under the Montreal Protocol, as the Kigali Amendment to the Montreal Protocol to eliminate hydrofluorocarbon (HFC) gases was negotiated. The Kigali Amendment, named after the negotiations in the capital of Rwanda, is an important sectoral agreement that, after seven long years of talks, "includes specific targets and timetables to replace HFCs with more planet-friendly alternatives, provisions to prohibit or restrict countries that have ratified the protocol or its amendments from trading in controlled substances with states that are yet to ratify it, and an agreement by rich countries to help finance the transition of poor countries to alternative safer products."[15] In particular, the goal of the Kigali Amendment is to phase out all HFCs by the year 2050, so as to avert 70 billion tons of CO_2-equivalent greenhouse gas emissions between 2020 and 2050.[16]

Although climate change was and remains the elephant in the global environmental room, other environmental issues showed similar tendencies. Consider, for example, the forests regime. In the aptly titled book *Logjam*, Humphreys provides a comprehensive overview of global cooperation on forests until the mid-2000s or so: "The failures, and few successes, of global forest politics . . . [do] not augur well for the future of the world's forests."[17] Although the increased emphasis on climate change has since brought some relief in the form of the REDD+ initiative—the snappy acronym for the convoluted phrase "countries' efforts to reduce emissions from deforestation and forest degradation, and foster conservation, sustainable management of forests, and enhancement of forest carbon stocks"—and countries such as Brazil have made progress in reducing rates of deforestation, the global regime for forest conservation remains underdeveloped and weak.[18]

One regime that has continued to make some progress, albeit at a slow pace, is the international chemicals regime. A major breakthrough in the control of hazardous chemicals was the Stockholm Convention of 2001, a late product of the heyday of global environmental politics in the 1990s. After three years of negotiations, this agreement entered into force in May 2004 and banned the production and consumption of nine hazardous chemicals, such as the insecticide Dieldrin. It also imposed restrictions on potentially harmful substances such as DDT. The significance of the Stockholm Convention lies with a global effort—one that has met with considerable success—to impose a blanket ban on those substances that are clearly harmful to humans and the environment, and for which better alternatives are available.

More recently, a rare exception to the generally slow pace of global environmental progress, again from the broad chemicals regime, was the Minamata Convention on Mercury. Following a decision by the Governing Council of UNEP in 2009, the negotiations were concluded in Minamata—the Japanese city that gave name to the Chisso-Minamata disease, a neurological syndrome caused by mercury poisoning—in October 2013. Similar to the earlier Stockholm Convention, the Minamata Convention bans certain products containing mercury by the year 2020.[19] Equally important, the convention mandates the installation of best available technology and the application of best environmental practices within five years for new sources of mercury. The Minamata Convention therefore not only adopts a defensive posture by aiming to ban the most harmful products but also encourages the spread of the best technologies and practices available for limiting mercury emissions.

Overall, though, progress in multilateral environmental treaty making is unimpressive. In their assessment of major new environmental treaties, Susskind and Ali record the Minamata Convention as the only new effort since the Stockholm Convention in 2001.[20] Conca counts fourteen new agreements after the Johannesburg summit (2002) but considers all of them except the Minamata Convention as extensions or amendments of existing regimes, instead of genuinely new efforts: "Most of these accords simply fill in details on existing treaty regimes . . . there are, as of this writing, no significant, ongoing talks that promise to yield another such accord on a previously unaddressed challenge."[21] Thus, with the exception of the Minamata deal and the more recent successes such as the Paris Agreement and the Kigali Amendment, the new century has so far been a difficult one in global environmental politics. Gone are the days when multilateral environmental treaties emerged from continuous negotiations on multiple issues with the support of all or most key players.[22]

Against this backdrop, issues of critical importance to emerging economies and the developing world more broadly appeared in the limelight.[23] This development is important because it shows that the structural changes in international political economy that are now shaking global environmental politics not only are about the degree of international environmental cooperation but also guide the focus and scope of environmental diplomacy. As negotiators, governments, and stakeholders adjust to new realities, they move in directions that promise greater likelihood of success than the traditional multilateral model focused on green global issues. An important part of this move is the increased emphasis on the concerns of emerging economies.

One such issue was the role of North-South finance in global environmental politics. As developing countries began to play a more and more important role in global environmental negotiations, questions of North-South began to loom larger and larger. If the Montreal Protocol saw transfers of a few billion dollars, and the entire budget of the Global Environment Facility in the 1990s was not much larger, in the 2000s developing countries raised the stakes. They not only demanded hundreds of billions of dollars in climate and other environmental finance but also insisted that such dollars should be completely "additional" to conventional development assistance.

Consider, for example, the climate negotiations in Doha, Qatar, in December 2012. At this meeting, a group of vulnerable least developed countries declared that the number proposed at Copenhagen, U.S. $100 billion annually by 2020, is not enough to support climate adaptation. As David Kaluba, chief economist of Zambia's Ministry of Finance, put it: "We are being very conservative. . . . One hundred billion is very minimum compared to the task that is ahead of us, and mind you, climate change is not an issue of the future."[24] But so far, industrialized countries have not even delivered on the $100 billion promise, which was to be met by 2020.

Kaluba is not alone in insisting on adaptation as the cornerstone of the future of climate finance. As Dr. Saleemul Huq, director of the International Center for Climate Change and Development in Dhaka, writes, "The main reason for this change in advice is the fact that while we have been coming to COP after COP every year to make the same arguments for help over and over again, climate change has become a reality of the present and ceased to be a problem of the future. Hence the most vulnerable countries need to look to their resources to finance adaptation, and possibly even Loss and Damage as they sometimes reach the limits of adaptation, as much as possible."[25] Reflecting on the slow and erratic progress of global negotiations on adaptation finance, Huq reminds the international community of the grim ground realities in the vulnerable countries of the world: "This is not to say that they should not keep pursuing the developed countries to fulfil the pledges they have made over time but that reality on the ground now trumps negotiations at [Conferences of Parties]." In his view, climate adaptation is an urgent priority, and it is already too late to avoid dealing with adaptation, given how fast the global climate is changing.

The emphasis on adaptation among both emerging economies and least developed countries makes a lot of sense. These countries, many of which are highly vulnerable to climate change, are aware of the changing realities of the global atmosphere, as they are already experiencing these effects in a way that few commentators could have seen two decades ago. They also rightly note that they have not contributed to the problem as much as industrialized countries, especially when the responsibility for greenhouse gas emissions is adjusted per capita. In such a circumstance, these countries both realize the objective urgency of financing adaptation and regard their demands as ethically justified.

More generally, an important and illustrative pattern in global environmental politics of the past decade is the increasing bilateralization of green and brown aid. As Bayer and Urpelainen show, environmental aid has, despite calls to the contrary in the context of multilateral cooperation on climate change, become increasingly bilateral: "As concerns about climate change . . . and the bargaining power of emerging developing economies have grown, donors have reacted by shifting their focus from multilateral to bilateral aid provision."[26] The results of this study show that as emerging economies grow more and more powerful, the North-South difficulties of multilateral environmental financing are compounded.

In particular, donors' willingness to offer funds for multilateral causes decreases as the ability of emerging economies to determine the use of such funds increases. Multilateral environmental financing in particular suffers because when donors allocate funds through multilateral channels, they understand that the collective managers of these funds are highly sensitive to the global environmental deterioration brought about by a bargaining or implementation failure. In contrast, bilateral funding often has ancillary motivations that reduce a donor's sensitivity to the recipient's power to destroy. In this context, the appeal of multilateral funding relative to more traditional bilateral dealings is diminished. Therefore we see a shift from multilateral to bilateral environmental funding over time. This development is troubling, however, as bilateral funding is hardly an optimal system for solving collectively important global or regional problems. When countries give environmental assistance on a bilateral basis, they may fail to consider the interests of other countries and instead focus on benefits to the recipient and the donor only.

Over time, the legitimacy of brown issues in global environmental politics has also grown. Practitioners increasingly recognize the legitimacy of concerns such as clean water, sanitation, solid waste management, and, perhaps most enthusiastically, energy poverty. These problems, which continue to complicate the lives and harm the health of billions, have recently grown in salience and importance because they are near and dear to the hearts of many governments of emerging economies. Indeed, one central consequence of the ever closer environment-development linkages has been the recognition of these concerns. Industrialized countries can no longer afford to just pay lip service to brown issues and human development, as efforts to secure the participation of emerging economies in global environmental governance now hinge on embracing the brown issues.

The third megatrend is the increasingly close relationship between energy and environmental issues. Because fossil fuels are the source of about four-fifths of all greenhouse gas emissions and are used to fuel and power economic growth everywhere in the world, energy conservation and clean energy deployment have emerged as the central challenges of global environmental governance in the first two decades of the twenty-first century. In fact, some detractors of the conventional approach to climate change, especially the Kyoto Protocol and the failed Copenhagen Conference of Parties, have advocated energy access as a core component of a strategy that would bring emerging economies onboard:

We believe that leaving more than a billion people without access to electricity by 2030 would represent policy failure. If energy access is to be expanded to include a majority of those without access today, while meeting expected growth in global energy demand in the rest of the world, the costs of energy will necessarily have to come down. The higher quality fossil fuels are in already tight markets. If the attempt is made to satisfy this new demand from these initially, as would be probable, the opposite is more likely to occur. Costs would rise. Alternatives to fossil fuels will therefore have to become cheaper. For this to happen, innovation is required.[27]

While this approach may initially appear problematic from the perspective of climate mitigation, a deeper analysis of the building blocks needed for effective, pragmatic, and politically feasible climate action leads to a different conclusion. As long as the number of people without basic electricity access—including people with low-quality electricity service[28]—in the world remains high, the notion that emerging economies would voluntarily impose constraints on their ability to gain energy access is a fantasy. The only practical solution to the problem of climate change, then, is to construct a narrative around sustainable human development—a development that prevents runaway climate change *and* ends energy poverty in the near future. Efforts to scale up clean energy without progress toward universal access to modern energy are unlikely to succeed, but any plan to end energy poverty with fossil fuels is increasingly under pressure in a carbon-constrained world.

While the world struggles to halt global warming, new environmental problems are emerging. One is the effect of plastic debris on the oceans.[29] Plastic is a useful material because it is so durable, but this very feature also makes it an environmental problem. Most of the litter found in the oceans is now plastic, and the most important source of it is consumer products. Plastic debris in the oceans kills fish and other marine species that eat the material or become entangled in it. There is no treaty on plastic debris, and the problem illustrates the difficulty of global environmental governance in a world of emerging economies. Both the production and consumption of plastics is now shifting to Asia, and Asian countries also import vast quantities of plastic waste from elsewhere in the world. Recycling of plastic remains limited, however, due to weak regulations and limited institutional capacity.

All told, global environmental politics is moving into a new direction. Fundamental changes in world politics and international political economy have paralyzed the twentieth-century machinery for multilateral treaty making. The gap has been filled with alternative approaches focused on brown environmental issues, such as energy access, and a renewed focus on decentralized, nonbinding forms of cooperation. To understand this shift, I now explore changes underneath, in the deep undercurrents of the global system.

CHANGES IN THE SYSTEM

The key changes in the system of global environmental politics are summarized in table 3.1. The number of players has increased from the baseline of late twentieth-century global environmental politics, and the new entrants have a lot of power to destroy but relatively weak environmental preferences and limited institutional capacities. At the same time, financial resources mostly remain in the hands of traditional industrialized countries. While the twentieth century saw both simple and complex situations, depending on the role of natural resources in developing countries, the transformation of global environmental politics has now produced a more uniform setting characterized by mostly complex situations.

The first key change is the number of players. In the previous chapter, I surveyed a range of environmental issues and concluded that for many key problems of the day, the number of truly pivotal countries was relatively small. This observation no longer holds in the twenty-first century.

TABLE 3.1 Core Features of the System in Twenty-First-Century Global Environmental Politics

Variable	Value	Change
Number of players	High	Increase
Average environmental preferences	Medium-low	Decrease
Average institutional capacity	Medium-low	Decrease
Distribution of structural power	Emerging economies hold most power to destroy; industrialized countries hold most financial resources	Less even

The number of relevant players is now much higher, and growing, across the board. These players are more diverse, less enthusiastic about the environment, and more limited in their institutional capacities to formulate effective domestic environmental and energy policy.

The initial, and so far most consequential, change in the set of players is China's emergence. In 1990 China was only the world's fifth-largest economy (purchasing power parity), even though its population was by far the largest. In 2000 China was the second-largest, and by 2015, the largest.[30] Between 1990 and 2010 China's energy consumption per capita increased 767 kilograms of oil equivalent (koe) to 1,881 koe,[31] and between 1990 and 2010 China's coal consumption increased from 1,123 million short tons to a staggering 3,606 million short tons.[32] These numbers reveal the gigantic scale of the Chinese economic boom. A billion people escaped abject poverty in a triumph of human development, but the resources required for this feat also transformed the landscape of global environmental politics, as China sped past the United States to become the world's leading consumer of resources and producer of pollution.

With these changes, China's position in global environmental politics has grown increasingly important, and there is by now a huge body of literature on China's positions in global environmental negotiations.[33] China is widely recognized as a key player across a large number of global environmental issues: "Future environmental diplomacy concerning almost every environmental issue will depend heavily on the role played by China. . . . China is increasingly becoming aware of its shifting position in global environmental politics."[34] At the same time, China's state apparatus has faced—and often overcome—high barriers to mitigating the environmental destruction brought about by four decades of rapid economic growth.

More recently, India has followed China's lead. In 1990 India's economy was only the eighth-largest in the world by purchasing power parity, despite having the world's second-largest population. By 2015 India was the world's third-largest economy, far ahead of Japan and behind only the United States and China. Although India's per capita energy consumption remains low, the change has been rapid, from 365 koe to 600 koe between 1990 and 2010. Perhaps even more notably, the change has accelerated in recent years, as the consumption was only 479 koe as recently as in 2005. In 1990 India's total coal consumption was only 248 million short tons, but by 2010 it had increased to 700 million short tons.[35]

These numbers are massive, but the scale of economic—in particular, industrial—activity in India remains clearly smaller than in China. While such numbers have often led observers to focus on China at the expense of India, they mask the important reality that the expansion of India's energy use, and thus emissions, is not a thing of the past, but in all likelihood the big energy-environment story of the first half of the twenty-first century. Where a naive observer sees India paling in comparison to China, an astute, forward-looking analyst sees tremendous potential for transformative change in the South Asian energy economy.

India's positions in global environmental negotiations have also drawn a lot of attention, both because of India's growing importance and because India's traditional position has not been very cooperative.[36] India has traditionally adopted a tough pro-South, anticolonial position in global environmental negotiations, accusing industrialized countries of hypocrisy and insisting on their unconditional leadership.[37] While these approaches have not had a decisive impact on negotiation outcomes in the past, India's economic *emergence* has changed the country's position. Now that India does have the power to change negotiation outcomes, all eyes are on Delhi's position across a wide span of global environmental negotiations.

Other emerging economies have also become increasingly important. While much of today's emphasis has been on middle-income countries such as Brazil and South Africa, we also see the growing importance of a new batch of large countries, including Vietnam, Bangladesh, Indonesia, and Nigeria. All these countries are growing wealthier over time, even though their development has not drawn the same kind of sustained attention as China and India's economic growth. Consider, for instance, Vietnam. Between 1990 and 2010 the country's GDP per capita (constant U.S. dollars, 2010 prices) increased from $446 to $1,334.[38] Between 2010 and 2015, during the great global coal boom, Vietnam built over 8,000 megawatts of coal-fired power generation capacity—half of that built in the United States.[39]

Among the least developed countries, we also see movement in recent years. The annual rate of economic growth in countries considered "low income" by the World Bank exceeded 5 percent between 2004 and 2010 and remained above 4 percent every year from 2011 to 2015.[40] In contrast, between 1983 and 2000 the average growth rate in this group exceeded 5 percent only once, in 1996, and was actually negative in 1992–1993. The East Asian experience notwithstanding, these numbers show how recent the economic boom in the global South actually is.

To understand how significant these implications are, consider research by economists at the University of California, Berkeley. They note that contemporary estimates of the potential for growth in energy consumption may be biased downward, because "above a first threshold income level, we see rapid increases in [appliance] ownership. . . . A large share of the world's population has yet to go through the first transition suggesting there is likely to be a large increase in the demand for energy in the coming years."[41] If billions of poor people begin to purchase energy-consuming devices such as refrigerators and automobiles within a short period time, and if these devices are durable, then we may see a dramatic upward shift in global energy consumption in the coming decades. Unless this surge in demand is met entirely with clean energy sources, the consequences for pollutants and hazardous waste are breathtaking.

While the global economic recession caused by the COVID-19 pandemic in 2020 may slow economic growth in emerging economies, this is not a solution to the problem. Emerging economies will have to continue to pursue economic growth to alleviate poverty, and slower economic growth in these countries sets back human development. It may also weaken global enthusiasm for sustainable development. The global community will need to grapple with the challenge of reconciling economic growth and sustainability for decades to come.

The countries in which the poorest people live are also beginning to assert themselves in negotiations. Consider, for example, the leading countries of sub-Saharan Africa. Over time, African countries have become increasingly coherent and assertive in their climate negotiation positions. Their capacity to negotiate has improved as negotiators have accumulated experience, and Africa's newly found economic dynamism certainly cannot hurt. Although Roger and Belliethathan attribute Africa's improved performance in global climate negotiations to negotiation capacity and discount the importance of growing power to destroy, a closer inspection of their evidence shows that they are looking at the wrong indicators:[42] it is not Africa's *current* but *future* greenhouse gas emissions that determine this negotiating bloc's structural power. Africa's growing power in climate negotiations does not reflect its current emissions, but the potential for spectacular emissions growth in the future under high levels of economic growth.

Thus the set of players in global environmental politics is very much in flux. China and India are already established players, the rest of the emerging economies are also asserting themselves, and now there is a large number of countries on the verge of becoming pivotal players. Although China and India are the most important players because of their massive populations, the fact remains that billions of people in Africa and Asia are now reaping the benefits of robust economic growth, with potentially massive implications for the global environment.

The fundamental reason why the number of relevant players has increased is the expanded power to destroy among the developing world. Given the nature of today's environmental problems, the combination of large populations and rapid economic growth creates a lot of power to destroy. Even if most developing and emerging economies have small environmental footprints today, these footprints are growing rapidly, and, based on the logic of income thresholds in appliance and vehicle ownership, their future growth may be faster than that of today. While China's rise has left the impression that there is one new major player in town, the future is more likely to see the appearance of at least a dozen major players. None of them individually is as important as China or India, of course, but together their potential for environmental degradation is massive and cannot be ignored in any credible analysis of global environmental politics in the twenty-first century.

When we aggregate individual cases into an overall picture, the change is striking. Table 3.2 illustrates these patterns by looking at typical indicators of power to destroy in ten emerging economies: population, energy consumption, GDP per capita, and greenhouse gas emissions. The table compares these patterns over time—in the years 1990 and 2014—to reveal a momentous change. Over time, growth in the global South has been extremely fast and completely overtaken developments in the global North. Of the ten countries under consideration, all except Indonesia and Myanmar—countries that have made considerable progress in reducing emissions from deforestation over the past two decades—have grown their

TABLE 3.2 Changes in Power to Destroy in Ten Emerging Economies

	1990				2014			
	Population	Energy p.c.	GDP p.c.	GHG	Population	Energy p.c.	GDP p.c.	GHG (2010)
Asia								
China	1,119	767	731	3,893	1,364	2,237	6,104	11,184
India	853	352	542	1,387	1,296	637	1,640	2,770
Indonesia	178	544	1,653	1,165	255	884	3,693	745
Bangladesh	103	120	400	127	155	229	951	178
Vietnam	65	271	446	99	92	660	1,579	279
Philippines	60	463	1,526	96	101	474	2,613	160
Myanmar	41	254	191	875	52	369	1,257	325
Africa								
Nigeria	93	695	1,369	163	176	764	2,550	292
Ethiopia	46	438	207	67	98	493	449	183
Tanzania	25	382	494	95	50	497	846	234

Note: Population is given in millions of people; GDP per capita in thousands of U.S. dollars, 2010 constant prices; energy consumption per capita in kilograms of oil equivalent; total greenhouse gas emissions in megatons of CO_2 equivalent (2010).

Source: World Development Indicators, http://data.worldbank.org/.

emissions. Some, like China and Vietnam, have almost tripled their emissions, and India and Tanzania have also seen very rapid growth in emissions over time.

While there has been remarkable change in the distribution of power to destroy, the basic environmental preferences have changed only slightly. Case studies of emerging economies and other developing countries show that while the governments of these countries are no longer as suspicious and reluctant to engage in global environmental negotiations, they still prioritize economic growth and poverty alleviation. For example, Najam characterizes the evolution of the global South's participation in international environmental negotiations as transitioning from contestation, to participation, and more recently to engagement.[43] Since around the time of the Rio conference in 1992, developing countries have supported broad environmental protection measures but have subsumed environmental protection under the right of economic development.[44] Indeed, the concept of sustainable development exists partly to sell the idea of environmental protection to countries whose top priority is developing their economy.

For concrete data on preferences on international environmental policy, consider data I collected with Tana Johnson on the World Trade Organization's Committee on Trade and Environment (CTE).[45] The CTE is a special advisory committee that considers the environmental aspects of the multilateral trade regime. In particular, the committee gives countries and international organizations an opportunity to discuss and debate trade-related environmental policies. The committee's decisions are not binding, but they can inform policy formulation in the General Council of the WTO, and studies of the CTE show that it has played an important role in supporting the WTO's trade-environment integration.[46]

For the period 1995 to 2011, we coded all substantive statements made by representatives of WTO members in all meetings of the CTE. The key variables of interest were the frequency of pro-South and protrade statements, and we compared the frequency of such statements across World Bank income groups (low income, lower middle income, upper middle income, high income). We found that while high-income countries make protrade statements only 10 percent of the time, low-income countries make such statements 24 percent of the time. If anything, the difference in pro-South statements is even more striking: high-income countries make such statements only 11 percent of the time, whereas low-income countries do so 36 percent of the time. The BASIC countries—Brazil, South Africa, India, and China—also showed interesting patterns: they made protrade statements 22 percent of the time and pro-South statements 32 percent of the time. To summarize, we found that the unity of developing countries remains strong: developing countries continue to make pro-South and protrade statements at a much higher rate than do industrialized countries. The difference holds both for the least developed and for the vocal BASIC quartet. This result is consistent with the idea that the North-South gap remains wide in discussions of the trade-environment nexus.

Another analysis of countries' preferences, this time focusing on international climate negotiations, is found in the work of Federica Genovese.[47] As she shows, developing countries continue to exhibit uniformly different preferences from industrialized countries. She conducts both qualitative and quantitative text analysis of official national submissions by countries for the Kyoto Protocol meetings in 2001–2004 and the meetings in 2008–2011 on the future of the climate regime. In both time periods, country positions follow the traditional North-South distinction, with industrialized countries submitting positive, proambition statements and countries in the global South sending more conservative statements with a different focus. Again, we see a familiar pattern: a wide gap remains between the industrialized and developing country parties on today's most pressing environmental problem, climate change. While many industrialized countries, and especially European leaders such as Germany, tend to use positive language emphasizing the importance and possibility of climate protection, many developing country parties instead use language that highlights the importance of avoiding impediments to economic development: " 'Strong' countries use the negotiations to discuss international targets and leadership. 'Weak' countries, by contrast, rarely miss the occasion to focus their documents on responsibility, sovereignty, and compensation."[48]

There are exceptions, of course, to this general pattern. During the presidency of George W. Bush in 2001–2008, for example, the United States was less proenvironment than during Democratic presidents Clinton and Obama. During Bush's tenure, the United States tried to undermine the

Kyoto Protocol by forming the low-ambition Asia-Pacific Partnership[49] and threatened to stop funding the GEF.[50] The United States was widely recognized as an obstacle to meaningful environmental cooperation at the global level, and there was much frustration about President Bush's lack of interest in protecting the planet. After President Obama's inauguration, in turn, the United States again joined the high-ambition coalition against climate change. It was during the Obama years that the United States formulated new environmental regulations to control carbon dioxide emissions, imposed new efficiency standards to reduce emissions from transportation, and played a constructive role in negotiations on the Paris Agreement. One of the key achievements of the Obama administration on the road to Paris was a bilateral climate agreement with China. When President Trump took the oath, the U.S. executive again took an anticlimate turn and began to distance itself from the international community. President Biden then reversed course again, bringing the United States back to the Paris Agreement.

These exceptions do not reflect a fundamental shift in preferences, however, but the changing costs of achieving environmental improvements through business as usual or, at best, modest behavioral adjustments. Although the positions of specific countries may fluctuate over time and reflect changes in both their position in the world economy and domestic conditions, there is little evidence of genuine meshing of traditional northern and southern countries. The official positions of specific industrialized countries fluctuate as different political parties win elections over time, and such fluctuations are amplified in polarized societies, such as the United States.[51] Such fluctuations are ephemeral, however, as changes in the ruling coalition simply produce policy fluctuation around a relatively stable, slow-moving average. At the same time, we see much less evidence of similar fluctuations among emerging economies. In these countries, the consensus frame is a hybrid of sustainable development and green growth, with a very strong emphasis on economic expansion and poverty alleviation.[52]

To the extent that some emerging economies have made major investments in the green economy, domestic motivations appear strong. China's spectacular expansion of renewable electricity generation appears to be largely driven by the urgent need to replace coal-fired power plants with less polluting and less water-intensive alternatives, along with energy security considerations. Already the country's Energy Policy of 2012 noted that

> vigorously developing new and renewable energy is a key strategic measure for promoting the multiple and clean development of energy, and fostering emerging industries of strategic importance. It is also an urgent need in the protection of the environment, response to climate change and achievement of sustainable development. Through unswerving efforts in developing new and renewable energy sources, China endeavors to increase the shares of non-fossil fuels in primary energy consumption and installed generating capacity to 11.4 percent and 30 percent, respectively, by the end of the 12th Five-Year Plan.[53]

This enthusiasm for low-carbon energy is welcome, but it does not indicate a willingness to sacrifice economic growth for the environment.

In the future, developing countries will continue to "graduate" into the group of industrialized countries. At this stage, both canonical theories of the environmental Kuznets curve[54] and the historical record, such as the case of Chile's industrialization and eventual OECD membership,[55] suggest a coming change in the government's environmental preferences. In practice, however, key emerging economies—both present and future— are many decades from such graduation. Additionally, even if their conventional emissions—say, sulphur—begin to decrease, a clever analysis of the relevant cross-national data over decades shows that the evidence is weaker for pollutants such as carbon dioxide.[56]

Even if China's emissions do peak because of a decrease in reliance on coal for industrial uses and electricity generation, it remains an open question whether the displacement of industrial activity from China to other emerging economies results in a compensating emissions boom, akin to China's own CO_2 explosion in the first decade of the 2000s. The growth in renewable power generation suggests that the world has a good chance of avoiding such an emissions boom, but growing energy demand will make it difficult for emerging economies to avoid growth in their greenhouse gas emissions. Increasingly affordable clean technology and growing environmental problems, such as heat waves and floods, will promote sustainable development in emerging economies, but economic growth will remain the primary goal.

The most fascinating nonchange in the rapidly evolving landscape of global environmental politics is institutional capacity. Although some emerging economies, such as China, have made marked progress in improving their institutional capacity for environmental policy, such capacity mostly remains lagging. The striking feature of economic growth in today's emerging economies is that countries have attained it in spite of limited improvement in institutional capacity. Their growth story is very different from the standard story of the East Asian developmental state.[57]

The data shown in figure 3.1, again based on Worldwide Governance Indicators, offer support for this prediction. The graph shows changes in the estimated values of three particularly important dimensions of governance: government effectiveness, regulatory quality, and control of corruption. The first available year is 1996, and the comparison year is 2019. The comparisons readily reveal that there is no overall pattern of improvement: most countries have backslid with respect to at least one indicator.[58] The only two countries that have improved across the board are Ethiopia and Myanmar. And yet, as we will see in chapter 6, they both suffer from serious political challenges—an internal conflict in Ethiopia and a military coup in Myanmar.

One plausible reason behind the relatively slow pace of change is that economic growth in emerging economies does not depend on a competent Weberian bureaucracy today. The economic growth that emerging economies have achieved does not reflect fundamental changes in the ability to protect the environment and natural resources. Emerging economies have benefited from opportunities afforded by technological progress, an open international economy, and economic reforms that have allowed the private sector to make profitable investments in previously closed societies with pervasive inefficiencies and unexploited opportunities. For my purposes, the key characteristic of such growth is that it is possible—even at relatively high levels—without comprehensive, crosscutting institutional capacity at the national level. Improved technology, openness to trade and investment, and liberalizing economic reforms do not generate growth in all circumstances, but overall they have proven to

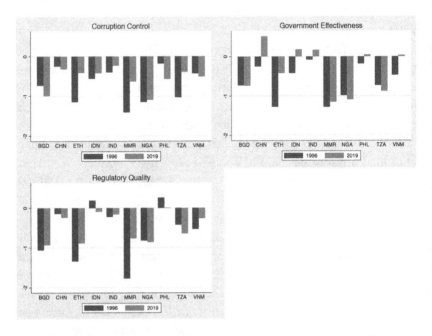

FIGURE 3.1 Changes in institutional capacity in ten emerging economies. The scores range from −2.5 to 2.5, with higher values indicating better governance. The countries (ISO3 codes) are Bangladesh (BGD), China (CHN), Ethiopia (ETH), India (IND), IDN (Indonesia), Myanmar (MMR), Nigeria (NGA), Philippines (PHL), Tanzania (TZA), Vietnam (VNM).

Data source: 2020 Worldwide Governance Indicators, https://info.worldbank.org/governance/wgi/.

be a good solution to economic problems around the world. This is good news for poverty alleviation without doubt, but it also means that much of today's economic growth is not something governments overseeing it can manage. The environmental cost of each unit of economic expansion is therefore high.

To the extent there has been institutional development, it has focused on sectors that are directly relevant to industrialization and infrastructure development. As emerging economies have made institutional reforms, whether grudgingly under external pressure or willingly to promote economic growth, their focus has been on liberalizing policy changes that produce rapid economic gains. Today's most important emerging economies, China and India, initiated a series of ambitious reforms in 1978 and 1991, respectively, but these reforms were largely focused on promoting investment, enhancing export competitiveness, and gaining access to modern technology.[59] In both cases, policy makers' overriding priority was to allow private business expansion, to enhance productivity, and to catch up with the rest of the world in the utilization of modern technology. Environmental reforms, to the extent they were made, followed much later and were less ambitious.

In many cases, economic growth has also been possible in spite of limited institutional capacity. Here the contrast between China and India is particularly insightful. In China, the administrative machinery has played a major role in policy design and experimentation, and the role of the bureaucracy in economic growth has always been central.[60] China's economic reforms have been managed by a competent and developing bureaucracy, and policy experimentation across China's provinces allowed the state to find good solutions to emerging problems in an adaptive fashion. In India, the opposite is true in many sectors. Many of the great achievements of India's reforms in 1991 have been those of the state withdrawing from a sector of the economy and allowing internal and external competition to guide outcomes. India's success in generating economic growth seems to be focused on those sectors in which the state has been able to reduce its presence through privatization and competition, and thus to allow the private sector to improve productivity and create value.[61]

Unfortunately, much of the discussion in the field of development on weak institutional capacity is focused on so-called fragile states. Many scholars of sustainable development have drawn attention to the association between lacking institutional capacity and environmental deterioration. Conca, for example, notes that local environmental quality has often deteriorated in areas suffering from civil war or the breakdown of law and order.[62] When national and subnational governments lose their capacity to govern, the societies under their watch become vulnerable to environmental destruction, and not least because of illicit activities. Civil war and breakdown of law and order are phenomena that enable economic actors to exploit natural resources, dispose hazardous waste, and pollute without any legal responsibility or accountability.

This pattern is important because it raises the troubling possibility that we have yet to see the worst of the consequences of limited institutional capacity. When emerging economies manage to grow their economies—an achievement that is virtually impossible under civil war or the breakdown of law and order—they all but ensure that economic expansion produces maximal environmental deterioration. If China stands out as an emerging economy with an unusually high level of institutional capacity for environmental protection, it is far from clear that India and other emerging economies will be able to pivot the way China has on key issues, such as renewable energy deployment. In the worst case, China's relatively high degree of success leaves an overly rosy impression of the future of global environmental politics in a world of emerging economies.

EXPLAINING THE TRANSFORMATION OF GLOBAL ENVIRONMENTAL POLITICS

Emerging economies' growing structural power, in combination with relatively weak environmental preferences and stubbornly low institutional capacity, has changed global environmental politics in three important ways. First, the likelihood of cooperation is decreasing, making global environmental negotiations more difficult. Second, the depth of cooperation is decreasing, making bottom-up approaches to cooperation with weak commitments more appealing and competitive than ever. Finally, as an ancillary implication, global environmental cooperation is increasingly driven by emerging economies' activism and based on a narrative about sustainable human development, instead of environmental protection per se. All three changes are linked to structural changes in international political economy more generally.

Global environmental negotiations in the twenty-first century have been difficult. Compared to the steady stream of new environmental treaties on key global and regional issues, the trickle in the first years of the twenty-first century is particularly underwhelming. Since the Johannesburg summit in 2002, there has been little new environmental cooperation, and the coming years do not promise to change this state of affairs fundamentally. The most important exceptions to this pattern are the Minamata Convention, which is arguably an important advance but benefited greatly from the availability of simple sectoral solutions, and the Paris Agreement, which we have seen to be consistent with the shifting focus of global environmental politics, as negotiators adapt to changing realities by focusing on flexible and decentralized solutions that respect national sovereignty and do not commit national governments to goals they might fail to meet.

These difficulties are directly related to the growing number of players with structural power but weak environmental preferences and limited institutional capacity. The growing number of important parties with substantial power to destroy and relatively weak environmental preferences in global environmental negotiations has made bargaining and enforcement increasingly difficult. The problem is worse for the lack of institutional capacity among these parties, as they might not be able to protect the environment even if they wanted to do so.

The new, dual distribution of structural power has created added difficulties. Emerging economies are powerful not only thanks to their ability to destroy resources, but also because they understand that industrialized countries continue to hold most of the financial resources and technological capabilities. This distribution of resources creates difficulties in negotiations, as emerging economies demand financial and technological transfers to compensate for the cost of reducing their environmental footprint. It is not just that emerging economies have become more powerful, but the continued asymmetry in ability to finance environmental and energy projects actually encourages countries like China, India, and others to bargain hard. If they succeed, they can expect direct material gains in the form of financial assistance and technology transfers.

If the newly powerful countries held strong environmental preferences and adequate institutional capacity to solve their environmental problems, their growing number and power to destroy might not raise insurmountable obstacles to environmental cooperation. Alas, the combination of weak environmental preferences and limited institutional capacity amplifies the negative changes that new players and the changes in structural power have generated. I will consider each in turn.

The lack of a fundamental change in the environmental preferences means that when their power to destroy grows, the threat to sacrifice the environment for economic growth is credible. A government overseeing a giant economy with great potential for emissions growth need not raise concerns about emissions or resource consumption if both the society and the political elite have a steadfast commitment to environmental protection, whether because of concerns about resilience or out of an intrinsic interest in protecting the environment. Unfortunately, today's booming economies are not overseen by governments that are ideologically committed to protecting the planet or under domestic political pressure to do so. These governments are instead facing severe pressure to maintain economic growth, alleviate poverty, and deliver substantial economic gains to the powerful interest groups that make or break national leaders.

Limited institutional capacity adds yet another complication. On the one hand, even if some emerging economies were willing to change their environmental policies, their lack of institutional capacity would prevent them from enacting and implementing effective policies to achieve this goal. On the other hand, limited institutional capacity also complicates environmental negotiations about compensating emerging economies for the costs of environmental protection. Emerging economies would demand additional payments from traditional industrialized countries, while these countries would hesitate to make such payments out of worries about diversion.

The second important change is that where negotiations have generated environmental cooperation, we increasingly see bottom-up action. To the extent that negotiations have achieved results, those results have mostly emphasized a bottom-up approach that diverges from the legalistic multilateral model of the late twentieth century. The best example of this shift is the Paris Agreement, which allows governments to set their own targets but provides for monitoring, peer pressure, and upgrading of these targets over time. While the trend in the decades following the Stockholm summit of 1972 was toward increasingly legalized multilateralism, recently this approach has produced few results, and public attention has increasingly turned toward alternatives. The decentralized alternatives are no longer considered inferior or illegitimate; quite the contrary, many scholars and practitioners now see them as a perfectly adequate way forward.[63] Beginning with the early example of "Madisonian climate policy,"[64] many scholars now see virtue in decentralized action, with the Paris Agreement on climate change being the most celebrated example.

Domestic political developments in the industrialized world complicate this story, but not in ways that would detract from the general thrust of my argument. Across the liberal democracies of the industrialized world, we see changes in governments' environmental policy positions, at both the domestic and the international levels. Such is the nature of democracy, and nothing in this fluctuation is inconsistent with the idea that industrialized countries continue to see, on average, high levels of support for environmental protection, and especially when the level of support is measured in willingness to pay in comparison to the rest of the world.

To understand this point, consider the implications of U.S. withdrawal from the Paris Agreement. On June 1, 2017, President Trump announced that the United States would withdraw from the Paris Agreement, and he was universally condemned by the international community for this decision. This decision has much in common with President George W. Bush's similar, if much less flamboyant, de facto exit from global climate cooperation under the Kyoto Protocol. The circumstances, however, are very different.

In the early 2000s the United States was both the largest emitter and politically the most important player in the climate regime. Effective climate action without the United States was inconceivable, and early scholarship on the Kyoto Protocol even found it puzzling that other industrialized countries would ratify it without the United States.[65] Today, however, the world has changed. The United States is a highly polarized country, and many U.S. states, cities, and businesses have announced their support for the Paris Agreement. Even a total U.S. withdrawal did not prevent other countries from moving forward, as both U.S. emissions and their share of the global total have continued to decrease. President Biden's return to the Paris Agreement in early 2021 was welcome news globally, but it did not have any fundamental impact on energy, environmental, or climate policy around the world.

Today the United States is neither the largest emitter nor politically the most important player. China is now a more important emitter than the United States, and the rapid decrease in U.S. carbon dioxide emissions because of energy efficiency, natural gas, and modern renewables suggests that American emission trajectories may benefit the global climate regardless of Trump's antics. At the same time, China's increasingly ambitious investments in renewable energy are widely recognized across the world, and now all eyes are on India as the next frontier for global climate policy. So while Bush's exit was a fatal blow to global climate cooperation,

Trump's more flagrant policy approach was much less of a threat to the Paris Agreement, both because of innovative treaty design and because the world has changed.

In general, global environmental politics has again found the spirit of the 1971 Ramsar Convention on Wetlands. Of all the major multilateral environmental treaties, Ramsar shows how technocrats can negotiate treaties that impose no binding obligations on members nor require major financial investments. Today's discussions on climate change, deforestation, and a wide range of other issues are eerily reminiscent of the negotiation history of the Ramsar Convention documented by Matthews.[66] Although today's environmental negotiations are not the exclusive privilege of technocrats, the now standard approach of avoiding political controversies and difficult, costly commitments also occurred in the Ramsar talks in the shadow of the Cold War. The people in the room may have changed, but the core features of the approach remain the same.

The resurrection of the Ramsar approach is both bad and good news. Some environmentalists are observing the reduced ambition and increased flexibility of global environmental cooperation with concern, pointing to the fact that even the largest possible impact of today's approaches is far from what they consider prudent. While this claim is probably true, a more productive approach would have to consider the potential—and likely—outcomes under the alternative: a traditional multilateral approach emphasizing targets and timetables. This thought experiment shows the return to Ramsar in a more favorable light. In a world of emerging economies, a rigid approach based on relatively homogeneous preferences among a small number of key players would probably result in no cooperation at all, as we saw in the debacle of the Copenhagen Accord of 2009.

The Paris Agreement of 2015 has been more productive. Even though it has so far failed to deliver rapid emissions reductions, this just shows how difficult global environmental cooperation is when the set of players is large and diverse. When solving the problem requires the participation of a large number of countries that are neither willing nor able to enact costly national policies, the top-down strategy holds little hope. If governments were to negotiate binding commitments, the important players would simply not join the agreement; those who did would not make much progress towards implementation. Decentralized action, respecting the sovereignty and variegated preferences of participating governments, is thus necessary. Without making it easy for emerging economies to join and participate, given their limited institutional capacity and low willingness to sacrifice economic growth for the environment, there are few good alternatives to decentralized action outside the scope of narrow, sectoral problems that afford simple technological fixes.

The growing number of players is itself related to the bewildering complexity of today's "regime complexes."[67] From biodiversity to climate change, top-down regimes tend to be replaced by collections of relevant, interlocked regimes that are often not very strongly coordinated.[68] Such complexes are not surprising in the presence of a large number of players with diverging preferences.[69] When solving global environmental problems requires the participation of a large number of diverse countries that face a host of daunting problems in implementation, it is understandable that top-down regimes tend to be replaced by amorphous constellations of sub-regimes often populated by nonstate actors. Although some of this complexity can be attributed to the growth of private governance and nonstate activities, the growing number of pivotal governments might be an equally potent contributor to this proliferation. When governments cannot agree on fundamental common rules for a single regime, smaller groups may make attempts at governance. Taken together, these attempts generate regime complexes over time, as different groups not only attempt to achieve their preferred governance arrangements but also respond to the initiatives of others. Even in the case of climate change, we saw this dynamic when President Bush negotiated the Asia-Pacific Partnership on Clean Development and Climate as a strategic response to the Kyoto Protocol.[70]

Institutional capacity also plays a role here. Because the lack of institutional capacity means that many countries are unable to implement the policies required, regime proliferation and fragmentation reflect the essential difficulty of making progress in diverse regional and social conditions. A global, uniform regime with binding commitments on all kinds of countries would not be feasible in the presence of a large number of countries with limited institutional capacity. While some countries with a high level of institutional capacity may prefer to move forward in a small group of capable and committed actors, others may prefer a regime that requires limited institutional capacity or may even focus on improving such capacity as a core activity. The divergence of institutional capacities in world politics thus creates an opening for regime complexity.

The growing role of nonstate actors in global environmental politics today is also related to the rise of the emerging economies. The absence of robust implementation architectures of ambitious, legally binding commitments creates an opportunity for alternatives, such as private governance. When governments fail to commit to policies or implement them, a space opens for the entry of nonstate actors, be it through delegation by governments or independently.[71] Sometimes governments see value in letting the civil society perform a certain task, such as product certification; in other times, the civil society proactively begins to govern an issue because there is a vacuum left by the lack of interstate cooperation.

Such delegation of authority is likely related to the rise of emerging economies. First, the difficulty of forging effective multilateral treaties in the twenty-first century creates an opening for the civil society. The barren environmental treaty landscape of the early twenty-first century suggests ample opportunities for private governance, as pressing environmental problems go unheeded because of cooperation failures. Second, as newly powerful developing countries create challenges that traditional systems of governance fail to address, there is an opening for civil society and private actors with capabilities or activities in these emerging economies. Countries like China and India open new opportunities for civil society groups because their nascent and immature environmental policies create the demand for capable and knowledgeable third parties.

Emerging economies' growing power is the third notable change in global environmental politics that I want to highlight. Gone are the days when it was enough to observe the positions of the United States and Western European countries to predict the broad contours of negotiation outcomes with a high certainty. Today, all eyes are on countries like China and India, given their structural power and pivotal role in negotiations. These countries' power to destroy has not just made global environmental cooperation more difficult but has also shifted the emphasis of environmental cooperation from the priorities of wealthy industrialized countries toward the priorities of the global South. From mercury negotiations to the Copenhagen Accord and the Paris Agreement, we have seen that emerging economies have played a pivotal role in the negotiations, determining both the possibility of a cooperative outcome and its content.

While the role of structural power in contributing to this shift is obvious and requires no explication, the role of the relatively weak environmental preferences of emerging economies is somewhat subtler but at least as important. The changing constellation of environmental preferences among pivotal players drives developing countries to adopt more aggressive negotiation positions. Emerging economies are empowered by their structural power, but it is their weak environmental preference that pushes them to oppose industrialized countries' proposals. Considering only those countries that are pivotal for negotiation outcomes and policy implementation, the rise of emerging economies means that the gap between proponents and detractors of an aggressive, ambitious approach is growing. The power shift favors those with relatively weak environmental preferences, raising new barriers to global environmental cooperation.

Because the preferences of emerging economies remain quite different from those of traditional industrialized countries, the focal points in negotiations have thus changed. Today more than ever before, concerns about the global environment revolve around sustainable development and green growth—concepts that place economic development at the heart of the global environmental agenda. Far from constraining the global economy, green growth takes the pursuit of profit to the next level by turning environmental conservation into business.[72]

This change in concerns is understandable in the light of the deeper transformation of the world economy. If emerging economies are now pivotal, securing their support requires focusing on issues that are of interest to them. Unless global environmental governance promises real benefits to governments with sovereign authority to formulate environmental and energy policy in emerging economies, the relevance of such governance to solving the world's great environmental problems and avoiding threats to human civilization will be minimal. Any frame that fails to secure the support of emerging economies dooms negotiations to a failure, resulting in further global environmental degradation.[73]

GLOBAL ENVIRONMENTAL POLITICS IN THE TWENTY-FIRST CENTURY

A careful evaluation of major trends in global environmental politics leads to a somewhat depressing conclusion: the world is moving in a troubling direction, with global environmental institutions doing less to halt the deterioration of ecosystems than they used to in the last decades of the twentieth century. Today, negotiations across the board have a large number of relevant players. Emerging economies hold most of the power to destroy, and their weak environmental preferences and limited institutional capacity ensure both that environmental deterioration is a real threat and that negotiations to stop it are difficult. To the extent that environmental cooperation has produced success, it has been based on the bottom-up strategy of Paris, and the making of major multilateral regimes which has been limited to just one exception, the Minamata Convention on Mercury.

The broad shift from top-down treaty architectures towards a more flexible, bottom-up approach reflects structural transformations in the world economy and international relations. The rapid rise of emerging economies with large populations, robust economic growth, relatively weak environmental preferences, and limited institutional capacity has decimated the foundations of the twentieth-century model of environmental treaty making. When the number of pivotal parties with lots of power to destroy is large, and neither their preferences nor institutional capacities are very favorable to ambitious environmental action, the idea of first negotiating and then enforcing binding commitments is simply not tenable. Even if this strategy somehow survived multilateral negotiations—in reality, it has not—it would fail when key emerging economies would simply either chose not to or would fail to comply with their treaty obligations.

The good news is that policy makers have recognized this shift. Treaties such as the Paris Agreement and summits like Rio+20 show that policy makers are aware of the new realities of global environmental politics, and that they are adapting their strategies to new realities. While the results leave much to be desired, the regime is nonetheless a substantial improvement over the alternative of banging one's head against the wall if continuing to rely on rigid top-down strategies developed in the 1970s and the 1980s.

4

THE EVOLUTION OF THREE GLOBAL
ENVIRONMENTAL REGIMES

T he previous two chapters have looked at the evolution of global environmental politics writ large. While such a broad overview is necessary for an analysis of the changes effected by the rise of emerging economies, the inevitable lack of detail raises the possibility that the view from above obscures important scope conditions, causal mechanisms, and limitations of the argument. An argument about the shifting logic of global environmental politics would, after all, not be worth much unless it can help us understand changes in specific issue areas and regimes.

Having reviewed broad changes in global environmental politics, I now examine the trajectories of three important global environmental regimes: chemicals, biodiversity, and climate change. Krasner defines regimes as "principles, norms, rules, and decision-making procedures around which actor expectations converge in a given issue-area."[1] The three regimes under investigation all play an important role in global environmental politics. The chemicals regime governs the global and regional use of potentially hazardous chemicals in industrialized society. The biodiversity regime protects globally valuable species, ecosystems, and habitats from destruction. The climate regime, finally, focuses on mitigating the ultimate global environmental problem, that is, human-caused atmospheric change due to emissions of greenhouse gases.

Because all three regimes emerged in the late twentieth century and remain central to the architecture of global environmental politics, they offer an opportunity to explore within-regime variation over time. I examine differences in the likelihood and depth of cooperation both across the three regimes and over time. I summarize the extent of global cooperation for each regime and identify the drivers behind this variation. The trajectories of these regimes have been quite different. While the chemicals regime has gradually expanded over time and achieved a high degree of success in dealing with many toxic and hazardous substances, the biodiversity regime has been weak and mostly a disappointment to conservationists. The climate change negotiations have been the most difficult of all, but they have also shown that governments adjust to new realities and change their approach in the face of new North-South realities, even as progress remains slow and the obstacles frustrating.

The comparison of changes over time across three regimes offers two kinds of insights. The first is whether the broad patterns of evolution in global environmental politics are also present in specific regimes. Across the three regimes, I expect the growing importance of emerging economies with relatively weak environmental preferences and limited institutional capacity to complicate negotiations, produce a shift away from top-down negotiations, and increase the salience of development issues in the negotiations. As the number of emerging economies with considerable structural power grows, negotiations should move toward a new dynamic that makes traditional multilateralism hard to sustain.

The second is that I can observe a *differential* evolution depending on the nature of the issue area. The three issue areas differ across their characteristics, such as the difficulty of cooperation and the width of the North-South gap in initial negotiation positions. Some areas of global environmental politics could lend themselves to the analysis I have taken more readily than others; in some areas, the theory could turn out to be impotent or, in the worst case, even misleading. By interrogating the theory in specific contexts, we can learn not only to appreciate the scope of the theory but also to improve our understanding of the internal logic and consistency of the theory, as the performance of the theory in different circumstances reveals strengths, weaknesses, and hidden causal mechanisms.

I first review the evolution of each regime and consider the explanatory power of my argument. I show that all three regimes have faced the same pressures originating from the growing power of emerging economies, but differences in issue characteristics have produced differential responses. In all three cases, the rise of the emerging economies has strained the traditional multilateral model—one that all three regimes embraced from the very beginning—and given rise to difficult North-South conflicts. In all three cases, diverging environmental preferences and variation in institutional capacity have complicated the negotiations.

The implications of these shifts, however, have been quite different, as shown in table 4.1. The chemicals regime has survived relatively well, as the regime's narrow focus on specific products and processes with considerable potential for technology innovation has enabled continued cooperation despite changes in the balance of power, preferences, and institutional capacity. The biodiversity regime has suffered, but there has been little change because the regime was always one that favored the developing countries, given their almost total control of the disputed natural resources. The climate regime, finally, is the perfect storm: it shows how deepening North-South conflicts have forced a complete change of direction in negotiations—one that recognizes the substantial bargaining power of emerging economies with limited institutional capacity, and adopts institutional approaches—in particular, the Paris Agreement—that accept the new realities.

TABLE 4.1 Three Regimes in Global Environmental Politics

	Twentieth century	Twenty-first century
Chemicals regime	High level of cooperation; focus on industrialized countries	High level of cooperation; compensation and exemptions for developing countries
Climate change regime	Relatively low level of cooperation; transatlantic conflict	Low level of cooperation; greater emphasis on sovereignty, flexibility
Biodiversity regime	Very low level of cooperation; North-South conflicts	Very low level of cooperation; North-South conflicts

Note: The table shows a stylized comparison of the three regimes' trajectories in global environmental politics.

A DEGREE OF SUCCESS: THE CHEMICALS REGIME

The chemicals regime is among the more successful global environmental regimes,[2] as cooperation has been frequent and has reached the kind of depth that mitigates the problem in a meaningful way. Over time, it has made an important contribution to international efforts to protect ecosystems and human health from hazardous chemicals. Major treaties under the chemicals regime have supported a transition toward cleaner and safer chemicals, and countries have complied with their key provisions to an impressive extent. The Stockholm Convention of 2001 alone imposed a global ban on a number of highly hazardous chemicals, and all available evidence suggests that the enforcement of the ban has been a success.

Perhaps even more strikingly, the chemicals regime is the *sole exception* to the rout of multilateral treaty making since the Johannesburg conference in 2002—the Minamata Convention on Mercury stands out as the only major new multilateral treaty negotiated since September 11, 2001. Although we have seen that multilateral treaty making has come to a grinding halt in global environmental politics, the chemicals regime has generated a new treaty on an issue area that is both politically salient and entirely new, as there were no existing treaties whatsoever on mercury before the Minamata Convention. While global environmental politics remained in paralysis and the December 2009 outcome of the Copenhagen summit marked the nadir of the domain, the mercury negotiators had begun their work and made steady progress, without much fanfare, toward a new treaty on an important environmental problem that did not currently fall under any regime or alternative governance architecture at the international level.

The first major multilateral treaty under what was to become the chemicals regime is the Basel Convention on Hazardous Waste (1989).[3] The issue of international trade in hazardous waste had emerged when environmental regulations in the industrialized world raised the costs of domestic processing of hazardous waste to high levels. As Clapp notes, "Because of its extreme need for foreign exchange, the African continent was a popular target for waste traders in the mid-1980s, as shipping costs were not prohibitive, and dumping fees were particularly low."[4] So instead of processing hazardous waste in a safe way at the source, be it in Europe or North America, industries commissioned waste traders—many of whom were of rather questionable repute—to deal with the problem.

The environmental costs of this practice were and continue to be serious. In 1988, for example, A.S. Bulk Handling, a Norwegian shipping company, "dumped 15,000 tons of a substance officially listed as 'raw material for bricks' in an abandoned quarry on Kssa, a resort island near Conakry."[5] Soon after the dump, however, visitors to the resort noticed that the vegetation of the lush resort had begun to shrivel, and "a Government investigation discovered that the material was incinerator ash from Philadelphia, the first shipment under a contract to dispose of 85,000 tons of chemical wastes in Guinea." Assisted by Norway's honorary consul, Sigmund Stromme, the shipping company had negotiated in bad faith a deal to depose an entirely harmless substance in the abandoned quarry and instead dumped a highly toxic load of hazardous waste, hoping to avoid being caught because of Guinea's limited enforcement capabilities. And the practice continues to this date, as waste traders now dump ever-increasing loads of electronic waste in African nations.[6]

Recognizing the severity of the hazardous waste problem, in 1987 the United Nations Environment Programme (UNEP) initiated preliminary negotiations on a global, legally binding treaty to govern trade in hazardous waste. The stage was set in Basel for the final negotiations at a Conference of Plenipotentiaries in March 1989 where 116 countries were represented. In the negotiations, some of the least developed countries and their environmentalist allies demanded a blanket ban on trade in hazardous waste, but industrialized countries opposed this view and preferred a regulated approach.[7] This cleavage is natural, as the industrialized countries had little material interest in reducing trade in hazardous waste. As long as the industrialized countries were able to dump their hazardous waste in the developing world, they would avoid the high cost of safely processing the toxic materials.

Given these cleavages and disagreements, the final Basel negotiations were quite controversial. The negotiation outcome, however, was clearly favorable to countries supporting the regulatory approach instead of a blanket ban. Indeed, the Basel Convention is in many ways quite a weak treaty. It only regulates the transportation of waste between countries without mandating proper disposal; it does not provide for assigning liability and compensation; and it has no rules for enforcement.[8] These design features show that the proponents of a modest treaty focused on strengthening the regulatory capacity of the least developed countries had the upper hand in the negotiations. They secured a treaty that regulated, but did not impede, trade in hazardous waste.

The core principle of the Basel Convention is the principle of informed consent. The convention does not ban trade; instead, it requires waste traders from member states to inform the recipients of hazardous waste about shipments in advance and to request consent for the shipment. Thus it is designed to help potential recipients of hazardous waste make informed decisions about whether and how to accept these imports. A particularly important element of this approach is to stop *illegal* transfers of hazardous waste, as many of the problems created by hazardous waste cannot be controlled when such waste is dumped without authorization and without regard for domestic policies.

Given that the Basel Convention required few actual behavioral changes, it is not surprising that it entered into force in May 1992, after twenty countries had ratified it.[9] As of October 30, 2016, the Basel Convention had 184 parties—virtually every country in the world. Interestingly, as Marcoux and Urpelainen note, low institutional capacity predicts prompt ratification: "Countries that enjoyed greater bureaucratic quality were significantly less likely to ratify the Convention in a given year than were countries with lower bureaucratic quality. Our theory offers the following interpretation: international treaties that improve regulatory capacity in developing countries also improve the ability of developing countries to capture rents from those activities."[10] So although the developing world did embrace the rhetoric of a blanket ban, their behaviors belie a different interest—strengthening regulatory capacity to turn trade in hazardous waste into a net gain.

Cooperation on hazardous waste ran into serious trouble, however, in the negotiations for the Ban Amendment of 1995.[11] Dissatisfied with the limited scope and low ambition of the Basel Convention, a coalition of vocal environmental groups and developing country governments demanded a blanket ban on trade in hazardous waste. In a move akin to later negotiations under the broader chemicals regime, these advocates thought that a blanket ban would be the only effective solution to the socioenvironmental problems that hazardous waste creates.

The Ban Amendment, however, proved controversial and never succeeded in securing the support of enough countries for entry into force.
Among industrialized countries, major exporters of hazardous waste, such
as Australia and the United States, opposed the ban. More important,
though, many *emerging economies* also opposed it. As Marcoux and Urpelainen show, countries such as South Africa and India have explicitly stated
that they oppose a blanket ban because they prefer to continue trade in
hazardous waste.[12] While some commentators, such as O'Neill, thought at
the turn of the millennium that the hazardous waste regime was "converg-
ing on the principle that waste trading from richer to poorer nations
should be banned,"[13] the reality is that the Ban Amendment has not entered
into force because the number of countries willing to ratify it is too low.

Regional efforts toward a ban have also failed. In 1991 African countries negotiated the Bamako Convention on the Ban of the Import Into
Africa and Control of Transboundary Movement and Management of
Hazardous Wastes Within Africa, a treaty that entered into force in 1998,
after ten countries had ratified it. The Bamako Convention remains a
paper tiger, however, with no active secretariat or any evidence of efforts
to enforce the ban on imports.

Ever since the Ban Amendment negotiations, the hazardous waste
regime has achieved little. Without the controversial Ban Amendment,
the original Basel Convention has settled into a low-ambition equilibrium
focused on capacity building and technical assistance. While the convention has made an important contribution in enhancing capacity, it
remains a modest treaty that does not by any means aim to "solve" the
problem of trade in hazardous waste. Instead, the Basel Convention operates at the margins. At the same time, new challenges such as electronic
waste have emerged, and the regime has not been able to respond effectively. In 2007, for example, the Basel Action Network, an NGO focusing
on the problem of hazardous waste, wrote in a provocative article titled
"Time to Realize the Global E-Waste Crisis" that "developing countries
will never be able to manage even their own waste sustainably unless they
can convert their informal sector, and that will never happen as long as it
is so easily fed by our waste exports. As long as gross cost externalization
is allowed via the global toxic waste export trade, the horror show will
continue. The Basel Convention and its export ban is there for a reason.
It's time for us all to become law-abiding global citizens."[14]

In sum, the hazardous waste regime shows how the sovereign governments of the world, while paying lip service to the idea of a blanket ban, mostly preferred to let individual nations to decide for themselves how to deal with hazardous waste. The Basel Convention, which enhanced national regulatory capacities, was these governments' treaty of choice, whereas the much more ambitious Ban Amendment died a quiet death because of a lack of political support.

The next two major chemical treaties that came into being were the Rotterdam Convention and the Stockholm Convention. These two treaties were a response to the increasingly widespread recognition that the unregulated use of chemicals could pose a threat to public health and the environment. As Selin notes, "Hazardous chemicals pose significant environmental and human health risks. . . . Global cooperation is necessary to address the full range of environmental and human health risks stemming from hazardous chemicals, as many important issues fall within the realm of international law."[15] By the mid-1990s industrialized societies had become thoroughly chemicalized. According to the European Environmental Bureau, a white paper by the European Commission in 2001 estimated the global production of chemicals to be at 400 million tons and, perhaps more significantly, that there were over a hundred thousand chemicals in the European market, with potentially serious consequences for the environment and human health:

> Serious knowledge gaps exist about the adverse impacts of these chemicals and too often action has only been taken after widespread damage has been done (well-known examples include: asbestos, DDT, PCBs, benzene, etc.). Many of these chemicals have caused—and still cause—serious damage to human health and wildlife through their continued release into the environment. Not only do hazardous chemical substances threaten environmental safety and thus biodiversity at the global level but they are also increasingly to cause serious health problems. The incidence of some major diseases (e.g., various types of cancer, multiple allergies and lower fertility) have increased significantly over the last decades and scientific research has shown clear evidence that continuous exposure of human beings and wildlife to multiple toxic chemical pollutants causes serious health problems.[16]

The Rotterdam Convention on the Prior Informed Consent Procedure for Certain Hazardous Chemicals and Pesticides in International Trade (1998) resembles the Basel Convention in that it also emphasizes the principle of informed consent. According to Selin, "The history of the Rotterdam Convention dates back to the 1980s with the development of a voluntary [prior informed consent] scheme." While international organizations initially created various voluntary codes of conduct, in March 1996 the official negotiations toward what was to become the Rotterdam Convention began. In the negotiations, countries such as Australia and the United States advocated for limiting the scope of the treaty to the most hazardous pesticides, while the European Union and many developing countries argued for a comprehensive treaty. Some developing countries even wanted a blanket ban on hazardous chemicals, but "the idea of a ban received little support from most countries." At the same time, developing countries demanded that the principle of common but differentiated responsibilities be considered, but the industrialized countries successfully rejected this demand.[17]

Given the preferences of different parties, the negotiations focused on prior informed consent (PIC). In practice, the rules for adding chemicals on the list became a linchpin of the talks, as the "discussions included questions about the number of countries that needed to submit notifications, the number of different regions these countries had to be from, and how to define these regions." In the final text, the Rotterdam Convention requires prior informed consent for a list of chemicals and establishes a procedure for expanding this list: "The Rotterdam Convention stipulates that a party that has taken regulatory action banning or severely restricting any chemical of a category not explicitly excluded under the treaty is required to notify the secretariat about such action. For a banned or severely restricted chemical to be included on the PIC list, at least one party . . . from at least two PIC regions must have taken regulatory action and must have submitted individual notifications to the secretariat."[18]

The treaty does not impose a ban on any of the substances listed but instead allows the treaty parties to choose their own national legislation and then requires that exporters both inform the importers of incoming products and abide by national legislation. Similar to the Basel Convention, the treaty is designed to help importing nations to control imports and enforce national legislation—it does not in any way restrict legal trade in these substances.

The Rotterdam Convention entered into force on February 24, 2004, ninety days after 50 countries had ratified it.[19] As of October 28, 2016, as many as 155 countries had ratified it, testifying to the success of the treaty. The treaty is almost global, and the only major economies that remain outsiders are the United States and Turkey. And while the absence of the United States may initially appear troubling, the global logic of information sharing means that the consequences of missing one major industrial economy are not that serious, provided others continue to participate. In practice, virtually any chemical used in the United States is also in the European Union, and because European chemical standards tend to be much more stringent than their American counterparts, EU participation enables developing country parties to gain access to a wealth of information about potentially hazardous chemicals and their regulation. Thus any chemicals that the United States might export are, in fact, indirectly covered by the PIC procedure.

In contrast to the Basel Convention, the regulation of hazardous chemicals did not stop at prior informed consent. In fact, the official negotiations on the Stockholm Convention on Persistent Organic Pollutants (2001) began in June–July 1998, only months after the negotiations on the Rotterdam Convention had been successfully concluded. In fact, "many of the same people who had participated in the [earlier] negotiations . . . were also negotiating the Stockholm Convention."[20]

An interesting feature of the negotiations on the Stockholm Convention was that they were, at least initially, relatively harmonious. Selin notes that "dominating industry interests in Europe and North America— like their home governments—backed the expansion of these regulations to the global level so that their competitors and chemicals producers across the world would operate under similar restrictions."[21] This desire for global coverage, in turn, reflects technological innovation, national legislation, and regional agreements such as the Convention on Long-Range Transboundary Air Pollution, which does impose restrictions on persistent organic chemicals.

The combination of preexisting national and regional restrictions on the use of hazardous chemicals in the world's largest chemical markets— Europe and the United States in particular—gave the chemical industry an incentive to promote similar regulations elsewhere, so that they could market their expensive but profitable new innovations on a global scale. Without such blanket bans, consumers of chemicals outside the already regulated markets might have continued to use the older alternatives, which were cheaper but more hazardous, and a global blanket ban was the easiest way to stop this bifurcation of the chemical market into regulated and unregulated segments.

The Stockholm Convention, then, adopts a more heavy-handed approach than the Basel or Rotterdam Conventions: it bans products. The treaty lists a set of particularly hazardous products for a blanket ban and includes a mechanism for expanding this list. It also contains exemptions and phase-outs for developing countries, along with provisions for capacity building and financial assistance. An interesting feature of the Stockholm Convention is that it adheres to the principle of common but differentiated responsibilities, as the treaty recognizes "the respective capabilities of developed and developing countries, as well as the common but differentiated responsibilities of States as set forth in Principle 7 of the Rio Declaration on Environment and Development."[22]

Similar to the Basel and Rotterdam Conventions, the Stockholm Convention quickly entered into force, on May 17, 2004—only a few months after the Rotterdam Convention.[23] As of December 9, 2021, 185 countries have ratified it. The United States again remains absent, but the logic of a blanket ban ensures that this absence is hardly a fatal blow on the treaty. The vast majority of the world's countries, including the large chemical consumers China and India, have imposed bans—caveats and exceptions notwithstanding, of course—on the regulated substances on the treaty list. As a result, it is highly unlikely that American exports of dangerous chemicals, virtually all of which are banned or heavily regulated by domestic legislation in any case, would find their way to the markets of developing country signatories. Such an outcome would require the illegal smuggling of banned, outdated, and not very profitable chemicals by American exporters on a spectacular scale.

After the Stockholm Convention in 2001, the chemicals regime saw a decade of standstill. Similar to other regimes in global environmental politics, for a decade no new treaties were created, though early talks on a mercury convention did begin only a few years after 9/11, with a voluntary effort in 2003 and the Global Mercury Partnership in 2005.[24] Having achieved the double victory of the Rotterdam and Stockholm Conventions, the regime came to a grinding halt in the aftermath of the 9/11 terrorist attacks and the resulting increase in conflict in world politics. The reason, however, was not a lack of need. While the Rotterdam Convention had created a basic framework for information sharing and the Stockholm Convention had imposed a ban on a set of particularly hazardous persistent organic pollutants, the vast majority of the world's chemicals were not yet subject to any international cooperation beyond the principle of informed consent. Instead, the thriving chemicals regime fell victim to the more general malaise of political conflicts in a hostile international environment shaped by President George W. Bush's neoconservative unilateralism and the rapid rise of the emerging economies that resulted in North-South conflicts across the board.

Below the global level, however, chemical regulation continued to evolve through regional cooperation. Although global cooperation on chemicals came to a halt soon after the Stockholm Convention negotiations were completed, pioneers at the national and regional level continued to develop new rules, regulations, and legislation. A particularly important development was the comprehensive European Union directive in 2006 on mandatory testing of chemicals, REACH (Registration, Evaluation, Authorisation, and Restriction of Chemicals).[25] The politically controversial feature of REACH is its scope: it would govern all chemicals on the market—over a hundred thousand of them and counting. While REACH is a regional regulation, in practice the vast size and diversity of the European chemicals market means that just about every chemical in the world would have to be tested. Any American, Japanese, or Saudi Arabian manufacturer of chemicals intending to sell their product in the pivotal European market would have to comply with the REACH regulations or be excluded from the market. Given that Europe remains the world's largest market for many advanced and profitable chemicals, the possibility of a major chemical company's not exporting a new chemical innovation to Europe is rather remote. Thus REACH is an example of a uniform regulation shaping outcomes at the global level.

At the global level, the Minamata Convention on Mercury was negotiated in 2014. The convention regulates mercury emissions in a comprehensive way by banning both new mercury mines and their use in various products and processes. The treaty covers both the production and consumption of mercury and imposes a series of requirements for the use of best available technologies in processes that could emit mercury. As the official treaty website explains, "Major highlights of the Minamata Convention include a ban on new mercury mines, the phase-out of existing ones, the phase out and phase down of mercury use in a number of products and processes, control measures on emissions to air and on releases to land and water, and the regulation of the informal sector of artisanal and small-scale gold mining. The Convention also addresses interim storage of mercury and its disposal once it becomes waste, sites contaminated by mercury as well as health issues."[26]

In the negotiations, some traditional North-South conflicts erupted, but with a twist.[27] China and India initially found support for their opposition to binding constraints on the use of mercury from the United States and some non-EU industrialized countries, while the EU and the African Group advocated for a legally binding treaty. When President Obama took office in the United States, the U.S. negotiation position changed and the prospect of a deal emerged.[28] At the end of the negotiation process, China also switched its position and a treaty with binding rules was possible. The Minamata Convention entered into force on August 16, 2017, after the European Union and seven EU members—Bulgaria, Denmark, Hungary, Malta, the Netherlands, Romania, and Sweden—ratified the treaty on May 18 and brought the number of ratifications to fifty.[29] Here, again, we saw a rapid move from negotiations in 2014 to ratification and entry into force in only three years.

While the Montreal Protocol is usually considered a separate regime, it has important implications for the global governance of chemicals and thus warrants a comment. As noted in chapter 2, the Montreal Protocol is a treaty that has phased out many ozone-depleting chemicals and continues to do so. Similar to the Stockholm Convention, the modus operandi of the Montreal Protocol is to focus on specific substances on the treaty's list and to reduce their use. Because the protocol has proven to be a success, it has recently experienced mission creep, with ever more chemicals being brought in regardless of whether they are directly relevant to ozone depletion. For example, HFC regulations took a major step forward in October 2016 under the Montreal Protocol. The Kigali Amendment, discussed earlier, is embedded in the Montreal treaty architecture, although the HFC negotiations focused on a climate issue. In this case, countries of the world found a way to solve the problem of a non–carbon dioxide greenhouse gas by going outside the cumbersome, polarized, and conflict-prone UNFCCC architecture.

Based on this concise review, the global chemicals regime has reached a high degree of success. Although the regime has faced the same challenges as global environmental politics more generally, negotiators have time and again found ways to negotiate effective and enforceable agreements. Over time, both the production and consumption of various chemicals have grown dramatically outside the traditionally dominant OECD bloc. In 2016 China alone was responsible for 40 percent of *all* global sales of chemicals, while the rest of Asia excluding South Korea and Japan held 14 percent. Between 1995 and 2014 Europe's share of global chemicals sales decreased from 32 percent to 17 percent, but not because of decreasing sales: over the same period, total sales increased from 326 billion to 551 billion euros.[30] The growing economic clout of emerging economies has increased their structural power in global negotiations on the governance of chemicals, but at the same time their institutional capacity has not reached the levels of the industrialized countries.

Indeed, the most interesting and important feature of the chemicals regime is that despite the growing power of emerging economies, multilateral cooperation has moved forward at a relatively rapid pace. With the exception of a decade-long paralysis after the Stockholm Convention of 2001, the regime has succeeded in broadening and deepening global environmental cooperation on the governance of chemicals. The Minamata Convention and the Kigali Amendment stand out as some of the most promising negotiation outcomes among all, and not just environmental, treaties in the second decade of the new millennium.

Why was the chemicals regime relatively successful and, in fact, one of the few bright spots in environmental multilateralism? The answer to this question lies with three key characteristics of the issue area. The first is that replacing outdated pesticides, herbicides, and other dangerous chemicals is not prohibitively expensive. As Ovodenko notes, the chemicals regime focuses on a specific sector with a high degree of oligopolistic industry concentration and a proven track record of technology innovation.[31] The industry is relatively easy to control from a regulatory perspective and, as Marcoux and Urpelainen suggest, actually can expect to profit from bans on old technologies—as they create demand for new, more expensive products.[32] Indeed, Clapp remarks that the chemical industry was an enthusiastic supporter of the Stockholm Convention, which created an opportunity to introduce new, profitable products to the global market.[33]

The second characteristic is that providing developing countries with flexibility in implementation is easy in this issue area. The chemicals regime has never been about deep changes to economic structures; it has always focused on governing, regulating, and managing specific products. Thus, providing flexibility to developing countries requires only phase-outs, temporary exemptions, and modest sums in financial assistance: "the chemicals regime recognizes the particular problems of developing countries. . . . [They] are given more time to phase out the use of regulated chemicals and deal with contaminated equipment."[34] In the end, these phase-outs and exemptions also do not compromise the efficacy of the regime, as other countries move first and market forces begin to displace outdated chemicals in any case.

Finally, implementing these treaties does not actually require much institutional capacity. Banning products is among the easiest things a government can do, especially when production is concentrated in a small number of large enterprises operating within a handful of countries. Although domestic authorities still have to enforce chemical bans, doing so is much, much easier than imposing more sophisticated regulations. If a manufacturing plant is found to produce a certain chemical, or if someone imports a banned chemical, the case is open-and-shut, and a punishment can be administered. Similarly, the users of chemicals are liable. Because the manufacturing and distribution of chemicals exhibits economies of scale, detecting illegal activity is comparatively easy. What is more, producers of safer alternatives have an incentive to monitor and report violations, as well as to lobby for stringent oversight by authorities.

The rapid ratification of the Basel Convention and the quiet death of the Ban Amendment illustrate this logic. When the Basel Convention was negotiated, it rapidly gained the support of the developing world and most industrialized countries. This success is not surprising, as the Basel Convention promises concrete gains to developing countries with few costs. Although some countries used the soapbox afforded by the negotiations to campaign for a blanket ban, it is notable that virtually all of them did ratify the Basel Convention in the end. The promises of easy regulatory gains and opportunities to deter illegal imports of hazardous waste were attractive, while the cost of participating in the treaty was virtually zero, as nothing in the treaty prevented governments from importing hazardous waste, and external financial support was available for the cost of implementation.

The Ban Amendment, which would completely ban trade in hazardous waste, on the other hand, carries high costs and thus has failed to gain widespread support. The amendment would have done something much more fundamental: instead of banning or regulating a specific product, it would have affected a huge number of industries that currently generate hazardous waste. The costs would have been high, and the promise of profits from new products would not have been there. As Marcoux and Urpelainen find, although many developing countries adopted aggressive bargaining positions calling for a ban in the initial negotiations, the wide gap in their enthusiasm for actually ratifying the Basel Convention and for ratifying the Ban Amendment shows that the enthusiasm for regulation is much broader than the enthusiasm for a ban.[35]

The Rotterdam and Stockholm treaties, similarly, have rapidly gained the support of most of the world, including both industrialized and emerging economies. Although the two treaties exhibit major differences in their design, with one adopting the principle of informed consent and the other imposing blanket bans, they have not proven particularly controversial in the global arena. As both treaties focus on specific technologies produced by a small number of industries for which cleaner, less harmful—and profitable—substitutes are available, the implementation and enforcement of these treaties are not politically controversial.

The Minamata Convention, finally, promises concrete gains to a large number of countries. The fact that the treaty was negotiated in 2014, following the years of negotiations that went into this complex deal, shows that the chemicals regime recovered from the 9/11 shock very quickly—an impressive achievement in and of itself. The Minamata Convention is unique in the twenty-first century in that it focuses on an entirely new environmental problem—one not governed by any treaty—and manages to produce an effective, enforceable treaty that covers multiple aspects of the problem, regulating the behavior of both mercury producers and users.

A particularly striking feature of the negotiations on the Minamata Convention is how China's position changed and enabled an effective global deal.[36] While both China and India were initially hostile to mercury restrictions, over time China's structural transformation and growing domestic institutional capacity contributed to a shift in their negotiation position. Thus China began to support restrictions on the production and consumption of mercury, splitting the traditional coalition of the emerging economies in the global South and sealing the deal. While the change of the U.S. position was a simple question of domestic politics, the Chinese change of position was much more significant in that it reflected a change in economic structure and, as a result, isolated India.

At the same time, the robust institutional architecture of the Montreal Protocol further contributes to the success of the chemicals regime. Whenever a specific hazardous chemical falls under the authority of the Montreal Protocol, negotiators can consider this institutional setting—a treaty architecture with a proven track record, if there ever was one—for formulating procedures and rules for governing its production and consumption. The existence of the Montreal Protocol thus created an avenue for progress even for the regulation of specific greenhouse gases. These achievements, however, were based on the sectoral logic of banning specific substances and replacing them with modern alternatives—a logic that would not apply to other climate change issues, such as reducing carbon dioxide emissions across the economy.

The chemicals regime is an example of how certain issue characteristics and appropriate institutional design allow meaningful North-South cooperation even in a world of emerging economies. The chemicals regime can thus be seen as an instance in which the problems created by the rise of emerging economies can be overcome because issue characteristics facilitate the kind of North-South deal that is necessary for credible and effective cooperation over time. The chemicals regime does not impose high costs on developing countries, as they (mostly) do not produce their own chemicals and gain benefits from upgrading in any case. Where high costs threaten to derail cooperation, treaties can afford flexibility with modest side payments and policies such as graduated phase-outs. Effective cooperation also does not depend on high institutional capacity, as implementation and enforcement often take the form of blanket bans.

UNDERWHELMING: THE BIODIVERSITY REGIME

The biodiversity regime is a collection of treaties and related instruments that focus on protecting species, ecosystems, and habitats. Compared to the chemicals regime, it is more complex. The protection of biodiversity is a complicated global challenge, as almost any human activity could potentially threaten species, ecosystems, and habitats. Here I begin with early treaties on trade in endangered species and wetlands protection but emphasize the central role of the United Nations Convention on Biological Diversity (CBD) of 1992. Besides direct efforts to conserve biodiversity, the regime also includes measures against deforestation as an important, if legally separate, subregime. This regime does not have a flagship convention. Instead, it relies on a complex architecture of relatively weak, and often informal, instruments.

Unfortunately, the contrast between the biodiversity and chemicals regimes is stark. While the chemicals regime has made considerable progress toward global environmental sustainability over three decades, the biodiversity regime has had little impact on national policies and outcomes. Countries have, time and again, failed to negotiate meaningful treaties that would move the needle. Although the global effort to conserve biodiversity goes back a long way and is among the first global regimes to emerge, its overall achievements are quite limited. Even though the scientific and economic case for protecting habitats and avoiding deforestation is strong, the international community has made little progress on this front. I shall argue that the North-South distribution of power to destroy and financial resources is a key problem.

To understand the problem with the biodiversity regime, the first step is to consider the issue characteristics. They could hardly be more different from chemicals. Similar to energy, biodiversity is a difficult issue to address largely because the expansion of human society and economic activities is enough to contribute to species extinction through habitation loss. While some species, such as elephants, are threatened because they are specifically hunted, the less dramatic combination of population and economic growth is a much more significant factor overall. Another factor contributing to biodiversity loss is rapid climate change. Although species can adjust to slow changes in temperature, today's change is so fast that evolutionary adaptation through genetics cannot keep up. As

Kolbert explains in her "unnatural history" of the ongoing sixth extinction, humans destroy vast forest areas to feed themselves, enable invasive species to move around the globe, and, "having discovered subterranean reserves of energy, . . . change the composition of the atmosphere."[37] With the exception of fossil fuels, there is no single product or process that is driving biodiversity loss. Almost everything we do—human life itself—contributes to the problem.

Broadly defined, the biodiversity regime is one of the first global environmental regimes. Early treaties in this global complex include the Ramsar Convention of 1971 and the Convention on International Trade in Endangered Species (CITES) of 1965. The Ramsar Convention, named after the Iranian city in which it was negotiated, was to protect international wetlands while CITES was to stop illegal exports and imports of endangered species. These two treaties turned out to be quite illustrative for understanding the biodiversity regime more broadly.

Although this interpretation is perhaps not very charitable, the Ramsar Convention is basically a treaty that allows interested countries to list wetlands of ecological importance and thus highlight their salience. Negotiated by technocrats, the convention—"the first of the modern instruments seeking to conserve natural resources on a global scale"—lists wetlands and encourages governments to protect them.[38] It does not contain specific provisions for enforcement or even require that countries adopt specific measures to protect wetlands. Instead, it requires countries to designate wetlands—at least one—worthy of protection as "wetlands of international importance for the Convention List."[39] The treaty does benefit from monitoring activities by the treaty secretariat, as well as peer review by the parties, in a logic that bears resemblance to the much more recent Paris Agreement on climate change.

Negotiated even earlier, the CITES agreement is a treaty to create a licensing system on trade in species that are already threatened by extinction or might be threatened in the future without restrictions on trade. It "works by subjecting international trade in specimens of selected species to certain controls. All import, export, re-export and introduction from the sea of species covered by the Convention has to be authorized through a licensing system. Each Party to the Convention must designate one or more Management Authorities in charge of administering that licensing system and one or more Scientific Authorities to advise them on the effects of trade on the status of the species."[40] The key feature of CITES, then, is that it focuses on trade in species. It does not impose any requirements on domestic legislation on the conservation of biodiversity or species but instead controls their exportation and importation across borders. This approach is similar to those adopted in the Basel and Rotterdam Conventions of the chemicals regime.

While both the Ramsar Convention and CITES turned out to be functional treaties, during the Cold War there was virtually no other movement on biodiversity conservation. It was only toward the end of the grand East-West confrontation that deforestation became a major environmental issue, as campaigners in the industrialized world began to realize the magnitude of the destruction in countries like Brazil and Indonesia. The conservation of biodiversity within countries did not even appear among the core issues on the global environmental agenda.[41]

In 1992 the Earth Summit breathed new life into a nascent, dormant regime. The combination of the rapidly rising salience of deforestation, the end of the Cold War, and the twenty-year milestone of the Stockholm Conference of 1972 reinvigorated a stagnant regime, as biodiversity appeared next to the issue of climate change at the summit. The biodiversity negotiations focused on two issues: deforestation and the use of biological resources. While the negotiations on a global forestry convention failed, the Earth Summit did give rise to the Convention on Biological Diversity. I shall start my review with the CBD and return to the murkier case of forests after that.

An integral component of the Earth Summit outcome, the CBD is a canonical framework treaty that does not yet impose specific restrictions on countries but instead lays the international legal foundation for future protocols. Article 1 of the treaty text states the objectives of "the conservation of biological diversity, the sustainable use of its components and the fair and equitable sharing of the benefits arising out of the utilization of genetic resources."[42] This bundle of objectives simultaneously highlights conservation, economic value, and equitable sharing of benefits as goals.

From the very beginning, the CBD brought to life North-South conflicts. As Harrop and Pritchard note, "Negotiations for the CBD were fraught with conflicts concerning its core objectives and its priorities. The debate was particularly marked by the divide between North and South perspectives, primarily regarding environment and development imperatives. For industrialised states the aim was to promote *conservation . . .* developing countries . . . stressed that the goal was for the sustainable use of biological resources."[43]

This brief summary again highlights the fundamental North-South cleavage in global environmental politics: Is the goal to conserve the global environment, or is the goal to ensure that it can be sustainably utilized for economic gain over time? Not surprisingly, wealthy industrialized countries mostly advocated for conservation, while the poorer developing countries that held sovereign authority over the key resources favored a focus on sustainable development.

The contentious negotiations did produce a framework convention that entered into force on December 2, 1993, after thirty countries had ratified it. The convention listed a set of key principles, created a Conference of Parties as the highest decision-making body, agreed on voting rules, and established a set of supporting bodies such as the Subsidiary Body on Scientific, Technical and Technological Advice and the treaty secretariat. As a framework convention, however, the CBD does not impose specific rules or requirements; rather, it is a platform for future action.[44]

Although the idea of a global framework for biodiversity conservation is a noble one, the reality of the CBD has been disappointing. Since 1992 the Biodiversity Convention has generated little activity: "After 18 years, only two protocols have been created."[45] Given the vast challenge of species extinction and habitation loss—the "sixth extinction"[46]—this lack of activity is remarkable and hints at profound problems in global cooperation to solve the problem.

The history of the CBD appears even more troubling when we consider two protocols within it. The first is the Cartagena Protocol on Biosafety to the Convention on Biological Diversity, which essentially regulates trade in genetically modified organisms (GMO) by endorsing the precautionary principle and requiring prior informed consent on all imports of genetically modified organisms.[47] Although a GMO focus may appear somewhat odd given the CBD's emphasis on biodiversity conservation, the Cartagena Protocol reflects widespread fears about the environmental and public health effects of genetically modified foods especially among the European public. For advocates of measures to constrain GMO use in agriculture, the Cartagena Protocol is thus about biosafety—making sure that genetic modification does not threaten bio-diversity or human health.

In 1994, only a year before the birth of the WTO, discussions on a biosafety protocol to regulate GMO trade began.[48] The EU, which had adopted strict restrictions on GMO use in 1990, began a major push for a biosafety protocol in 1998, and the last negotiations in Montreal produced a final text on January 29, 2000. While the United States and other propo-nents of GMO use in agriculture had opposed the very idea of a biosafety protocol and the notion of prior informed consent based on the precau-tionary principle, "in the final text of the Cartagena biosafety protocol . . . the EU achieved virtually all of its aims. Perhaps the most significant victory was the adoption of an international, binding protocol in the first instance, considering the initial unlikelihood of such agreement."[49]

The Cartagena Protocol entered into force on September 11, 2003, after fifty countries had ratified it.[50] Once the protocol entered into force, there was a sharp increase in ratifications as many countries realized that the treaty architecture was the new status quo.[51] A tipping point was reached when the ratification requirement was met, and other countries rushed to ratify the treaty to avoid being left outside. As of December 2021 there were already 173 parties to it, with notable nonparties including Austra-lia, Argentina, Canada, and the United States—all major exporters of genetically modified agricultural products.[52]

While the basic idea of the Cartagena Protocol sounds fine, in practice it soon became a weapon in transatlantic warfare on agricultural trade. Far from advancing collective global interests by adopting a universal framework for regulating genetically modified organisms based on sci-ence, it became a deeply contested treaty and gave rise to a regulatory con-flict between the United States and the European Union. As Schneider and Urpelainen show, this time the primary conflicts were not about North-South issues but about the transatlantic disagreement on GMO regulation.[53] American agriculture has for decades increasingly relied on the genetic modification of crops by agricultural giants such as Monsanto, whereas the European Union has imposed a de facto ban on GMO pro-duction. These differences in regulation reflect decades of differential exposure to environmental threats and regulatory failures.[54] At the inter-national level, their primary consequence was a fundamental conflict on

GMO regulation, with a strong consumer-producer consensus in favor of strict regulations in Europe—and an equally strong consensus against them in the United States.

Given the clear transatlantic split, the Cartagena Protocol is an exception from the general pattern in that North-South politics did not in fact play much of a role in its negotiation, ratification, or implementation. Moreover, it is also an exceptional environmental protocol in that it is not clear how it is related to biodiversity conservation. While opponents of GMO production highlight the risk of contamination, proponents suggest that if genetic modification can improve productivity, it can feed the world's population at a lower environmental cost.

Here, the trade-off is not so much between the economy and the environment; rather, stakeholders disagree on whether the problem is too much or too little GMO production in the world. To expect such a protocol to stop the sixth extinction, then, appears ill-founded regardless of whether one supports or opposes genetic manipulation. The question of biosafety—a label that the opponents of the Cartagena Protocol detest—is largely orthogonal to the much bigger threat of species extinction.

The second protocol of the CBD is the Nagoya Convention on Access to Genetic Resources and the Fair and Equitable Sharing of Benefits Arising from Their Utilization to the Convention on Biological Diversity.[55] The primary goal of the Nagoya Convention is to ensure that the benefits from the use of genetic resources, such as plants with medical value, are shared according to criteria such as fairness. To achieve this goal, the convention provides a set of rules based on the principle of informed consent, with special attention paid to indigenous rights. Put simply, the main goal of the convention is to ensure that extractors and users of genetic resources operate under clear and transparent rules. The convention protects governments with genetic resources against exploitation, but it also generates gains for users of genetic resources by clarifying their rights and obligations.

In 2002 the Johannesburg summit initiated the talks. The Nagoya negotiations "resulted from dissatisfaction with the regime on access and benefit sharing (ABS) under the 1992 CBD," as "developing countries pursued the most ambitious policy objectives, aiming at an effective implementation of the benefit sharing objective of the CBD."[56] The North-South cleavage was highly salient, as developing countries sought to ensure that the biotechnology industry, which was and still is heavily concentrated in the industrialized world, would not reap the vast majority of the gains from biological resources. The key to the success of the negotiations—measured simply as the adoption of the protocol—was a change in the EU's position, which moved away from adamant rejection of any binding rules to a moderate position that still favored corporate interests but now accepted the need for binding rules—a major demand of the rather unified southern front.[57]

The Nagoya Protocol was adopted in October 2010, opened for signature in February 2011, and entered into force in October 2014. As of December 2021, there were 132 parties to the protocol.[58] While the United States and Japan are missing from the list, perhaps more troubling is the fact that Brazil, the country with more biodiversity than any other, has not ratified the agreement. Despite Brazil's active involvement in the negotiations of the Nagoya Protocol and the signing of the agreement, since 2012 the ratification process has stalled in the Brazilian Congress, where the agribusiness lobby has mounted opposition to the treaty.[59]

The final text of the Nagoya Protocol is a North-South compromise that makes some concessions to the developing countries but ultimately favors the biotechnology industry. Of greater import, however, is the fact that the protocol focuses on sharing the benefits of biotechnology exploitation, instead of addressing the core issue of conservation. While the protocol may have indirect benefits because it creates a legal regime for biodiversity exploitation and thus may encourage conservation efforts by developing countries, it is far removed from the central challenge of stopping habitation loss and species extinction.

The Nagoya Conference of Parties also introduced the Aichi Biodiversity Targets for 2011–2020, named after Aichi prefecture in Japan, where Nagoya is located.[60] The twenty Aichi targets provide a framework for biodiversity protection and lay the foundation for national biodiversity targets and action plans, which almost all countries in the world had submitted by the end of 2020. This move points to an emphasis on national action, but the Aichi approach lacks an institutional foundation for monitoring and enforcing these actions.

To summarize, the growth of the biodiversity regime under the CBD is a disappointment to anyone worried about biodiversity loss. Compared to the chemicals regime, the convention has given birth to only two weak, highly idiosyncratic protocols that put little pressure on governments to actually stop biodiversity loss.

At the UNCED, countries also tried to negotiate a global regime to stop deforestation. Against any meaningful yardstick, the resulting sub-regime has been a momentous failure. There is no formal convention on deforestation, and the subsequent global efforts to address the issue amount to little more than flailing. As Dimitrov put it in 2005, "Virtually no progress was made over fifteen years of debates, the differences appear irreconcilable, and key players offer no indication they may change their positions in the foreseeable future."[61] His prediction has proven correct.

The problem of deforestation is very similar to that of biodiversity loss, for the issue is again that of land conversion. Deforestation in a given area occurs when forest cover is cleared faster than it is being renewed elsewhere. The proximate causes of deforestation include fires, logging, and land clearing for purposes such as agriculture, settlements, and infrastructure. The underlying causes, however, are more complex. As Geist and Lambin explain based on an extensive literature review, "Proximate causes are human activities or immediate actions at the local level, such as agricultural expansion, that originate from intended land use and directly impact forest cover. Underlying driving forces are fundamental social processes, such as human population dynamics or agricultural policies, that underpin the proximate causes and either operate at the local level or have an indirect impact from the national or global level."[62] While policies can either encourage or discourage deforestation,[63] the fundamental pressures are related to high demand for forest products and agricultural land on local, national, and global scales.

At the Earth Summit in 1992, negotiations on a forests convention succumbed to North-South politics.[64] Industrialized and developing countries disagreed on whether forests should be considered a global commons or national resources. Not surprisingly, developing countries which owned most of the contested resources advocated for national ownership and sovereignty. In the third preparatory committee meeting in August–September 1991, Malaysia's representative accused the industrialized countries of using "nebulous terminologies" such as *global commons* to assert control over forests in the developing world.[65] Developing countries also vigorously argued for financial compensation, a claim rejected by the EU, the United States, and Japan.

In 1995, the international community made another effort to structure a global forests regime, the Intergovernmental Panel on Forests (IPF). In the coming years, the IPF was replaced by the Intergovernmental Forum on Forests (IFF) and, finally, the United Nations Forum on Forests (UNFF). These name changes did little to mitigate the conflicts standing in the way of a global convention, and it was only in 2007 that the UNFF produced a nonbinding consensus document on forests—"but without specific targets for performance."[66]

As a result of these failures, international efforts to regulate forests now include a somewhat confusing variety of international governmental and nongovernmental organizations, but overall the regime remains very weak. Humphreys provides a thorough but depressing review of global cooperation in this area: "The unwritten rules of diplomacy mean that the environmentally destructive policies of governments and their corporate allies are rarely criticized, except in veiled form. There has been no sustained dialogue on the deep political, social and economic drivers of forest degradation. To compound the problem, policy responses have been framed within, and thus delimited by, the core assumptions of neoliberalism."[67] This assessment highlights the fact that the forest regime has drawn on soft instruments, such as voluntary certification, instead of trying to impose restrictions on the destruction of forest resources by agricultural and industrial interests.

Scholars have noted, for example, that independent certification of forest products has played a role in efforts to protect forests.[68] In essence, the fragmented certification system aspires to allow consumers to purchase forest products that are extracted in a sustainable manner. Issues related to the certifier's credibility notwithstanding, certified forest products are produced in a way that stops, or at least slows down, the loss of forest cover. Unfortunately, certification is a voluntary measure that does little to constrain illegal logging and land clearing. It also does not fully remove the global demand for legal but unsustainable forest products at a low cost.

The certification efforts have not managed to stop global deforestation. While rigorously assessing the effectiveness of specific certification schemes in specific areas is a major challenge and few rigorous studies exist, at the global level it is clear that deforestation continues at a rapid pace. Between 2000 and 2012 the net loss in forest area globally was 1.5 million square kilometers.[69] At the same time, the entire area of forests certified by the Forest Stewardship Council (FSC), a leading certifier, was only 1.84 million square kilometers in 2015.[70] Thus the area covered by a leading certifier is barely enough to account for what was lost over a period of twelve years. Once we consider the fact that forest certification probably has at best a marginal impact on deforestation and could also cause negative spillovers, as deforestation is displaced to noncertified areas, it is hard to be very optimistic about forest certification.

Recently, REDD+ has emerged as the linchpin of the forest regime. Standing for "reducing emissions from deforestation and forest degradation," the original REDD was initially proposed in 2005 in Montreal. Because the Kyoto Protocol's CDM did not allow forestry projects, many developing countries from the Coalition for Rainforest Nations led by Costa Rica and Papua New Guinea demanded a system to encourage and reward forest protection in developing countries. In 2007 the expanded REDD+ architecture was adopted under the Bali Action Plan for a comprehensive global climate regime to replace the Kyoto Protocol.

Under this program, countries with forest resources can convert their value as carbon sinks into money through the sale of carbon credits.[71] Managed by the UNFCCC, the program offers financial incentives for the protection of forests as carbon sinks, with a strong emphasis on the monitoring, reporting, and verification of results. Without going into the details, the basic idea is that REDD+ allows developing countries to claim credits from forest projects that provide evidence for avoided emissions, following official methodological guidelines.[72]

Given the global scope and complexity of REDD+, a thorough assessment of its effectiveness will likely be a long time coming. Early assessments, however, give reason for cautious optimism while raising a few key challenges. Pasgaard et al. conducted a thorough literature review and a global expert survey to assess the record of REDD+, finding "a common but cautious faith in REDD+ to achieve economic, natural and political co-benefits." They note that there seems to be a tension between the actual—often complex—drivers of deforestation on the ground and the logic of REDD+ projects. They also identify problems related to the sharing of localized cobenefits between different stakeholders such as local communities, private investors, and national governments.[73]

More important, REDD+ remains limited in scale. A true breakthrough in halting global deforestation would require bringing the vast majority of the world's threatened forests under a carbon credit system. As long as REDD+ remains a pilot program with limited coverage, it cannot play a major role in stopping deforestation even if the outcomes from implementation are excellent at the local level. The problem is that a comprehensive carbon credit system would require someone—in practice, the wealthy industrialized countries—to finance the conservation efforts that protect the carbon sinks. Here, the international community again faces the North-South conflict over burden sharing and financial responsibility.

As we can now see, the few bright spots in the biodiversity regime have been imported from the climate regime. As concern over climate change has increased in the industrialized world, the idea of using forests as carbon sinks has begun to make an impact, though it is too early to say how large and sustainable these benefits are. Given that industrialized countries are much more concerned about climate change than they are about deforestation, the prospects for forest conservation as a climate mitigation measure are brighter than the prospects of forest conservation for its own sake.

Having offered an admittedly cursory review of the international forest regime, a comment on national policy is in order. National efforts have proven more significant in countries with major biodiversity resources, but even here the picture is ultimately mixed. While major biodiversity hotspots have adopted various policies to reduce deforestation, the track record of these policies has been varied. Their potential for generating positive outcomes in these countries is clearly much larger than that of the lackluster international forest regime, but the obstacles to policy success remain severe. To see this logic, consider Brazil and Indonesia.

Historically, Brazil's policies have contributed to deforestation, as the government encouraged settlers to move into rainforest areas with subsidies, credit, and infrastructure.[74] More recently, however, the Lula government, which held office between 2003 and 2010, initiated a series of policies to counter deforestation. The most important of these was the Priority Municipalities program, which put municipalities with high deforestation rates under heavy surveillance and enforcement of laws against illegal deforestation.[75] While some of Brazil's success in reducing the rate of deforestation at the time can be attributed to commodity price changes and other external factors, the evidence also suggests that the Priority Municipalities program certainly contributed.[76] While deforestation rates have recently begun to rise again, the Brazilian case nonetheless shows the power of national policy.

Indonesia's government has also recently made efforts to reduce deforestation, but with little success. Between 2000 and 2014 Indonesia lost a staggering 12 percent of its tree cover—more than any major country in the world: "First come the loggers; clear-cutting and burning follow, to make way for palm-oil or timber plantations."[77] Indonesia's decentralized governance structure has made it very hard for small districts to protect forests, and both loggers and palm-oil cultivators exceed their land quotas with impunity. So while Brazil's Priority Municipalities program shows the effectiveness of carefully crafted national policy, Indonesia's experience shows the difficulty of implementing policies without adequate state capacity.

Overall, this short history reveals a depressing trajectory. Although the biodiversity regime was among the first to appear, with the Ramsar Convention negotiations beginning well before anybody had even thought of a global environmental summit, the Earth Summit in 1992 revealed the tremendous difficulty of negotiations in this issue area. With most of the relevant biodiversity resources controlled by a small number of large developing countries and the industrialized countries unwilling to invest substantial sums in protection, the negotiations produced a weak CBD that, if anything, grew softer and softer over time. The CBD itself has given rise to only two tangential protocols, and the legally distinct international forest regime remains even weaker. To date, the biodiversity regime has failed to achieve much.

The most credible explanation for the depressing trajectory of the biodiversity regime is twofold. First, large developing countries have always controlled the key resources. The industrialized countries had limited bargaining power to begin with—the only resource at their disposal was money, and so far research suggests that their willingness to pay for biodiversity conservation is actually quite low.[78] My overview of biodiversity negotiations shows, with the exception of the almost immaterial Cartagena Protocol, very difficult North-South conflicts have prevented meaningful cooperation on the core issue of habitat loss. Industrialized countries have always prioritized the needs of the biotechnology industry, while developing countries—led by emerging economies such as Brazil and Indonesia—have insisted on a strict interpretation of national sovereignty over natural resources.

Second, and relatedly, the bargaining power of large developing countries—in particular, emerging economies—has increased over time. As these countries have grown their economies and the demand for natural resources has exploded, securing their collaboration without massive financial transfers has become more and more difficult. Industrialized countries never showed a high willingness to pay for biodiversity, and the expanding scale of economic activity in the world's biodiversity hot spots has driven a wedge between the low availability of financial resources and the high cost of protection.

The relevance of this argument can best be seen in counterfactual reasoning. Over time, climate change has brought a great deal of additional urgency to halting deforestation. In an ideal world, this urgency would have increased industrialized countries' willingness to pay and resulted in a new consensus for a grand forests deal. But because global demand for natural resources, including timber and meat, has grown rapidly, the total cost of protecting vast swaths of forests in countries like Brazil, Indonesia, and Malaysia has grown. The financial investment required to implement REDD+, which is the international community's best hope for effective action, on scale would be nothing short of staggering.

Financial support on the requisite scale seems highly unlikely. Martin describes how Ecuador tried to secure major financial compensation from donors in exchange for forgoing the development of oil resources under Yasuni National Park, a global biodiversity hot spot.[79] President Rafael Correa ultimately abandoned the scheme because industrialized countries were unable to put together his demand for U.S. $3.6 billion to compensate the country for the value of the oil underneath the national park. The sums required to implement REDD+ globally would be several orders of magnitude larger.

The most compelling explanation for the early success of the Ramsar and CITES architectures is that the costs of these treaties were simply not very high. Both treaties are narrow and technical, and they actually impose very few restrictions on domestic policy. Their rules were focused on idiosyncratic issues (Ramsar) or left national policy entirely untouched (CITES), and thus finding a compromise was not that difficult even in the conflictual environment of the Cold War and the recent decolonization of the majority of the world.

When governments tried to negotiate a more ambitious regime on biodiversity more generally, conflicts erupted. The evolution of the United Nations CBD is a good example: although this framework treaty was supposed to be followed by effective protocols on specific issues, only a few were negotiated over time, and they did not focus on the key problem of biodiversity conservation. Instead, they focused on the more manageable and less conflictual—at least in the North-South sense—issues of GMO regulation and intellectual property rights over genetic resources.

Over time, these conflicts grew more and more difficult to manage. As the economic power of large developing countries like Brazil and Indonesia grew, the cost to industrialized countries for compensating these countries to protect their forests increased rapidly. Despite an urgent need to deal with deforestation, very little was achieved. Even carbon credits have, in the end, done little to protect forests. While their effectiveness in specific areas may be high—rigorous assessments remain few—their aggregate global effect is bounded from above to a frustratingly low level even with highly optimistic assumptions.

Industrialized countries' interest in biological resources, such as plants with medical uses, has not contributed to solving this problem. Corporate interests do not support the notion of biodiversity and habitat as "common heritage."[80] Instead, they prefer restricting access and securing a monopoly over economically valuable resources. They also do not have an interest in those vast areas that do not promise to generate profits. Thus corporate interests are not a potential counterbalance to sovereignty-based claims over natural resources.

All told, the failure of the biodiversity regime highlights the central role of the power to destroy in global natural resource governance. The resources in question have been under the control of a number of countries with power to destroy from the early years of global environmental negotiations. As a result, international cooperation has stalled. The countries with biodiversity and forest resources have seen little reason to surrender their national sovereignty, and the industrialized countries have not been willing to offer sufficient compensation for protection. This status quo has complicated negotiations for half a century, and there is little reason to believe the situation will change any time soon.

THE WORLD'S GREATEST PROBLEM:
THE CLIMATE REGIME

Climate change is the ultimate testimony to the difficulty of North-South cooperation. Because mitigating climate change requires major changes in energy production and consumption, as well as land use, climate change presents a much deeper and broader governance challenge than most environmental issues. As widespread awareness about the dangers of climate change coincided with the rise of China and other emerging economies, the problem of stopping global emissions growth is to a large extent a question of decarbonizing the growth trajectories of these emerging economies. It is simply not possible to stop the global temperature from increasing unless emissions growth in emerging economies can be brought to a halt.

Overall, climate negotiations have proven difficult, and both the likelihood and depth of cooperation have remained low. In the early years, industrialized countries led the pack and negotiated the UNFCCC and the Kyoto Protocol. The rise of the emerging economies, and China in particular, then derailed the process and contributed to painfully slow and inconsistent progress between the Kyoto negotiations in 1977 and the Copenhagen talks in 2009. Since then, the level of cooperation has remained low, but negotiators have become increasingly savvy and realized that any global agreement must respect national sovereignty and avoid imposing burdensome obligations on countries. This logic underpins the 2015 Paris Agreement on climate change.

In the early years of climate cooperation, North-South considerations took the back seat. As discussed in some detail in chapter 2, negotiators at the first UNFCCC COP in 1995 were so confident about the secondary role of the developing countries that the so-called Berlin Mandate set for international climate negotiations the target of only reducing the emissions of developed country (Annex I) parties to the UNFCCC. Instead of trying to negotiate a deal that would provide for emissions reductions in the developing world in the near future, the COP-1 negotiation outcome set a legal rule for focusing the Kyoto Protocol on industrialized countries. As a result, the vast majority of the world's population remained, for all practical purposes, outside the dominant international treaty architecture for climate change.

In the negotiations on the Kyoto Protocol, North-South concerns began to appear, though mostly thanks to domestic politics in the United States. In fall of 1997 the U.S. Senate unanimously passed an infamous resolution that effectively prevented the United States from joining any climate agreement that would not constrain emissions growth in countries such as China and India. In the negotiations, these concerns were ignored because the global South refused to agree to any negotiation outcome that would impose binding restrictions on their emissions. As Aldy and Stavins put it,

> The Kyoto Protocol provides no means for developing countries to take on emission targets and engage in international emission trading, because some of the largest developing countries actively opposed a voluntary accession mechanism at the 1997 Kyoto negotiations. . . . The Kyoto Protocol severely limited opportunities for developed countries to leverage finance of low-cost emission abatement in developing countries (e.g., domestic cap-and-trade, fossil fuel subsidy reform, and building codes) through international emission trading under emission targets.[81]

From a North-South perspective, the most important issue on the table concerned this principle of common but differentiated responsibilities, which had first appeared in the UNFCCC negotiations in 1992. Although this notion initially sounds innocuous and, to many people, fair, it had significant implications for the logic of the Kyoto negotiations both before and after December 1997. Given China's rapid economic growth and its corresponding increase in greenhouse gas emissions, as well as the prospect that countries like India were to soon follow, the idea that developing countries would do nothing to reduce their greenhouse gas emissions was clearly anachronistic by the Bali COP in 2007.

While the decision to exclude China, India, and other developing countries looks bizarre from today's viewpoint, at the time the logic of focusing on industrialized countries made sense. With the exception of emissions from land use and deforestation—think of Brazil and Indonesia here— even China remained a relatively minor player. Chinese carbon dioxide emissions were 21 percent of the world total in 2005 but only 14 percent in 1995. Following the model of the Montreal Protocol, negotiators placed a high premium on the universal acceptance of the Kyoto Protocol, and such acceptance would have been all but impossible if developing countries had faced legally binding constraints on their emissions. And while excluding the developing countries obviously increased the likelihood of U.S. hostility, Vice President Al Gore personally flew to Kyoto to convince other countries that the Clinton administration remained committed to the approach. As he said in his speech on December 8, 1997, at the conference,

> You have shown leadership here, and for that we are grateful. We came to Kyoto to find new ways to bridge our differences. In doing so, however, we must not waiver in our resolve. For our part, the United States remains firmly committed to a strong, binding target that will reduce our own emissions by nearly 30 percent from what they would otherwise be—a commitment as strong, or stronger, than any we have heard here from any country. The imperative here is to do what we promise, rather than to promise what we cannot do.[82]

For a long time negotiations did continue to focus on the transatlantic conflict, even as the world was changing and North-South conflicts became increasingly apparent. Gore's promise of U.S. leadership in the climate regime lost its relevance when President George W. Bush, a Republican, chose Dick Cheney as his vice president. In a speech in June 2001 worth quoting in length, Bush made it clear that the United States opposes the emission reductions enshrined in the Kyoto Protocol:

> This is a challenge that requires a 100 percent effort; ours, and the rest of the world's. The world's second-largest emitter of greenhouse gases is China. Yet, China was entirely exempted from the requirements of the Kyoto Protocol. India and Germany are among the top emitters. Yet, India was also exempt from Kyoto. These and other developing countries that are experiencing rapid growth face challenges in reducing their emissions without harming their economies. We want to work cooperatively with these countries in their efforts to reduce greenhouse emissions and maintain economic growth.[83]

As late as the Montreal climate meeting of 2005—the first under the Kyoto Protocol, which entered into force earlier in that year—almost all the attention focused on the implementation of the Kyoto commitments. The

Earth Negotiations Bulletin, which tracks global environmental negotiations, offers the following summary:

> The most urgent objective in Montreal was to implement the Kyoto Protocol. The Protocol's entry into force in February 2005 may have made it a legal instrument, but without the formal adoption of the Marrakesh Accords, which set out the technical details that are key to its functioning and integrity, the utility of the Protocol and its mechanisms, at least in the near-term, would be greatly reduced. Many felt that without the Accords the entire Protocol could unravel and the delicate balance reached at COP 7 in Marrakesh in 2001 would be difficult, if not impossible, to re-establish.[84]

One of the few areas in which North-South cooperation bore fruit was the Clean Development Mechanism, which allowed industrialized countries to purchase carbon credits from climate mitigation projects in the global South. The idea of this controversial and complicated mechanism was to reduce abatement costs by ensuring that low-cost projects in countries such as China and India—by far the largest users of the CDM—were accessible.

The problem, of course, was that it is very hard to say whether a certain project actually reduced emissions relative to the counterfactual without the project. The effect of any given project would have to be compared against a counterfactual baseline: How would emissions have changed without the project? The fundamental problem of such an exercise is that one can only observe the outcome with the project, and not without.

Not surprisingly, there were many issues with the CDM. As Wara and Victor noted in an early analysis of the CDM, it was common for countries to give carbon credit for phony projects that did not actually reduce emissions at all, such as HFC plants in China or India that were built with the express goal of later dismantling them for carbon credits.[85] While Bayer and Urpelainen note that the CDM has over time served an important purpose in extending clean technologies to developing countries,[86] the fact remains that reducing greenhouse gas emissions in the global South remains very difficult without nationwide policies to cap these emissions. The tens of thousands of projects implemented under the CDM may or may not have reduced emissions, depending on whether the projects would have been implemented regardless, what the quality of implementation was, and whether they caused the displacement of emissions elsewhere.

Problems or not, the CDM did prove to be a popular device for minimizing the cost of emissions reductions. By 2009 nearly 1,500 CDM projects were undertaken by developing countries, and over 4,000 projects were in the pipeline. The CDM executive board issued a total of 275 million certified emission reductions (CERs). It is easy to see why the CDM was so popular: it allowed developed countries to undertake emissions reduction projects in developing countries where abatement costs were low in return for CERs that could be used to comply with their emissions reduction targets. The developing countries received the direct benefits of these projects, which included increased employment and energy efficiency. The majority of the projects were undertaken in just two countries: India and China.

Over time, North-South difficulties began to mount, and climate cooperation came to a standstill. The entry into force of the Kyoto Protocol in 2005 following Russia's ratification did raise the question of the next steps, and in 2007, at the Bali Conference of Parties (COP13), countries agreed on the Bali Action Plan to create a binding treaty. The goal was ambitious, as it left negotiators with only two years before the Copenhagen climate summit in 2009 to achieve it. The principle of common but differentiated responsibilities took a particularly prominent role in the Bali Action Plan. The plan emphasized proper burden-sharing among all members and reiterated the goal of protecting the environment while promoting sustainable development. More broadly, the Bali Action Plan stressed the need to consider specific national circumstances and capabilities when distributing the responsibilities among participating states.[87]

One key demand from the developing countries has been technology transfer.[88] For the Bali Action Plan, for example, "the G77 and China, the principal developing country bloc . . . put forward a comprehensive proposal under which developed countries would finance efforts along the full technology chain, from basic research to the construction of high-tech factories in developing countries." These demands can be rationalized with reference to capabilities or historical responsibility for climate change.

Industrialized countries have raised objections to technology transfer, citing both the financial cost and problems with intellectual property rights.[89] While developing countries see technology transfer as both necessary and fundamentally just, industrialized countries argue for commercial approaches and reject the argument of historical responsibility, focusing instead on emerging economies' growing emissions.

Another, closely related issue that has fueled controversies is climate finance.[90] Developing countries make demands for mitigation finance, arguing that they lack the resources to decarbonize their economies and, again, noting historical responsibility. They also increasingly argue for adaptation finance as a necessary means to avoid current and future damage from climate change. Even the measurement of climate finance commitments has created conflict and confusion, as industrialized countries use loose definitions and ambiguous reporting requirements to label various projects as climate finance.[91] Developing countries argue for strict definitions of climate finance to prevent industrialized countries from redefining their existing development assistance as climate-related. Such redefining, after all, would allow industrialized countries to claim that they are doing their share without actually investing any new and additional funds.

Expectations for Copenhagen were high. The economic competitiveness of renewable energy had increased and, in the United States, the ambitious climate agenda of the Democratic president Barack Obama—at least relative to his predecessor, the Republican Bush—contributed to optimism. Alas, climate advocates were in for a bitter disappointment.[92] The Copenhagen negotiations almost failed to produce any treaty at all, as major emitters were unable to agree on burden sharing, climate finance, monitoring, and enforcement. China, India, and other emerging countries refused to accept binding commitments, and a legally binding treaty without such constraints for all countries was a nonstarter for the industrialized countries. A small group of countries, such as Bolivia, even tried to sabotage the negotiations, to the delight of the Saudi Arabian delegation. In the end, negotiators achieved a last-minute deal on a Copenhagen Accord.

Far from a global treaty, the accord was essentially a list of voluntary, nonbinding promises by interested countries.[93] Countries did submit their promises, but they were far from comprehensive climate strategies. China, for example, simply reiterated its pre-existing domestic policies; India specifically noted that it does not consider the accord binding.[94] The gap between these documents and the much more detailed plans that the countries submitted under the Paris Agreement of 2015 is wide.

The Copenhagen Accord moves the climate regime toward a decentralized approach. The Kyoto Protocol was based on what scholars call a "targets and timetables" approach,[95] but in the end the treaty achieved little, as the United States did not ratify it and few countries actually faced demanding targets for emissions reductions. Because the Kyoto Protocol also did not have a working enforcement system,[96] it did little to encourage countries to reduce their emissions, except through symbolic politics. The Copenhagen Accord was a radical move in that it turned this approach on its head: now countries did not negotiate their commitments, but each country simply announced one.

Although the Copenhagen Accord itself was a frustration and a disappointment for advocates of climate action, it created an opening for a new approach based on decentralized action. In the next set of meetings in Cancun and Durban, negotiators set the goal of reaching a global agreement by 2015.[97] The hope was to recover from the Copenhagen debacle based on a fresh start.

The approach worked. If the Copenhagen Accord was frustrating to many climate advocates, the mood in the aftermath of the Paris Agreement was, to put it mildly, euphoric. Between the Copenhagen and Paris summits, negotiators converged on a "pledge and review" approach. Countries, again, were able to propose their own goals in what are known as Nationally Determined Contributions, but this time the contributions would be collectively reviewed on a regular basis, at five-year intervals. The idea here would be to achieve what Hale calls the "ratchet up" approach:[98] public scrutiny would encourage governments to propose increasingly ambitious commitments over time, allowing the global community to achieve effective climate change mitigation over the coming decades. While countries again submitted their own targets, the Paris Agreement established a system and schedule of peer review, so as to put reputational pressure on countries to first meet and then upgrade their targets over time. The Paris Agreement also set ambitious global targets for mitigating the rise of global temperatures and emphasized the importance of climate finance, with industrialized countries reiterating their commitment to mobilizing U.S. $100 billion per year by 2020.

In sum, the Paris Agreement is a sophisticated version of the Copenhagen Accord. It can be criticized for being weak,[99] but it is still far more likely to yield gains than the Kyoto Protocol or the Copenhagen Accord. In Paris, negotiators basically accepted, in a deep and meaningful way, that they would not be able to challenge the national sovereignty of major emitters. The international community recognized that binding commitments are very, very difficult to sustain under the anarchic international system. They did not, however, give up. They did not just let governments do anything they want but instead created a system of peer review to encourage the progressive deepening of decarbonization over time. This move toward a sovereignty-based treaty architecture amounts to recognizing the inherent difficulty of climate change as a problem and then setting realistic goals for the depth of cooperation to avoid a total failure along the lines of the Copenhagen talks in 2009.

In the aftermath of the Paris deal, October 2016 turned out to be a pretty good month for climate mitigation. First, the International Civil Aviation Organization (ICAO) achieved a deal on carbon offsets for aviation emissions relative to a 2020 baseline. Somewhat unexpectedly, countries negotiating under the ICAO umbrella agreed to offset the growth of emissions from the sector. While the ICAO deal, called the Carbon Offsetting and Reduction Scheme for International Aviation (CORSIA), does not force emission reductions on the aviation industry itself, it does require that the sector offset the future growth of emissions with projects in other sectors, be they renewable energy or energy conservation. In other words, CORSIA allows global aviation emissions to grow as global air traffic continues to increase but requires that they be offset with emissions reductions elsewhere. A possible explanation for this agreement is the fear of a mushrooming of unilateral aviation schemes, such as the earlier aviation carbon market of the European Union, which proved politically controversial.

The key limitation of this deal, of course, is that it depends on offsets bringing new life to the CDM. Still, the fact that a deal on aviation, a sector with troubling potential for emissions growth over time as more and more people begin to travel around the world, was possible only a year after the Paris Agreement is reason for cautious optimism.

Second, under the Montreal Protocol negotiators arrived at the Kigali Amendment on HFC emission reductions. The Kigali Amendment, as discussed previously, focuses narrowly on specific substances in a certain sector, but HFC emissions are so important that the overall effect on climate change is large. At the same time, the amendment does virtually nothing to facilitate the much thornier negotiations on carbon dioxide emissions. Similar to the aviation deal, the Kigali Amendment is a narrow agreement that solves a very important sectoral problem. It directly mitigates climate change by enabling HFC emission reductions, but it does not have clear positive spillovers for the more challenging and fundamental task of reducing carbon dioxide emissions.

These changes in the negotiations correlate closely with changes in the explanatory variables of my argument. As we can see, in 1995 it was still perfectly reasonable for negotiators to agree on the principle of common but differentiated responsibilities, legally locking in the idea that only industrialized parties to the UNFCCC would have to act. In the coming years, the flaws inherent in this principle were revealed as virtually all growth in greenhouse gas emissions came from developing countries. While the Montreal COP of 2005 still mostly ignored these issues, as countries were focused on implementing the troubled Kyoto Protocol, by the Bali summit in 2007 it was clear that the future treaty framework would have to consider China and other emerging economies.

The change in the global distribution of greenhouse gas emissions gave developing countries a huge amount of bargaining power. At the time of the Berlin Mandate (1995), developing countries were able to secure a good negotiation outcome for the curious reason that everyone considered them irrelevant. As their centrality to climate mitigation became clear to everyone, however, they started to make demands for provisions such as climate finance—with some success. By the time of the Bali Action Plan (2007), and certainly after the derailing of the Copenhagen COP (2009), the emerging economies were firmly in charge of the UN negotiation process—and thus the future of the planet's atmosphere.

But the fundamental preferences of developing countries did not change. Despite rapid economic growth in the global South, none of the key emerging economies had undergone a profound socioeconomic transformation that would make concerns such as environmental protection comparable in importance to economic growth and poverty alleviation. Furthermore, rapid economic growth in emerging economies has not led to equal improvements in institutional capacity. Thus climate policy at the national level in emerging economies remained for the most part a major challenge.

This challenge can be seen in the national goals that governments set in the aftermath of the Paris negotiations.[100] Of the first 160 Intended Nationally Determined Contributions that countries submitted, 122 included a climate finance component, and 64 requested a specific amount of money for implementation. From Ethiopia to India and Indonesia, many key emerging economies explicitly conditioned their more ambitious climate plans on finance for mitigation and adaptation. For many countries, such as Vietnam, the gap between unconditional and conditional commitments is wide: compare promises of 8 and 25 percent reductions relative to business-as-usual emission growth by 2030. For others, such as India, any action would be conditional on climate finance, technology transfer, and capacity building.

Under these conditions, deep North-South conflicts on climate finance are a cause for concern. When the OECD released a report on climate finance in 2017 for the Katowice, Poland, negotiations on a rulebook for the Paris Agreement, it claimed that public funds for climate finance had reached U.S. $57 billion in 2017.[101] This number includes grants, loans, and export credits. The idea that climate finance would include loans—money that developing countries have to pay back—and export credits—money that supports industrialized country exports—contradicts the idea that climate finance would constitute additional support for climate adaptation and mitigation beyond what is already included in development assistance. Indeed, the OECD report does not even mention additionality as a criterion.[102] This kind of accounting does not bode well for the idea that developing countries would ratchet up their emission pledges and meet their conditional commitments.

In 2020 countries submitted updated climate targets under the Paris Agreement. According to the Climate Action Tracker, at the end of the 2020 calendar year, thirty-four countries, including the EU, had submitted new targets. Of the eleven analyzed, four increased ambition and seven did not. An additional nine countries proposed new targets. Of the seven analyzed, four had proposed stronger targets and three did not.[103] These patterns suggest a split on climate change. Some countries are increasingly enthusiastic about climate action, while others are dismissive or outright hostile. Even among the more enthusiastic countries, it remains to be seen whether the long-term targets turn into concrete action.

Where low-hanging fruit has been available to reduce greenhouse gas emissions *without* fundamental structural transformations, cooperation has been much easier. The aviation and HFC deals of October 2016, for example, were possible because they avoided the whole issue of difficult behavioral change. They focused on narrow sectoral considerations, and while I do not want to downplay the importance of skilled negotiation in securing cooperation in these sectors, the distributional conflicts and enforcement problems cutting across these specific negotiations are not comparable to those that are at the very core of energy and land use debates. In contrast, when negotiations center on broad issues of energy consumption and land use, intractable conflicts between industrialized and emerging economies severely constrain diplomatic options and force an overall low level of cooperation.

The key question thus remains: Can climate cooperation reduce emissions from the energy sector and land use, the two most difficult, demanding, and absolutely crucial sectors? So far, everything we have seen suggests that achieving these goals will be much more difficult than securing small but significant victories in specific sectors. Virtually all the concrete successes of the climate regime have come from narrow sectoral wins, such as the Kigali Amendment and the agreement to offset aviation emissions, whereas nothing comparable has been achieved to deal with deforestation and energy use. Where success has emerged in the energy space, for example, the credit should go to national policies motivated by domestic considerations of political survival.[104] Indeed, Mildenberger finds that the distributive politics of domestic climate action—in particular, the distribution of costs and benefits across interest groups—provides a powerful explanation for variation across climate policy ambition across countries.[105] The evolution of the climate regime suggests that negotiators increasingly recognize the importance of domestic factors, and not least among emerging economies struggling to meet their energy needs.

To summarize, difficulties in global climate cooperation mounted over time as the global South's importance grew relative to Europe and the United States. Although many of the initial difficulties in global climate cooperation were related to transatlantic disputes and the obstinacy of the U.S. Republican Party, economic realities and executive action by President Obama allowed the United States to achieve significant emissions reductions over time. When the transatlantic conflict began to be overshadowed by the North-South conflict, negotiators were forced to look for an alternative, and they returned to the idea of decentralized, bottom-up climate action. While this approach is modest in ambition, it is suited to an international political economy of emerging economies. To put it bluntly, the targets and timetables approach is not feasible when a number of emerging economies are struggling to meet their energy needs at a time of rapid economic growth without a high level of institutional capacity.

The growth of emerging economies has also contributed to the growing importance of brown issues in the climate regime. One consequence of the move away from top-down regimes with targets and timetables for greenhouse gas emissions is that the dimensionality of climate negotiations has increased. Concerns with energy access, air pollution, water access, land deterioration, and energy security have grown increasingly important. The discourse on such cobenefits, supported by the UN Sustainable Development Goals, has grown much more prominent over time and will likely continue to gain credibility as the structural power of emerging economies continues to increase.

In this environment, progress in clean technology becomes increasingly important. As long as countries are unwilling to sacrifice short-term economic growth for protecting the environment, technologies that are fully or almost competitive with polluting alternatives are essential for success. Many of the world's largest economies, from China and Japan to the European Union, have formulated long-term goals of carbon neutrality. While these targets are not by any means easy to achieve, the decreased cost of renewable power generation and electric vehicles, and the promise of similar progress in other sectors, suggests that the targets are not impossible either. China's ambitions will likely serve as a litmus test for other emerging economies. If China cannot stay the course, it seems unlikely that India and others would set such targets any time soon. If China takes decisive action to decarbonize, however, other emerging economies will be under growing pressure to follow suit and will reap the benefits of improved clean technologies from China's investments.

Another manifestation of this change in the negotiations is the growing importance of adaptation in the wider patchwork of dynamic climate governance. More than ever before, adaptation is a key consideration in discussions over climate finance.[106] Developing countries, including many emerging economies, recognize adaptation as an urgent challenge and insist that industrialized countries offer support. The (Intended) Nationally Determined Contributions of the developing country parties typically condition their mitigation ambition on generous external financial assistance.[107] These developing countries set a low level of ambition unilaterally and then condition much more aggressive activities on climate finance. Indeed, countries like Bangladesh are often explicitly combining adaptation and mitigation in their national climate strategies.[108]

A concrete illustration of this demand is the emergence of the concept of "loss and damage" in the negotiations. The concept refers to the idea that despite realistic mitigation and adaptation measures, many countries will still be vulnerable to the effects of climate change and thus dealing with the losses and damages from these effects arises as a policy question. As Huq, Roberts, and Fenton note, the concept appeared already in 1991 "when Vanuatu proposed an international insurance pool to compensate small island developing states for the impacts of sea-level rise."[109] The Doha COP in 2012, in turn, agreed to address the issue under the UNFCCC framework in a decision known as the Doha Gateway. The whole notion of loss and damage is another move away from the conventional, mitigation-based framing of the problem. The policy solutions to loss and damage are either based on adaptation or compensation and insurance strategies, and in each case the pressure is on the wealthier countries to assist their poorer counterparts.

These changes not only are necessary but also inspire hope. The international community is slowly learning how to deal with the problems of global environmental politics in a world of emerging economies. Climate change shows that negotiators can collectively adjust their expectations and strategies over time, as they recognize and process the new realities. While the task ahead remains daunting and there is ample reason for worry, it cannot be said that negotiators are not aware of the issues and finding new ways to overcome them. The overall level of cooperation on climate change still remains low, but fundamental distributional conflicts between industrialized and emerging economies make higher levels of cooperation currently unattainable. While global concern with climate change continues to grow and clean technology improves, a dose of pragmatism about climate politics is welcome news.

COMPARING REGIME TRAJECTORIES

The chemicals regime is the narrowest of the three, with a ready supply of technological solutions in a concentrated, oligopolistic industry. The biodiversity regime covers a much broader socioeconomic domain, and yet most of the relevant natural resource—biodiversity—is concentrated in a handful of tropical countries with large rainforest territories. Climate change, in contrast, is the ultimate general environmental problem, for almost everything we do—and nothing more so than rapid economic development through industrialization—holds great potential for greenhouse gas emissions.

If the chemicals regime is a relatively successful one, then biodiversity exemplifies almost complete failure, and climate change shows the momentous difficulty of North-South cooperation when the stakes are high. The success of the chemicals regime, however, should not be primarily attributed to political will, entrepreneurship, or skilled treaty design. Even though all these factors appear to have facilitated the positive, productive outcomes we have seen, the fact is that the problem was never a very difficult one to solve. In the case of chemicals, a low cost of participation and the promise of concrete gains—often in the form of enhanced institutional capacity and improved local environmental quality—have enabled continued North-South cooperation in an otherwise barren landscape of global environmental politics.[110] Because the global governance of the chemicals is about specific products in a narrow sector, policies such as bans and phase-outs are suitable for cooperation. They do not require much institutional capacity, are not very expensive, and open opportunities for technology innovation.

In these circumstances, the drivers of change in my analytical model are understandably of limited import. Even though the number of pivotal countries has clearly increased, this increase does not make the banning of a number of already outdated industrial chemicals, pesticides, and herbicides much more difficult. To the extent that some emerging economies are manufacturing these outdated chemicals and depend on them because of their lack of access to advanced technology, the empirical record on the effectiveness and political acceptability of exemptions, phase-outs, technical assistance, and financial support is unusually clear: these simple and practical strategies work when the goal is to break a narrow, sectoral gridlock in the negotiations.

In the case of biodiversity, we see the difficulties that the growing structural power of emerging economies can create in global environmental politics. Biodiversity has always been among the most difficult issues for cooperation, given that large developing countries have always owned virtually all of the relevant resources, and the willingness of industrialized countries to pay to protect them has been minimal. Over time, the importance of biodiversity has been increasingly recognized, and certainly the link between land degradation, deforestation, and climate change has breathed new urgency into the stalling biodiversity negotiations.

As large developing countries have turned into powerful emerging economies, these complications have grown worse. While the world has seen much progress in many domains, such as controlling deforestation in Brazil despite population growth and the country's continued dependence on extensive agriculture for export revenue, this progress cannot be attributed to carefully negotiated, politically robust global regimes. Instead, progress reflects specific achievements in different national contexts. What is more, the progress that we have seen remains uncertain, fragile, and piecemeal. To say that the world has found a genuinely workable solution to the triple problem of deforestation, habitat destruction, and biodiversity loss would be a gross overstatement.

With climate change, we see these same difficulties in action. Given the scope and magnitude of the challenge, North-South conflicts have colored the negotiations at least for a decade. Before that, in the twentieth century, these conflicts were ignored and suppressed because of myopia among the negotiators. When the Berlin Mandate was formulated in 1995, negotiators still genuinely believed that they could make meaningful progress on climate change while excluding emerging economies from commitments.

Today negotiators face a completely different reality. Global climate cooperation has moved away from binding, top-down global treaties toward decentralized, bottom-up cooperation on a voluntary basis, with negotiators giving up on the idea of strict enforcement and using the weaker pledge-and-review approach as a substitute. This response has been a rational, if perhaps convoluted and erratic, response to the changing realities. In fits and starts, the climate regime has moved toward greater "fit" to the characteristics of the problem.[111] National sovereignty and the primacy of economic development are now the cornerstones of international climate negotiations, and the voices opposing these principles have been all but silenced.

The comparison of the trajectories of these three regimes thus reveals the narrow conditions under which North-South cooperation remains feasible in a world of emerging economies. When negotiations are focused on specific issues and simple solutions such as blanket bans are available and inexpensive, the difficulties of North-South cooperation can be circumvented with an array of phase-outs, exemptions, technical assistance, and financial transfers. For regimes that are narrow and require nothing more than technological fixes, the rise of emerging economies has been important, but not in a profound sense. In these issue areas, conventional approaches and solutions continue to produce satisfactory solutions, even though emerging economies can now secure better side payments for their participation than they would in an alternative world of economic paralysis in the global South. Issues that resemble chemicals have a "problem structure"[112] that mitigates the negative impacts of emerging economies' rise on global environmental cooperation.

When such easy solutions are not available, North-South cooperation is very difficult—and increasingly so over time. If the negotiations must do more than create the space for the diffusion of technological fixes in a specific sector, making progress in a world of emerging economies is a daunting challenge. The pivotal players refuse to accept constraints on their national sovereignty or limits to the quest for economic growth, and their ability to carry out their promises is compromised by limitations of institutional capacity. As a result, negotiators find it very difficult to agree on measures that would go beyond business as usual. As the Paris Agreement shows, there is still scope for bottom-up actions without strict enforcement, but the conventional approach of targets and timetables is simply no longer viable. Similarly, negotiators have made progress in addressing specific sources of climate change, such as HFC emissions under the Kigali Amendment, but such progress has proven frustratingly elusive in dealing with greenhouse gases more generally. The best evidence of progress comes from dramatic cost reductions in key technologies, such as wind and solar power. These lower costs will not erase North-South conflict over climate mitigation itself, but they create opportunities for decarbonization without economic sacrifice, thus reducing the level of cooperation required. Here, again, we see the importance of problem structure as a mediating factor.

5

CHINA AND INDIA IN GLOBAL ENVIRONMENTAL POLITICS

In global environmental politics, two countries in Asia—both emerging economies—have captured the popular imagination. China, the world's factory, is a credible contender for world leadership in the twenty-first century, with potential for replacing the United States as the center of gravity in world politics.[1] And while few people see immediate potential for hegemony in India, South Asia's democratic giant, it has lots of untapped growth potential in the coming decades.

For these reasons, no credible analysis of global environmental politics can ignore China and India. The first half of this book focused on global environmental politics writ large and the evolution of three important regimes, and now I will shift my perspective again and consider the experiences, views, and futures of specific emerging economies. Doing so is both analytically worthwhile, for a country-specific analysis offers an opportunity to link international governance to realities on the ground, and substantively necessary, as China and India are the two biggest pieces of the puzzle in twenty-first-century global environmental politics. Research design aside, it is impossible to even begin to understand today's great environmental challenges without considering China and India in particular.

China and India are quite clearly the two most important countries for the future of global environmental politics, but for very different reasons. China today is a heavily industrialized country with considerable institutional capacity, and global efforts to halt environmental deterioration are dependent on its ability to reduce resource use and pollution. In 2011, for example, China produced a staggering 28 percent of all carbon dioxide emissions—a clear indication that any efforts to mitigate climate change are bound to fail if Chinese emissions continue to grow.[2] For better or worse, China is the world's factory and has contributed the most to the growth in global environmental stress in recent decades. On the other hand, considering China's relatively high level of institutional capacity, the government does have the tools to improve the situation.

India, on the other hand, is still a mostly agricultural economy. However, its economic growth prospects in the medium run are quite bright. According to the United Nations, the country is on the verge of replacing China as the world's most populated nation.[3] Because of its massive and expanding population, India's ability to mitigate the environmental impacts of its economic growth will be critical for the success of global environmental cooperation. If India's population and economy continue to grow rapidly without massive investments in environmental protection, the security threats at the national, regional, and global levels are serious, and policymakers across the world are increasingly paying heed to this reality.

Unfortunately, India still lacks institutional capacity. In Levy's categorization, India is the quintessential competitive regime that suffers from significant limitations of capacity for effective public policy: "India's endemic corruption, and continuing difficulty in providing infrastructure and public goods, signal that it is only partway along the trajectory from personalized- to rule-of-law competitiveness and then sustainable democracy. It is troublingly difficult to find twentieth century examples of countries that have managed a sustained, incremental evolution along the trajectory, open throughout."[4] If such problems of incomplete transition raise concerns about India's ability to sustain economic growth, one can only imagine how they shape policy formulation in a secondary issue area, such as environmental policy.

My comparison of China and India is based on a set of quantitative indicators and qualitative analyses of both countries. I pay particular attention to comparing the institutional capacities of the two countries using both objective criteria, such as the aforementioned Worldwide Governance Indicators and budgetary data from environmental ministries, as well as evidence from country experts who have commented on Chinese and Indian governance based on extensive empirical research. This wealth of different data allows me to establish and relate environmental preferences, power to destroy, and institutional capacity to domestic environmental policy and global environmental negotiations. Most of my research draws on existing literature, as an original investigation of either China or India would require a focused study. After measuring preferences, power to destroy, and institutional capacity, as well as domestic and international environmental positions, I link them by demonstrating how changes in the fundamentals were followed by changes in policy at domestic and international levels alike.

As I review the evolution of Chinese and Indian positions in global environmental politics, I argue that the most important changes over time are related to the massive expansion of each country's structural power. Domestic political preferences have changed less, though China's rapid economic growth has already increased the salience of domestic environmental problems. At the same time, a much more significant difference between China and India on a global scale is their institutional capacity to solve environmental problems: unlike China, India has very little capacity to implement effective environmental policies. China's economic growth has been accompanied by impressive growth in institutional capacity, including in the field of environmental policy, whereas India's growth has occurred essentially despite capacity limitations and the lack of fundamental governance reforms. As much as China's phenomenal growth story has contributed to environmental degradation, the outcome could have been a lot worse without growth in institutional capacity and evolving domestic preferences.

The bad news for the planet is that the next batch of emerging economies will have institutional capacities more like that of India than that of China. The good news is that if emerging economies follow China's lead and manage to improve their institutional capacity, along with a growing environmental awareness, then a more sustainable future is possible.

CHINA'S RISE AND GLOBAL ENVIRONMENTAL POLITICS

Although China's rise to the top of the world economy initially appears straightforward, drawing lessons from the Chinese case for global environmental politics in general turns out to be difficult. Compared to most emerging economies, China has achieved a relatively high degree of institutional capacity. Because of this, China's economic growth has slowly translated into a degree of success in environmental protection. Thus, over time China shown that it can mitigate and limit environmental deterioration from rapid economic growth. Although China's environmental track record looks bad from the outside, the evidence suggests that it could have been much worse without the accumulation of policies to minimize damage from industrialization, and economic expansion more generally.

China's story as an emerging economy begins with the end of the communist era.[5] China's phenomenal economic boom began in 1978 with Deng Xiaoping's economic—but not political—reforms. When Chairman Mao Zedong died in 1976, Deng's reform faction won the resulting competition for power and initiated a series of economic reforms that shook the world.[6] Beijing let farmers own land to increase productivity, introduced new technology into the stagnant industry, created export-oriented industries, restored merit as a criterion for promotions in the bureaucracy, allowed foreign direct investment, modernized education, and gave provincial leaders strong incentives to maximize local economic growth—among many other initiatives.

These reforms generated rapid economic growth over the next three decades, turning China into the world's undisputed industrial powerhouse.[7] Between 1978 and 2015, China's per capita income grew by at least 6 percent every year except 1989 (2.6 percent) and 1990 (2.4 percent). In 2007 the growth was a spectacular 13.6 percent. Industrial value added in 2010 constant prices grew from U.S. $88.5 billion in 1978 to $4.12 trillion in 2015—almost a fiftyfold increase in less than four decades.

However, China's economic growth has also contributed to climate change. Between 1990 and 2018 China's greenhouse gas emissions increased from 3.3 gigatons to 13.4 of carbon dioxide equivalent. Because of this increase, China is the world's largest emitter, well ahead of the United States.[8] But a significant portion of China's total emissions stem from exports of products consumed elsewhere in the world. In 2017 China's emissions would have been 13 percent lower if they were counted based on consumption, instead of production, of goods.[9] In other words, almost two gigatons of China's greenhouse gas emissions originate from manufacturing of products consumed by people outside China.

In the early days of the economic reform, environmental concerns were decidedly secondary for the Beijing government. Due to China's extreme poverty and the threat that it posed to the survival of the communist regime, economic growth was the overriding priority. China's primitive economy generated environmental problems mostly due to poverty and inefficiencies in industry, as environmental pollution or resource depletion were not yet a serious concern for prosperity of the society. China faced much more immediate threats to economic growth and political stability than environmental deterioration.

To be sure, some of this timidity in environmental policy was an unfortunate cultural legacy of the Mao era. During Mao's time, Chinese environmental policy consisted of a host of efforts to conquer nature:

Mao's voluntarist philosophy held that through concentrated exertion of human will and energy, material conditions could be altered and all difficulties overcome in the struggle to achieve a socialist utopia. In concert with the militarization of other aspects of life, Maoist ideology pitted the people against the natural environment in a fierce struggle. To conquer nature, the power of ideas was unleashed through mass mobilization in political campaigns, often accompanied by the use of military imagery.[10]

Mao's regime considered population growth a blessing despite China's history of severe famines, built huge hydroelectric dams at a high environmental and social cost, and created a massive deforestation problem with the wood-fired backyard furnaces during the Great Leap Forward in 1958–1960. Indeed, Elizabeth Economy maintains that this pattern of exploitation dates back to imperial China: "Through the centuries, the relentless drive of China's leaders to amass power, consolidate territory, develop the economy, and support a burgeoning population led to the plundering of forests and mineral resources, poorly conceived river diversion and water management projects, and intensive farming that degraded the land."[11] Thus when China's economic emergence began with the Deng era reforms, the country had already lost much of its originally spectacular environmental wealth and abundant natural resource endowment. Centuries of myopic abuse culminated in Mao's war against nature.

Toward the end of the 1980s, China began to take some initial steps toward an "environmental state."[12] As Sims states, "the key contextual factor for China's contemporary environmental officials is the sweeping economic reforms initiated in 1978 by the late Vice Premier Minister Deng Xiaoping, who took charge following nearly three decades under Mao Zedong's idiosyncratic rule. Reforms entailed both economic liberalization and decentralization initiatives."[13] In the 1980s China's environmental governance still retained its rigid, top-down approach that excluded civil society and maintained tight Communist Party control. Although China had established a National Environmental Protection Office in the aftermath of the Stockholm Conference in 1974 and formulated an Environmental Protection Law in 1979, it took the country at least until the mid-1990s to create a capable environmental administration. The 1980s saw the first efforts to prepare for environmental protection, but it was only in the mid-1990s that China began to actually invest in the implementation of environmental policies.

Less than a decade after China's economic growth began, the government saw the need to prepare for environmental problems, but this realization was converted into action only a decade later. As Mol and Carter note, until 1997 public environmental investments as a percent of total GDP hovered around 0.6 percent, but then surged by 2001 as they had exceeded a full 1 percent.[14] Given rapid economic growth, this doubling of share equaled the tripling of actual expenditure. Administrative reforms also gave environmental causes a much-needed political boost: "In 1998, as part of sweeping administrative reforms that reconstituted many institutions within Chinese bureaucracy, then premier Zhu Rongij elevated the [environmental] agency from its long-time subcabinet status to ministerial rank, changing its name from the National Environmental Protection Agency to the State Environmental Protection Administration."[15]

China's international positions followed the same basic logic. In the early years of China's participation in global environmental regimes, the country's positions did not move far from the general position of the G-77 bloc. China maintained a high profile in the negotiations but focused on a defensive effort to avoid onerous commitments that would compromise economic growth. As long as China's economy remained small, such a defensive strategy was successful, and Beijing drew little criticism on the international scene. As Miller puts it, China "insists on linking accession to environmental treaties to assistance in making the transition to alternative technologies. . . . China emphasizes its willingness to cooperate in the evolution and implementation of global environmental regimes, provided it receives the requisite financial and technical assistance."[16]

In climate negotiations, China has also always been a strong advocate of the principle of common but differentiated responsibilities, arguing that industrialized countries must lead climate mitigation activities because of their greater wealth levels and historical responsibilities—in the case of the United Kingdom, for example, going back to the industrial revolution—for global warming.[17] Economy notes, for example, that "to many international observers at the [Earth Summit of 1992] Rio conference, China was an inflexible obstructionist, intent on allying the developing countries against the advanced industrialized nations to prevent an international agreement on climate change, one of the key topics of the gathering."[18]

Over time, however, domestic demand for environmental protection began to grow. As China's breakneck industrialization increased resource consumption and pollution, the degradation of water and air quality, as well as forest depletion, began to create societal instability. The expansion of industry without stringent environmental regulations began to pose a threat to public health and the quality of life. According to data compiled by Liu and Diamond,[19] for example, among 142 countries examined, China's overall environmental sustainability rank was 129th, and the country now faces major problems in five environmental categories: air, land, fresh water, oceans, and biodiversity. In her analysis of China's environmental problems, Economy speaks of "the enormous toll the reform period has taken on the environment . . . threatening to the Chinese leaders, protests over polluted water, damaged crops, air pollution, and forced settlement contribute to the increasingly pervasive social unrest already confronting them."[20]

Concrete, if perhaps extreme, examples of these problems are not difficult to find. On December 8, 2015, at 7 a.m. local time, the municipal government of Beijing declared a three-day "pollution red alert," forcing construction sites, factories, and power plants to close.[21] Local pollution levels were almost fifteen times higher than those recommended by the World Health Organization, as environmental inspectors wandered around the city to ensure that people and organizations complied with the ban on polluting activities. A clear sign of China's rising environmental consciousness was the wildly popular *Under the Dome* documentary, a self-financed film from 2015 on the country's air pollution problems.[22] Although it was banned by the government, it sparked huge interest in the problem of air quality in the country.

Another highly visible example of the consequences of China's industrial boom is the disappearance of rivers. China's failure to protect its rivers has contributed to hardship in the agriculture, industry, service, and residential sectors. While China had over fifty thousand rivers with "significant catchment areas" in the 1950s, only twenty-three thousand were left in 2013. Because of excessive extraction for industry, agriculture, and other uses, there was simply not enough water left for a river.[23] In describing the "death of the Huai River," for example, Economy notes that "in 1999 and 2000, the Huai ran dry for the first time in twenty years. . . . The local economy was hit hard with crops ruined and thousands of tons of fish dead."[24]

For the longest time, however, these growing domestic demands did not translate into changes at the international level. Although domestic demands for environmental protection grew, changes in China's negotiation positions lagged behind, as the regime's primary concern remained the possibility that industrialized countries would try to impose new restriction on China's economic growth strategies. Environmental constraints on trade were a particularly salient threat, as "China sees her need as having global environmental arrangements in place that allow her to continue to grow, and key to this is maintaining openness in the global economy, and without environmentally motivated trade restrictions, so as to allow for continued high export growth and continuing FDI inflows as she and others take on environmental commitments."[25]

The lack of change in China's negotiation positions was easy to see in the case of climate change. Until the December 2009 summit in Copenhagen, China retained the G-77 position, emphasizing the importance of industrialized country leadership, making demands for huge financial and technological transfers, and repeating the mantra of common but differentiated responsibilities over and over again. China "pushed hard to preserve the integrity of Kyoto and demanded strong targets and actions solely from Annex 1 states under the principle of [common but differentiated responsibilities]. . . . China held staunchly to this position, which did nothing to offend its sovereignty, while it significantly extended its domestic energy and climate policy commitments to tackle global warming."[26]

At Copenhagen itself, maintains Bodansky, "China was much more assertive than previously, reflecting its emergence as a global power."[27] A striking illustration of this new, assertive bargaining position is found in Beijing's "decision to assign a lower-level official to summit talks [with the United States] even though the premier was in the conference center"—a diplomatic insult and a signal of supreme confidence in one's bargaining power.[28] China's role in the conference was that of the bad guy, and the country flexed its muscle to make sure it would not be subjected to any emission reduction targets or carbon constraints that would undermine economic growth based on industrial production.

After the Copenhagen conference, however, China's positions began to shift. The change was so fast that it surprised many commentators. In 2014 Presidents Barack Obama and Xi Jinping made a joint announcement on climate change, and, for the first time, China officially stated that it "intends to achieve the peaking of CO_2 emissions around 2030 and to make best efforts to peak early and intends to increase the share of non-fossil fuels in primary energy consumption to around 20% by 2030."[29] China's contribution to the Paris negotiations in December 2015, its Intended Nationally Determined Contribution (INDC), was submitted on June 30, 2015, and strived for "the target to peak CO_2 emissions by 2030 at the latest, lower the carbon intensity of GDP by 60% to 65% below 2005 levels by 2030, increase the share of non-fossil energy carriers of the total primary energy supply to around 20% by that time, and increase its forest stock volume by 4.5 billion cubic metres, compared to 2005 levels."[30] In September 2020 Xi Jinping further announced that CO_2 emissions would peak before 2030 and, more significantly, that China would achieve carbon neutrality by 2060. While achieving carbon neutrality in four decades will be a daunting challenge, Xi's directive suggests that China's leadership increasingly views the low-carbon transition as a necessity. The target is a distant one, though, and achieving it requires rapid action to reduce China's dependence on coal.

The Minamata mercury negotiations show a similar pattern. While India retained its traditional positions and put brakes on the negotiation process throughout, China made a dramatic departure from its earlier position during the fifth and final negotiation session. Not only did China accept mandatory control requirements for new sources of mercury, but it also relaxed its opposition to strict timetables for control requirements on existing sources. As Stokes, Giang, and Selin demonstrate, China's changing negotiation position can be attributed to growing domestic concern about air pollution, the country's completion of the basic industrialization process, and increased domestic scientific and technical capacity.[31]

More generally, China's changing positions reflect, first and foremost, the country's deep economic transformation. Until the Copenhagen conference in 2009, China's industrial economy grew rapidly and the country's demand for coal and other fossil fuels expanded. By 2011, however, the growth in coal demand began to slow down, and in 2014 coal use actually fell.[32] According to World Bank data, over 47 percent of China's GDP came from the industrial sector in 2006, but by 2015 this number had collapsed to below 41 percent.[33] As China's economy increasingly moves away from industrial to services and commercial growth, the importance of expanding resource consumption for the country's prosperity decreases, following the pattern of the environmental Kuznets curve.[34]

At the same time, changes in the government's preferences have been much slower. Although the Chinese economy is no longer as dependent on the continued expansion of fossil fuel use and an environmental civil society exists, there has not been a fundamental change in Beijing's outlook. The Chinese government continues to prioritize economic growth and considers environmental issues mostly as a challenge to be managed, as opposed to a goal worth pursuing even in the absence of social pressure. For example, the new environmental protection law (EPL) was enacted in January 2015. While ostensibly the law restricted business from polluting and overusing natural resources, more specific legislation regulating these resources overrode the EPL, rendering it toothless. Other countries with federal structures facing similar problems have fixed them by making environmental monitoring and protection the responsibility of the federal government. Today the monitoring and enforcement of environmental standards in China are the responsibility of lower levels of government, which encourages a race to the bottom as these levels favor economic growth over environmental protection. Despite the Chinese government's public proclamations to protect the environment—and China's citizens—civic groups and individual citizens are not able to file lawsuits against the government if environmental standards are not maintained.[35]

From the perspective of the Chinese Communist Party, environmental problems are essentially a question of political survival. After Mao's death and the beginning of the reform era, the regime placed its hopes on rapid economic growth, but as Gilley shows, rapid social change in China over time has provoked dissatisfaction and undermined the government's legitimacy.[36] According to Economy,

> In China, social discontent is evident everywhere. It is expressed in forms as diverse as labor unrest, mounting peasant protest, and increased ethnic violence. As the government has diminished its role in guiding the economy, its role in managing the society has decreased as well. For this reason, it retains few levers to shape public opinion and action, with the exception of suppression or media and Internet censorship. It is this discontent, if mobilized throughout the country and more specifically directed at the Communist Party, that the Chinese authorities fear.[37]

In this telling, environmental problems are but one type of social unrest that threatens the long-term survival of the Communist Party leadership in Beijing. Environmental awareness is closely linked to the political challenge of sustaining authoritarian rule in a wealthier and more educated society, and thus the regime's responses to environmental problems are inherently colored by this political perspective. Even solutions to global environmental problems, notably climate change, can be framed as efforts to deal with local environmental degradation, such as air pollution from industry and power generation or groundwater depletion.[38] Renewable energy, for example, not only reduces carbon emissions but also contributes to cleaner air and reduces water stress.

The most interesting feature of the Chinese case is that institutional capacity has been relatively high and growing over time.[39] Although China began to build an environmental administration only after Mao's death in 1976, by the mid-1990s the Chinese environmental administration had over a 100,000 employees. Thereafter the country's total investment as percentage of GDP began to grow rapidly as a result of policies and regulations. Between 1991 and 2004 the number of environmental employees increased from about 70,000 to over 150,000. Environmental spending as a percentage of GDP grew from less than 0.6 percent in 191 to almost

1.4 percent between 1981 and 2004, despite exceptional GDP growth. In recent years the trend has continued, as the budget of the Ministry of Environmental Protection grew between 2009 and 2016 from U.S. $168 billion to $480 billion—a threefold increase within seven years.[40]

Gilley proposes that China's environmental policies reflect the core features of the "authoritarian environmentalism" model, the merits of which "are its ability to produce a rapid, centralised response to severe environmental threats, and to mobilise state and social actors. However, where state actors are fragmented, the aims of 'eco-elites' can easily be undermined at the implementation stage. Moreover, the exclusion of social actors and representatives creates a malign lock-in effect in which low social concern makes authoritarian approaches both more necessary and more difficult."[41] Interestingly, this model of authoritarian environmentalism would score high for national institutional capacity but face difficulties in decentralized implementation and, more important in my view, in building social support for environmental protection.

Another way to understand China's issues is to consider how problems in Chinese policy implementation tend to originate from political economy issues. The first problem is the still awkward relationship between central and provincial governments. Under China's system of "fragmented authoritarianism,"[42] Beijing devolved considerable decision-making powers to provincial decision makers, unlocking local innovation and endowing local leaders with high-powered incentives. The cost of this approach, of course, is that it raises complications related to "environmental federalism."[43] If local leaders have very strong incentives to increase their economic performance, they may adopt policies that generate local economic growth at a high environmental cost. Because pollution travels across provincial boundaries, people living in other provinces suffer from this environmental damage, but provincial leaders ignore these damages because their careers primarily depend on local economic growth. They may consider local environmental damage to the extent it threatens political stability and undermines economic growth, but they have little reason to consider the effects of pollution outside their own jurisdiction.

The second important issue is the political clout of state-owned natural resource and heavy industries. In China, these sectors remain politically powerful and have often been able to thwart environmental regulations. Their direct connections with key policy makers and importance for local economies provides them with enough political clout to avoid the enforcement and implementation of environmental policies set by the national government. A study of compliance with China's environmental disclosure requirements for municipalities across 113 cities, for example, finds that large firms in polluting industries contribute to noncompliance with the rules: "We find that the more a city's economy is dominated by large firms, the more it resists centrally mandated disclosures about pollution sources. By contrast, cities whose economies comprise smaller firms are more willing to impose onerous requirements on these firms. Furthermore, this negative effect on environmental transparency is most pronounced if the city's single largest firm is in a highly polluting industry."[44]

To illustrate this logic, consider the effect of China's decision to decentralize the approval of the environmental assessments for coal-fired power plant projects to the provincial level in March 2015. According to Myllyvirta, Shen, and Lammi, China's dramatic expansion in permits given for the construction of coal-fired power plants in 2015–2016 reflects this decision. This leaves local authorities to consider the immediate economic benefits of construction and electricity generation while discarding the broader societal costs, including negative effects on China's international reputation.[45] Indeed, the permitting of coal-fired power plants exploded so rapidly that in October 2016 China took the extreme step of canceling coal-fired power plants that were already under construction.[46]

This second example of the construction of coal-fired power plants is particularly telling about the true nature of China's "authoritarian environmentalism."[47] Given China's systematic orientation toward economic growth, provincial leaders have strong incentives to maximize short-run economic development regardless of the long-run costs.[48] Because much of the damage caused by the pollution from coal-fired power plants and the negative reputational effects at the international level accrue to other provinces in China, these leaders ignore the cross-province negative externality—and perhaps even the long-run damage to their own province—and myopically focus on maximizing local economic growth at any cost through investments in power generation capacity.[49]

In a similar vein, China has also participated in a number of projects to design, finance, and construct coal-fired power plants elsewhere in the world. As Peng, Chang, and Liwen note, "By the end of 2016, China had been involved in 240 coal-red power projects in 25 of the 65 countries along the Belt and Road [a Chinese initiative for connectivity among Eurasian countries], with a total installed capacity of 251,054 MW." Even as China has made progress toward reducing its own reliance on coal, it has continued to fund hundreds of projects in countries such as India and Indonesia, thus becoming "one of the important players in the development of global coal-fired power projects."[50]

At the same time, China's general strategy in multilateral institutions has been to emphasize the benign and responsible nature of the country's rise, that is, to portray China as a "responsible power."[51] This narrative emphasizes the beneficial side of China's rise, such as new opportunities to embrace multilateralism and respect for other countries' sovereignty. In the case of climate change, renewable energy policy and constraints on carbon dioxide emissions are examples of China as a responsible power, whereas large-scale financing of coal-fired power plants in other countries contradicts the very notion of responsible state behavior in the era of climate change.

China's efforts to present itself as a climate champion run parallel to commercial considerations. The country's industrial might help it gain a leading position in global wind and solar technology markets from the very beginning.[52] For example, between 2008 and 2013 China played a critical role in the worldwide, 80 percent decrease in solar panel prices.[53] By 2016 it had cornered the global market for solar modules, producing a whopping 71 percent of the global total.[54]

Despite China's mixed international energy record, the central government's ability to enforce environmental policies in China has clearly grown over time. Zhang evaluates the success of a central enforcement program that began in 2007 and "was established . . . to curtail perceived widespread data falsification and to enhance the quality of emission data, the basis for assessing local compliance with targets."[55] This analysis finds that the central government largely managed to achieve the goals of the program, though data quality remains poor, and the central government has seen more success in reducing deliberate overreporting by local authorities than in enforcing proper accounting and reporting practices more generally.

Practitioners also recognize China's growing capabilities in enforcing environmental law and implementing effective policies. Barbara

Finamore, a senior attorney and Asia director of the Natural Resources Defense Council, notes that "the game-changing amendments to China's bedrock Environmental Protection Law (EPL) that went into effect in January 2015 put powerful new tools into the hands of environmental officials and the public, providing a strong legal foundation to China's pollution control efforts." The revisions impose severe penalties on violators, add environmental protection as an explicit criterion to performance assessment, and provide civil society organizations with the ability to sue polluters. These changes address core weaknesses of China's environmental protection system by strengthening the polluter-pays principle, encourage local officials to take environmental quality into consideration as they seek career advancement, and harness the power of nongovernmental organizations.

The link between China's growing institutional capacity and increasingly progressive positions in global environmental negotiations is not hard to see. In the case of mercury, and chemical regulation more generally, China's growing capabilities in using environmental science to inform feasible and effective policies prompted a 180-degree shift from an obstructionist position to a cooperative stance.[56] In the case of climate change, China's ability to rapidly expand the use of renewable energy and clean technology through coordinated government policy has made low-carbon growth a realistic prospect.[57] While institutional capacity itself is not enough to shape a country's contributions to global environmental governance, it can reduce the cost and uncertainty surrounding the environmental policies required to achieve mitigation goals. In the case of mercury, institutional capacity allowed China to commit to phase-out goals; in climate change, it created an opportunity for low-carbon development as a solution to a host of problems ranging from energy security to air pollution and rapidly growing greenhouse gas emissions.

To summarize, China's rapid economic transformation has created massive domestic and global environmental problems. But because of a combination of domestic concern about the effects of environmental degradation and a relatively high level of institutional capacity, China has not been paralyzed by the problems. Both China's domestic policies and international positions have reflected a growing demand for environmental protection, and the softening of China's negotiation stance on issues such as mercury and climate change has been essential for progress in global environmental cooperation. These changes, however, do not reflect a fundamental rethinking of the environment as a policy issue. China's primary concern remains to avoid new constraints on economic growth, exports, and domestic policy formulation. Meanwhile, global environmental protection is often a convenient frame for the pursuit of local environmental improvements such as clean air and water conservation.

If recent history is an indicator, China's future positions on environmental issues will continue to evolve toward an increasingly pro-green position, though with the twist that internal sovereignty remains sacred. China's shift toward an increasingly service-oriented economy will reduce the pressure on the environment, as economic growth would no longer depend as much on converting material inputs into industrial products for exportation. At the same time, the country's institutional capacity enables the government to respond meaningfully to environmental problems, though political economy problems related to the core logic of the authoritarian environmentalism—decentralization, political clout of state-owned heavy industry, and lack of inclusion of societal interests—will remain an issue. If China's authoritarian turn continues and Beijing centralizes control, these political economy problems may also worsen and contribute to lackluster environmental policy performance because of a lack of inclusivity and rent-seeking by polluting industries.

A MODERNIZING INDIA IN GLOBAL ENVIRONMENTAL POLITICS

India's trajectory is in some ways similar to China's, but there are also several important differences. While India's economy has grown rapidly, the economic transformation has been slower and much less complete than China's. It has also not been driven or accompanied by the kind of institutional capacity-building in which China has excelled. For these reasons, India remains decades behind China in the extent of both economic transformation and achievement in environmental protection.

It is important to note that this Indian trajectory of development is closer to the experiences of most emerging economies, both so far and likely in the future, than that of China's. With limited capacity for environmental protection, most emerging economies are bound to follow

India's pattern of rapid but uncontrolled economic growth with limited success in environmental protection. While capacity limitations may prevent emerging economies from maximizing their economic growth the way China did, they also mean that each step forward will likely generate more environmental deterioration than it would have under China's high-capacity conditions.

To date there is no academic consensus on the timing of India's economic transformation. Although some scholars attribute the key policy changes to the economic reforms that Prime Minister P. V. Narasimha Rao's government enacted in 1991 as a response to the country's balance-of-payments crisis,[58] others note that the Indian economy had broken out of the underwhelming "Hindu rate of growth" equilibrium by the early 1980s.[59] At any rate, India's economic performance improved significantly toward the end of the twentieth century: The average annual growth rate was only 3.9 percent in the 1960s and decreased to 2.9 percent in the 1970s. In the 1980s, however, it increased to 5.6 percent, and it stayed there during the 1990s. Between 2001 and 2010 the annual growth rate increased to 7.4 percent, and it remained at 6.7 percent between 2011 and 2015.[60]

Although India's economic rise is not as spectacular as China's, the overall picture is still bright. Measured in constant 2010 U.S. dollars, India's GDP per capita increased from $394 in 1980 to $1,751—almost a fivefold increase. Although India is not an industrial powerhouse, industrial value added grew from $76.6 billion in 1980 to $665 billion in 2015—almost by an order of magnitude.

In the early years, India's environmental policies were very weak, both on paper and, even more so, on the ground. Although India had some environmental protections on water and air quality, they were not comparable to those in industrialized countries, and enforcement was virtually nonexistent. As Reich and Bowonder note, until 1976, when "the Constitution of India was amended in ways that provided for the first time a strong constitutional basis for protection of the environment and strengthened the power of the state and the judiciary to intervene in environmental matters," India's environmental policies were ad hoc and haphazard. Although India has since formulated a series of laws ranging from forest protection to the control of industrial pollution, Reich and Bowonder found in the early 1990s that "India's lack of an overall environmental policy or a well formulated set of priorities is a major obstacle to effective implementation"—an assertion that holds true to this date.[61]

The weak environmental policies certainly reflected India's extreme poverty. To the end of the twentieth century, India remained a country with widespread abject poverty. The Census of India in 2001 paints a grim picture, for example. At that time, only 65 percent of Indians were literate and only 56 percent of households were electrified. With every third Indian illiterate and almost half living without electricity at the turn of the millennium, it is not surprising that environmental concerns were not at the top of the Delhi government's agenda. For the vast majority of India's population, the lack of basic economic amenities and opportunities, from employment and education to electricity, have historically been a more salient concern than global environmental threats.

The Census of India in 2011 shows that the country's development continues at a brisk pace. Between 2001 and 2011 the country's literacy rate increased from 64.8 to 74.0 percent; the household electrification rate increased to 67 percent—not including off-grid solar power. By 2020 almost every home had a grid electricity connection, and the literacy rate was approaching 80 percent, again highlighting India's progress.

The lack of domestic interest in environmental protection could also be observed in India's international positions. In a broad survey of the country's bargaining positions in global environmental negotiations around 1990, Rajan concludes that "the limited domestic political interest in global environmental issues and the limited impact of non-state actors left the government with a considerable degree of autonomy in policy formulation." He further notes that the Indian government had two consistent goals across the different negotiations: "defensive goals, to do with preserving sovereignty, ensuring equity, and reducing vulnerability; and more assertive goals, to do with securing economic benefits and exercising more power in the international system."[62] Neither set of core goals includes the protection of the global environment.

If anything, India was more vigorous and vocal than other developing countries in opposing environmental constraints on economic growth. As Jasanoff noted in the immediate aftermath of the Earth Summit of 1992, India's "resistance quickly mounted against causal paradigms propagated in the North which cast India as a leading contributor to the present problem of global warming."[63] India's argument was that because the country's per capita greenhouse gas emissions were low and most of the population still lived in poverty, the country needed enough carbon space for economic development. Accordingly, wealthy industrialized countries, which had built their wealth on fossil fuels for centuries, should reduce their emissions to allow India's emissions to grow.

To an extent, India's aggressive position also reflects the country's history as a colonial subject in the erstwhile British Empire. India's democratic political system with a free media also encouraged attacks on industrialized countries for domestic political reasons.[64] Given that India had a long history of fighting against foreign domination, culminating in Gandhi's nonviolent struggle against Great Britain and the chaotic partition of the country in 1947, the Indian domestic discourse on global environmental politics contains ample anticolonial and anti-imperial rhetoric. Although India is now an independent nation—and fiercely proud of it—the ghost of the British Empire remains alive in public debate and politics. Right or wrong, Indian elites continue to invoke their freedom fight in discussions of global environmental politics, reminding the representatives of industrialized countries both about the realities of life in a poor country and that Mahatma Gandhi, India's great leader of the nonviolent *satyagraha* movement, never believed that the lifestyles of industrialized nations were sustainable.

As a famous report authored by Anil Agarwal and Sunita Narain for the Centre for Science and Environment, an environmental organization based in New Delhi, puts it, the climate change policies proposed at the Earth Summit would be "a case of environmental colonialism."[65] A key conceptual distinction underpinning this accusation of environmental colonialism is that between "luxury" and "survival" emissions. As Narain explains, reflecting on her early intervention into the debate on climate change, "the world needed to differentiate between the emissions of the poor—from subsistence paddy cultivation or animal rearing—and that of the rich—say, from the cars. Survival emissions weren't, and couldn't be equivalent to luxury emissions."[66]

An important insight into Indian environmental politics from this anecdote concerns the relationship between civil society and the political and economic elites. While India's ecological movement has exploited the country's democratic institutions to thwart the threat of government oppression, on many issues the most vocal, radical environmentalists actually sing to the government's tune. When Agarwal and Narain accused the West of environmental colonialism, they also put a stamp of approval on the Indian government's early position in climate negotiations, which said that climate change is a problem caused by industrialized countries. While Agarwal and Narain, along with other Indian environmentalists, often give their government a hard time in all environmental affairs domestically, their anti-Western positions also gave the country's powerful and wealthy elites a modicum of legitimacy as they fought against the very idea of global climate cooperation. This particular overtone of environmentalism in the global South is very important, for it shows that genuine environmental concern need not always result in outcomes that the American and European environmentalist mainstream would approve of.

I have personally witnessed this tension in the Indian environmental debate. A few years back, in 2013, I visited a scientific institute in the city of Bangalore in the southern state of Karnataka. In a meeting with the institute's team—a fantastic group of talented scholars—I noted that India had often opposed measures such as monitoring and verification in climate negotiations. The remark split the group into two equal halves, with one half nodding enthusiastically and making spirited arguments for environmental sustainability and the domestic benefits of low-carbon development. The other half, however, accused me of being unfair; mistakenly taking me for an American (I am a Finnish citizen), they asked me how many emissions my lifestyle generated. Having just recently flown into Delhi from New York City, where I lived at the time, I had to concede the point.

Although India's rhetoric has grown softer over time, with fewer references to colonialism or imperialism, the basic combative posture remains intact. Joshi uses data from twenty-two interviews with Indian policy makers and civil society in Delhi, along with participant observation from the Copenhagen climate summit, and finds that "India's self-identification as a developing country or with the imaginary of the Global South is a key feature of its climate politics. . . . International distributive justice has been a key aspect of North–South environmental politics, reflected in the South's claims to development and emphasis on holding the North accountable for contemporary environmental crises." She further notes that among her interviewees, "even the few respondents who felt that the gravity of the impending climate crisis might necessitate that all countries undertake mitigation measures were hesitant to agree to absolute emission targets for India in light of development concerns. Consequently India seems unwilling to budge from its basic original positions, as its participation in current climate negotiations and national-level debates continue to reveal."[67]

Other scholars concur with this assessment of continuity: India's climate politics—and global environmental politics more generally—are strongly influenced by the legacy of the Third World movement and Indira Gandhi's prominent role in the Stockholm conference of 1972. As Dubash puts it, "Indian climate politics is, in large part, a story of remarkable continuity. The dominant frame of 'climate equity'—understood predominantly in a North-South contest around dividing up a global commons—was established relatively early. This frame has also had the effect of shaping climate politics around engagement with the international negotiation context, insulating Indian domestic political and policy spaces from considering climate concerns."[68] Although India has increasingly embraced sustainable energy and recognized the importance of energy conservation, these decisions are made under an overarching framework of global equity and an emphasis on the country's sovereign right to pursue economic development.

In a more recent assessment, Dubash applies this reasoning to India's role in the Paris Agreement. In an article aptly titled "Safeguarding Development and Limiting Vulnerability," he notes that the bottom-up architecture finalized in Paris "should allow India to safeguard development and explore more linkages between development and climate objectives. . . . The Paris Agreement provides a framework within which India could productively engage its interests, even while it by no means guarantees their realization."[69] While the move away from common but differentiated responsibilities and the principle of equity in the Paris Agreement has provoked criticisms in the Indian debate, the Paris Agreement does afford India with flexibility to pursue economic development through the cobenefits of climate action.

One way in which climate concerns have penetrated the Indian policy debate is the discourse of "cobenefits."[70] Many actions that mitigate climate change by reducing greenhouse gas emissions also generate a host of other benefits. Energy efficiency, for example, can achieve economic savings, and the Indian state has, among other things, launched initiatives to promote the use of efficient lighting technologies.[71]

A prominent example of the increasingly central theme of cobenefits is found in India's ambitious renewable energy targets. Under the Paris

Agreement, India has set for itself a goal of 175 GW of renewable power capacity, not including large hydroelectric facilities.[72] Almost the entire target would be achieved with installations of solar (100 GW) and wind (60 GW) power. These targets, however, are not primarily driven by concerns with climate change, but rather by the national imperative to provide abundant power for agriculture, industry, commerce, and homes. Investment in renewables expands generation capacity, enhances energy security in a volatile regional context, and reduces air pollution—all concrete benefits that feature prominently in the Indian public policy debate.

The mercury negotiations—another key example of China's structural transformation and the resulting change in negotiation positions—also show India's slow rate of change. As we saw in the previous chapter, a key reason for India's stubborn opposition to new mercury rules was the country's lack of technological and institutional capacity for alternatives. While China's position shifted rapidly over the span of less than a decade of negotiations, India's lack of structural transformation in the economic sphere prevented a similar change. At the fifth round of negotiations, when China pivoted and began supporting a treaty on mercury, "India was less constructive . . . and was reluctant to commit to implementing any emissions control technologies above existing standards. India obstructed contact group attempts to operationalize broad concepts like source thresholds. India also objected to consensus on final negotiating packages on mercury phase-out dates, without China's support."[73]

Overall, then, the changes that have materialized seem to mostly reflect reduced costs of action or the availability of side benefits, instead of a deeper change in the valuation of the environment. India's local environmental problems have reached alarming levels, and, as a result, political pressure to act has mounted. Where these problems have threatened mobilized interest groups and/or a relatively inexpensive solution has been available, a piecemeal solution has sometimes been found. A more fundamental change in societal preferences is missing, however, and domestic economic considerations remain the leadership's overriding priority.

The concrete problems that Indian policy makers, and the society more broadly, face in dealing with constraints on greenhouse gas emissions can be seen in an insightful study on how increasingly stringent climate mitigation plans would influence the affordability of clean cooking fuels.[74] Their conclusion is sobering: "Our most stringent mitigation scenario increases clean fuel costs 38% in 2030 relative to the baseline, keeping 21% more South Asians on traditional stoves or increasing the minimum support policy cost to achieve universal clean cooking by up to 44%." Although these numbers are subject to great uncertainties and depend to a great extent on the details of the policy design, the very possibility of such outcomes illustrates the difficult problem that India faces in balancing between development and environment.

India's position in global environmental negotiations is interesting because the country's power largely stems from the promise—or, more appropriately, threat—of *future* power to destroy. Although India remains a very poor country, we have seen previously that it was the world's third largest economy by purchasing power parity in 2015. With the world's second largest population and a low level of industrialization, India's bright economic future promises to bring staggering increases of energy consumption. As noted in the introduction, India's energy demand will increase by 70 percent by 2040 under current policies.[75] These predictions are uncertain, as India's energy consumption continues to change with domestic and international economic conditions. If India manages to meet its growing power demand with cleaner alternatives to coal, the outlook for global climate mitigation is much brighter than under the alternative. India's success in growing its renewable power generation capacity through wind and solar installation at rapidly decreasing costs offers hope, as a focus on renewables would allow India to power its economy without the massive environmental side effects that relying on coal would cause.

But while it is hard to predict exactly how India will evolve, the more important point is that the potential for environmental degradation is colossal, and much depends on domestic policy. If India's gamble on a massive expansion of renewable energy succeeds, the country may power its economy and society without the coal boom that China had to go through. But if India fails to develop robust policy and regulatory frameworks to deal with new power sources, along with investments in smart infrastructure such as intermittent solar and wind, the country's air quality may continue to deteriorate for years to come.

Although international environmental issues are increasingly the subject of a public debate in India, the government and domestic political elites have largely kept their defensive posture in global environmental negotiations. India's vibrant democracy has given rise to a large number of ecological resistance movements,[76] but the political elite's overriding concerns remain economic development and, closely related, political survival. Environmental issues have come to the forefront only in isolated cases, such as public alarm about air pollution in the winter in the capital city of New Delhi and dirty water in the religiously significant river Ganges.

Consider recent problems with air quality in Delhi, India's sprawling capital. On December 23, 2015, the air quality index in the city had reached the level of "430–435 . . . an emergency health warning, according to the pollution monitoring agency."[77] While the causes of such extreme air pollution are manifold and depend on complex atmospheric processes that move pollution around across long distances, the municipal government led by Arvind Kejriwal did declare, as an emergency measure, an "odd-even scheme" to reduce pollution from the congested city's traffic. Under this scheme, vehicles were allowed on the road only on odd (even) calendar dates if the last number of their license plate was odd (even).

The merits of this emergency measure have been debated, but the more important consideration is how the emergency measure did not lead to any longer-term solutions. Although the air pollution problem gave rise to outrage and public debate, it seems fair to say that neither the municipal nor the central (federal) government adopted any long-term measures to act on the problem. As soon as the air pollution decreased after the end of the cold season, the problem disappeared from the public agenda almost entirely. Even though air pollution frequently appears in the news and is discussed in the media, India is far from embracing improved air quality as a common aspiration and dream.

India's problems with environmental policy are but one example of a much broader governance challenge in the country. This problem was recognized a long time ago by Wade, who wrote about the frequent, politically motivated transfers of bureaucrats: "While one should certainly not assume that corrupt government is therefore bad government any more than honest government is therefore good government, the discussion of what the transfer leads people to do does provide *prima facie* grounds for concluding that its effects are strongly regressive, that it skews the output of departments far from the optimum almost however the optimum is defined."[78] In an explicit comparison of governance in China and India, Bardhan observes that India's competitive democracy may have—the reforms of 1991 notwithstanding—contributed to a disappointing growth record because of a lack of long-run investment: "India's experience suggests that democracy can also hinder development in ways not usually considered by democracy enthusiasts. Competitive populism—short-run pandering and handouts to win elections—may hurt long-run investment, particularly in physical infrastructure, a key development-related bottleneck in India. Such political arrangements make it difficult, for example, to charge user fees for roads, electricity, and irrigation, discouraging investment in these areas."[79] While India's democratic political system has successfully kept aspiring dictators at bay, it has also resulted in clientelism, populism, and myopia in policy.

A striking illustration of India's political culture is the rise of criminal politicians. As Vaishnav notes, a large and growing number of Indian parliamentarians, members of state assemblies, and even union and state ministers face pending criminal charges—often for serious crimes ranging from murder to electoral fraud and grand corruption.[80] Indian voters support criminal candidates who promise to protect their voters in India's unpredictable and harsh society; political parties expect gains from criminal candidates who have access to illicit sources of campaign funding; and criminal candidates expect to profit from being in a position of authority, with the ministerial portfolio being the ultimate prize. In such a setting, it is obvious that environmental sustainability is not the first thing on the minds of incumbent politicians—if they competed for office for personal gain, then one would expect their emphasis to be on rent seeking.

More generally, India's problem with institutional capacity stems less from administrative limitations and more from political economy problems, such as political intervention and corruption. If anything, India inherited a relatively capable administrative structure from the British colonial era, as the Imperial Colonial Service became the Indian Administrative Service (IAS). The problem is not so much that India does not have capable administrators or a functioning bureaucratic structure, but that corruption and political manipulation of government agencies make policy implementation and enforcement difficult.

The other important aspect of India's domestic demand for environmental protection are grassroots movements of ecological activism.[81] Because of India's democratic constitution, the country offers good opportunities for local ecological movements that often fight against problems such as deforestation, hydroelectric dam construction, or water pollution.

Unlike the strict constraints that Mao's regime placed on the environmental civil society in China, Indian environmental organizations have always benefited from a host of constitutional protections and legal rights that have allowed them to challenge the state apparatus and economic interests. For example, it would be hard to imagine how the famous Chipko "tree hugger" movement that began in 1973 in the state of Rajasthan could have survived in communist China under Mao's repressive rule. The same goes for a large number of similar movements, such as the mobilization against dams[82] and activism in support of indigenous peoples' rights.[83] In India's democratic system, the courts have played an important role in enabling environmental activists to challenge government and private-sector efforts that contradict laws in the books.[84]

The problem with these movements, however, is that they are localized and often emphasize "not in my backyard" environmental politics instead of more programmatic approaches to national environmental protection. Although ecological movements have met with lots of success in individual struggles against dams, mines, forest clearing, and violations of tribal rights—to name a few—their ability to effect more fundamental changes in the Indian system of governance has been much more limited. As a result, ecological movements have won quite a few defensive battles against the state, but they have failed to launch a systematic offensive to force the Indian state to create a robust system—a set of enforceable rules—of environmental protection across the country. In his survey of India's participation in global environmental negotiations, Rajan notes that "NGOs also generally had very limited influence over government policy . . . there was very little public criticism of government policy by NGOs."[85]

The most fundamental difference between China and India is, indeed, the wide gap in their institutional capacity. Unlike China, India simply does not have the institutional capacity to implement effective policies across the country. Both the central government and, in particular, many of India's state governments rely on bureaucracies that have limited resources and suffer from endemic corruption.[86] Because of this lack of institutional capacity, India faces severe implementation difficulties. Even if the government was committed to solving the country's environmental problems, it might not be able to make progress. In this regard, India does offer a compelling illustration of what Levy calls a "competitive regime."[87] India has a relatively robust system of free and fair elections and an independent judiciary, but the ability of the bureaucracy to effect lasting change on the ground is limited by endemic corruption, political manipulation, and the resulting lack of frontline implementation capacity.

India's federal structure adds further constraints. In a pertinent analysis, Busby and Shidore consider India's ability to mitigate climate change across different sectors of the economy. Besides emphasizing standard technical considerations and market structure, they note that "sectors in which the central government shares rule-making authority with states/ provinces or local governments or are primarily a state or local responsibility are more fragmented and increase the collective action costs of mitigation."[88] As an example of how this fragmentation constrains India's ability to act, they note that the power sector—a key source of greenhouse gas emissions, given India's dependence on coal-fired thermal power plants—is governed both by central and state governments, meaning that policy reforms are difficult to achieve. In particular, the central government's efforts to reform policy can be defeated by state governments that fail to take concrete action.

India's lacking capacity in environmental policy can also be directly observed by looking at environmental spending. Earlier we saw that China's budget for its environmental ministry had increased to U.S. $480 billion by 2016, but in the meantime India's environmental ministry had to do with $351 million—a hundredfold difference.[89] Although some of the difference can be attributed to factors such as China's strategy of transferring funds to provinces through the ministry and differences in institutional structure, it is still striking that India, a country with a population of 1.3 billion, spends less than half a billion dollars through the central environmental ministry. This lack of resources all but prevents India from developing, executing, and enforcing a coherent set of national environmental policies—and this is ignoring the fundamental political economy constraints discussed previously.

Reflecting on India's participation in the Earth Summit in 1992, Jasanoff took a careful look at India's opportunities and challenges for environmental protection. Among her many interesting findings, two stand out as quintessential for understanding the problem of institutional capacity. The first is that "insensitivity to feasibility consistently leads Indian lawmakers to create new governmental obligations without providing the institutional infrastructure needed to meet them."[90] In her telling, India's relatively centralized legislative institutions, the workings of which have deep historical roots going back to the British colonial administration and Prime Minister Nehru's ambitious plans for socialist planning in India's first years as an independent nation, formulate legislation that is then not implemented because of institutional capacity constraints on the ground. The second is that "India's federal structure and highly decentralized framework of administrative decision making raise additional institutional barriers to the effective implementation of regulatory mandates."[91] Even clear improvements in the institutional capacity of the federal administration might not result in much improvement in environmental protection on the ground, as key enforcement and implementation responsibilities actually lie with the state governments—many of whom suffer of even more severe constraints than the federal government.

A useful, if sobering, illustration of India's lack of capacity is the captive society. Because the Indian state does a poor job at providing adequate electricity supplies, good primary education, and basic health care, Indians are increasingly turning toward private alternatives—if they can afford them. India's income distribution is extremely unequal, and the lack of a broad tax base means that the still small middle class pays for a large share of total government expenditure. Frustrated with the low quality of public services, well-off households may choose to evade taxes and use the savings to procure private services, with potentially chaotic consequences in case these private services generate negative externalities.

From an environmental perspective, the use of diesel generators as a substitute for grid electricity is a particularly clear illustration.[92] Because India's electric grid offers an intermittent supply with regular blackouts and voltage fluctuation, many enterprises and households have invested in diesel generators as backstop solutions.[93] These diesel generators are inefficient and generate large quantities of air pollution. Controlling them with regulations is virtually impossible because they are sold in private markets and it is unclear how many generators there are in use. Markets for illegal sales of diesel are robust and thriving, meaning that fuel quality regulations are ineffective. This turn toward private alternatives could further undermine the capacity of the state, as wealthier citizens no longer depend on public services and may choose to evade taxes. Breaking the vicious cycle would require a concentrated, coordinated plan by the central and state governments, but the challenge remains daunting. If citizens trusted the government, there would be policy space for ambitious reforms; but if the government did a better job with policy implementation, citizens might learn to trust the public sector. This chicken-and-egg problem, as we have seen, has had serious environmental and economic consequences in the captive Indian society.

For the grand plan of replacing coal-fired power generation with renewables, India's institutional capacity issues are particularly troubling. As Tongia notes in his comment on increasing the share of renewable power generation,

> India's grid is weak and unstable, and instead of having a reasonable reserve margin (typically 15–20% in the west), there is a shortfall in the grid, officially in the range of 5% or so, but actually much higher. Even the Grid Code is modest, recommending (but not mandating) only a 5% margin. The grid is kept afloat through massive load-shedding (feeder-level supply cuts). . . . There are other technical reasons why the Indian grid is weak, including lack of ancillary services (systems designed to keep the grid stable, instead of just pricing kilowatt-hours), and even a lack of time-of-day pricing for bulk procurement of power. There are few peaker plants (which would operate only some 5–10% of hours in a year), since there isn't sufficient incentive for these.[94]

Although this discussion may seem technical, the issues identified here mean that improving India's ability to absorb intermittent renewable power requires massive improvements and upgrades to the electric grid—a feat the Indian power sector has not managed to achieve in the past.

Given that India's most important contribution to climate mitigation promises to come from a massive scale-up to renewables with 175 GW of capacity aimed by the year 2022, institutional capacity for grid management is critical. While a June 2017 study by the National Renewable Energy Laboratory finds that India's electric grid can accommodate this expansion, the positive result hinges on assumptions of effective governance and optimal siting of wind and solar power.[95] If such assumptions are not met because of limited institutional capacity and political constraints on effective, consistent policy formulation and implementation, India's ability to rapidly displace coal-fired power generation with renewables remains in doubt.

In climate policy more broadly, India's institutions are at the early stages. According to Pillai and Dubash, India's climate institutions are opportunistic, with political leaders prioritizing "traditional development objectives but [sometimes using] the language of mitigation."[96] The opportunistic, nonstrategic layering of climate institutions on a complex administrative apparatus has resulted in an incoherent system of climate policy making, with different parts often at cross purposes and lacking a long-term goal.

India's problems with institutional capacity are best seen by contrasting them with China. In the case of mercury negotiations, India continued with an obstructionist position even after both the United States and China chose to support aggressive mitigation targets.[97] In the case of climate change, India's traditionally obstructionist position has slowly begun to change as the pressure to expand coal-fired power generation capacity has disappeared, but great uncertainties surround India's ability to expand renewable energy use. The successor of the Indian Planning Commission, NITI-Ayog, estimated in June 2017 that India's coal-fired power generation would more than double by the year 2040 without specific efforts to decarbonize the power sector.[98] While India's energy policy is certainly moving in the direction of lower carbon intensity, and a doubling of coal-fired power generation appears increasingly unlikely, lacking institutional capacity creates great uncertainties around the country's energy future. Considering India's institutional challenges, it is simply not possible to say whether the country's fledgling efforts to claim a climate leader's mantle amount to concrete and effective action. At the same time, India's economic trajectory also remains uncertain as the economy struggled throughout Prime Minister Modi's first term from 2014 to 2019 and suffered a heavy blow during the 2020 coronavirus pandemic. If the Indian economy fails to grow in the short run, its greenhouse gas emissions will not increase as much—though for a troubling reason, as the Indian economy cannot continue to alleviate poverty without robust economic growth.

To summarize, the Indian energy-environment trajectory shows how economic growth shapes outcomes in the absence of adequate institutional capacity. Thus India's recent evolution is a useful heuristic for future changes in global environmental politics. Unlike China, the vast majority of the world's emerging economies share India's weakness in institutional capacity; if anything, many of them have even weaker bureaucracies. In the 2019 Worldwide Governance Indicators, India's government effectiveness score is 0.17, putting it at the 60th percentile—in the middle of the worldwide distribution.[99] While such indicators are not necessarily perfect, the contrast to China is stark: in 2019 China's score was 0.52, putting it at the 72nd percentile.

As countries that share India's characteristics grow economically, the world faces a set of challenges that might not resemble those similar to China's rise. Because of a lack of institutional capacity, the next generation of emerging economies faces difficult implementation challenges, which is not good news for humanity. If countries like India fail to expand their economies because of their lack of institutional capacity, then their ability to end poverty is compromised, and the human consequences of this failure would be tragic. But if such countries manage to grow their economies without institutional capacity, then their ability to mitigate environmental degradation is compromised—with serious consequences for the health of ecosystems and poverty alleviation around the world. The only truly positive trajectory is one of economic growth with rapid improvements in institutional capacity to enable effective environmental protection when it is needed most. The lack of such a trajectory in present-day India is perhaps the single darkest cloud on the global scale; it is also the single most important opportunity to change course in the future.

COMPARING CHINA AND INDIA: KEY SIMILARITIES AND DIFFERENCES

The key differences between China's and India's evolving roles in global environmental politics are summarized in table 5.1. The most important similarity between the two countries is the unlocking of potential for economic growth. Both China and India were for decades held back by their rigid, inward-looking economic policies. As these policies were gradually removed, the countries' economic performance improved rapidly. And as their economies grew, their importance in global environmental politics became increasingly clear as well.

TABLE 5.1 China and India in Global Environmental Politics

	China	India
Domestic environmental policy	Medium; growing stronger over time	Weak; growing stronger over time, slowly and inconsistently
Global environmental negotiations	Increasingly cooperative, but economic growth and sovereignty remain nonnegotiable	Mostly reluctant, except when cooperation is close to costless
Structural power	Explosive growth (economy, population)	Rapid growth (economy, population)
Environmental preferences	Medium; growing stronger over time but slowly and inconsistently	Medium-weak; growing stronger over time but slowly and inconsistently
Institutional capacity	Medium; growing stronger over time	Medium-weak

Note: The table shows a stylized comparison of the two countries' trajectories in global environmental politics.

Thus the structural power of both countries has increased over time. China began its economic transformation soon after Mao Zedong's death in 1976, years earlier than India, and has since then grown more rapidly and consistently. By 2016, four decades after China's break with the past, the country's economy was many times larger than India's by any reasonable measure. So while both countries have clearly earned the coveted title of an emerging economies, it is important to recall that China's economic development has been much faster than India's. There is still widespread poverty in China, but it is nothing compared to the poverty of rural India. The Chinese economy, however, is now slowing down, and rapid economic growth in the future is much more likely to come from India. Whether one considers China an economic miracle or not, the country appears to be constrained by the force of gravity in its economic development: it is much easier to grow fast when poor than when rich. China's industrial expansion has reached the point at which the country is struggling to move into an innovation economy, following the examples of Japan, South Korea, and Taiwan. But where China's authoritarian resolve may have proven beneficial for some aspects of industrialization, it may not furnish the same benefits as the country's growth prospects begin increasingly to depend on human capital, technological progress, and creativity.

The origins and development of Chinese and Indian government preferences in global environmental politics follow similar trajectories as well. Both governments were initially hostile, even though the Chinese government maintained a lower profile thanks to the lack of democratic domestic politics and a free media. Over time, both countries have slowly, and often grudgingly, begun to appreciate the environmental costs of uncontrolled economic development. Because China has made much more progress toward modernization, such concerns are more prevalent there. Both China and India have reached a point at which the costs of environmental deterioration to the society are extreme, but China has proven to be both economically and institutionally better positioned to deal with these problems than India.

The most critical difference is institutional capacity. While China and India have both grown rapidly, China's growth has been to a much greater extent the product of "developmental" intervention by the state apparatus.[100] China's institutional capacity not only has allowed the country to industrialize rapidly but also has provided the government in Beijing an opportunity to deal with the negative externalities of industrialization at a breakneck pace in a way India could not. My review of the Chinese and Indian trajectories of economic expansion and the accompanying efforts to govern environmental problems shows quite clearly that China has done much more to mitigate the negative environmental externalities of economic growth. In India, environmental deterioration has been limited by the inherent limits of the country's economic development; in China, decisive policies to limit the damage have prevented an environmental apocalypse. This difference in institutional capacity means that the uncertainties and obstacles to India's low-carbon future are greater than those that Chinese policy makers face.[101]

Based on this summary of similarities and differences in the Chinese and Indian trajectories, we can now begin to explain, understand, and assess the trajectories of these two giants. To begin with, China's faster economic growth plays an important role in explaining the differences.

China's great impact on the global environment is mostly driven by the country's large and heavily industrialized economy. The primary reason why China has captivated the imagination of the international community is the massive scale of the country's achievements. Industry is a key contributor to many environmental problems, certainly climate change, and the world's factory has thus been under intense scrutiny for decades.

If India had industrialized earlier, it would have almost certainly had to expand its coal consumption and consume greater quantities of natural resources. While India's growth rates are also impressive in a global comparison, the fact remains that the South Asian giant awoke a decade later than China and has since grown at a slower pace. Moreover, India's growth has been much less based on heavy industrialization than China's. On the other hand, India's environmental governance framework leaves much to be desired. India's main advantage is that because it is industrializing later, it has access to clean technologies that China could not use two decades ago. Most important, India can generate affordable solar power and deploy electric vehicles. Neither technology was commercially viable in 2001, when China joined the World Trade Organization.

Fundamentally, it is not surprising that government preferences in China and India are moving in the same direction. In both countries, economic growth remains the overriding priority, and the legitimacy of the regime largely depends on economic growth rates. Only extremely serious environmental problems have been enough to induce the governments to act in each country. In both countries, political elites understand that their political survival—whether in democratic elections or not—now requires sustaining economic growth.

We should not, however, lose sight of important differences in political institutions and histories. Although China's authoritarian institutions have created difficult problems related to information collection and decentralization, overall China's performance in environmental management has grown over time. In the admittedly unrealistic counterfactual with equally rapid economic growth in the absence of institutional capacity, China's environmental problems would likely be much, much worse than they are today. The other counterfactual is equally unfathomable: without institutional capacity, China might have remained much poorer than it is today. It is simply not possible to imagine a world in which China could attain environmentally sustainable economic growth without high levels of institutional capacity.

In India, the combination of democratic political institutions and a colonial history shape the domestic politics of the global environment. While the literature on environmental policy finds that democracies, when compared to autocracies, are more likely to enact and implement effective environmental policies,[102] India's lack of implementation capacity and politics challenges have made the country an exception to the rule. Environmental issues are not major electoral concerns, and policies impressive on paper do not deliver concrete results on the ground. Indian elections still tend to revolve around issues of caste, religion, clientelism, and local development—with environmental problems far below the radar. While growing problems with air pollution have begun to change this picture in urban areas, such as New Delhi, the Indian public debate has a long way to go until environmental problems reach the level of salience that is now common in many industrialized countries and China.

Although Indian political institutions provide greater opportunities and access to ecological movements, these have only appeared to deal with specific local issues. While institutions such as courts have given local ecological activists a degree of protection against state power, more proactive campaigning for state and federal policies has been virtually absent. One way to understand India's vibrant ecological movement is that it is basically a form of resistance. Similar to Gandhi's nonviolent freedom movement, India's ecological democracy can boast great achievements in preventing, halting, and delaying ecologically destructive forms of economic development, such as dam infrastructure or forest clearing. The Indian environmentalists' achievements in building an institutional framework for governing the nation's environmental future have, however, been much less impressive.[103]

Will India's economic growth create more problems than China's? On the one hand, China has been such a major source of pollution simply because of its economic success—relative to the kind of problems that India would create and face at equal growth rates, China's growth has actually been benign to the environment. China's institutional capacity has allowed the country to devise policy solutions to the environmental problems created by industrial growth, and these policy solutions have allowed China to avert some of the potential environmental degradation that the country's rapid industrialization could have caused. Although China's environmental impact may appear massive, it actually understates China's full power to destroy as the world's factory.

Without policy interventions, the damage would have been worse. On the other hand, India has a late-mover advantage. Over time, clean technologies have become more affordable. India can already power its economy with solar power, and the coming years hold promise for electric vehicles and battery storage of electric power. These late-mover advantages may dampen the negative effects of India's governance challenges. If clean technology is cost-competitive, a lack of institutional capacity may not be a completely insurmountable obstacle.

Nonetheless, improvements in India's institutional capacity—and, looking forward, the institutional capacity of other emerging economies—are essential for improving the quality of global environmental cooperation. The Chinese story is a clear warning about environmental destruction under rapid economic growth in large, poor countries, but it understates the severity of the threat. If I am right to contend that most of the emerging economies of the future will look more like India than China, then the Chinese experience with the environmental costs of rapid industrialization will leave too rosy an impression. The problems might be more severe, and the governments most likely will be much less capable in solving them. The most important silver lining here is the increasing competitiveness of clean technology, from renewable power generation to electric vehicles. If India can draw on competitive clean technology that simply was not available during China's rise at the turn of the millennium, some of the damage caused by limited institutional capacity could be avoided.

To some degree, the requisite institutional capacity is going to develop thanks to positive spillovers from other policy areas, such as infrastructure. Countries like India cannot grow at a rapid pace without improvements in institutional capacity, and the priority of economic growth means that governments do have incentives to act, no matter how complicated and difficult such action is. If India and its followers are to achieve China's level of economic development, they must invest in building more efficacious institutions to govern the economy and society, and such investments may contribute to the quest of sustainability through cross-sectoral spillovers.

In the end, comparing China and India highlights two possible futures for global environmental politics. Both present tremendous challenges, but the Chinese way forward brings more hope. Although China still struggles with institutional capacity constraints and environmental awareness remains bounded, the country's direction is a positive one. China's environmental policy benefits from the country's impressive achievements in clean technology, be it solar panels, electric vehicles, or high-speed rail.

India, on the other hand, remains far from embracing sustainability, and this is because of both institutional capacity constraints and weak environmental preferences. India's best hope is to tap into newly available clean technology, which it has already done to a great extent in renewable power generation and energy efficiency.[104] One can only hope that India's late start in rapid economic growth gives clean technology such an overwhelming advantage that the net result is sustainable development.

As the next chapter shows, the next batch of key emerging economies are currently on the Indian trajectory.

6

THE RISE OF THE REST

My goal in this chapter is to explore the implications of the rise of the next batch of emerging economies for global environmental politics. I provide an overview of environmental issues and policy in nine emerging economies. This whirlwind tour traces changes in emerging country positions in global environmental politics and evaluates their importance. The nine cases are assessed against my model in table 6.1.

As my primary illustrations, I have chosen four countries: Vietnam, Philippines, Indonesia, and Nigeria. These countries all have large populations and thus would have substantial power to destroy with economic growth. Given that South and Southeast Asia are the world's economically most dynamic regions, with the largest potential for growth in the short run, three of the four illustrations are from this area. Sub-Saharan Africa, on the other hand, is the final frontier for rapid economic growth, with early signals of an economic surge on the horizon.[1] Among the four countries, Indonesia and Nigeria are rich in natural resources, while the Philippines and Vietnam have less abundant natural resource endowments. All four countries are at least as wealthy as India on a per capita basis and thus already qualify as emerging economies.

In all four cases, we see a clear and consistent relationship between a country's economic growth and its role in global environmental politics. Although both Indonesia and Nigeria have received their fair share of

TABLE 6.1 Nine Countries in Global Environmental Politics

	Power to destroy and relevance in global environmental politics		Environmental preferences	Institutional capacity
	Twentieth century	Twenty-first century		
Indonesia	Major player: natural resources	Major player: emerging economy	Weak	Weak
Nigeria	Major player: natural resources	Major player: emerging economy	Weak	Weak
Vietnam	Mostly insignificant	Major player: emerging economy	Weak	Moderate
Philippines	Mostly insignificant	Major player: emerging economy	Weak	Weak
Brazil	Major player: natural resources	Major player: emerging economy	Moderate	Moderate
Bangladesh	Mostly insignificant	Future player: emerging economy	Weak	Weak
Myanmar	Mostly insignificant (despite natural resources)	Future player: emerging economy	Weak	Very weak
Ethiopia	Mostly insignificant	Future player: emerging economy	Moderate	Weak but growing
Tanzania	Mostly insignificant	Future player: emerging economy	Weak	Weak but growing

criticism for specific issues such as illegal deforestation and socioenvironmental destruction from oil drilling, and both have been accused of obstructionism under the OPEC banner, their importance in global environmental politics has stemmed from their exceptional abundance of natural resources. These two countries thus illustrate the conditions under which developing countries have played important roles in global environmental politics from the beginning.

In contrast, Vietnam and the Philippines played hardly any role in global environmental politics until the end of the twentieth century, mostly because they did not have natural resource endowments of global importance. Since then, however, all four countries have shown the crucial pattern of development that underlies everything in this book. Over time, economic growth puts the natural environment, both domestically and internationally, under tremendous stress, and a perverse consequence of this newly found power to destroy is an increase in a government's bargaining power and importance in global environmental politics. The more damage emerging economies could do simply by neglecting environmental protection, the more pivotal they become in the negotiations.

I include Brazil because its rainforests afford it an unusually important role in global environmental politics.[2] Although Brazil's economy already grew in the twentieth century, it provides a good illustration of the challenges of international cooperation over natural resources. The Brazilian case demonstrates the persistent difficulty of protecting forest resources that are largely controlled by one country.

I next focus on another batch of four: Bangladesh, Myanmar, Ethiopia, and Tanzania. These countries are from South and Southeast Asia or sub-Saharan Africa. They are all less wealthy than India, but their recent economic performance suggests that their consumption of energy and resources will increase in the future. Bangladesh, Ethiopia, and Tanzania have all sustained high economic growth rates over time. Although none of the three has abundant natural resources, their large populations and growing economies virtually guarantee that they will play pivotal roles in global environmental politics in the future. Myanmar also offers a particularly interesting illustration, as the country was, until very recently, a closed economy that had suffered decades of civil war.

These four countries are clearly behind Vietnam, Philippines, Indonesia, and Nigeria on the critical trajectory from a least developed country to a fully industrialized society. However, they all show potential for economic emergence. Their position and role in global environmental politics may change as they begin to wield power to destroy and thus face major new governance challenges related to energy, resources, and environment—the kinds of challenges they have not had to deal with in the past.

Importantly, all these countries face the problem of limited institutional capacity, as all have a spotty track record of trying to deal with their past and present environmental problems. While Ethiopia and Tanzania show promising signs of growing institutional capacity, and Vietnam has made significant progress over the past decades, Bangladesh appears to be stagnating, and Myanmar even shows some signs of backsliding. Based on these trends, Myanmar in particular emerges as a potential source of concern in the future—if the country manages to continue on a trajectory of rapid growth, the lack of institutional capacity may result in high levels of environmental deterioration.

The analysis also shows a precarious political situation in Myanmar and Ethiopia. Myanmar saw a military coup in early 2021 that may hamper economic growth, especially if the country goes back to autarky after less than a decade on the democratic path. Ethiopia's civil conflict in the Tigray region could, if not resolved, cut short a promising trajectory of economic development in the early twenty-first century. These cases highlight the difficult and uncertain path to economic development and caution against premature celebration of a global end to poverty.

GROWING GIANTS

I first examine the trajectories of Indonesia, Nigeria, Vietnam, the Philippines, and Brazil in global environmental politics. For each country, I describe their natural resource endowments, population size, and salient societal features. I then look at their past and present environmental policies at both the national and international levels. In a more speculative move, I finish by characterizing their likely future trajectories, as predicted by the combination of fundamentals, history, and recent developments. An analytical comparison and a holistic assessment follow in the next section.

To establish the basic facts of the first four cases, table 6.2 compares these four countries across a set of key indicators. The first four indicators

TABLE 6.2 Country Characteristics for Five Countries (2014)

	Indonesia	Nigeria	Vietnam	Philippines	Brazil
Population	255	176	92	101	203
Energy per capita	884	764	660	474	1,496
GDP per capita	3,693	2,550	1,579	2,613	11,951
GHG (2010)	745	292	279	160	1,331
Resource rents	4.8	10.7	7.2	2.9	3.3
Forest cover	52.3	24.8	45.0	23.4	60.5

Note: Population is given in millions of people; energy consumption per capita in kilograms of oil equivalent; GDP per capita in thousands of U.S. dollars, 2010 constant prices; total greenhouse gas emissions in megatons of CO_2 equivalent (2010); natural resource rents in percentage of GDP; forest cover as percentage of total area.

Source: World Development Indicators, http://data.worldbank.org/. For Brazil, greenhouse gas emission number is corrected with data from CAT (2020).

we have already seen in table 3.2. All four emerging economies are large and populous, have achieved a relatively high GDP per capita, consume large amounts of energy, and together generate more than two gigatons of greenhouse gas emissions (CO_2 equivalent).[3]

Based on this brief overview, it should be clear that all four countries hold tremendous potential for shaping the global environment and global environmental politics, but for very different reasons. To structure the discussion of these similar yet diverse countries, I begin with Indonesia and Nigeria, the two emerging economies with substantial natural resource endowments. I demonstrate that the role of each country in global environmental politics has begun to change because of rapid economic growth.

NATURAL RESOURCES AND ECONOMIC GROWTH: INDONESIA AND NIGERIA

Of the four economies under consideration, Indonesia and Nigeria have been in the limelight in global environmental politics for some time, though not because of their growing economies. Instead, both countries have played important roles in specific environmental negotiations because of their huge natural resource endowments. Both are major producers of oil and natural gas, while Indonesia is also home to some of the world's largest and biologically most diverse forests. Nigeria has been in the spotlight because of the environmental destruction from oil exploration and extraction in the Niger delta, while Indonesia's rainforest destruction has drawn the attention and ire of the international community for decades. Today, however, the two emerging economies are also increasingly important as producers and consumers, and this change of status is increasing their salience in global environmental talks.

Nigeria is Africa's most populous nation, with a head count of about 200 million today. Compared to other countries in sub-Saharan Africa, Nigeria is also relatively wealthy, with a GDP per capita of U.S. $2,550 in 2014. Although much of this wealth originates from oil exports, the country is more industrialized than most sub-Saharan African countries. In 2015, 20 percent of GDP came from industry and 59 percent from services.[4]

Although Nigeria has experienced economic diversification over time, the defining feature of the nation's economy remains oil production. In 1956 Shell and British Petroleum found large quantities of oil in Oloibiri in the Nigerian delta, and commercial production began in 1958. In 2015 Nigeria's proven oil reserves stood at 37 billion barrels and production at 1.75 million barrels per day.[5] The country joined the oil exporter club OPEC in 1971 and has remained a member ever since, despite considerable domestic political turmoil.

Nigeria's economy remains completely dependent on oil exports. Between 1965 and 1979, the country's oil production rose to 2,306 thousand barrels per day—ahead of Libya's 2,139. Although production peaked at 2,527 thousand barrels per day in 2005, it remained at 2,389 barrels per day in 2014.[6] In the same year, fuel exports—for practical purposes, oil—constituted 91 percent of all merchandise exports, and this ratio has remained above 90 percent every year since 1974.[7]

Nigeria has a long history of political turmoil, with multiple swings between authoritarian rule and democracy since the country's independence in 1960. After independence, the country adopted liberal democratic institutions, but in 1966 a military coup by the so-called Young Majors threw the country under authoritarian rule. It remained under military rule except for a brief interlude that followed the free elections of 1979 and lasted until the end of 1983, when the Nigerian Second Republic was again overthrown in a military coup. In May 1999, however, Nigeria again held free elections: "The death of Nigeria's brutal dictator Sani Abacha in June 1998 led to the election of Olusegun Obasanjo the following year and launched Nigeria's fragile and incomplete move toward democracy."[8] Since then, Nigeria has remained a democracy, without authoritarian backsliding but with considerable growing pains.

Because of the oil in the delta areas, the country has been in the limelight in global environmental politics for decades, well before its economy amounted to much more than pumping oil. Ever since oil production began in 1958, the ecological damage, human rights violations, and civil conflict caused by a scramble for the black gold have featured prominently in international environmental affairs. Both Nigeria's leaders and international oil majors, especially Shell, have been heavily criticized for their actions in the delta areas. According to Cayford, "Other fields have been found throughout the country, but the Niger delta region as a whole accounts for roughly 90 percent of Nigeria's oil. . . . The effect of this production on the local environment has been dramatic."[9] Direct environmental harms include oil spills and air pollution from flares; the indirect effects comprise violence and forced displacement. Over decades of military rule, the indigenous peoples of the Niger delta paid a steep price for Nigeria's petro-wealth.

A good example of these issues is oil production in Ogoniland. The Ogonis, an indigenous people living in the Niger delta, had suffered from the environmental effects of oil production in the delta areas since 1958. In 1990 the writer Ken Saro-Wiwa organized the Movement for the Survival of Ogoni People to lead protests. After three years of intense campaigning by the movement, Shell decided to pull out of Ogoniland in May 1993. The decaying oil infrastructure continued to cause environmental problems, however, and the conflict between the Ogonis and the Nigerian government continued. In November 1995 Saro-Wiwa and eight other leaders of the Ogoni uprising were executed, with the government accusing them of murders of other Ogoni chiefs. Saro-Wiwa's family sued Shell in 1996 for human rights violations, and in 2009 the case was settled out of court for a compensation of U.S. $15.5 million.

Except for the criticism focused on delta oil production, Nigeria has not traditionally played a major role in global environmental politics. The country has remained entirely passive in global environmental negotiations, except for supporting—or at least quietly accepting—various efforts by Saudi Arabia and OPEC, which Nigeria joined in 1971, to undermine the climate regime. Nigeria has ratified all the major multilateral treaties, from the Montreal Protocol to the Kyoto Protocol and the Stockholm Convention, but it has not played a particularly significant role in any of the negotiations or shown leadership in implementation over time. Exploring Africa's regional powers in international climate negotiations, for example, Nelson notes that "thus far Nigeria has not played the leadership role that one might expect."[10] Based on population and economic size, the country would be a natural leader in the African climate coalition, but in practice it has mostly maintained a low profile in global environmental negotiations.

In the future, however, Nigeria's importance in global environmental politics is bound to increase. Although Nigeria has faced political and economic turmoil both historically and recently, its population and economy are on a path of expansion. GHG emissions increased from 163 million to 292 million tons of CO_2 equivalent between 1990 and 2010, an 89 percent increase. With rapid population and economic growth, there is every reason to believe that this pollution expansion will continue. Although Nigeria remains dependent on oil exports, there are signs of economic diversification. In 2015 the service sector had grown to 58.8 percent of the total economy—well ahead of the oil sector (9.8 percent). Modern sectors such as telecommunications are thriving, creating jobs and opportunities for value creation beyond fossil fuels.

This is not to say that Nigeria's economic expansion is guaranteed. Its fragile political institutions and economic dependence on fossil fuel exports have created lots of uncertainty. Still, such crises have come and gone in Nigeria for half a century, and over time the country has grown wealthier. Nigeria's uneven trajectory remains a source of concern, but so far the country has managed to muddle through every time. At the very least, it can be said that Nigeria's potential for economic expansion is substantial.

Africa has historically played a relatively minor role in global environmental politics, but Nigeria's emergence promises to change all this. The country's large population, growing economy, fossil fuel resources, and leadership position in sub-Saharan Africa make it a bellwether for

Africa's future in global environmental politics. As Radelet notes, for the people of Nigeria and West Africa more broadly, much hangs in the balance with Nigeria's future.[11] If the country manages to consolidate its political institutions for stability and tap into its potential for economic growth, its vast size not only will enable it to make a significant contribution to Africa's structural power but also in all likelihood will generate positive spillovers to other economies. Nigeria could catalyze growth in other African economies as well, given its size and potential as a market for African exports of goods and services.

There are early signs of Nigeria's growing interest in global environmental governance. It was, for example, among the first fifty countries to ratify the Paris Agreement.[12] According to then-minister of environment Amina Mohammed, who announced Nigeria's decision to ratify the agreement, Nigeria's Intended Nationally Determined Contribution (INDC) was among the most ambitious and comprehensive in Africa. The INDC clearly states a 20 percent mitigation target relative to business as usual and promises to increase the target to 45 percent conditional on adequate international assistance. The targets are based on a particularly aggressive effort to decarbonize Nigeria's troubled power sector by 2030, with more than half of the planned reductions coming from that sector.[13]

For Nigeria, institutional capacity remains a major challenge. As we saw in figure 3.1, Nigeria's government effectiveness score in 2019 was below that of all other emerging economies analyzed in this book, except for Myanmar. The much smaller and poorer Ethiopia and Tanzania both perform much better. The picture in the field of environmental policy remains equally bleak. Although Nigeria has begun building an environmental policy framework after democratization, progress has been slow and uneven, and there is a wide gap between laws on the books and their implementation on the ground. A World Bank analysis of Nigerian environmental policy in 2006, for example, notes that "many gaps and weaknesses still remain. A more strategic approach focused on priorities may be lacking, and implementation of policies on the ground has been very weak. The levels of education and awareness regarding the links between poverty, growth and environmental sustainability are often limited, leading to low political support and interest for sustainable management of resources."[14]

These capacity constraints, together with political risk stemming from fragile democratic institutions, raise concerns about Nigeria's ability to produce economic growth in a sustainable fashion in the future. Even though Nigeria's economic diversification is welcome news and reduces the country's dependence on oil exports, the lack of institutional capacity means that growing wealth levels could generate large negative externalities. As the emerging Nigerian middle class purchases cars, air conditioners, and bigger homes, the country's natural capital could come under threat without an effective environmental policy.

Similar to Nigeria, Indonesia is a true giant in its region, Southeast Asia. A country of islands, Indonesia has the fourth largest population in the world, standing at 237 million in 2010 and still growing rapidly. The country is also relatively wealthy, with a GDP per capita of U.S. $3,693 in 2014. A G-20 member, it is highly industrialized, with industry and services each responsible for 43 percent of GDP in 2015.[15]

Indonesia's natural resource endowments are remarkable. The country has been blessed—or cursed, depending on one's perspective—with large amounts of oil. An OPEC member from 1962 to 2008, Indonesia was a major oil exporter in the second half of the twentieth century, though since then a combination of falling output and increasing domestic consumption have turned it into a net importer. Its daily oil production peaked at almost 1.7 million barrels in 1977 and has decreased steadily since 1995; in 2013 Indonesia produced only 826,000 barrels per day— about half of the peak.[16] Indonesia has thus gone from being a major petro-state to a net importer of oil. What is more, the country has abundant endowments of natural gas and coal. While oil production has historically dominated gas production, by 2002 the energy content of gas production exceeded that of oil production, and in 2012 the country produced about 1.5 million barrels of oil equivalent per day of natural gas, that is, almost twice the energy content of oil.[17]

As demand for coal grew in China and elsewhere in the 2000s, Indonesia became a major coal producer. Annual production rose from only 11 million tons in 1990 to 458 million tons in 2014, making the country the fifth-largest producer after China, the United States, India, and Australia.[18] While domestic demand remains well below supply, in November 2016 the head of the coal division of Indonesia's energy ministry, Hersonyo

Wibowo, said that the country expects domestic demand to grow fast, so that more and more coal would be used at home, especially for power generation.[19] Such a development would trigger a rapid increase in carbon dioxide emissions and air pollution. Encouragingly, Indonesia has recently begun to explore ways to reduce its dependence on coal and requested international transition finance to support the effort.

Indonesia's most significant environmental problem is deforestation. The country's rainforests are among the largest and most diverse on the planet. For decades, however, their area has decreased greatly because of illegal logging and land clearing for palm oil production. While 65 percent of Indonesia's land area was covered by forests in 1990, this had decreased to 52 percent by 2010. Although the annual decrease has diminished since 2000, the trend remains clear: Indonesia's rich forest heritage is disappearing rapidly. Proximate causes of deforestation include oil palm and timber plantations, forest-to-grassland conversion, small-scale agriculture and plantations, and logging roads.[20] Indonesia has tried a wide range of approaches to stop deforestation, from enforcing rules against forest fires and land clearing to restoring peatlands and banning primary forest clearing. The results have been mixed, however, as these policies have not been effectively enforced in Indonesia's highly decentralized political system.[21]

Indonesia's political history can be divided into the ironclad authoritarian rule of generals Sukarno and Suharto from the country's independence in 1945 until abrupt democratization in 1998.[22] Between 1967 and the Asian financial crisis in the late 1990s, General Suharto's political survival was never seriously threatened. But Indonesia's serious economic difficulties in 1997 contributed to political tension, as influential leaders began to blame Suharto for the country's dire straits, and by May 1998 the general had lost his political support and was forced to resign. After democratization, Indonesia has gone through extensive decentralization, and today the country's political system relies heavily on the autonomy of provinces.[23] In general, Indonesia's democracy has proven to be robust, with free and fair elections.

In the past, Indonesia's role in global environmental politics was all but defined by international concern about deforestation and, to a much lesser extent, the country's role as a major oil and gas producer. In an early analysis of the politics of deforestation in Indonesia, Dauvergne notes that "environmentalists stress the impact of destructive logging and large development projects, and the role of foreign companies and international organizations that encourage and finance these activities. Aid agencies, multinational corporations, international finance, and Third World elites, motivated by profit maximization and the international market, all contribute to destructive forest activities."[24] While he is careful to consider other causes of deforestation as well, for my purposes it is notable that already at the end of the Cold War, the international environmental community had identified Indonesia as a problem.

Internationally, Indonesia has historically played a minor role in global environmental politics outside the specific areas noted. To my knowledge, the country did not play a major role in any of the major global environmental treaties covered in chapters 2 and 3. Indonesia has promptly ratified all the typical global treaties, beginning with the Montreal Protocol in 1987 and including more recent accords such as the Stockholm Convention the Nagoya Convention and the Minamata Convention.

Today Indonesia is undergoing an economic transformation and is widely considered among the leading emerging economies globally. The country is already moving away from an industrial to a service-based economy, with the share of agriculture down to 13.5 percent by 2015 and services up to 43.3 percent.[25] Indeed, despite the depletion of oil resources, Indonesia has maintained a per capita growth rate of over 2 percent every year since the Asian financial crisis. It has emerged as the leading economy of Southeast Asia, with lots of potential for industrial and service expansion in the future.

Indonesia's role in global environmental politics has also begun to change, which can be best seen in the case of climate change. Michaelowa and Michaelowa, for example, note that "in the mid-2000s, the Yudhyono government developed national as well as provincial climate change mitigation plans. . . . The Indonesian INDC [for the Paris Agreement] defines a mitigation target of 29% below [business as usual] by 2030 which would be increased to 41% if international financing is provided."[26] According to Indonesian civil society, "Being a developing country with so much promise for economic growth and development, the international community applauded Indonesia for this daring target, which became a game-changer in the stagnant climate negotiations at the time [in 2009]."[27] In the future, then, Indonesia's role in global environmental politics will likely undergo a profound transformation. As Indonesia's INDC for the Paris Agreement already shows, the country now recognizes climate change as a major issue and has adopted a fifteen-year emission target.

If the country's economy continues to thrive, as it has done in the past, Indonesia will increasingly play a major role in Southeast Asian climate politics—not just as a rainforest nation or an energy producer, but as an economic powerhouse and a consumer of large quantities of energy and natural resources. If Indonesia retains its dynamism as Southeast Asia's largest economy, the country's power to destroy will increasingly come from energy and natural resource use, as opposed to energy production.

Although Indonesia has made impressive economic progress and succeeded in the consolidation of democratic political institutions, exceeding some of the more pessimistic expectations in the aftermath of the Asian financial crisis, the country's institutional capacity remains a source of concern. The country does reasonably well in general government effectiveness, but regulatory quality and the control of corruption moved in the wrong direction between 1996 and 2010. As we have seen, for example, Indonesia's rapid deforestation largely stems from the government's inability to bring the problem under control in a highly decentralized system of governance that prevents the rigorous enforcement of the laws in the books.

Overall, then, Indonesia's story is in many ways similar to that of Nigeria. While Indonesia's economic trajectory has not been as tumultuous as that of Nigeria, the country has undergone a relatively recent democratization and, since then, reaped the benefits of a remarkable economic transformation. As a result, Indonesia is no longer significant only as a rainforest nation or an oil exporter but as a large and growing economy with potential to destroy. While Indonesia has more institutional capacity than Nigeria and faces less political and economic risk, the fact remains that the government has been unable to stop deforestation, and this failure under tremendous international pressure hints at problems in capacity for effective environmental policy.

Nigeria and Indonesia illustrate the consequences of the economic diversification and growth of resource-dependent economies. These countries' economic destiny has always been shaped by natural resources. Nigeria is often seen as an example of the "resource curse,"[28] whereas

Indonesia seems to have governed the resource wealth in a somewhat more productive and sustainable fashion. And yet both countries have made progress toward economic diversification, the emergence of a middle class, and industrialization with a thriving service sector. As a result, their importance for global environmental politics no longer lies with natural resources alone. Both countries hold the potential for a major economic transformation and could thus come to hold the power to destroy because of their energy and resource consumption—and not just because of their natural resources.

INTO THE SPOTLIGHT: VIETNAM AND THE PHILIPPINES

Vietnam and the Philippines have traditionally maintained a low profile in global environmental politics. Neither country has played an active role in key global negotiations, but recently they have both faced increasing pressure to protect the environment and become more active in global environmental politics. Because their natural resources are less abundant than those of Nigeria and Indonesia, their path in global environmental politics has been more linear and straightforward: it is only now that the countries have become important players in their own right.

When the Vietnam War ended in April 1975 with the capture of Saigon by the North Vietnamese Army, the country had been ruined by a decade of brutal warfare. Vietnam's GDP per capita was U.S. $389 (2010 prices) in 1984, making the country one of the poorest in the world. In 1986, however, the socialist government launched an ambitious reform agenda, *Doi Moi*, as a response to a serious economic crisis in the early 1980s.[29] Since then, the economy has grown rapidly: between 1990 and 2015, GDP per capita has grown by at least 3 percent every year, with a record growth of 7.8 percent reached in 1995, a decade after the beginning of the reforms.[30]

Vietnam is not a country endowed with massive natural resource wealth. It has oil, gas, and coal reserves, but it is not a major producer of fossil fuels. Vietnam also exports some minerals and wood products, but again the scale of this activity pales in comparison to more major players, such as Indonesia or Nigeria. The country does export substantial quantities of seafood, coffee, and rice.

Instead of natural resources, Vietnam's quick economic growth mostly stems from rapid industrialization. In 1985 Vietnam's industrial value added (constant 2010 U.S. dollars) amounted to a puny $5.8 billion, but by 2015 it had increased to $52.8 billion—almost a tenfold increase. Vietnam exports textiles, electronics, machinery, and wooden products. Between 1990 and 2010, industrial value added as a percentage of GDP grew from 22.7 to 32.1 percent, having peaked at 38.6 in 2006, during the global economic boom. Services remained approximately stable, at 38.6 percent in 1990 and 36.9 percent in 2010.

An important feature of Vietnam is the country's closed society and authoritarian political system. The Vietnam War was won by the communist regime of North Vietnam, and although the country has embraced market reforms ever since, political liberalization has not come forth. Vietnam's Polity IV score has remained at –7 since unification in 1975, showing that the country is a stable authoritarian regime. The primary threat to regime survival appears to be a future economic crisis. As a recent assessment of "nontransitions" to democracy suggests,

> we can expect the communist regimes in China and Vietnam to enter the danger zone if the population stops pragmatically accepting them, due to the onset of an economic crisis. In such a situation, workers and peasants will conclude that they have nothing to lose but their chains. By itself, however, that will not be enough. The vast majority will not be willing to rise up against their rulers unless their expectations for political reform have first been frustrated. . . . It is hard to imagine a scenario in China or Vietnam where expectations for reform are stimulated from the outside.[31]

Historically, Vietnam's environmental problems mostly originated from the inefficiencies and flaws of socialist planning. When Vietnam was still a very poor country, the scale of economic activity itself did not raise serious environmental issues; instead, the problems were related to bad management. In their overview of Vietnamese environmental policy, Beresford and Fraser state:

In fact the traditional socialist economy has inbuilt mechanisms leading to enormous waste of resources and inhibition of technical change, both of which clearly have important implications for the environment. The key feature of this type of economy which, more than anything else, has been responsible for environmental degradation, has been the overwhelming emphasis given to growth of produced output value. It is an emphasis arising out of the economic backwardness of the socialist countries relative to the capitalist world and a desire to prove the superiority of socialism.[32]

Although Vietnam's small economy limited the scale of destruction, environmental degradation per unit of production was enormous because of inefficiencies in the planning system.

The other important feature of Vietnam's socialist environmental policy, of course, is that rules and regulations for private economic activity were mostly unnecessary. Environmental management was directly incorporated into planning and was largely ignored. As Vietnam began the process of economic modernization in the 1980s, the focus of environmental policy thus shifted.[33] The economic reforms themselves improved input-output efficiency in the economy, but the government also enacted a series of policies to protect the environment. The move away from a socialist economy meant that the government could no longer directly control all economic activity but instead had to enact policies and regulations both for private and state-owned enterprises.

Internationally, Vietnam remained almost entirely outside the realm of global environmental politics until the end of the Cold War.[34] When the Stockholm summit was held in 1972, Vietnam as a unified country did not even exist. Until the Rio summit in 1992, Vietnam participated in virtually no environmental treaties at all. It was only after that summit that it became active, ratifying in rapid succession key treaties such as the Montreal Protocol and the UNFCCC in 1994.

Recent developments, however, suggest a very different future trajectory. Given Vietnam's large population, industrial expansion, and bright economic prospects, the country is bound to play an increasingly important role in global environmental politics. If Vietnam continues on the path of rapid industrial expansion and growing standards of living, the country's demand for energy and resources is bound to expand rapidly in the coming years.

Signs of change can already be seen in both domestic environmental policy and participation in global processes. Vietnam's INDC for the Paris Agreement, for example, promises an 8 percent reduction relative to business as usual by 2030 even without any international support, and a 25 percent reduction conditional on bilateral and multilateral support.[35] In the baseline, the government estimates emissions to increase from 246.8 million tons of carbon dioxide equivalent in 2010 to 787.4 million tons in 2030. One important reason for this expected growth is the central role that coal expansion is to play in Vietnam's energy planning. The National Power Development Masterplan for 2011–2020 emphasized coal, and Vietnam's electricity monopoly estimated that the country would add thirty-one new coal-fired generation plants to its January 2017 total of twenty.[36] In July 2020, however, the Vietnam Energy Institute announced that the coming decade would shift the focus from coal to renewables and natural gas, suggesting a major change in policy focus.[37]

Compared to most emerging economies, Vietnam's institutional capacity is relatively high. The general indicators, such as government effectiveness and corruption, are in the middle of the pack. While corruption has grown worse over time, government effectiveness in general has improved. Vietnam's environmental policy capacity has also clearly grown over time thanks to focused efforts, in a pattern resembling that of China. While Vietnam does face the issue of possible pressure to democratize in the future, so far the country's political regime appears stable.

To summarize, Vietnam resembles China, only a decade earlier. Its economy has grown over time, and there has been some improvement in institutional capacity. The government has also become more engaged in domestic and international environmental policy, but it remains to be seen if this generally positive trajectory continues in the future.

The Philippines used to have large tracts of primary forests, but those were lost decades ago during the authoritarian era.[38] Between 1900 and 1988 the country's forest cover decreased from 21 million hectares to 6.5 million according to government estimates. As over 10 million hectares were lost by 1970, the battle against deforestation was mostly lost before it appeared on the global environmental agenda. The country is not a major producer of fossil fuels, though it does have an active mining industry and generates large amounts of geothermal power. Mines in the Philippines produce gold, nickel, copper, and chromite in particular.

The political history of the Philippines since American rule ended in 1946 can be divided into an initial spell of partial democracy that lasted from 1946 until 1972, when President Marcos declared martial law and ruled as a dictator until 1986. At that time, the Philippines democratized, and it has remained a presidential democracy ever since. The Fifth Republic of the Philippines had seen six regimes by the end of 2016.

While the Philippines inherited a set of environmental policies from the colonial era, the year 1977 was a watershed, as the president formulated the law for "Philippine Environmental Policy." For the first time, this law created a general framework for environmental governance in the country. Pertinently, Magallona and Malayang note that "these legislative developments came in the wake of the United Nations Conference on the Human Environment in Stockholm in 1972. The Stockholm Conference proved to be a consolidating influence in the making of an integrated approach to environmental protection and it gave impetus to a more unified national action towards this objective."[39]

At the international level, the Philippines has mostly remained a passive player. It has never played a prominent role in any environmental negotiations. While the country has been shaped by the heightened international attention to environmental issues at least since the Stockholm summit in 1973, it has not played a very active role in these negotiations and instead remains a passive member of the Group of 77.

In the future, however, the Philippines is bound to play a more important role. Rapid population growth and economic expansion all but guarantee that the country's environmental footprint will increase over time. The country is already well past the industrialization stage. Value added from services has increased from 43.6 percent of total GDP in 1990 to 59.0 percent in 2015. GDP per capita (2010 constant prices) increased from U.S. $1,526 to $2,640 between 1990 and 2015, with particularly rapid growth in the 2000s.

For example, the Philippines' INDC predicts that without additional government policy, emissions would grow over threefold relative to 1990 and over twofold relative to 2010 by 2030.[40] While the INDC promises a whopping 70 percent reduction relative to business as usual conditional on international assistance, the document does not actually report the projected emissions without climate policy. Initially, the Filipino government also emphasized the necessity of coal-fired power generation to meet the country's soaring power demand. In October 2020, however, its Department of Energy announced a moratorium on new coal-fired power plants, suggesting a possible shift away from coal.[41]

Moreover, the climate policy debate within the Philippines remains turbulent. In July 2016 President Rodrigo Duterte, who had earlier built a reputation as an outspoken opponent of climate policy, softened his position and noted that "addressing climate change shall be a top priority but upon a fair and equitable equation. It should not stymie our industrialization."[42] With this move, Duterte brought his position in line with the consensus view in the global South—climate policy is important and every country should contribute, but only to the extent that these contributions do not compromise economic growth and poverty alleviation.

The Philippines' institutional capacity situation is somewhat contradictory. On the one hand, the country performs well in general government effectiveness and has always been among the highest in our sample of emerging economies, increasing from −0.18 to −0.05 between 1996 and 2019. At the same time, corruption and regulatory quality have grown worse over time.

The country also seems to thrive in the specific field of environmental policy, as consistent progress in legislation, and implementation thereof, shows. The Philippines has for decades been relatively active and capable in domestic environmental policy. Since the early 1970s the country has built a relatively effective system of environmental policy. The government has often shown willingness to go against influential economic interests. In February 2017, for example, it ordered the closure of twenty-three mines mostly producing nickel, citing concerns about environmental degradation, human rights, and public health.[43] These mines account for half of Filipino nickel output and one-tenth of all world output.

Overall, the Philippines' case resembles Vietnam's development, with the exception of early and so far robust democratization. The country has a large population, and the economy is expected to grow in the short and medium run. These changes likely will turn the Philippines into an increasingly important player in global environmental politics, especially relative to the country's low profile in the past. What remains to be seen is how much the Philippines government is willing to do to reduce the country's growing pollution burden.

Though they are at very different levels of economic development, both Vietnam and the Philippines face a similar challenge: providing their growing economies with enough energy and natural resources to continue improving living standards and performance in human development. Vietnam approaches this challenge under stable authoritarian rule, while the Philippines is a liberal democracy. Both countries are bound to play a more important role in global environmental politics in the future.

SOVEREIGN POWER OVER THE AMAZON RAINFOREST: BRAZIL

Brazil plays a unique role in global environmental politics because it controls most of the Amazon rainforest. From the early days of global environmental negotiations, Brazil has advocated for agreements that respect national sovereignty and acknowledge economic development as a legitimate need. Political volatility has made Brazil a challenging partner in global environmental politics despite its advanced economy and potential, if sometimes politically compromised, institutional capacity.

Unlike the other countries explored in this chapter, Brazil achieved middle-income status a long time ago. Already in 1960 its GDP per capita had reached U.S. $3,417—higher than that of Indonesia in 2010. It grew to $8,349 by 1980 and then, after two decades of stagnation, to over $20,000 by 2007. Although the Brazilian economy depends heavily on natural resources, it is also industrialized and service-oriented. In 1960 Brazil's agriculture, forestry, and fishing sectors still amounted to 18 percent of total GDP, but this number had decreased to 4 percent by 2010.

Before 1985 Brazil was a military dictatorship. In 1964 a military coup removed President Goulart from power. The repressive military regime stayed in power for twenty-two years, aided by Brazil's strong economic performance throughout the 1970s. As economic difficulties compounded in the early 1980s, however, the military lost its popular support and eventually lost power to the Brazilian Democratic Movement Party in 1985. By 1988 Brazil's democratic government had drafted a new constitution, which entered in effect in 1990. Since then, Brazil has been a democratic polity.

Brazil's power to destroy is exceptional. Approximately 60 percent of the country is covered by forest, and Brazil controls the vast majority of the Amazon rainforest. The destruction of this rainforest is a major driver of global climate change. In 2010, 29 percent of Brazil's greenhouse gas emissions came from forestry and land use changes. At that time, Brazil's population stood at 196 million. Brazil also has large domestic oil and mineral reserves.

Deforestation is the most important global environmental problem in Brazil. Before democratization, the military regime encouraged, and even subsidized, migration into the Amazon both to exploit domestic natural resources and to secure the vast area against invasions by other countries in the region.[44] The government built roads, subsidized settlements, and provided inexpensive credit to cattle ranchers. Because of these measures, large-scale land clearing and logging resulted in rapid deforestation beginning in the mid-1970s. By 1989 the Brazilian Amazon had lost over 150,000 square miles of forest cover, or about 10 percent of the initial total,[45] and another 64,000 square miles were lost between 1990 and 2000.

During President Lula's tenure, 2003–2010, the federal government took decisive action to halt deforestation. In 2004 Brazil created the DETER satellite system to monitor deforestation in real time, and in 2007 the Ministry of the Environment identified a list of "priority municipalities" with high levels of deforestation.[46] These municipalities saw increased enforcement activity, including fines for noncompliance with forestry laws based on satellite observations. Brazil also increased the area under protection by 50 percent, to cover half of the total forest area.[47] These measures alone brought deforestation down by 35 percent relative to predicted levels.[48]

Since Lula's tenure ended, Brazil's commitment to halting deforestation has wavered. Lula's successor, President Rousseff, struggled with an ailing economy and low approval ratings. Rural landowners made major political gains and controlled 40 percent of the seats in the Brazilian Congress between 2015 and 2018. This change of fortunes forced the impeachment of Rousseff in August 2016. Her successor, President Temer, gave major concessions to the rural constituency, from reducing the size of protected areas to offering amnesty to farmers and ranchers who had been fined for deforestation. In October 2018 Jair Bolsonaro, a right-wing populist, won the elections and continued to encourage deforestation in the Brazilian Amazon.

Another major environmental concern in Brazil pertains to dam construction. In 2016 Brazil had constructed 87 GW of hydroelectric generation capacity, which accounted for more than 70 percent of all electricity generated in the country.[49] For decades, environmentalists and indigenous peoples have expressed concern about the negative impacts of dam construction, ranging from displacement to loss of biodiversity.

Brazil has been a major player in global environmental negotiations on deforestation, biodiversity, and climate change for a long time. Indeed, the Earth Summit was hosted in Rio de Janeiro in 1992. When international concern about deforestation exploded in the mid-1980s, nationalist forces in Brazil argued that the governance of the Brazilian Amazon was not anyone else's business and accused industrialized countries of colonialism.[50] One reason why the Earth Summit did not produce a forest convention was the North-South conflict about national sovereignty over forests, and Brazil was among the most vocal voices in favor of national self-determination. In the negotiations under the Intergovernmental Panel on Forests, and later at the Intergovernmental Forum on Forests, Brazil, alongside the United States, led the coalition against a global, legally binding forest treaty.

In climate negotiations, Brazil's initial position emphasized the importance of historical emissions.[51] Brazil argued that industrialized countries were responsible for a vast majority of global warming, and that treaties such as the Kyoto Protocol should allocate burden based on historical responsibility. But thanks to success in reducing deforestation, the Brazilian position became increasingly cooperative, and Brazil emphasized the importance of financial support for carbon sinks in forestry. A coalition of "Baptists and bootleggers"—environmentalists and businesspeople—supported international climate policy, as it would create opportunities in carbon finance and low-carbon development.[52] Against this backdrop, Brazil went to the Paris negotiations in 2015 with an INDC that promised to reduce the country's greenhouse gas emissions by 37 percent by 2025 relative to a 2005 baseline. In doing so, it became the first non-OECD country to promise absolute emissions reductions.

After the Paris Agreement, Brazil's position again reversed. As the country's own policies again began to permit, and even encourage, forest clearing and logging, Brazil no longer supported ambitious decarbonization plans. President Bolsonaro, in particular, expressed skepticism about the Paris Agreement and threatened to leave it, following the U.S. withdrawal.

This flip-flopping is closely related to Brazil's institutional capacity in environmental policy. Although Brazil's high per capita income and a long history of statehood have given rise to a generally capable bureaucracy, political interference and instability undermine its ability to protect the environment. When Brazil's top leadership was committed to stopping deforestation during Lula's regime, it was able to equip the Brazilian Institute of Environment and Natural Resources (IBAMA) with sufficient resources to identify and punish rule violators. But when this commitment ended, the bureaucracy rapidly lost its capacity to act and violations went unpunished, even before the Brazilian government officially reversed course.

To summarize, Brazil demonstrates the difficulties of international cooperation on natural resources. Except for a brief, self-interested honeymoon period during President Lula's rule, Brazil has been a staunch advocate of national sovereignty. Brazil's position has always emphasized the importance of self-determination and refused any responsibility for climate change and deforestation. These preferences, combined with a politicized bureaucracy, have made Brazil a difficult partner in global environmental negotiations.

THE NEXT BATCH OF EMERGING ECONOMIES IN GLOBAL ENVIRONMENTAL POLITICS

Brazil aside, turning back to the four other countries discussed previously, all are socially, economically, and politically diverse, and all share a few core features that underscore their growing importance in global environmental politics. They have large populations and robust economic growth, which have over time contributed to growth in resource depletion and pollution, while limitations of institutional capacity have inhibited their governments from controlling the negative externalities of population and economic growth. Nigeria and Indonesia are undergoing a transformation in the source of their power to destroy, while Vietnam and the Philippines are only now starting to build up their structural power.

Historically, power to destroy was unevenly allocated across the four emerging economies. All four started on a relatively low level, but Indonesia and Nigeria had, thanks to their fossil fuel and biodiversity assets, more structural power than Vietnam and the Philippines. Through their membership in OPEC, Indonesia and Nigeria also increased the strength of the petro-states in global environmental politics. While Indonesia and Nigeria have not emerged as OPEC leaders, their membership has legitimized OPEC's efforts to sabotage global climate negotiations.

Over time, all four countries have emerged as important players in global environmental politics. Their growing economies have added to their power to destroy, and, in the case of climate change, all now belong to the group of major emitters. Efforts to protect the planet and human civilization from runaway global warming would suffer a major blow if any of these countries failed to participate, cooperate, and mitigate in the future. While Indonesia remains particularly critical thanks to its large but rapidly decreasing rainforests, the other three emerging economies are also now important and should not be ignored.

The consequences of this growing power to destroy for global environmental politics are now becoming apparent. As these countries face growing pressure to act, both by complying with international treaties and by implementing national environmental policies, they are now also in a position of strength, as their power to destroy enables them to demand reciprocal concessions from the rest of the world. Indonesia and Nigeria are now globally important for many more reasons than just their resource endowments. Indonesia is Southeast Asia's largest economy and shapes the growth of energy use and economic activity in that region in a decisive fashion; Nigeria is Africa's most populous country and a potential economic leader—or, in the worst case scenario, a major source of economic trouble and political turmoil in all of West Africa. Vietnam and the Philippines are dealing with rapidly growing energy demand, and their ability to do so without expanding their coal use would make a notable dent in the growth of global carbon dioxide emissions.

At the end of the day, there are good reasons to expect robust economic growth in these countries in the future. All have weathered many political storms and economic crises over the past decades, and yet their economic trajectories have remained on upward trajectories. While uncertainties remain in the short run for any particular country, it is unlikely that these countries would not collectively continue to grow, in terms of both wealth and political power, in the future.

As for institutional capacity, the historical baseline was again low in all four countries. None had the capacity to effectively manage their environmental challenges. All four countries share a history of dictatorship, and authoritarian rule arguably contributed to their troubling record of environmental destruction. Although the limited scope of economic activity and abject poverty mitigated these countries' total environmental footprint, the environmental cost for each unit of GDP was very high because of extreme inefficiencies, be it due to Nigeria's total disregard of the effects of oil production in the Niger delta or Vietnam's philosophy of extreme natural resource extraction for industrialization at all costs.

Today, however, there is substantial variation in institutional capacity among the four, as we saw in figure 3.1. Government effectiveness has improved in Vietnam, the Philippines, and Indonesia, whereas developments in Nigeria have been much less positive. Regulatory quality and corruption, though arguably secondary indicators, tell an even more troubling story, with many losses across the countries.

Much hinges on improvements in institutional capacity. Although all four countries have made some progress on this front, severe challenges remain, as we have seen relatively slow growth in institutional capacity to manage environmental issues. Although the overall indicators described in figure 3.1 are generic and crude, my review of the track record of environmental policy reveals a similar picture. Countries like Vietnam and the Philippines have made some progress over time, though by very different means. The sectoral picture in Indonesia is more troubling, as the country's decentralized institutional structure and endemic corruption hamper efforts to stop deforestation. Nigeria's situation is perhaps the worst of them all, with little evidence of any progress on effective environmental policy to date.

This slow growth of institutional capacity has meant that governments have faced real difficulties in keeping their own power to destroy at bay. The combination of rapid economic growth and an expanding population has created environmental pressures that national governments have failed to mitigate to any significant degree. With the partial exception of Vietnam and the Philippines, overall we see four manifestations of the Indian story: economic growth has not been accompanied by sufficient growth in institutional capacity, whether in general or specifically in the environmental sector.

Improving institutional capacity is a central consideration for the meaningful engagement of these emerging economies in global environmental politics. All four countries can realize gains from improved management, with sizable positive spillovers at the regional and global levels. To the extent that strategic policy interventions can turn the ship around and help these four gigantic economies improve their institutional capacity, the prospects for sustainable development could improve significantly.

THE NEXT COHORT OF EMERGING ECONOMIES

When investigating the role of Bangladesh, Myanmar, Ethiopia, and Tanzania in global environmental politics, a common pattern emerges: economic growth is creating new policy challenges and encouraging increasingly active participation in international diplomacy. On the one hand, international pressure to protect the environment is increasing; on the other hand, governments in these four countries are beginning to realize that external support can prove valuable in national environmental management.

Table 6.3 compares the four countries across a set of key indicators. Again, the first four indicators are from table 3.2. All four countries are

TABLE 6.3 Country Characteristics for Four Countries (2014)

	Bangladesh	Myanmar	Ethiopia	Tanzania
Population	155	52	98	50
Energy per capita	229	270	493	497
GDP per capita	951	369	449	846
GHG (2010)	178	325	183	234
Resource rents	1.1	7.8	13.4	5.1
Forest cover	14.5	46.4	15.5	54.7

Note: Population is given in thousands of people; energy consumption per capita in kilograms of oil equivalent; GDP per capita in thousands of U.S. dollars, 2010 constant prices; total greenhouse gas emissions in megatons of CO_2 equivalent (2010); natural resource rents in percentage of GDP; forest cover as percentage of total area.

Source: World Development Indicators, http://data.worldbank.org/.

large but much poorer than the four emerging economies discussed earlier. Their energy consumption and GHG emissions also tend to be very low, though Myanmar tends to produce higher emissions because of deforestation. Indeed, of Myanmar's total GHG emissions, only 4 percent come from carbon dioxide—the country has one of the lowest per capita emissions on the planet.

RAPID TURNAROUNDS: BANGLADESH AND MYANMAR

Bangladesh and Myanmar are neighbors, but their country characteristics are quite different. Bangladesh is an exceptionally densely populated territory that gained its independence from Pakistan in 1971 and has since oscillated between democratic and autocratic rule. Myanmar, a vast country with a comparatively small population and abundant but untapped natural resources, was a closed military dictatorship until very recently. Both countries have, however, recently shown signs of robust economic growth.

Beginning our review with Bangladesh, we see a long history of abject poverty that has recently begun to change. Bangladesh had achieved a GDP per capita of U.S. $760 (2010 prices) in 1990, still clearly behind India's GDP per capita of $1,346.[53] Industrial output remained at 26 percent in that year, whereas services had increased to 56 percent, in a pattern akin to that of India. A key driver of Bangladesh's economy is the textile industry, which has emerged as the country's keystone industry for international markets.

An interesting twist of Bangladesh's growth story is the country's relatively rapid human development. A *Wall Street Journal* article in 2015, noting India's much higher GDP per capita, compares the attainment of human development between the two neighbors and finds that Bangladesh now beats in India in most indicators.[54] Most important, life expectancy in Bangladesh is now seventy-one years—a whopping five years more in India. The mortality rate for children under five years of age in Bangladesh fell to 0.041 by 2013, whereas India remains at 0.053. While this difference is not dramatic, it is highly unfavorable when one remembers that the average Indian had a 50 percent higher income than the average Bangladeshi in 2013. Since then, the gap has continued to shrink, and during the COVID-19 pandemic the Indian economy contracted much more sharply than the Bangladeshi economy.

Though fertile for agriculture, Bangladesh has few natural resources and is also highly vulnerable to environmental degradation. The country's population density is among the highest in the world, standing at 1,237 persons per square kilometer in 2015. What is more, Bangladesh is a low-lying country that is among the most vulnerable to climate change—in particular, sea level rise and extreme weather. The country can feed a large population because of the fertile landscape and monsoon rains, but the landscape is also extremely vulnerable to flooding. According to an environmental risk assessment by the consulting firm Maplecroft in 2011, for example, ranked Bangladesh as the world's most vulnerable country based on "exposure to climate-related natural disasters and sea-level rise; human sensitivity, in terms of population patterns, development, natural resources, agricultural dependency and conflicts; thirdly, the index assesses future vulnerability by considering the adaptive capacity of a country's government and infrastructure to combat climate change."[55]

The political history of Bangladesh is also tumultuous. The country declared its independence from Pakistan in March 1971, and by the end of the year the Pakistani troops, which were handicapped by the lack of a land corridor between (West) Pakistan and Bangladesh, had been beaten by an intervention launched by India's prime minister, Indira Gandhi. Although Bangladesh initially adopted a secular democratic constitution, by 1975 the military was in complete control of the country, and it was only in 1991 that the country's democratic political institutions were restored. In 2007 the president declared state of emergency, and the country again plunged into autocracy. Although the emergency ended almost immediately, Bangladesh's democracy never made a full recovery and remains a partial democracy at best, with flaws in the electoral process and oppression of political participation. In 2013 the country's Polity IV score was 4, closer to the democratic than the autocratic end but far from the status of a liberal democracy.

Given constant political turmoil in Bangladesh, for decades there was little environmental policy to speak of, except for interventions supported by foreign donors.[56] Independent Bangladesh inherited and adopted the East Pakistan Water Pollution Ordinance of 1970, extending it into a more

general Environmental Pollution Control Ordinance in 1977 and establishing a Pollution Control Board. It was only in 1992, however, that a comprehensive National Environmental Policy was formulated, after the
democratization of the country and the formation of an environmental
ministry in 1989. Since then, the country has slowly built its institutional
capacity, often with donor support.

In the past, Bangladesh's role in global environmental politics was limited to being a mostly passive victim of environmental threats and hazards. While Bangladesh has historically played a minor role in global environmental politics at best, because of its high level of vulnerability it has
spearheaded the calls for climate finance focused on adaptation. According to Saleemul Huq, a leading Bangladeshi scholar of climate policy, by
2001 "Bangladesh has been able to participate only nominally" in global
climate negotiations.[57]

At the same time, population growth has contributed to ever-stronger
pressures on natural resources, as the country's population per square
kilometer has soared from 853 in 1991 to 1,237 in 2015. Although the rate
of population growth has recently decreased because women give birth
to fewer children, the population remains decades away from stabilizing.

The consequences of this expanding economy are tangible and a cause
for concern both from an environmental and from a public health perspective. Consider, for example, the construction of coal-fired power
plants in Bangladesh. While Bangladesh has historically relied on natural gas for most of its power needs, in February 2017 the country planned
six coal-fired power plants with a total capacity of about 5,000 MW.[58] If
Bangladesh cannot find cleaner alternatives to coal for power generation
in the future, the consequences for global warming and air pollution will
be significant. The country's high population density, dependence on
farming for livelihoods, and vulnerable natural resources such as the
mangrove forests of the Sundarbans exacerbate the potential damage that
coal-fired power generation could cause. In August 2020 Bangladesh
announced plans to review coal-fired power generation and reduce future
capacity expansion.[59]

Bangladesh's government has not remained inactive with regard to
environmental policy. In the twenty-first century the country has enacted
a number of new environmental policies, including a renewable energy
policy in 2008, a climate change strategy in 2009, and a biodiversity act

in 2012.[60] These new policies help the government prepare for threats and risks in a future characterized by vulnerability. The policies reflect the country's growing environmental pressures, with an expanding economy and higher population densities.

The climate change strategy, formulated in the run-up to the infamous Copenhagen summit, sheds light on the politics of climate change in Bangladesh.[61] The strategy formulates a ten-year program "to build capacity and resilience of the country to meet the challenge of climate change." Of the five pillars of the strategy, only one is focused on mitigation; under that pillar, the emphasis is on efficient production, and the strategy even specifically promotes "maximising coal output and managing coal fired power stations in a carbon-neutral way." For Bangladesh, climate change remains a threat that requires adaptation and resilience, while mitigation is considered only when compatible with broader development goals, and energy security in particular.

In a similar vein, Bangladesh's INDC is not very ambitious. The plan only promises to reduce greenhouse gases from "the power, transport, and industry sectors" by 5 percent below business as usual, a target that can be increased to 15 percent upon adequate international assistance.[62] Again, international assistance, economic growth, and adaptation are important motives: "In selecting the actions set out above, Bangladesh has prioritised those which fit with the growth priorities set out in our national development plans. In addition, Bangladesh has captured the synergies between mitigation and adaptation, not only by prioritising those adaptation activities with significant mitigation co-benefits, but also by seeking to minimise the carbon footprint of adaptation portfolio as a whole."

The question of institutional capacity is an intriguing one in Bangladesh. On the one hand, the typical governance indicators listed in figure 3.1 suggest stability, with no change in government effectiveness and countervailing changes in the secondary indicators of regulatory quality (+) and control of corruption (–). The general picture is one of uneven performance and muddling through, consistent with the country's turbulent political trajectory since independence.

On the other hand, the aforementioned examples of environmental legislation suggest that Bangladesh is making progress in the field of environmental protection. Bangladesh stands out as a promising example for least developed countries that are now beginning to see bright economic futures, possibly because the country's severe and chronic vulnerability makes investment in disaster preparedness both an absolute necessity and a goal that donors would be willing to support. To summarize, Bangladesh is on the verge of an important transition. While the country remains mostly known for its vulnerability to environmental disasters, it is also a dynamic economy with substantial power to destroy. The country has never had many natural resources, so most of the potential for destruction will come from the general increase in the use of energy as living standards rise, industrialization continues, and the middle class expands.

Myanmar is an unusual case because of its political history. Until 2010, the country remained closed to the outside world under the control of a military dictatorship. Although the country had held free elections in 1990, the military dictatorship, which had ruled since 1962, refused to accept the results. Since 2010 elections, however, the country has made a series of ambitious economic and political reforms that have created a surge in economic growth. Although the 2010 election and the 2012 by-election did not meet the standards of free and fair elections, the elections in 2015 were openly contested and brought to power Aung San Suu Kyi's National League for Democracy with an absolute majority.

Since 2015, however, Myanmar has struggled with democratic consolidation. Nominally a democracy, Myanmar politics remain heavily influenced by the military, and elections have not been accompanied by robust civil rights. In 2017 tensions between the majority Buddhist population and the Rohingya Muslim minority intensified. International observers, including the United Nations, have criticized the Myanmar government for ethnic persecution, which has caused hundreds of thousands of Rohingya Muslims to flee to neighboring countries. In February 2021 these pressures led to a military coup, raising global concern about Myanmar's democratic future.

Historically, Myanmar's economy has depended on agriculture and natural resource extraction. Until the end of the Cold War, Myanmar remained a very poor country, with virtually no economic growth to speak of. GDP per capita peaked at U.S. $232 (2010 prices) in 1985 and then decreased to $187 in 1991—below 1979 and only slightly above that of war-ravaged Ethiopia at the time.[63] Almost the entire economy was based on subsistence farming, and the few commodities exported were essentially natural resource rents, such as natural gas or jade. Since the end of the

Cold War and the country's failed experiment with totalitarian socialism, economic growth has been rapid. In 2014 the country's GDP per capita had increased to $1,257 (2010 prices)—almost seven times that of 1991. This growth performance makes Myanmar one of the best-performing economies on the planet.

Myanmar's natural resource endowments are substantial beyond its status as the world's most important jade producer. Half of the country remains under forest cover, mostly primary forest with high densities of biodiversity. Myanmar is large relative to its population and has both oil/gas and minerals, as well as untapped hydropower potential. Until very recently, however, most of these resources remained untapped because of the closed economic system and internal conflict, and now commentators worry about a possible resource curse:[64]

> If the impacts of investments in the natural resources sector can be properly assessed and managed, and the revenues can be dealt with accountably and transparently, the potential benefits could be enormous. Wealth from natural resources could fund a substantial part of Myanmar's transition, if managed well. Unfortunately, the track record for this internationally is quite low, with few countries having succeeded in avoiding 'resource curse' issues.[65]

In the past, Myanmar's role in global environmental politics has also been minimal. Myanmar—then Burma—inherited a forest management system from the British colonialists. Similar to the colonial rulers, the government of independent Myanmar was much more interested in maximizing natural resource revenue in the short run than in sustainable forestry in the long run: "Pressure from Burma's leaders to maximize revenue has meant that foresters have been unable to balance forest exploitation and conservation."[66] After the military coup of 1988, pressures on the environment increased, as "the regime began indiscriminately exploiting the country's natural resources. . . . The institutional development for environmental governance falls behind the intensified uses and abuses of the natural environment in Burma."[67]

Because of Myanmar's closed political system, the country also did not participate in global environmental politics to any meaningful extent, though the country did ratify the standard multilateral treaties.

Its history in global environmental politics is one of almost total silence. The military regime was not an attractive target of criticism for environmental groups because the country was almost entirely self-contained and the regime had little interest in its international reputation.

Myanmar's economic and environmental future could be quite different, however. Consider, for example, Myanmar's energy scenario. According to a country report by the International Growth Centre at the London School of Economics, when it comes to the power sector, "Myanmar is now at the stage Vietnam was a decade or two ago, when it struggled to meet demand and avoid blackouts." Electricity consumption per capita is about one-sixteenth of Thailand's and about one-eighth of Vietnam's. Moreover, with rapid economic growth in the years to come and the country's limited natural gas supplies going to Thailand and China under long-term contracts, the country faces particular pressure to invest in coal-fired power capacity.[68] Needless to say, such a strategy would have substantial environmental impacts.

Myanmar's INDC raises doubts about the country's ability to contribute to climate mitigation. The government does not present any predictions about greenhouse gas emissions under business as usual, and all sector targets are only indicative of possible future trends. While Myanmar does propose some important policies, such as halting deforestation to protect the country's abundant carbon sinks, the targets are not precise or exactly quantified.

Myanmar certainly faces great challenges of institutional capacity. In figure 3.1 we saw that the country had made significant progress in regulatory quality and control of corruption between 1996 and 2019, but government effectiveness remained a significant problem. The country's transition from a closed military dictatorship to a young democracy has proven to be a momentous challenge, and one that the government simply has not solved yet. The military coup in 2021 underscores the risk of authoritarian backsliding, and it remains unclear how much a military leadership can do to improve Myanmar's policies on the environment and beyond.

Myanmar also faces a challenge of donor dependence. Since the democratization of the country, the government has faced shortages of institutional capacity, and donors have stepped in to fill the governance gap. Unless the country finds a way to enhance its own capacity to govern, it will remain dependent on donor interest, a volatile and unreliable source of funds and technical assistance for policy implementation. According to Rieffel and Fox, the donor rush to Myanmar could reduce government effectiveness, as "senior government officials spend many hours every day meeting with delegations from donor countries, not just their aid agencies but also their parliaments, corporations, international NGOs, media, etc. This stream of visitors is diverting key officials in Myanmar from crucial work on policy formulation and implementation."[69] In such an environment, a military coup does not help.

These challenges can be seen in Myanmar's efforts to promote rural energy access with off-grid solar power, such as solar home systems. When I visited Myanmar in March 2017, local researchers, businesses, and government officials told me that the government's donor-driven strategy had distributed hundreds of thousands of solar home systems in rural areas for free.[70] Because of this move, rural markets for solar home systems had failed to develop, as investors hesitated to put their money into a sector that could at any time be disrupted by another massive solar-for-free program. Here, the government's limited institutional capacity to formulate robust and consistent off-grid policies resulted in an expensive subsidy program that prevented a more sustainable solution to Myanmar's chronic rural electrification problem.

Although Bangladesh and Myanmar began their growth into emerging economies from very different backgrounds, they are both now on the verge of an economic transformation. Each country faces capacity constraints and political risks related to the stability and robustness of their democratic political institutions. But if these risks fail to stop economic growth, both Bangladesh and Myanmar are bound to be much more significant players in the global environmental politics of the twenty-first century.

EMERGING AFRICA: ETHIOPIA AND TANZANIA

The remaining two emerging economies on my tour are both from East Africa. Both Ethiopia and Tanzania have performed well over the past two decades, and Ethiopia's growth trajectory even resembles in many ways the first two decades of China's economic boom much earlier. Increased power to destroy has been an important consequence of successful economic development in these two East African economies. In what might qualify as good news, institutional capacity has improved in both, and Ethiopia has even adopted a green growth strategy to guide the country's official aspiration to become a middle-income country by 2025.

Ethiopia was, until very recently, known for its abject poverty and vulnerability. Often remembered for the tragic famines of 1973 and 1984, as well as the civil war that continued for decades until 1991, Ethiopia saw a decrease in GDP per capita throughout the 1980s and reached a nadir of U.S. $164 (2010 prices) in 1992—among the lowest in the world. After a decade of slow growth until 2003, the economy began to grow very rapidly, with annual real growth exceeding 10 percent on average between 2004 and 2015.[71] While Ethiopia's manufacturing sector has not grown very fast, both agriculture and services—often fueled by public investment—show spectacular gains over the past decade.

Ethiopia is a vast country with a large and growing population. The country's population is already well above 100 million today. The population density in 2013, however, was only 94.6 people per square kilometer. While this number is double the world average, it is well below India's (430.0) or even China's (144.6). Thus although Ethiopia's population is large in absolute terms, the country is not particularly densely populated.

Intriguingly, Ethiopia's natural resource endowments remain shrouded in uncertainty.[72] Extractive industries are nascent and contributed only 1.5 percent of GDP in fiscal year 2011–2012, but in fact most of Ethiopia's promising geological potential is yet to be explored. While it is unlikely that Ethiopia would ever become a resource-dependent economy, systematic exploration and exploitation of mineral wealth could fuel economic growth and, in particular, export revenue. On the other hand, as table 6.3 shows, Ethiopia has little forest cover left because of extensive deforestation over time.

Politically, Ethiopia remains an authoritarian country. Although the end of the brutal civil war in 1991 brought down Mengistu's Marxist dictatorship, Ethiopia cannot be described as a democratic country. In 2015 the country's Polity IV score remained at −3, closer to the authoritarian than the democratic end of the scale. Although Ethiopia has elections and political parties, the political system is not truly competitive, and constraints on executive power are minimal. The winner of the civil war, the

Ethiopian People's Revolutionary Democratic Front, has ruled the country since then.

In the past, Ethiopia's domestic environmental policies were minimal. Given its extreme poverty and continuous civil war since 1974, the country simply was not in a position to formulate a coherent national environmental strategy. The initial cornerstone of the Ethiopian strategy was the Mengistu regime's rural development policy, "an ambitious program of agrarian reform intended to transform rural social economic and political institutions and spur agricultural development, increase food security and address environmental problems, including deforestation and soil erosion." Formulated against the backdrop of the disastrous 1974 famine, "the net effect of the [regime's] actions, was to lessen farmer's incentives for good natural resource management by decreasing both the security of land tenure and the profitability of agriculture. At the same time it appears to have reduced, instead of increased, food security in many areas."[73]

In global environmental politics, Ethiopia has historically also had a profile in negotiations on adaptation and resilience to climate change and erosion. Consider, for example, Ethiopia's infamous 1985–1988 "reclamation program"—the last period of Mengistu's rural development policy. After the Mengistu regime's collectivist rural policies had failed to prevent—and may have even contributed to—the disastrous 1984 famine, donors and NGOs joined forces with the regime to stop environmental degradation in the countryside. The program was based on a narrative that saw Ethiopia in a Malthusian trap of dwindling natural resources under extreme population pressure. According to Hoben, the dominant narrative used to run as follows:

> Long ago when there were fewer people in Ethiopia, indigenous farming systems and technology enabled them to make a living without seriously depleting their natural resources. Over the present century human and animal populations have grown. Indigenous farming systems have been unable to keep up. Population has exceeded carrying capacity, causing ever-increasing and perhaps irreversible environmental damage. Only a massive investment in environmental reclamation can reverse this process. People are unable to make this investment without outside assistance because they do not know how and because they are too poor to forego present for future income or to provide for their children.[74]

In this telling, Ethiopia's environmental degradation would be a simple and direct consequence of population growth, and only aggressive intervention by the socialist state would solve the problem. The program fit the preconceived notions of donors and civil society about the causes of environmental degradation, while the top-down approach focusing on resource mobilization coincided with the Marxist regime's ideology. The result, on the other hand, was needless human suffering without environmental improvements.

All this is now in the past. Among the four countries in this second batch, Ethiopia shows perhaps the clearest signs of a momentous economic transformation. Although it must be acknowledged that Ethiopia's economic growth is partly related to the country's low baseline, a decade of annual growth rates in excess of 10 percent in real terms remains an exceptional achievement, rarely seen outside the East Asian growth miracles. Given this economic boom, the Ethiopian government has every reason to be confident about the country achieving the coveted status of a middle-income economy within only a few years, by 2025, according to the country's official target. The economy has continued to grow across all sectors, and although it remains primarily agrarian, the early signs of industrialization are already there. Although agricultural productivity has grown very fast, industrial growth has been even faster: industrial value added was 13.9 percent of total GDP in 2004, then decreased to 10.2 percent by 2010 during the country's agricultural boom, but has since then reached a new peak of 16.3 percent in 2015. From primary education to life expectancy, all other development indicators also point to a bright future.

In the future, these changes create great potential for environmental stress. The green growth strategy of Ethiopia in 2011 notes that "if Ethiopia were to pursue a conventional economic development path to achieve its ambition of reaching middle-income status by 2025, GHG emissions would more than double from 150 Mt [carbon dioxide equivalent] today to 400 Mt in 2030. Ethiopia's development could result in unsustainable use of natural resources, in being locked into outdated technologies, and in losing an ever-increasing share of GDP to fuel imports. Ethiopia would lose the opportunity of making its development sustainable."[75] In this scenario, the use of fossil fuels and other natural resources would grow rapidly, as Ethiopia would invest in conventional technologies and find itself trapped in a high-carbon economy.

Against this backdrop, Ethiopia's INDC has drawn a lot of praise. Drawing heavily on the country's aforementioned green strategy, the INDC states that "in the long term, Ethiopia intends to achieve its vision of becoming carbon-neutral, with the mid-term goal of attaining middle-income status."[76] The INDC aims to reduce emissions by 64 percent relative to the baseline in 2030.

An interesting feature of Ethiopia's emergence is that the country has in fact seen major gains in institutional capacity. In 1996 the government effectiveness score was –1.28, and among the emerging economies covered in this book, only Myanmar had as weak a score—even Nigeria came ahead at –0.98. In 2019, however, Ethiopia's score had increased to –0.42 while Nigeria's had declined to –1.09. These spectacular gains raised Ethiopia ahead of Bangladesh, Myanmar, Nigeria, and Tanzania. Indeed, Ethiopia's strategy for green growth is itself an interesting example of this improvement, as it seems highly unlikely that the Ethiopia of the past could have developed a national strategy for green growth.

For Ethiopia, the authoritarian political system remains a source of risk. While the system has allowed the effective mobilization of both internal and external resources, pressures to democratize could result in political instability, such as riots or a coup. So while Ethiopia's recent effectiveness as a state partly stems from authoritarian institutions, these same institutions are perhaps the most important source of uncertainty with regard to the country's otherwise bright economic future. If democratization pressures continue to accumulate and the government fails to manage the democratic transition, some of the recent progress could be reversed. In late 2020, for example, Ethiopia saw armed conflict in the Tigray region, a troubling sign of instability. Ethiopia's autocratic leadership has an impressive economic record, but it remains to be seen whether this state of affairs is sustainable in the long run.

To summarize, Ethiopia is a positive example of how emerging economies can combine the pursuit of wealth with environmental sustainability. The country's excellent economic performance has provoked a positive response by the government, with a comprehensive and credible strategy for green growth. The strategy has also been supported by external donors, showing how the international community can have a positive impact on the development strategies of the youngest emerging economies. However, the internal conflict in Tigray remains a major source of political risk for Ethiopia's sustainable development.

Unlike Ethiopia, Tanzania has historically exhibited a pattern of relative political and economic stability. The country gained independence in December 1961, and Julius Nyerere, the iconic leader of African socialism, was elected president the next year. Since then, Tanzania's revolutionary party, Chama Cha Mapinduzi (CCM), has held power and, in a continent plagued by widespread civil conflict, avoided the outbreak of political violence. Tanzania did move into a democratic political system with regular elections in 1995, but the country's Polity IV score remains at −1, closer to the authoritarian than to the democratic end of the spectrum. Formal democratic institutions notwithstanding, Tanzania remains a single-party system that has yet to see a regime change—legislators come and go, but the hegemonic CCM remains firmly in control.

Economically, Tanzania has grown slowly but steadily, perhaps thanks to the absence of civil wars and societal conflict. Similar to much of sub-Saharan Africa, Tanzania reached its economic low point in the early 1990s, with a per capita GDP of U.S. $458 (2010 prices). While this is not an impressive per capita income by any meaningful indicator, it is still almost three times as much as Ethiopia's at the time. Since then, Tanzania's GDP per capita has almost doubled, reaching $842 (2010 prices) in 2015. While this growth trajectory does not shine like Ethiopia's or China's, it is still a respectable achievement. It is also notable that Tanzania appears to have succeeded in industrializing, as the share of industrial value added has grown from 15 to 26 percent over the same time period, while the share of services has remained virtually unchanged, going from 40 to 42 percent.

In Tanzania, national environmental policy has largely focused on the management of forest resources. Tanzania formulated a national environmental framework only in 1997, two years after the first elections in the country:

> The National Environmental Policy, 1997 provides a framework for making fundamental changes that are needed to bring environmental considerations into the mainstream of decision-making in Tanzania. It also

seeks to provide policy guidelines and plans and gives guidance to the determination of priority actions, for monitoring and regular review of policies, plans, and programmes. It further provides for sectoral and cross-sectoral policy analysis thus exploiting synergies among sectors and interested groups.[77]

Unfortunately, this national framework has not been very successful. As Maro notes, the policy "has not had much impact on environmental conservation and management."[78] Although the framework appears comprehensive on paper, implementation has been patchy and slow. For example, it took Tanzania until 2004 to even formulate an Environmental Management Act for the implementation of the framework.

Tanzania has ratified all the standard multilateral environmental agreements and participated in initiatives to reduce deforestation. At the international negotiations themselves, Tanzania's influence has been the most pronounced when the country chaired the Group of 77 in the international climate negotiations. In his book *Survival Emissions*, Mark Mwandosya, who chaired the group on behalf of Tanzania in the climate negotiations leading up to the Kyoto Protocol, notes that Tanzania focused on maintaining the unity of the Group of 77. At the critical Ad Hoc Group for the Berlin Mandate, held in Bonn in March 1997, "Tanzania applied intense pressure and persuasion to get the AOSIS [Alliance of Small Island States] and petroleum-exporting countries to find a middle ground for the sake of the unity of the group."[79] Although Tanzania's contributions to the content of global environmental politics are not substantial, the country has thus played a facilitating role in the internal negotiations of the Group of 77.

Tanzania lacks Ethiopia's star power in economic development, but it has maintained impressive growth rates over relatively long periods of time, with few signs of slowing down. The *Economist*'s Intelligence Unit expects annual economic growth to remain above 5 percent until 2021, throughout the five-year forecast period.[80] In practice, a growing and increasingly wealthy population would materialize into growing demand for energy and natural resources. According to CoalSwarm, an international NGO that keeps track of coal-related developments around the world, Tanzania has over 1,500 MW of coal-fired power capacity planned.[81]

If Tanzania's population continues to grow and economic performance remains solid, growing energy demand will put pressure for more power generation capacity in this young emerging economy.[82] Between 1963 and 2012 the population grew from 11 to 45 million, and at current rates it will exceed 100 million in 2035. Although it seems very unlikely that the population will continue to grow at such a rapid rate, given the experiences of other countries, the very high baseline of historical growth means that it is still likely to continue growing very fast, acting as a large multiplier for the impact of per capita growth on the environment.

Similar to Ethiopia, Tanzania thus faces important policy choices in the future. If it decides to pursue a green growth strategy, perhaps following Ethiopia's lead, it could become an important leader in Africa's increasingly vigorous participation in international environmental politics. On the other hand, if Tanzania adopts a more confrontational strategy, it may face more external pressure to reduce its environmental impact in the future. Tanzania's long history of stability and gradual democratization, which have facilitated environmental policy making, have recently faced headwinds. President John Magafuli, who came to power in November 2015, has aggressively suppressed the political opposition and critical media. If democratic backsliding continues, Tanzania's role in global environmental politics could become more complicated.

Like many other rapidly growing economies, Tanzania is grappling with the question of coal-fired power generation capacity. Based on data from interviews between March and August 2016, Jacob found that Tanzania had over 1,800 MW of coal-fired power generation capacity in development. According to his analysis, Tanzania's policy makers consider coal an important component of a national development strategy that combines economic development, energy access, and energy security. He further notes, however, that political and rent-seeking considerations play an important role in Tanzania's policy formulation, as "the current and ongoing investments in coal and natural gas mean that the quantity of resource rents likely to accrue to the Tanzanian state, ruling elite factions, state bureaucrats, and their patron-client relations will be massive."[83]

Internationally, Tanzania has not joined Ethiopia in making an unconditional national commitment to a sustainable growth strategy. It does not have a comprehensive strategy for sustainable growth, and its INDC repeatedly emphasizes the necessity of external support for mitigation efforts. A particularly interesting feature of Tanzania's INDC is that the baseline is defined as "national efforts without support for the intended contribution," implying that Tanzania's contributions are fully dependent on external support.[84] Unlike many other countries, Tanzania states that it has no intention to act to bring down emissions relative to the business as usual unless external donors offer generous assistance for climate mitigation measures.

Tanzania's institutional capacity remains limited and depends heavily on external assistance by donors. Similar to Ethiopia, Tanzania's governance indicators have generally improved over time, with government effectiveness increasing from −0.73 to −0.58. While this improvement is not as impressive as Ethiopia's, which has surpassed Tanzania (−0.42 versus −0.58), the direction is nonetheless positive. While Tanzania has almost no past experience with environmental policy, since democratization the country has begun to enact and implement national environmental policies. In addition it has increased participation in international environmental negotiations, especially as far as climate adaptation and deforestation are concerned.

In sum, Tanzania and Ethiopia come from very different backgrounds. While Tanzania has enjoyed a long period of peace and political stability, Ethiopia has gone through decades of civil war and famines. Since the end of the Cold War, however, Ethiopia has caught up with Tanzania through exceptional economic growth in agriculture and services, with major public investments. Although these two East African emerging economies have followed very different pathways to economic development and poverty alleviation, both are now facing difficult policy choices related to energy, natural resources, and even pollution. Ethiopia's high institutional capacity has allowed the country to claim leadership through an official and widely publicized green growth strategy, but its civil conflict raises concerns about the future. Tanzania's key strategic decisions on energy and the environment remain to be seen.

A NEW GENERATION OF EMERGING ECONOMIES IN GLOBAL ENVIRONMENTAL POLITICS

Compared to Indonesia, Nigeria, Vietnam, and the Philippines, the next batch of emerging economies have begun their economic transformations more recently. Bangladesh, Myanmar, Ethiopia, and Tanzania are all showing signs of taking off economically. With no return to an agrarian economy in sight, these transitions are recent, and their full effects will be seen over decades, not years. While these four countries may not shape global environmental politics in the next five to ten years, there is little doubt that they will be pivotal players after another two to three decades.

Historically, none of the four countries had much power to destroy. Only Myanmar had a relatively abundant resource base, but because of the country's isolation from the world economy, the rate of natural resource exploitation remained relatively low. The other three countries were mostly known for their large, growing, and poor populations. While Tanzania has been able to avoid civil war throughout its history as an independent nation, all other countries in the sample have suffered from intense violence. The extreme example is Ethiopia, which saw a civil war continue for over two decades. None of these countries had much power to destroy in the twentieth century, even though Myanmar could have played a role in issues such as deforestation under a different political and economic system.

Over time, the power to destroy among these countries has begun to grow, but it remains at a low level. None of the four countries can yet be called a major source of environmental deterioration with massive power to destroy, but all are showing unmistakable signs of economic dynamism. The combination of rapid economic growth and an expanding population results in exponential aggregate growth rates. As a result, the significance of these countries in global environmental politics will increasingly shift away from that of passive victims of environmental deterioration to that of an emerging economy trying to minimize environmental stress without sacrificing the goal of economic development.

In all four countries, economic growth remains a top national priority— and understandably so, given high levels of extreme poverty. Although the four have different political institutions, in all of them the regime's legitimacy remains dependent on sustaining rapid rates of economic development. These governments face the pressing challenge of reducing poverty and sustaining economic dynamism, but they are also increasingly realizing that they face external pressure to minimize the environmental impact of their growth. Under the assumption that economic growth continues unabated, improvements in institutional capacity are a necessity for better, more sustainable environmental outcomes. As Myanmar and

Ethiopia show, however, political risk remains a major issue for emerging countries, and years of progress could be reversed in a military coup or internal armed conflict.

All four countries show varying degrees of success in public policy formulation across sectors, but the development of institutional capacity has, in general, not kept abreast of economic growth in environmental management. Ethiopia's example shows that even relatively poor countries can formulate national plans to promote green growth, but the other countries under investigation have made much less progress on this front. Vietnam's recent environmental policies also show promising signs, but it remains to be seen whether they can stop the tide of new coal power plants and other investments that would contribute to environmental degradation.

One key issue is that all four countries remain dependent on donors to an extreme degree, and it is not at all clear whether they would be able to devise effective strategies and policies to protect the environment without sustained external assistance. Even Ethiopia's low-carbon development strategy has benefited heavily from external donor support, with the UNDP and the Global Green Growth Institute playing major supporting roles. The hope is that economic growth creates the resources needed for autonomous capacity for environmental policy, so that the role of external support can decrease over time without compromising progress in policy formulation.

Fortunately, improving institutional capacity is easier at the early stages of an economic transformation. It is not yet too late to avoid negative policy traps and bad equilibria in these countries, provided indigenous institutional capacity can improve. All this, of course, depends on avoiding a return to the bad old days of civil war (Ethiopia) and autarkic military rule (Myanmar).

THE FUTURE OF EMERGING ECONOMIES IN GLOBAL ENVIRONMENTAL POLITICS

Across these nine diverse economies, we see consistent evidence of the combination of rapid economic and population growth leaving governments with a potent weapon: the power to destroy the global environment.

Unfortunately, this power to destroy is a double-edged sword, as low levels of institutional capacity all but force governments to contribute to global environmental destruction—willingly or unwillingly. Countries with natural resource endowments have contributed to global environmental destruction for decades, regardless of whether their economic growth accelerated in the twentieth century (e.g., Brazil) or in the twenty-first century (e.g., Indonesia). As a result, they have also played important roles in global environmental politics, though mostly focused on natural resources. Countries that have benefited from economic growth have recently begun to shape global environmental politics.

A particularly important implication of these trajectories is the appearance of new players in global environmental politics. In the twentieth century only Nigeria, Indonesia, and Brazil among the nine countries could be considered major players with power to destroy, and even their influence was limited to a narrow of range issues specifically related to their abundant forestry and fossil fuel endowments. Since then, however, all nine have become increasingly important for global environmental politics, and to the extent negotiators ignore them, they do so at their own peril. All nine are on track to exert a considerable influence on the global environment within a decade or two.

To be sure, this rapid economic growth is not set in stone. Ethiopia and Myanmar show that economic growth is precarious and political backsliding remains a possibility. Across all nine economies, the COVID-19 pandemic has wrought havoc, with Brazil and Myanmar being among the worst hit countries anywhere in the world. Emerging economies as a group will likely continue to grow and thrive, but some of them may lose momentum in the short and medium run. None of this negates the transformation of global environmental politics, except in a worst case scenario with persistent slow growth in emerging economies across the world.

Like India, these nine countries are still handicapped by their limited institutional capacity. Even Vietnam, which has rapidly achieved impressive heights in many sectors of social and economic policy, such as rural electrification, suffers from severe institutional problems in environmental governance, and most of the other countries are plagued by such problems to a much greater extent. Without significant improvements in institutional capacity, all nine will struggle with their ability to implement their environmental plans, notably NDCs under the Paris Agreement of

2015. These limitations in institutional capacity are an ominous sign for the future: if emerging countries can grow rapidly without corresponding developments in institutional capacity, how can their governments and the rest of the international community protect the planet and human civilization from grave environmental threats? The conclusion of this book explores possible solutions to this problem.

CONCLUSION

Bringing It All Together

The central argument of this book is not complicated: robust economic growth in emerging economies has changed the basic logic of global environmental politics. The number of relevant players has increased significantly, as the structural power—in particular, the power to destroy—of emerging economies has grown thanks to energy and resource consumption. This surge of structural power has come, however, without rapid growth in pro-environmental preferences among the governments of emerging economies. Similarly, accumulation of institutional capacity for national environmental policy and the implementation of treaty commitments have been slow.

This constellation of changes has complicated environmental negotiations. In the twentieth century, industrialized countries were able to address most environmental concerns because the rest of the world had little power to destroy. But when it came to natural resources controlled by developing countries, such as rainforests, progress was minimal. In the twenty-first century, developing countries' power to destroy has greatly increased and is no longer limited to the control of natural resources.

These changes force us to reconsider the orientation of global environmental politics in a new century. The negotiation of environmental accords is a difficult challenge when the number of relevant players is high and many of them have the power to destroy without strong, pro-environmental preferences or institutional capacity to act. Such complex situations used to be limited to natural resource management but now the run the gamut of global environmental politics. When the number of relevant players with power to destroy is high and preferences are heterogeneous, the conventional approach based on multilateral treaties with top-down commitments is unlikely to work. This approach requires that negotiators can agree on commitments and then collectively enforce them, but these are tall orders in a world of emerging economies. Fundamental distributional conflicts and the difficulty of limiting environmental deterioration during rapid economic growth raise high barriers to mutually agreeable deals, and if negotiators do achieve such deals, enforcing them will be difficult.

The problem is further compounded by the lack of domestic institutional capacity for environmental policy. A key dimension of twentieth-century global environmental politics was the relatively high degree of institutional capacity across the key players—in most instances, industrialized countries. In early twenty-first-century global environmental politics, such a degree of institutional capacity is no longer present, as many emerging economies have achieved impressive growth rates without the kinds of Weberian bureaucracies that industrialized countries have taken for granted for a century. While China's rise has been accompanied by growing institutional capabilities in environmental and energy policy, future emerging economies are expected to be more like India and less like China. Their economies continue to grow, and the lack of improvement in institutional capacity means that efforts to mitigate the environmental harm caused by economic expansion will often fail.

In this concluding chapter, I summarize the key claims made in this book. I recap my argument concerning the drivers of global environmental cooperation and remind the reader of the empirical evidence for this argument. A discussion of the implications of the argument for the academic study of global environmental politics follows. I claim that the rise of emerging economies calls for a reorientation of the field toward environmental policy making in large developing countries with limited institutional capacity. While recent scholarship has spilled much ink on international environmental institutions and nonstate alternatives to national policy, this collection of theory and evidence sheds little light on the most important environmental challenges of this century—how to mitigate the environmental impacts of rapid economic growth in emerging economies with limited institutional capacity. Reaching out to scholars of international relations, I also call for more research on the role of external support and international linkages in solving this vexing problem.

Global environmental politics was born out of a collective realization that our lives on this blue planet are supported by complex ecological systems threatened by economic activity, often hundreds or thousands of miles away. Diverse human societies everywhere survive, and often thrive, by using nature's resources for meeting their basic needs—and more.

Billions around the world aspire for modern living standards, and never have they been as close to reaching this goal as they are today. Humanity's grand challenge for this century is to devise a new global environmental politics, one that enables all human beings to lead good lives and to pursue happiness—without preventing other humans, future generations, and all living beings from doing same.

SUMMARY

In my stylized model of global environmental politics, four key variables shape the extent and nature of international environmental cooperation. With a focus on national governments as the key actors in global environmental politics, the model emphasizes the number of pivotal players with structural power, the distribution of this power across them, the degree of environmental preferences among them, and their institutional capacity to enact and implement effective environmental policies. The combination of these four variables characterizes the setting for global environmental cooperation, shaping the likelihood of cooperation, the outcomes it produces, and the distribution of gains from it.

In the twentieth century, the constellation of these key variables was mostly, but not entirely, favorable to global environmental politics. Because industrialized countries were responsible for the majority of environmental deterioration, the basic logic of international environmental cooperation was often one of negotiations and implementation among a relatively small number of pivotal governments. This group already had strong interests in environmental protection and a high level of institutional capacity to comply with treaties, along with other effective national environmental policies. In these simple situations, the likelihood of success in multilateral treaty formation was relatively high. Because the number of players was low and their preferences were relatively homogeneous—at least relative to what was on the horizon in the twenty-first century—finding mutually agreeable solutions based on reciprocal environmental cooperation was not that difficult. Negotiations could focus on the concerns of a small group of governments that had at least some interest in solving the environmental problem at hand. With high institutional capacity across the board, treaty compliance was relatively easy, as the cost and difficulty of implementing treaty commitments were ultimately not that high.

The empirical record supports the hypothesis. The Stockholm summit of 1972 launched an era of global environmental cooperation, with early success stories such as MARPOL and the Montreal Protocol generating enthusiasm about the prospects of global environmental cooperation. In the early 1990s the UNCED in Rio in 1992 released an avalanche of new environmental agreements, inspiring new initiatives for environmental protection across the world. The key exception to this pattern was the destruction of natural resources, such as rainforests and fisheries—issues in which developing countries' control of key endowments complicated cooperation from the very beginning. In these issues, efforts toward global environmental cooperation were frustrated as fundamental North-South conflicts made mutually beneficial bargains all but impossible.

Since then, the world has changed. If China could still be considered a minor player in global environmental politics in the fateful Berlin climate change conference of 1995, it was only because of myopia and a lack of understanding of a momentous shift in the world economy. By the early 2000s it was clear that China's phenomenal economic growth was the most important mover of global environmental deterioration, with the country's coal-fueled industrialization shifting the center of carbon pollution to Asia. Once people began to pay attention to China, they also realized that there were many other emerging economies that were moving into the same direction, if not as fast. India, with its billion people, would be the next emerging economy to change global environmental politics.

Today, the values of key variables in global environmental politics point to great difficulties. The number of relevant players has increased for environmental problems of all stripes, and their environmental preferences are far more diverse than in the twentieth century, with traditional North-South conflicts surfacing everywhere. Even more troubling is that most emerging economies have very low levels of institutional capacity for environmental governance, with the exception of China, a few other East Asian countries, and Latin American countries. In these circumstances, treaty negotiations promise to be difficult because a mutually agreeable treaty requires reconciling a wide range of diverging interests. Even if a treaty is negotiated and enters into force, implementation and compliance pose major challenges to a large number of pivotal countries with power to destroy—and little institutional capacity to prevent themselves from using this power on ecosystems and natural resources.

The record of early twenty-first-century global environmental politics shows how difficult cooperation is under these circumstances. Although the shock of 9/11 did throw sand into the wheels of the multilateral treaty machine, this temporary shock hid much graver threats to global environmental cooperation. Because the shock coincided with China's pollution boom and rapid economic growth across almost all developing economies, it was initially perfectly reasonable to hope that once the shadow of Osama bin Laden's terrorist attacks receded, the world would resume the regular programming of multilateral treaty making. Alas, these expectations proved deeply flawed, as the surge of the North-South conflict froze global environmental cooperation for years.

The few exceptions to this disappointing record originate from cooperation on narrow sectoral issues that can be solved with simple fixes, such as product bans or phase-outs. In the climate regime, we saw in October 2016 some success in the Kigali Amendment to phase out HFCs and, perhaps more controversially, in the ICAO aviation agreement. The Minamata Convention to deal with mercury pollution saw success after difficult rounds of negotiations because China's economic transformation and growing institutional capacity prompted Beijing to accept restrictions on the production and consumption of mercury.

Outside this select set of issues, the recent record is disturbing. In the climate regime, the Paris Agreement of 2015 finally recognized the difficulty of environmental cooperation in a world of emerging economies and allows governments to choose their own climate plans. While the move to the Paris architecture is itself a smart and necessary one, this is only inspiring because of lowered expectations: it would clearly be much better if the world could negotiate legally binding treaties that impose enforceable caps on greenhouse gas emissions. Unfortunately, such treaties are not possible given today's political realities. The same goes for the much less impressive performance of the global biodiversity regime, which has done virtually nothing to stop what Kolbert calls "the sixth wave of extinction."[1]

Most troubling of all, the future may bring even greater challenges, as the Chinese model of an emerging economy loses significance relative to the Indian model. The first decade of the 2000s was China's show, and the country's rapid industrialization caused much global environmental destruction. Over time, however, China's relatively effective bureaucracy began finding solutions to environmental problems. At the same time, as we saw in chapter 5, India's achievements in the field of environmental protection have been much less impressive. To the extent that future emerging economies are more Indian than Chinese in their ability to enact and implement national environmental policies, China's ability to mitigate its pollution boom may be the high road—and thus paint too optimistic a picture for the future. If India, and not China, is what the emerging economies of the future look like, then the environmental cost of economic growth will be high. This low-road scenario would raise the specter of rapid environmental deterioration and possibly result in catastrophic outcomes such as runaway climate change. Without such economic growth, however, global poverty alleviation would slow down, at a great human cost.

China's own efforts outside its boundaries highlight these dangers. While the country has invested in renewable energy and imposed strict regulations on domestic air pollution,[2] it has also financed hundreds of coal-fired power plants around the world.[3] These investments are not subject to the increasingly stringent Chinese environmental standards, so their potential contribution to air pollution, water scarcity, and climate change is substantial. China's overseas finance highlights the dangers of economic power without accompanying environmental safeguards.

Perhaps the greatest opportunity in global environmental politics is the rapid growth of clean technology. As wind power, solar power, battery technology, and electric vehicles continue to grow, emerging economies will face fewer stark trade-offs between the environment and economic development. Even in this scenario, institutional capacity will remain important. Managing intermittent renewables, deploying batteries on a massive scale, and developing a charging infrastructure for electric mobility will all require government policy, regulation, and implementation. Investments in institutional capacity will help emerging economies overcome barriers to clean technology.

RESEARCH ON GLOBAL ENVIRONMENTAL POLITICS: WHAT NEXT?

For scholars of global environmental politics, the pressing challenges of the twenty-first century call for a reorientation of both theoretical and empirical research. In the early part of the century, arguably the most salient trend in research on global environmental politics was a move away from state-centric analytical models and toward an increased recognition of the importance of nonstate actors.[4] Although these processes have proven important and the paralysis of state action in the first decade of the twentieth century remains a reminder of the fragility of state-centric approaches, the reality is that the future of global environmental politics depends, first and foremost, on the national policies of emerging economies. In this situation, scholarship on global environmental politics must reconsider its priorities and focus on the core challenge of understanding the roles, challenges, and opportunities of emerging economies in global environmental cooperation.

The priority area that requires scholars' dedicated, sustained attention is the political economy of domestic energy and environmental policy in emerging economies. As we have seen, understanding the policy choices and negotiation positions of emerging economies depends on recognizing the challenges of sustaining rapid economic growth under limited institutional capacity. While there is an older literature on environmental policy in the developing world,[5] with few exceptions this body of work does not address the momentous shift from the twentieth-century Third World to the twenty-first-century international political economy of emerging economies.[6] Much existing work on national environmental policy in developing countries focuses on the vulnerability and weakness of the Third World, while the core challenge of the twenty-first century is the peculiar combination of rapid economic growth without institutional capacity.

In other words, scholars of global environmental politics should invest much more time and effort in developing rigorous accounts of policy making under these conditions. To be useful for meeting today's challenges, future studies of environmental policy formulation at both the national and international levels should begin with assumptions that reflect the realities of policy formulation under limited state capacity and then introduce considerations such as negative externalities, interest groups, and the logic of international collective action.

Another priority area is understanding, and eventually removing, obstacles to improving institutional capacity. A common thread running through this volume is the importance of institutional capacity, but the literature on institutional capacity in environmental policy remains thin. While institutional development is now a staple of institutional development economics and a vibrant debate exists on how best to create institutional capabilities in challenging environments,[7] the literature on developing countries' institutional capacity in environmental and energy policy remains small.[8] This limited attention is unfortunate, as improvements in institutional capacity should be guided by systematic political economy theory subjected to difficult empirical tests. Developing the models and collecting high-quality data for empirical tests takes time, and time is the scarcest resource in global environmental protection today, given the disastrous consequences of failing to anticipate the environmental impact of rapid economic growth in emerging economies.

Scholars also need to look beyond formal environmental policy. As we have seen, policies that do not formally qualify as environmental often affect the environment to a large extent. Especially in the absence of systematic environmental governance structures, nonenvironmental policies can have major impacts. We saw examples in India, where free electricity to farmers has created a crisis of groundwater depletion; in China, where investment subsidies have contributed to the massive expansion of coal-fired power generation capacity; and in Brazil, where policies to populate the Amazon have contributed to deforestation. The returns for understanding the environmental effects of nonenvironmental policy in emerging economies are potentially large. Policies such as fuel subsidies, power sector reforms, natural resource management schemes, and agricultural programs have potentially huge environmental impacts. They are also policies that emerging economies must formulate to sustain their growth rates.

The final priority area that I want to emphasize concerns the role of international forces and global cooperation in supporting the sustainable development of emerging economies. Although the prospects for dealing with local brown environmental issues are brighter than those of solving global green problems, it is in the direct self-interest of the international community to contribute to national efforts to protect the environment in emerging economies. With national capacity building a key requirement for future success, now is the time to invest in research on how to build institutions and formulate policies for sustainable development. Many of today's emerging economies are at the stage where carefully crafted policies can prevent vicious cycles, such as dysfunctional environmental regulations or consumer subsidies that contribute little to poverty alleviation but encourage wasteful consumption of natural resources. This is a tremendous opportunity for social scientists looking for work that can make a positive difference in the world.

The primary insight from my broad overview is the importance of focusing on the policy priorities of governments in emerging economies. The balance of power in the world is shifting, with emerging economies now, and increasingly, holding most of the trump cards. International cooperation can best support environmental protection efforts by identifying national policy priorities and offering financial and technical assistance to address them. Efforts to impose an external agenda with conditionalities are much less likely to work now that emerging economies, which for decades have expressed concern about colonial legacies and exploitation, are such powerful players in world politics. Scholarship on international environmental cooperation should recognize this shift and focus on identifying and developing opportunities for cooperation under the new realities.

BETTER STRATEGIES FOR PROTECTING THE PLANET

The cause of today's rapid global environmental deterioration is much more fundamental than the prevailing logic of capitalism, the political power of business interests, or the resource curse. We see an outburst of global environmental problems because billions of people around the world are seeking better, more convenient, and less fragile lives. Protecting the planet from rapid and extensive environmental degradation will thus be human civilization's greatest and most important challenge in the twenty-first century. Not only is the moral case for ending poverty clear, but there is nothing the international community can do to stop the economic boom of emerging economies. The solutions must lie with mitigating the effects of economic expansion.

The bad news is that the challenge of dealing with the rapid economic expansion of emerging economies is massive. The time of universal, top-down environmental regimes is over. In a world with a high number of pivotal countries holding diverging preferences and often only limited institutional capacity, the whole notion of global environmental politics as an exercise in multilateral treaty making is an anathema. There is a clear need for a reorientation of not only research on global environmental politics but, more tangibly and significantly, the practice of international environmental cooperation. Contemporary and future environmental treaties only work if they are simultaneously attractive to emerging economies and can be implemented with limited institutional capacity. These concerns highlight the importance of increasingly strong emphases on dealing with brown environmental issues, resilient adaptation under environmental stress, and forward-looking efforts to build institutional capacity.

However, a realistic understanding of the priorities and interests of emerging economies need not be all gloom and doom. The rapid progress of renewable energy in the power sector is an example of how fast things can change. While the institutional capacity constraints of emerging economies underscore the inherent limitations of national policy, there are encouraging technological trends that can help the world avoid replicating the coal-fired environmental disaster that China's economic success caused.

Despite the limitations of institutional capacity—or perhaps because of it—it would be foolish to ignore the policy challenges that emerging economies face. As many are still at the early stages of their energy development and can still steer the ship, governments have an opportunity to avoid locking-in of polluting or wasteful development trajectories through bad decisions. Good decisions, however, require an understanding of the realities of policy formulation in emerging economies. The paragraphs that follow are dedicated to this understanding.

In emerging economies that grapple with the deep governance challenges accompanying rapid economic growth, it would be naive to expect governments to pass policies that sacrifice economic growth for environmental policies. The best hope for effective environmental protection in emerging economies is therefore a clear focus on domestic brown environmental issues that threaten the economy, society, public health, and the quality of life. Whenever domestic and international advocates of environmental protection can demonstrate the high human, economic, and social cost of environmental deterioration locally and in the short-to-medium run, the chances of success in the political process are that much higher.

The issues that generate enthusiasm in emerging economies are likely to be quite different from those that animated environmentalist mobilization in the Western world in the 1960s and the 1970s. Examples include rural electrification, access to drinking water, and agricultural extension. The use of renewable energy to provide power to remote rural communities, for example, is a cause behind which governments of emerging economies can rally. Similarly, measures to deal with the depletion and pollution of water resources are a political winner. Measures to make agriculture more sustainable and to enhance food security are also of great interest. In this sense, the frame of sustainable development—economic growth that respects natural boundaries and avoids ecological breakdown—is more important than ever.

In the case of climate change, the recent turn toward an increased focus on climate adaptation is promising in this regard. Many emerging economies, such as the South Asian giants of Pakistan, India, and Bangladesh, are very vulnerable to climate disruption because of water scarcity, their dependence on the monsoon, and already high summer temperatures. For such countries, climate agreements that promise tangible support for adaptation in the form of climate finance, technical assistance, and institutional support are more attractive than those that focus only on mitigation, as adaptation promises concrete gains in the short run given today's prevalent weather anomalies. Linkages to energy security could further increase the appeal of inter alia renewable energy and energy conservation policy.

A simple way to encourage emerging economies to cooperate is to ensure that global environmental agreements offer solutions to brown environmental issues. Although emerging economies have fared well over the past decades, all remain home to huge numbers of people living in dire poverty. The more that global environmental cooperation can contribute to the solution of problems of poor water and air quality, the more likely it is that emerging economies see value in participating and implementing their treaty obligations. When negotiators systematically include in global environmental agreements brown environmental issues ranging from air and water pollution to community resilience in the face of climate change, they lay the foundation for securing the interest and political support of emerging economies. This insight was originally recognized in the formulation of sustainable development by the United Nations in 1987, and recent developments have made it more important than ever.

As an example, consider again the fundamental challenge of dealing with climate change. Although it is scientifically and technically possible to consider an approach that emphasizes climate mitigation, a politically more palatable approach would ensure that climate mitigation activities are geared toward solving concrete brown problems on the ground, such as the hazardous levels of air pollution in India's capital or the damage that coal power plants do to mangrove forests in Bangladesh. Instead of seeing adaptation finance as a distraction from the main challenge of mitigation, adaptation should be considered as an important strategy for securing the support of emerging economies. Such agreements would further offer vulnerable countries support with climate adaptation, provided they make progress toward meeting their climate mitigation commitments. They would harness renewable energy to help vast rural populations in South Asia and sub-Saharan Africa gain access to domestic electricity.

Against this backdrop, industrialized countries' failure to honor their promise of U.S. $100 billion in climate finance by 2020 is deeply troubling. Emerging economies hold the power to destroy but need support in adapting to a rapidly changing, increasingly hostile climate. If industrialized countries do not provide the support they promised more than a decade ago, why should emerging economies increase their ambition? Industrialized countries' refusal to finance climate mitigation and adaptation in emerging countries is shortsighted, as it greatly complicates negotiations over global climate mitigation.

From a global environmental perspective, the main policy challenge is to link the solution of brown environmental problems to progress toward addressing green issues. If global environmental negotiators give up on halting environmental deterioration, then the attention to brown issues displaces, or crowds out, attention to green issues—hardly a desirable outcome in the long run. But if negotiators manage to negotiate agreements that address green issues by solving brown issues, then meaningful cooperation is possible in a world of emerging economies. The strategy of introducing brown environmental issues and human development concerns into global environmental politics should, in the language of negotiation theory, be seen as a "synergistic linkage."[9]

The point is not to replace green issues with brown ones, but to give brown issues a fair consideration to build trust among emerging economies and secure their commitment to mutually beneficial cooperation. For emerging economies, brown issues remain a tangible threat to human development, and it is perfectly understandable that the enthusiasm for solving them is greater than the interest in addressing green concerns at the global level. In an earlier stage of development, industrialized countries made the same choice, and it was only later that global concerns found their way, in fits and starts, onto the political agenda.

An encouraging, if preliminary, example of a successful framing of brown and green environmental issues is the United Nations Sustainable Development Goals. Of the seventeen broad goals set by the global community, some, such as goal 13 on climate change, are directly related to solving green environmental issues. Others are general development goals, such as goal 1 on poverty and goal 2 on hunger. But the most intriguing category concerns brown environmental issues. For example, goal 7 is to "ensure access to affordable, reliable, sustainable and modern energy for all."[10] This goal is an example of how a central development issue—energy poverty—can be linked to environmental quality by highlighting the role of renewable energy and energy efficiency in allowing all countries to provide their populations with access to modern energy.

The framing is powerful because it offers concrete developmental gains for emerging economies through sustainable energy policy. By linking energy access and renewable energy, goal 7 shows how emerging economies as well as least developed countries can expect direct gains—access to modern energy for their populations—from investment in clean sources of energy. Ideally, this linkage allays concerns about the green energy agenda possibly crowding out energy poverty as an issue. If industrialized nations can convince the governments of emerging economies that energy access is equally important to the deployment of clean energy, then the economic dynamism of renewables offers a win-win opportunity for both sides. But if industrialized nations only pay lip service to the energy access agenda, their strategy will likely backfire as emerging economies lose interest in it.

Besides the green-brown linkage, negotiators can make global environmental cooperation more effective by identifying narrow sectoral approaches that circumvent the thorny North-South politics of difficult structural changes. My model of global environmental politics has shown how difficult collective commitments on broad and deep economic changes are in a world of a large number of emerging economies with limited institutional capacity, but these barriers are much lower when negotiations are narrowly focused on specific sectors. When the focus of negotiations is narrow, effective solutions to the problems are often relatively simple policies that do not require massive changes in the growth trajectories of emerging economies. This is advantageous both because negotiating narrow deals on specific issues is easier and less costly than negotiating sweeping deals and because simple regulatory solutions require much less institutional capacity than comprehensive policy solutions. Although sectoral approaches are no panacea and will never be, they can provide relief and buy time to address the more central problems of energy use and resource consumption.

As we have repeatedly seen in the previous chapters, by far the most difficult North-South negotiations have concerned energy and resource use. Examples such as the ICAO agreement on global aviation emissions or the Kigali Amendment on an HFC phase-out show that when these issues are absent, the complications that emerging economies create can be avoided in standard bargaining. While climate negotiators have time and again failed to agree on burden sharing and thus reverted to voluntary pledges under the Paris Agreement, sectoral approaches have proven effective in mitigating climate change at the margins.

The ICAO agreement on global aviation does require an effective and credible mechanism for offsetting aviation emissions, but other than that it does not require specific policies by emerging economies or even restrict their ability to expand their aviation sectors in the future. The Kigali Amendment simply bans certain products. Although the ban raises the cost of services such as air-conditioning, the benefits in terms of avoided climate disruption are large, while various graduation clauses and exemptions significantly reduce the cost to the pivotal emerging economies, especially China and India. This sectoral approach has limited potential for solving the bigger issue of fossil fuels, but it shows that identifying and exploiting particular opportunities can bring the world closer to a sustainable state of affairs. As low-carbon technology continues to improve, cooperation opportunities in specific sectors and technologies offer a promising way forward.

Another essential improvement in policy formulation is the timely implementation of capacity-building programs. One of the great mistakes of the international community in the 1990s was the failure to see how pivotal China would be as soon as the early 2000s. India is now on the brink of becoming such a pivotal player, and there are billions of people living in other large, emerging economies, as we saw in chapter 6. Given that both India and other emerging economies lack the kind of institutional capacity that prevented an environmental disaster in China, the need for enhanced capacity-building efforts is urgent.

Capacity building is often criticized as a vague buzzword in development jargon—a concept without much meaning or relevance. While there is no denying that the term has been abused, the reality is that few things in sustainable development are as important as institutional capacity for domestic environmental policy. In the absence of institutional capacity, ambitious treaty commitments and grandiose plans for national policy mean little. As I have reviewed the environmental policies of different emerging economies, time and again I have seen that the lack of institutional capacity has raised fundamental barriers to more effective policies. Unless institutional capacity improves rapidly enough over time, the future of the global environment could be grim, as the turnaround in environmental policy that essentially saved China may fail to be realized elsewhere.

Fortunately, there are concrete solutions to the problem of capacity building. Governing the environment, energy, and natural resources requires a set of basic institutional capabilities that are very similar across brown and green issues, so it is politically expedient to build institutional capacity with decisive action to deal with emerging economies' brown issues as a first line of attack. What is more, as long as the international community understands the importance of capacity building, securing external support for dealing with brown issues should be much easier than one might think.

In particular, ignoring countries on the verge of sustained economic growth is dangerous. In the case of climate change, the myopic obsession with transatlantic disputes in the mid-1990s resulted in a variant of the generally laudatory principle of common but differentiated responsibilities that excused *all* emerging economies from any climate action. Given that China grew into the world's largest emitter—and by a wide margin—over the next two decades, this myopic formulation of ground rules for climate negotiations caused great confusion and led to years of delay in meaningful, substantive discussions about the roles and responsibilities of China, India, and other emerging economies. As we have seen, a large number of populous countries in South Asia, Southeast Asia, and sub-Saharan Africa have sustained impressive growth rates for years. Ignoring these countries now would be a mistake, as their power to destroy is likely to grow and will play a decisive role in global environmental politics in the medium run. In chapter 6 we saw nine examples of economic dynamism—and the power to destroy just around the corner. Although the world economy was hit by a pandemic that contributed to a global economic recession in early 2020, the long-run outlook for emerging countries remains unchanged.

In practice, governments can prepare for a new batch of pivotal emerging economies in several different ways. One of them is to commission international organizations and research institutes to conduct scenario analyses of the future power to destroy in countries that are currently too small to count but hold potential because of their large populations and growth prospects. Such scenario analyses can help negotiators assess possible sources of future environmental deterioration and begin engaging with the relevant countries before it is too late. Assessing the future emission pathways of different countries under varying policy scenarios is certainly not easy, but early analytical work can highlight gaps in and opportunities for international cooperation on low-carbon development in the emerging economies of the future.

A good example of such an assessment is Ethiopia's green growth strategy until the year 2025.[11] Formulated in 2011, the strategy notes that

"Ethiopia aims to achieve middle-income status by 2025 while developing a green economy" and infers that "if Ethiopia were to pursue a conventional economic development path to achieve its ambitious targets, the resulting negative environmental impacts would follow the patterns observed all around the globe." Based on analytical work done by government officials, the plan reviews the business-as-usual trajectories of different sectors of the economy, from the power sector to industry, transport, and livestock. The strategy then lays out a series of policies that would allow Ethiopia to reduce the environmental impact of the country's rapid economic growth. Since the launch of the original strategy, Ethiopia's systematic approach has drawn wide international attention and enabled the country to collaborate on implementation of the strategy with organizations such as the United Nations Development Organization and the Seoul-based Global Green Growth Institute.[12]

Where does this all leave us? Until very recently, almost all modern economic activity was concentrated in a handful of industrialized countries, and our assumptions about the nature of global environmental politics reflected this state of affairs. We saw some success in negotiations on pollution and many failures in negotiations on natural resources controlled by developing countries. All this has begun to change, as billions in the global South have finally found a way out of abject poverty. To achieve success in this situation, industrialized countries must support emerging economies technically, financially, and politically. Although emerging economies have had success in mitigating poverty, they still have a long way to go and will understandably prioritize economic development. That is only fair, given that both per capita resource use and pollution are much higher in the wealthy countries, where many people enjoy wealth that is unimaginable to most of the world's population.

Against this backdrop, the rise of right-wing populism and nationalism, exemplified by U.S. president Donald J. Trump, is troubling. If domestic politics in industrialized countries favors leaders who despise global cooperation and multilateralism, it is hard to see emerging economies fully engaging in global environmental negotiations. Industrialized countries must lead the way and, after all these decades, honor their promises to support poorer countries.

At the end of the day, global environmental politics in the twenty-first century is about finding ways for all humans—seven billion of us, and counting—to survive and thrive on a crowded planet. To prevent serious climate disruption and irreversible environmental degradation, both industrialized countries and emerging economies have a great deal of work to do. Industrialized countries must recognize their historical responsibility for environmental damage and acknowledge the developmental needs of emerging economies as fundamentally legitimate. Emerging economies must cultivate their environmental awareness and invest in institutional capacity to deal with their worsening environmental problems. The transformation of global environmental politics is both the greatest challenge and the greatest opportunity of our time.

NOTES

INTRODUCTION

1. "China's Thing About Numbers," *Economist*, January 2, 2010, http://www.economist .com/node/15179774.
2. See official U.S. White House announcement, September 25, 2015, https://tinyurl.com /9pzv4wtr.
3. See "China's Renewable Power Capacity Up 9.5% Year-on-Year in June," Reuters, July 25, 2019, https://tinyurl.com/3ynkwfa2.
4. International Energy Agency 2021, executive summary.
5. See World Bank, Data, http://data.worldbank.org/region/sub-saharan-africa, accessed May 9, 2021.
6. Vijay et al. 2016.
7. For example, see Greenpeace, "Palm Oil: Who's Still Trashing Forests?," March 3, 2016, https://www.greenpeace.org/usa/palm-oil-whos-still-trashing-forests/.
8. Kusumaningtyas and van Gelder 2017.
9. These numbers for 2010 are from an infographic available at Mercury Science and Policy at MIT, http://mercurypolicy.scripts.mit.edu/blog/?p=72, accessed June 7, 2021.
10. See Max Roser, "Economic Growth," Our World in Data, https://ourworldindata.org /gdp-growth-over-the-last-centuries/, accessed August 7, 2021. The data are in 1990 International Geary-Khamis dollars.
11. Shah et al. 2015.
12. Downie 1999.
13. See Kate Larsen et al., "China's Greenhouse Gase Emissions Exceeded the Developed World for the First Time in 2019," Rhodium Group, May 6, 2021, https://rhg.com /research/chinas-emissions-surpass-developed-countries/.
14. See Miller 1995.

15. In some cases, predominantly local problems become global in international negotiations. For example, some governments may express concern about endangered species in other countries (Sell 1996), even though the loss of these species would have no direct impact outside those countries. My definition of global environmental problems covers such issues.

16. Sprinz and Vaahtoranta 1994.

17. Tolba and Rummel-Bulska 1998.

18. Putnam 1988; Hughes and Urpelainen 2015; Mildenberger 2015.

19. Marcoux and Urpelainen 2013.

20. Keohane and Victor 2016.

21. Axelrod and Keohane 1985.

22. Barrett 1994b.

23. Axelrod and Keohane 1985, 226.

24. Fearon 1998.

25. Mitchell and Keilbach 2001.

26. Aklin and Mildenberger 2020; Hughes and Urpelainen 2015.

27. Waltz 1979; Axelrod and Keohane 1985.

28. In a related typology, Mitchell (2010, 30–33) classifies environmental problems as those of "degradation" and "overappropriation." The former is close to pollution; the latter, close to resource depletion problems.

29. In the case of mercury emissions, for example, Giang et al. (2015) find that most benefits from mercury emission reductions from China and India would benefit these countries. While mercury does travel across geographies even at the global level, most of the costs of mercury emissions are concentrated in the geographic region of the emission source.

30. Ostrom 1990.

31. E.g., Meadows et al. 1972.

32. E.g., Rockström et al. 2009.

33. Hicks et al. 2008.

34. Founex 1971.

35. Scholarship on environmental justice emphasizes unequal exposure to brown environmental problems, with a focus on industrialized countries (Bullard 1990; Brulle and Pellow 2006).

36. Beckerman 1992.

37. Barrett 2003.

38. Keohane 1984.

39. To apply this framework, one must assume governments are at least somewhat sensitive to environmental costs. In practice, distributive politics at the domestic level complicate this equation, as different interest groups disagree on the importance of environmental protection (Hughes and Urpelainen 2015; Mildenberger 2015).

40. Krasner 1991.

41. Axelrod and Keohane 1985.

42. Mitchell 1994.

43. Rowland 1973; Miller 1995; Najam 2005.

44. See http://www.indiragandhiuniversity.in/indiragandhi.html for the full text of the address (accessed April 16, 2021).

45. The twenty-first century will be very different from the previous one for many reasons. For example, the growing competitiveness of wind and solar power offers an important cause for optimism, as does the rapid decline in the use of coal. Rapid decreases in the cost of cleaner energy sources mean that even without policy, the power sector will decarbonize over time, though the pace of the transformation remains an open question. At the same time, the very notion of rapid population and economic growth in emerging economies puts ecosystems under unprecedented stress. These changing fundamentals set the baseline—business as usual—against which the contribution of global environmental cooperation can be assessed.

46. Pallas and Urpelainen 2012.

47. Green 2014.

48. Hadden 2015.

49. Hoel 1991; Barrett 1994b; Carraro and Siniscalco 1993; Miller 1995; Mitchell and Keilbach 2001; Najam 2005.

50. E.g., Ehrlich and Holdren 1971. In mathematical terms, $I = P * A * T$, where I refers to impact, P to population, A to affluence, and T to technology. This equation is a mechanical representation of environmental impact. It does not consider interdependencies between the components and fails to explicitly consider a wide range of factors, including culture and institutions (Brulle 2010). Yet it remains a useful first step toward assessing intervention points to halt environmental degradation.

51. Downie 1999.

52. This is not to say that poverty cannot lead to environmental destruction. For example, the use of inefficient technology in fuel combustion can contribute to air pollution.

53. Andrews, Pritchett, and Woolcock 2017.

54. E.g., Pritchett, Woolcock, and Andrews 2010; Levy 2014.

55. On the state-centric mode, e.g., Barrett 1994b; Mitchell 1994; Barrett 2003; on nonstate governance, e.g., Cashore 2002; Betsill and Bulkeley 2004; Green 2014; Hadden 2015.

56. E.g., Wolfram, Shelef, and Gertler 2012.

57. Even indoor air pollution mostly stems from the use of firewood or other traditional biomass as a cooking fuel.

58. Hale 2015.

59. Victor 2008.

60. Aklin and Urpelainen 2018.

1. INTERNATIONAL POLITICAL ECONOMY AND GLOBAL ENVIRONMENTAL POLITICS

1. Levin et al. 2012.

2. For excellent overviews of global environmental politics from the perspective of international relations, see O'Neill (2009) and Mitchell (2010). A basic introduction to the issues and processes at hand is found in Chasek, Downie, and Brown (2014).

3. E.g., Ausubel and Victor 1992; Barrett 1994b; Aidt 1998; Barrett 2003; Carraro and Siniscalco 1993; Mitchell and Keilbach 2001; Hovi, Sprinz, and Underdal 2009; Hoel and de Zeeuw 2010; Mitchell 2010.
4. Mitchell 2010, 2.
5. Barrett 1994b.
6. It is a basic premise of international law that countries are free to leave treaties at any time; in general, treaties also do not impose any obligations on nonmembers.
7. Barrett 1994b, 891.
8. Mitchell and Keilbach 2001, 892.
9. McEvoy and Stranlund 2009.
10. Hoel and de Zeeuw 2010; Urpelainen 2014.
11. Dai 2005.
12. Haas 1989.
13. Victor 2011.
14. Clapp and Dauvergne 2011, 2.
15. Grossman and Krueger 1995; Dasgupta et al. 2006.
16. Mani and Wheeler 1998; Porter 1999.
17. DeSombre 1995; Vogel 1995; Urpelainen 2010a; Saikawa 2013.
18. Krasner 1985; Lake 1987; Miller 1995.
19. See Group of 77, "About the Group of 77," United Nations, http://www.g77.org/doc/index.html##establish, accessed August 18, 2021.
20. See Bhagwati (1977) for an edited volume on the North-South conflict over NIEO written at the time of the debate.
21. Krasner 1985.
22. Rowland 1973.
23. Rowland 1973, 47.
24. Najam 2005, 307–8.
25. Miller 1995, 9.
26. Miller 1995.
27. Najam 2005.
28. Roberts and Parks 2007.
29. Newell 2005.
30. Hurrell and Sengupta 2012.
31. Roberts 2011.
32. Hochstetler and Milkoreit 2014.
33. Lukes 1974.
34. Downie 1999; Bayer, Marcoux, and Urpelainen 2014.
35. Ehrlich and Holdren 1971.
36. Here I am careful not to claim that power to destroy is unambiguously a good thing. Sometimes power to destroy originates from uncontrollable environmental destruction that hurts the economy and the people over time. Even then, however, power to destroy is a negotiation asset.
37. Davis and Socolow 2014.

38. Of course, not all power generation capacity is used to the fullest possible extent. In China, for example, the capacity factors of coal-fired power plants have decreased as the pace of construction has exceeded the demand for power. For a detailed discussion, see Lauri Myllyvirta, "China Keeps Building New Coal Plants Despite New Overcapacity Problem," Greenpeace Energydesk, December 7, 2016, https://tinyurl.com/k43cx4ft.

39. Nash 1950.

40. Bayer, Marcoux, and Urpelainen 2014.

41. I thank Fariborz Zelli for suggesting this formulation.

42. Haas 1980.

43. E.g., Allison 1972. The primary importance of bureaucracy in environmental policy is in the difficult challenge of implementing policies, and thus considerations of institutional capacity are central to my argument.

44. Olson 1993; Acemoglu 2003; Bueno de Mesquita et al. 2003; Besley 2005.

45. Urpelainen 2010b.

46. Franzen and Meyer 2010.

47. Environmental grassroots mobilization is widespread in poorer countries (Baviskar 1995; Martinez-Alier 2002; Hochstetler and Keck 2007; Shah 2010). It does not mean that governments of these countries do not have strong progrowth preferences. Indeed, the very reason for social mobilization in favor of environmental protection in emerging countries is typically that a local community perceives a threat to their livelihoods and lifestyle and mobilizes to demand protection because their government allows environmental destruction (Martinez-Alier 2002).

48. Grossman and Krueger 1995; Dasgupta et al. 2002; Stern 2004.

49. Dasgupta et al. 2006.

50. Aklin 2016.

51. Carson 2010, 3.

52. Sprinz and Vaahtoranta 1994.

53. Oye and Maxwell 1994.

54. Najam 2005.

55. Bullard 1990; Newell 2005.

56. Buntaine and Prather 2018.

57. Grindle and Hilderbrand 1995, 445.

58. Grindle and Hilderbrand 1995, 446.

59. For example, in some cases states delegate to nonstate actors and thus increase their capacity to act (Green 2014). In such cases, nonstate actors can augment state capacity, but the state's ability to delegate remains a potential limitation.

60. VanDeveer and Dabelko 2001, 18–19.

61. On the other hand, Mitchell (2010, 60) notes that the lack of capacity can sometimes also be a blessing for the environment, as it prevents governments from implementing projects that would cause a lot of environmental destruction. This perspective is of limited relevance in today's world, however, because governments have accumulated capacity for economic development, such as road construction or commissioning of

power plants; it is the lack of institutional capacity for sustainable development, environmental protection, and resource conservation that is the issue.

62. Hughes and Urpelainen 2015.

63. Scholars of epistemic communities have recognized scientific capabilities as an important factor in global environmental cooperation (Haas 1989; Stokes, Giang, and Selin 2016). These authors rightly point out that adequate scientific knowledge about environmental problems can be a powerful force for change when scientists actively communicate it to policy makers and have access to key decision makers. My argument about institutional capacity contains scientific knowledge and its use to inform policy formulation but is not limited to this aspect. Institutional capacity is a much broader concept that includes information about bureaucratic implementation capabilities, regulatory autonomy, administrative resources, and other aspects of the administrative structure that allow governments to pursue their goals with effective policies.

64. Ikenberry 1986; Hughes and Urpelainen 2015.

65. Ikenberry 1986, 112.

66. Hughes and Urpelainen 2015.

67. Krasner 1985; Killick 1989; Geddes 1994; Cheibub 1998; Sagar 2000; VanDeveer and Dabelko 2001; Andrews, Pritchett, and Woolcock 2017.

68. Herbst 2000.

69. Acemoglu, García-Jimeno, and Robinson 2015.

70. Geddes 1994; Saylor 2014.

71. Andrews, Pritchett, and Woolcock 2017.

72. Ostrom, Janssen, and Anderies 2007.

73. Aklin and Urpelainen 2014; Weidner and Jänicke 2002.

74. Shah 2009.

75. Dasgupta 1977.

76. Narayanamoorthy 2010, 550–51. The six states are Andhra Pradesh, Tamil Nadu, Rajasthan, Punjab, Karnataka, and Haryana. Meanwhile, states such as West Bengal have abundant groundwater resources that farmers for a long time were unable to access because of lack of power for electric pumps (Mukherji 2006).

77. Victor 2009.

78. Rocha, Assunção, and Gandou 2014.

79. Nepstad et al. 2014, 1118.

80. Cisneros, Hargrave, and Kis-Katos 2013.

81. See CITES, https://cites.org/, accessed July 18, 2021.

82. Reeve 2014, 247.

83. See Basel Convention, http://www.basel.int/, accessed July 17, 2021.

84. Marcoux and Urpelainen 2012.

85. Marcoux and Urpelainen 2012.

86. North 1990.

87. Urpelainen 2010a.

88. In a political economy approach to environmental protection, Cao and Ward (2015) note that stable democracies with high levels of implementation capacity have succeeded in controlling air pollution. They argue that democratic political institutions translate into

the provision of environmental public goods, such as clean air, only when levels of implementation capacity are high enough. This mechanical relationship, however, masks a more complex incentive problem in global environmental negotiations: countries with limited implementation capacity may use this handicap as an excuse to do nothing. In this sense, the simple approach in Cao and Ward likely understates the importance of institutional capacity in global environmental politics.

89. E.g., Ciplet, Roberts, and Khan 2015.

90. Hoffmann 2005, 92.

91. As Hoffmann (2005, 105) notes, "the major actors in the South (Brazil, China, and India) [initially] refused to sign the [Montreal Protocol]."

92. Hoffmann 2005, 92. While Hoffmann's focus is on how universal participation became a norm in the negotiations, for understanding the negotiation outcome it is much more significant to note that the number of players actually needed to solve the problem of ozone depletion was small throughout, and the cost of securing the support of China and India low.

93. Barrett's (1997) model of global cooperation under the Montreal Protocol emphasizes universal participation, but he assumes that all countries are relevant to the global outcome. In reality, if the vast majority of countries have little power to destroy, then the environmental outcomes generated by universal participation would be only slightly different from an agreement among the major players.

94. I am setting aside the issue of implementation for now, but it bears remembering that most issue linkages and side payments codified in a treaty are, in the spirit of reciprocity, usually conditional on the potential recipient's abiding by its environmental commitments.

95. Chayes and Chayes 1995.

96. Victor 2008, 1.

97. Note, however, that the ceteris paribus clause is unlikely to hold in any practical conditions. As I move to the empirical applications of the analytical model, I thus consider other fundamental drivers as well, with a particular emphasis on the increasing competitiveness of clean technology, such as modern sources of renewable energy.

98. Trancik et al. 2013.

99. E.g., Gerring 2004.

100. E.g., Christoff 2010; Hurrell and Sengupta 2012.

101. Vihma 2011.

102. International Energy Agency 2015.

2. GLOBAL ENVIRONMENTAL POLITICS IN THE AMERICAN CENTURY

1. Mitchell 2016.

2. The Congo agreement was the General Act of the Conference at Berlin of the Plenipotentiaries of Great Britain, Austria-Hungary, Belgium, Denmark, France, Germany, Italy, the Netherlands, Portugal, Russia, Spain, Sweden and Norway, Turkey, and the

United States Respecting: (1) Freedom of Trade in the Basin of the Congo; (2) the Slave Trade; (3) Neutrality of the Territories in the Basin of the Congo; (4) Navigation of the Congo; (5) Navigation of the Niger; and (6) Rules for Future Occupation on the Coast of the African Continent.

3. Dalton 1994, 36.
4. Carson 2002.
5. See "The History of Earth Day," http://www.earthday.org/about/the-history-of-earth -day/, accessed August 22, 2021.
6. Shabecoff 2003, 121.
7. Dunlap 1991.
8. Sohn 1973, 426.
9. Rowland 1973, 34–35.
10. Sohn 1973, 427.
11. Rowland 1973, 47.
12. Joshi 2016.
13. Najam 2005, 309.
14. Founex 1971.
15. For other achievements of the conference, see Sohn (1973).
16. Ivanova 2007.
17. See Declaration of the United Nations Conference on the Human Environment, Stockholm, June 16, 1972, https://legal.un.org/avl/ha/dunche/dunche.html.
18. Mitchell 1994.
19. Reeve 2014.
20. Levy 1993.
21. See Susskind and Ali (2014, 13) for a useful list of significant multilateral environmental agreements.
22. Skjaerseth 1992, 293, 294.
23. E.g., Litfin 1994; Benedick 1998; DeSombre 2000–2002; Parson 2003; Hoffmann 2005.
24. Solomon et al. 2016, 269.
25. World Commission on Environment and Development 1987.
26. Rio Declaration on Environment and Development, https://legal.un.org/avl/ha/dunche /dunche.html, accessed August 10, 2021.
27. See UNFCCC, Convention Documents, https://unfccc.int/process-and-meetings/the -convention/history-of-the-convention/convention-documents, accessed May 20, 2021.
28. Barrett 2008; Hoffmann 2011; Victor 2011.
29. Gupta 2010.
30. Article II, paragraph (b). The full text of the Berlin Mandate is available at UNFCCC, June 6, 1995, https://unfccc.int/resource/docs/cop1/07a01.pdf.
31. Article I, paragraphs (c) and (d).
32. For the full text of the resolution, see 105th Congress (1997–1998), S.Res.98, https://www .congress.gov/bill/105th-congress/senate-resolution/98/text.
33. McCright and Dunlap 2011.
34. Hovi, Skodvin, and Andresen 2003.

35. Shishlov, Morel, and Bellassen 2016.
36. Streck and Lin 2008.
37. Olson 1965.
38. These data are based on World Bank, World Development Indicators, http://data .worldbank.org/indicator, accessed March 20, 2021.
39. These data are based on the World Development Indicators.
40. Takao 2016, 41.
41. Takao 2016, 41.
42. Schreurs 2002, 251.
43. Schreurs 2002, 253.
44. Young 1999, 207.
45. Ivashchenko, Clapham, and Brownell 2011, 17.
46. Miller 1995; Najam 2005.
47. Krasner 1985.
48. Rowland 1973.
49. Najam 2005, 304.
50. Najam 2005, 312.
51. In the case of hazardous waste, developing countries, egged on by environmental groups such as Greenpeace, sought protection against an environmental hazard created by industrialized countries (Clapp 1994; Marcoux and Urpelainen 2012). While this pattern may initially appear inconsistent with my argument, most developing countries did not at the time produce any hazardous waste at all. They had nothing to lose from insisting on regulations and restrictions on illegal trade in hazardous waste, a practice that harmed their populations. As a result, there was no cost to them of adopting the Greenpeace rhetoric on hazardous waste.
52. Vogel 2003.
53. Bloom 1995.
54. Capstick et al. 2014.
55. Meyer, Frank, Hironaka, Schofer, and Tuma 1997.
56. Because of the efficiency of their economy, advanced industrialized countries captured a larger share of the world's GDP than their share of the world's energy use, resource consumption, or pollution. Even then, advanced industrialized countries remained far ahead of other countries.
57. World Bank, Worldwide Governance Indicators, http://info.worldbank.org/governance /wgi/index.aspx##reports, accessed February 9, 2021.
58. Founex 1971.
59. Aklin and Urpelainen 2014.
60. Selin 2010, 152.
61. Barrett 1997.
62. DeSombre 2000–2002.
63. Humphreys 1996.
64. Barrett 1994a; Bayer and Urpelainen 2013b.
65. Reeve 2014.

66.   Dickson 2002.
67.   Clapp 2001.
68.   Marcoux and Urpelainen 2012.
69.   Najam 2004, 133.
70.   Streck 2001; Clémençon 2006; Bayer, Marcoux, and Urpelainen 2014.
71.   Streck 2001.
72.   Clémençon 2006, 54.
73.   Bayer, Marcoux, and Urpelainen 2014.
74.   Clémençon 2006, 55.
75.   Roberts and Parks 2007.
76.   Conca 2004.
77.   DiMaggio and Powell 1983; Meyer, Boli, Thomas, and Ramirez 1997.
78.   Mitchell 1994, 427–28.
79.   Mitchell 1994, 452.

3. GLOBAL ENVIRONMENTAL POLITICS FOR
A NEW CENTURY

1.   "Obama's Dramatic Climate Meet," *Politico*, December 18, 2009, http://www.politico
     .com/story/2009/12/obamas-dramatic-climate-meet-030801.
2.   "How China and India Sabotaged the UN Climate Summit," *Der Spiegel*, May 5, 2010,
     https://tinyurl.com/22c64t9u.
3.   Jentleson 2007, 181.
4.   Kessie 2013.
5.   Drezner 2014.
6.   Drezner 2014.
7.   Vogel 2003.
8.   Eckersley 2007.
9.   See United Nations, Sustainable Development Goals Knowledge Platform, https://
     sustainabledevelopment.un.org/milestones/wssd, accessed March 21, 2021.
10.   Conca 2004, 122.
11.   See United Nations, Sustainable Development Goals Knowledge Platform.
12.   Ivanova 2013, 9.
13.   Axelrod and Keohane 1985. In October 2016 the International Civil Aviation Organi-
      zation (ICAO) also adopted a Carbon Offsetting and Reduction Scheme for Interna-
      tional Aviation. See ICAO, "Historic Agreement Reached to Mitigate International
      Aviation Emissions," October 6, 2016, https://tinyurl.com/j8ft37ew. The scheme, which
      begins with a voluntary pilot period in 2021, aims for carbon-neutral aviation growth
      beginning in 2020. Member states commit to offsetting any emissions growth relative
      to a year 2020 baseline.
14.   Hurrell 1994, 152.

15. United Nations Environment Programme, https://tinyurl.com/4ps9tn6p, accessed January 27, 2021.

16. See "Kigali: Deal on Cutting HFC Gases Is Second Big Step on Climate in a Year," *Indian Express*, October 16, 2016, https://tinyurl.com/yts9um67.

17. Humphreys 2006, 214.

18. Nepstad et al. 2014. See Forest Carbon Partnership Facility, "What Is REDD+?," https://www.forestcarbonpartnership.org/what-redd, accessed August 29, 2021.

19. Stokes, Giang, and Selin 2016.

20. Susskind and Ali 2014, 13.

21. Conca 2015, 81.

22. To be sure, one potential reason for the slow pace of progress is that many issue areas had a framework convention by the year 2000. I find this explanation dissatisfying as it fails to explain those issue areas that did not have such a framework (e.g., forestry) and the lack of progress in new protocol creation for concrete action.

23. Young 2002b; Hicks et al. 2008.

24. See Lisa Friedman, "Poorer Nations Demand More Aid to Deal with Climate Change," *Scientific American*, November 28, 2012, http://www.scientificamerican.com/article/poorer-nations-demand-more-aid-to-deal-with-climate-change/.

25. See Saleemul Huq, "Adaptation Finance: Climate Change's Forgotten Child," *Climate Change News*, November 15, 2016, http://www.climatechangenews.com/2016/11/15/adaptation-finance-climate-changes-forgotten-child/.

26. Bayer and Urpelainen 2014, 278–79.

27. Prins et al. 2010.

28. Chakravorty, Pelli, and Marchand 2014; Aklin et al. 2016.

29. Dauvergne 2018.

30. See International Monetary Fund, World Economic Outlook Database, October 2015, http://www.imf.org/external/pubs/ft/weo/2015/02/weodata/download.aspx, for IMF economic data.

31. See World Bank, Data, http://data.worldbank.org/indicator/EG.USE.PCAP.KG.OE, for statistics on per capita energy consumption.

32. Data from the U.S. Energy Information Administration, https://www.eia.gov/international/data/world, accessed October 6, 2020.

33. Najam, Huq, and Sokona 2003; Gupta and Falkner 2006; Christoff 2010; Allan and Dauvergne 2013; Downie 2015; Stokes, Giang, and Selin 2016.

34. Carter and Mol 2006, 339.

35. Data from the U.S. Energy Information Administration, https://tinyurl.com/56y2tr8e, accessed October 9, 2020.

36. Najam, Huq, and Sokona 2003; Benecke 2009; Vihma 2011; Michaelowa and Michaelowa 2012; Dubash 2013; Urpelainen and Vihma 2015; Stokes, Giang, and Selin 2016.

37. Miller 1995.

38. See World Bank, Data, http://data.worldbank.org/indicator/NY.GDP.PCAP.KD?locations=VN, accessed June 6, 2021.

39. Shearer et al. 2016, 10.

40. See World Bank, Data, https://tinyurl.com/yk9y9sp3, accessed June 6, 2021.

41. Wolfram, Shelef, and Gertler 2012, 134.

42. Roger and Belliethathan 2016.

43. Najam 2005.

44. Williams 2005.

45. Johnson and Urpelainen 2017.

46. Sinha 2013.

47. Genovese 2014.

48. Genovese 2014, 623.

49. Vihma 2009.

50. Clémençon 2006.

51. For political polarization in the United States along partisan lines, see Layman, Carsey, and Horowitz 2006; Fiorina and Abrams 2008.

52. To be sure, electoral politics in industrialized countries should not be taken for granted. Trump's presidency is but an example of a broader pattern of the rise of a populist anti-globalization, anti-immigration movement in the West. If the electoral success of this movement proves durable, then industrialized democracies' ability to act on global issues such as climate may be severely constrained.

53. China 2012.

54. E.g., Grossman and Krueger 1995; Urpelainen 2010b; Aklin 2016.

55. Mendy 2010.

56. Aklin 2016.

57. E.g., Woo-Cumings 1999.

58. Here, of course, it is important to remember possible bias from improved reporting over time.

59. Ahluwalia 2002; Lin, Cai, and Li 2003.

60. E.g., Yang 2003.

61. A theoretical foundation for understanding the relevant distinction between different growth trajectories can be found in Levy's work on the institutional foundations of economic development (Levy 2014, 33–35). He notes that both "dominant" (e.g., China) and "competitive" (e.g., India) political regimes in the developing world have seen economic growth, but the logics underpinning these growth strategies are different. In a dominant system, "rulers focus on strengthening their bureaucratic capability, without expanding the openness of the political or economic system." In a competitive system, these strategies are not available to rulers, who must continuously expend effort to retain their political support: "The emphasis is on addressing specific capacity and institutional constraints as and when they become binding. Sustaining growth involves continual crisis management, endlessly putting out fires in an environment that to the casual observer seems quite dysfunctional, but nonetheless defies the odds by sustaining continuing dynamism" (Levy 2014, 41).

62. Conca 2015.

63. Falkner, Stephan, and Vogler 2010; Hale 2011; Urpelainen 2013.

64. Victor, House, and Joy 2005.

65. See Hovi, Skodvin, and Andresen 2003.

66. Matthews 1993.

67. Raustiala and Victor 2004; Keohane and Victor 2011.

68. Johnson and Urpelainen 2012.

69. Urpelainen and Van de Graaf 2015.

70. Vihma 2009.

71. Green 2014.

72. A closely related trend is the "compromise of liberal environmentalism" (Bernstein 2012), whereby decision makers insist that environmental protection be compatible with the liberal world order and economic growth. I do not claim that this discourse, which surfaced at the Earth Summit in 1992, was exclusively caused by the rise of emerging economies. The emphasis on economic growth, however, was a necessary condition for any kind of progress in the negotiations, given the growing clout and shifting interests of emerging economies. Over time, this tendency has only grown stronger.

73. Incidentally, these considerations shed light on why the rights-based approach advocated by Conca (2015) has failed in the UN system. As long as emerging economies prioritize sovereignty over human rights, the prospects for a rights-based approach are weak in the future. Although bottom-up approaches, such as ecological and environmental justice movements in major emerging economies, can locally halt environmental degradation, these approaches suffer from the inherent limitation of spillovers. In communities and areas with robust and thriving ecological movements, locals may succeed in mitigating or even preventing environmental harm from infrastructure expansion or resource extraction, but every such success increases the economic pressure to build infrastructure or extract resources in other communities and areas.

4. THE EVOLUTION OF THREE GLOBAL ENVIRONMENTAL REGIMES

1. Krasner 1982, 185.

2. E.g., Selin 2010.

3. Earlier, the Convention on Long-Range Transboundary Air Pollution regulated chemical use in Europe and surrounding countries (Selin 2010). I start with the Basel Convention because it was the first global treaty in the regime.

4. Clapp 1994, 507.

5. "Waste Dumpers Turning to West Africa," *New York Times*, July 17, 1988, http://www .nytimes.com/1988/07/17/world/waste-dumpers-turning-to-west-africa.html.

6. See, for example, "The Burning Truth Behind an E-Waste Dump in Africa," *Smithsonian Magazine*, January 13, 2016, https://tinyurl.com/4yj8t5xn.

7. Clapp 1994, 511.

8. O'Neill 2000, 42–43.

9.   See UNEP, "Text of the Convention," http://www.basel.int/TheConvention/Overview /TextoftheConvention/tabid/1275/Default.aspx, accessed October 30, 2020.

10. Marcoux and Urpelainen 2012, 418

11. Marcoux and Urpelainen 2012.

12. Marcoux and Urpelainen 2012, 420.

13. O'Neill 2000, 41.

14. "Time to Realize the Global E-Waste Crisis," http://archive.ban.org/Library/Features /070700_ewaste_crisis.html, accessed March 22, 2021.

15. Selin 2010, 1–2.

16. See European Environmental Bureau, Chemicals, http://www.eeb.org/index.cfm /activities/industry-health/chemicals/, accessed March 22, 2021.

17. Selin 2010, 88, 94–95.

18. Selin 2010, 95.

19. See UNEP, Rotterdam Convention, Status of Ratifications, http://www.pic.int/Countries /Statusofratifications/tabid/1072/language/en-US/Default.aspx, accessed March 22, 2021.

20. Selin 2010.

21. Selin 2010, 141.

22. Selin 2010, 144.

23. See UNEP, Stockholm Convention, Status of Ratifications, http://chm.pops.int/Coun tries/StatusofRatifications/PartiesandSignatoires/tabid/4500/ Default.aspx, accessed March 22, 2021.

24. Selin 2014, 6.

25. See European Commission, Environment, Chemicals, REACH, http://ec.europa.eu /environment/chemicals/reach/reach_en.htm, accessed October 28, 2020.

26. UNEP, Minamata Convention on Mercury, http://www.mercuryconvention.org /Convention/tabid/3426/Default.aspx, accessed February 10, 2021.

27. Stokes, Giang, and Selin 2016, 6.

28. Selin 2014, 7.

29. See UNEP, "New Convention Calls Time on Mercury Poisoning," May 18, 2017, http:// www.unep.org/newscentre/new-convention-calls-time-mercury-poisoning.

30. These numbers are based on European Chemical Industry, "CEFIC Facts & Fig- ures 2016," https://www.feica.eu/search_results/wtag/statistics.

31. Ovodenko 2016.

32. Marcoux and Urpelainen 2014.

33. Clapp 2003.

34. Selin 2010, 164.

35. Marcoux and Urpelainen 2012.

36. Stokes, Giang, and Selin 2016.

37. Kolbert 2014, 2.

38. Matthews 1993, 4.

39. Matthews 1993, 5.

40. See CITES, "How CITES Works," https://www.cites.org/eng/disc/how.php, accessed November 1, 2020.

41. In 1983 the International Tropical Timber Agreement was negotiated, but it was more focused on trade and resource extraction than environmental protection (Humphreys 1996, 57).

42. Humphreys 2006, 191.

43. Harrop and Pritchard 2011, 475.

44. For an introduction, see Convention on Biodiversity, "Sustaining Life on Earth," September 16, 2009, https://www.cbd.int/convention/guide/default.shtml?id=intaction.

45. Harrop and Pritchard 2011, 476.

46. Kolbert 2014.

47. Gupta and Falkner 2006.

48. Rhinard and Kaeding 2006, 1033.

49. Rhinard and Kaeding 2006, 1042.

50. See the Convention on Biological Diversity website at https://bch.cbd.int/protocol/background/, accessed February 12, 2021.

51. Schneider and Urpelainen 2013, 18.

52. See the Convention on Biological Diversity website.

53. Schneider and Urpelainen 2013.

54. Vogel 2003.

55. See Convention on Biological Diversity, "The Nagoya Protocol on Access and Benefit-Sharing," https://www.cbd.int/abs/, accessed November 12, 2020.

56. Oberthür and Rabitz 2014, 46, 47.

57. Oberthür and Rabitz 2014, 49.

58. See Convention on Biological Diversity, "Parties to the Cartagena Protocol and Its Supplmentary Protocol on Liability and Redress," https://bch.cbd.int/protocol/parties/, accessed February 12, 2021.

59. Peschard 2017.

60. See Convention on Biological Diversity, "Aichi Biodiversity Targets," September 18, 2020, https://www.cbd.int/sp/targets/.

61. Dimitrov 2005, 2.

62. Geist and Lambin 2002, 143.

63. E.g., Hurrell 1991; Nepstad et al. 2014.

64. Humphreys 1996, 90–102. Davenport (2005) also emphasizes the importance of U.S. domestic politics as an insurmountable barrier. My own reading is that even without U.S. obstinacy, the North-South conflicts that surfaced would have prevented a meaningful global convention.

65. Humphreys 1996, 94–95.

66. McDermott, Levin, and Cashore 2011, 90.

67. Humphreys 2006, 214.

68. Cashore 2002; Gulbrandsen 2004.

69. Hansen et al. 2013.

70. FSC 2015.

71. Angelsen 2009.

72. For more information about REDD+, see the official program website at http://redd .unfccc.int/, accessed February 12, 2021.

73. Pasgaard et al. 2016, 167.

74. Hurrell 1991; Browder and Godfrey 1997; Chomitz 2007.

75. Rocha, Assunção, and Gandou 2014.

76. Nepstad et al. 2014; Rocha, Assunção, and Gandou 2014.

77. See "Despite Tough Talk, Indonesia's Government Is Struggling to Stem Deforestation," *Economist*, November 26, 2016, https://tinyurl.com/cy5bsw6x.

78. E.g., Bayer and Urpelainen 2013b, 2014.

79. Martin 2011.

80. Çoban 2004.

81. Aldy and Stavins 2012, 1043.

82. See the text of the speech at https://clinton3.nara.gov/WH/EOP/OVP/speeches/kyotofin .html, accessed February 12, 2021.

83. For the full text of the official speech on climate change, see White House, "President Bush Discusses Global Climate Change," June 11, 2001, https://georgewbush-whitehouse .archives.gov/news/releases/2001/06/20010611-2.html.

84. ENB 2005, 18.

85. Wara and Victor 2008.

86. Bayer and Urpelainen 2013a.

87. Honkonen 2009.

88. Urpelainen 2012.

89. Ockwell et al. 2010.

90. Ghosh and Woods 2009.

91. Roberts and Weikmans 2017.

92. Dimitrov 2010.

93. For more information on the accord, see UNFCCC, http://unfccc.int/meetings /copenhagen_dec_2009/items/5262.php.

94. All national submissions and comments relevant to the accord can be found at http:// unfccc.int/meetings/copenhagen_dec_2009/items/5276.php.

95. Victor 2011.

96. Barrett 2008.

97. Cancun 2010; Durban 2011.

98. Hale 2015.

99. E.g., Sharma 2017.

100. Zhang and Pan 2016.

101. OECD 2018.

102. See Romain Weikmans and Timmons Roberts, "It's Déjà Vu All Over Again: Climate Finance at COP24," December 6, 2018, Brookings, https://tinyurl.com/363db28a.

103. CAT 2020.

104. Bayer and Urpelainen 2016.

105. Mildenberger 2015.
106. Ciplet, Roberts, and Khan 2013.
107. For example, see Climate Action Tracker's analysis at https://climateactiontracker.org /climate-target-update-tracker/, accessed March 23, 2021.
108. GoB 2009.
109. Huq, Roberts, and Fenton 2013, 948.
110. For a quantification of the regional benefits of mercury abatement in Asia, see Giang et al. 2015.
111. Young 2002a.
112. Mitchell and Keilbach 2001; Mitchell 2006.

5. CHINA AND INDIA IN GLOBAL ENVIRONMENTAL POLITICS

1. Regionally, such a shift has already occurred, as China has surpassed both Japan and the United States as the dominant actor in East Asia.
2. See EPA, "Global Greenhouse Gase Emissions Data," https://www.epa.gov/ghgemissions /global-greenhouse-gas-emissions-data, accessed October 30, 2020.
3. See "India 'to Overtake China's Population by 2022—UN," *BBC News*, July 30, 2015, http://www.bbc.com/news/world-asia-33720723.
4. Levy 2014, 41–42.
5. As noted, however, some scholars attribute China's capacity to reform to a culture of "adaptive governance" dating back to the revolution in 1949 (Heilmann and Perry 2011).
6. Lin, Cai, and Li 2003.
7. The numbers in this paragraph are based on the World Development Indicators, http:// data.worldbank. org/indicator/NV.IND.TOTL.KD?locations=CN.
8. CAT 2020.
9. See Hannah Richie and Max Roser, "CO2 and Greenhouse Gas Emissions," Our World in Data, August 2020, https://ourworldindata.org/co2-and-other-greenhouse-gas-emissions.
10. Shapiro 2001, 3.
11. Economy 2011, 17.
12. Mol and Carter 2006.
13. Sims 1999, 1228.
14. Mol and Carter 2006, 154.
15. Economy 2011.
16. Miller 1995, 45.
17. Walsh et al. 2011.
18. Economy 2011.
19. Liu and Diamond 2005, 1181.
20. Economy 2011, 19.
21. Tom Phillips, "Beijing's 'Airpocalypse': City Shuts Down Amid Three-Day Smog Red Alert," *Guardian*, December, 8, 2015, https://tinyurl.com/rnkfx9kz.

22. See Chris Buckley, "Documentary on Air Pollution Grips China," *New York Times*, March 1, 2015, https://tinyurl.com/c9u87m34.

23. "All Dried Up," *Economist*, October 12, 2013, https://tinyurl.com/622zv8av.

24. Economy 2011, 7.

25. Tian and Whalley 2008, 2.

26. Christoff 2010, 647.

27. Bodansky 2010, 240.

28. See Peter Maer, "Impromptu Moments Shaped Copenhagen Accord," *Christian Science Monitor*, December 20, 2009, http://www.cbsnews.com/news/impromptu-moments -shaped-copenhagen-accord/.

29. See "U.S.-China Joint Announcement on Climate Change," https://obamawhitehouse .archives.gov/blog/2014/11/12/us-and-china-just-announced-important-new-actions -reduce-carbon-pollution.

30. See summary at Climate Action Tracker, http://climateactiontracker.org/countries /china.html, accessed September 27, 2020.

31. Stokes, Giang, and Selin 2016, 7, 9–14.

32. See Carbon Brief, "Official Data Confirms Chinese Coal Use Fell in 2014," February 26, 2015, https://www.carbonbrief.org/official-data-confirms-chinese-coal-use-fell-in-2014.

33. See Carbon Brief 2015.

34. E.g., Grossman and Krueger 1995.

35. Melanie Hart and Jeffrey Cavanagh, "Environmental Standards Give the United States and Edge Over China," Center for American Progress, April 20, 2012, https://tinyurl .com/j9bbz598.

36. Gilley 2008.

37. Economy 2011.

38. Peng et al. 2018; Zhang, Zhong, and Wang 2018.

39. Mol and Carter 2006.

40. I thank Michaël Aklin for the budgetary data

41. Gilley 2012, 300.

42. Lieberthal and Oksenberg 1988.

43. E.g., Baumol and Oates 1988.

44. Lorentzen, Landry, and Yasuda 2014, 183.

45. Myllyvirta, Shen, and Lammi 2016.

46. See "China Starts Cancelling Under-Construction Coal Plants," October 21, 2016, http:// energydesk.greenpeace.org/2016/10/21/china-coal-crackdown-cancel-new-power -plants/.

47. Gilley 2012.

48. Studies of China's "political budget cycles" show that local leaders try to maximize economic growth at the time of a possible promotion (Guo, 2009).

49. As Kostka and Nahm 2017 note, though, China's efforts to recentralize environmental governance have not always been successful, because of a lack of both interest and capabilities.

50. Peng, Chang, and Liwen 2017, 1.

51. Gao 2013.

52. Nahm and Steinfeld 2014.

53. See John Fialka, "Why China Is Dominating the Solar Industry," *Scientific American*, December 19, 2016, https://www.scientificamerican. com/article/why-china-is-domi nating-the-solar-industry/.

54. USCC 2017, 510.

55. Zhang 2017.

56. Stokes, Giang, and Selin 2016.

57. Liu et al. 2013.

58. E.g., Bhagwati and Panagariya 2013.

59. E.g., DeLong 2003.

60. See World Bank, Data, http://data.worldbank.org/indicator/NY.GDP.MKTP.KD.ZG, for annual growth rates since 1961, accessed September 10, 2021.

61. Reich and Bowonder 1992, 646, 650.

62. Rajan 1997, 250, 255.

63. Jasanoff 1993, 34.

64. Urpelainen and Vihma, 2015.

65. Agarwal and Narain 1991.

66. Narain 2016, 14–15.

67. Joshi 2013, 143, 136.

68. Dubash 2013, 191.

69. Dubash 2016, 1.

70. Mayrhofer and Gupta 2016.

71. For information about the Ujala scheme to distributed efficient LED lighting to house-holds, see http://www.ujala.gov.in/, accessed February 5, 2021.

72. For an assessment of India's Intended Nationally Determined Contribution, which contains the target, see Climate Action Tracker, http://climateactiontracker.org/countries /india.html, accessed February 5, 2021.

73. Stokes, Giang, and Selin 2016, 8.

74. Cameron et al. 2016.

75. IEA 2021, executive summary.

76. E.g., Baviskar 1995; Shah 2010.

77. Nikita Mehta, "Delhi Records Highest Air Pollution Levels in 2015," *Mint*, December 23, 2015, http:// www.livemint.com/Politics/81cRtCoabWnL8yQjc1NJxO/Delhi-records -highest-air-pollution-levels-in-2015.html.

78. Wade 1985, 485.

79. Bardhan 2009, 349.

80. Vaishnav 2017.

81. Gadgil and Guha 1993.

82. E.g., Baviskar 1995.

83. E.g., Shah 2010.

84. Rosencranz and Jackson 2003. These authors also note, however, that the court faces a dilemma. First, when it rules against the state, it undermines the authority and capacity

of environmental agencies. Second, when it rules against public opinion, it undermines its own legitimacy and support. For these reasons, the judiciary must carefully balance legal interpretation and political pressures.

85. Rajan 1997, 243–45.

86. Wade 1985.

87. Levy 2014.

88. Busby and Shidore 2017, 62.

89. Again, data provided by Michaël Aklin.

90. Jasanoff 1993, 39.

91. Jasanoff 1993, 40.

92. Joseph 2010.

93. Aklin et al. 2016.

94. Tongia 2015, 22.

95. Palchak et al. 2017.

96. Pillai and Dubash 2021.

97. Stokes, Giang, and Selin 2016.

98. NITI-Ayog 2017.

99. See 2020 Worldwide Governance Indicators at https://info.worldbank.org/governance/wgi/, accessed June 28, 2021.

100. Wade 2000.

101. If anything, comparisons between China and India may understate China's advantage. Indian institutions are formally similar to Western institutions, so they may appear more impressive than their Chinese counterparts from a Eurocentric perspective.

102. Bayer and Urpelainen 2016.

103. The differences in institutional capacity also have deep historical roots. With its Confucian tradition and a culture of meritocracy in administration, China always had a solid foundation of institutional capacity, and it is often overlooked that Mao's China achieved impressive heights in developing institutional capacity, notwithstanding missteps such as the Great Leap Forward and the Cultural Revolution. In India, on the other hand, governance capacity was a transplant of British colonialism. Although the first prime minister, Nehru, was a proponent of bureaucratic modernization and state-driven development, in the end India failed to develop the kinds of robust administrative structures that enabled countries such as Japan, South Korea, and Taiwan to coordinate investments in a way that generated rapid and robust economic growth.

104. Chaudhary, Krishna, and Sagar 2015; Nandi and Basu 2008.

6. THE RISE OF THE REST

1. Most countries in the region, including Brazil, have already reached relatively high levels of income. In the Middle East, the large economies remain dependent on exports of fossil fuels, and their future as emerging economies more generally remains subject to great uncertainty. Both regions are clearly relevant to North-South conflicts in global

environmental politics, but they are, overall, less important as drivers of the transformation under study than South Asian, Southeast Asian, and sub-Saharan African countries.

2. Hochstetler and Keck 2007.

3. I calculated the number by dividing total greenhouse gas emissions by world population based on World Bank data at http://data.worldbank.org/.

4. See World Bank, Data, http://data.worldbank.org/indicator/NV.SRV.TETC.ZS?locations=NG, accessed February 16, 2021.

5. See OPEC, "Nigeria Facts and Figures," http://www.opec.org/opec_web/en/about_us/167.htm, accessed December 20, 2020.

6. BP 2015.

7. See World Bank, Data, http://data.worldbank.org/indicator/TX.VAL.FUEL.ZS.UN?locations=NG, accessed March 28, 2021.

8. Radelet 2011, 54–55.

9. Cayford 1996, 184.

10. Nelson 2016, 122.

11. Radelet 2011, 158.

12. See "Nigeria to Ratify Paris Agreement in September," https://tinyurl.com/23zwuxh7, accessed June 18, 2021.

13. See Nigeria's INDC at NDC Registry, https://tinyurl.com/yznvjywu, accessed June 18, 2021.

14. WB 2006, v.

15. See World Bank, Data, http://data.worldbank.org/indicator/NV.SRV.TETC.ZS?locations=ID, accessed February 16, 2018.

16. PWC 2014, 10.

17. PWC 2014, 10.

18. BP 2015.

19. "Indonesia Targets to Halve Coal Exports by 2019 Amid Domestic Demand Spike," https://tinyurl.com/33zyt7wy, accessed April 2, 2017.

20. Austin et al. 2019.

21. Tacconi, Rodrigues, and Maryudi 2019.

22. Vatikiotis 1999.

23. Hofman and Kaiser 2006.

24. Dauvergne 1993, 500.

25. See World Bank, Data, http://data.worldbank.org/indicator/NV.AGR.TOTL.ZS?locations=ID.

26. Michaelowa and Michaelowa 2015, 506.

27. See "Positioning Indonesia's Climate Commitment on the Global Stage," https://tinyurl.com/ zzfsd62x, accessed June 18, 2021.

28. E.g., Ross 2012.

29. Van Arkadie and Mallon 2004.

30. See World Bank, Data, http://data.worldbank.org/indicator/NY.GDP.PCAP.KD.ZG?locations=VN, accessed December 5, 2020.

31. Saxonberg 2013, 301.
32. Beresford and Fraser 1992, 10.
33. Beresford and Fraser 1992, 10.
34. Bryant and Jessup 2002.
35. The INDC can be found at UNFCCC, "Nationally Determined Contributions," http://unfccc.int/focus/indc_portal/items/8766.php, accessed February 19, 2021.
36. Nishtha Chugh, "For Vietnam Coal Will Ensure a 'Cheap' Energy Future. Or Will It?," *Forbes*, January 31, 2017, https://tinyurl.com/3adv9j3x.
37. Institute for Energy Economics and Financial Analysis, "Vietnam May Cancel 17.1 GW of Planned Coal-Fired Power Projects, Push Renewables and Gas," https://tinyurl.com/6s9z8a9e, accessed October 30, 2020.
38. For deforestation in the Philippines, see Rhett Butler, "Philippines," July 14, 2014, http://rainforests.mongabay.com/20philippines.htm.
39. Magallona and Malayang 2001, 2, 3.
40. See Climate Action Tracker, "Philippines," http://climateactiontracker.org/countries/philippines.html, accessed February 19, 2021.
41. See "Philippines Declares Moratorium on New Coal Power Plants," *Climate Home News*, October 28, 2020, https://www.climatechangenews.com/2020/10/28/philippines-declares-moratorium-new-coal-power-plants/.
42. See "Duterte: Addressing Climate Change Is 'Top Priority' for Philippines," *Climate Home News*, July 25, 2016, http://www.climatechangenews.com/2016/07/25/duterte-addressing-climate-change-is-top-priority-for-philippines/.
43. Enrico Dela Cuz and Manolo Serapio Jr., "Philippines to Shut Half of Mines, Mostly Nickel, in Environmental Clampdown," *Reuters*, February 1, 2017, http://www.reuters.com/article/us-philippines-mining-idUSKBN15H0BQ.
44. Browder and Godfrey 1997; Moran 1993.
45. Laurance, Albernaz, and Da Costa 2001.
46. Rocha, Assunção, and Gandou 2014.
47. Nepstad et al. 2009.
48. Rocha, Assunção, and Gandou 2014.
49. IEA 2017.
50. Dimitrov 2005, 9.
51. Hochstetler and Viola 2012.
52. DeSombre 1995.
53. See World Bank, Data, http://data.worldbank.org/indicator/NY.GDP.PCAP.KD?locations=BD, accessed February 16, 2021.
54. See "How Poorer Bangladesh Outpaces India on Human-Development Indicators," *Wall Street Journal*, June 5, 2015, https://tinyurl.com/4d92k9y5.
55. See Verisk Maplecroft, "Climate Change Vulnerability Index," https://maplecroft.com/about/news/ccvi.html, accessed April 2, 2017.
56. Clemett 2006.
57. Huq 2001.

58. See Global Energy Monitor, "Bangladesh and Coal," https://gem.wiki/Bangladesh_and_coal, accessed February 19, 2021.

59. See Naimul Karim, "Bangladesh Looks to Cut Future Coal Use as Costs Rise," *Reuters*, August 7, 2020, https://tinyurl.com/ja3js39h.

60. Tarannum 2015.

61. GoB 2009.

62. See UNCC, NDC Registry, http://www4.unfccc.int/ndcregistry/PublishedDocuments/BangladeshFirst/INDC_2015_of_Bangladesh.pdf, accessed June 18, 2017.

63. See World Bank, Data, http://data.worldbank.org/indicator/NY.GDP.PCAP.KD?locations=MM, accessed February 19, 2017.

64. Ross 2012.

65. David Allen and Rainer Einzenberger, "Myanmar's Natural Resources: Blessing or Curse?," Heinrich Böll Stiftung, December 11, 2013, https://www.boell.de/en/2013/12/11/myanmars-natural-resources-blessing-or-curse.

66. Bryant 1996, 346.

67. Myint 2007, 189.

68. Dobermann 2016, 6, 5, 10.

69. See Lex Rieffel and James Fox, "Are Aid Donors Repeating Mistakes in Myanmar?," Brookings, March 16, 2013, https://www.brookings.edu/opinions/are-aid-donors-repeating-mistakes-in-myanmar/.

70. For more information about the subsidized solar home systems, see Ross 2015.

71. See World Bank, "The World Bank in Ethiopia," http://www.worldbank.org/en/country/ethiopia/overview, accessed February 16, 2021.

72. WB 2014.

73. Hoben 1995, 1011.

74. Hoben 1995, 1013.

75. Ethiopia 2011.

76. See NDC Registry, http://www4.unfccc.int/ndcregistry/PublishedDocuments/EthiopiaFirst/INDC-Ethiopia-100615.pdf, accessed June 18, 2021.

77. Pallangyo 2007, 30.

78. Maro 2008, 153.

79. Mwandosya 1999, 45.

80. See Economic Intelligence, "Tanzania," http://country.eiu.com/tanzania, accessed February 16, 2021.

81. See Global Energy Monitor, "Tanzania and Coal," https://www.gem.wiki/Tanzania_and_coal, accessed February 16, 2021.

82. Kristoffer Welsien, Jacques Morisset, and Waly Wane, "Can Tanzania Afford 100 Million Citizens in 2035?" World Bank Blogs, October 15, 2012, http://blogs.worldbank.org/africacan/can-tanzania-afford-100-million-citizens-in-2035.

83. Jacob 2017, 351.

84. The INDC can be found at UNCC, "Nationally Determined Contributions," http://unfccc.int/focus/indc_portal/items/8766.php, accessed February 19, 2021.

CONCLUSION

1. Kolbert 2014.
2. Jin, Peng, and Urpelainen 2020.
3. Hale, Liu, and Urpelainen 2020.
4. E.g., Betsill and Bulkeley 2004; Bäckstrand 2006; Biermann 2007; Andonova, Betsill, and Bulkeley 2009; Biermann, Pattberg, and Zelli 2010; Green 2014; Hadden 2015.
5. Jasanoff 1993; Clapp 1994; Broad 1994; Miller 1995; Sell 1996; Bryant and Bailey 1997; Najam 2005; Ivanova 2007.
6. Economy 2011 is one exception.
7. Killick 1989; Woo-Cumings 1999; Easterly 2006; Besley and Persson 2009; Saylor 2014; Acemoglu, García-Jimeno, and Robinson 2015.
8. Notable exceptions include Brown Weiss and Jacobson 1998; Marcoux and Urpelainen 2012; VanDeveer and Dabelko 2001; Sagar and VanDeveer 2005; Victor 2009; Joseph 2010.
9. Putnam 1988.
10. See United Nations, Sustainable Development Goals, http://www.un.org/sustainabledevelopment/energy/, accessed November 2, 2020.
11. Ethiopia 2011.
12. See, respectively, UNDP, Ethiopia, "Green Economy and Progress in Ethiopia," August 24, 2012, http://www.et.undp.org/content/ethiopia/en/home/library/environment_energy/publication_2.html; and GGGI, "Ethiopia Aims for a Bright, Green Climate Future," October 19, 2015, http://gggi.org/ethiopia/.

BIBLIOGRAPHY

Acemoglu, Daron. 2003. "Why Not a Political Coase Theorem? Social Conflict, Commitment, and Politics." *Journal of Comparative Economics* 31 (4): 620–52.

Acemoglu, Daron, Camilo García-Jimeno, and James A. Robinson. 2015. "State Capacity and Economic Development: A Network Approach." *American Economic Review* 105 (8): 2364–2409.

Agarwal, Anil, and Sunita Narain. 1991. *Global Warming in an Unequal World: A Case of Environmental Colonialism*. New Delhi: Centre for Science and Environment.

Ahluwalia, Montek S. 2002. "Economic Reforms in India Since 1991: Has Gradualism Worked?" *Journal of Economic Perspectives* 16 (3): 67–88.

Aidt, Toke S. 1998. "Political Internalization of Economic Externalities and Environmental Policy." *Journal of Public Economics* 69 (1): 1–16.

Aklin, Michaël. 2016. "Re-exploring the Trade and Environment Nexus Through the Diffusion of Pollution." *Environmental and Resource Economics* 64 (4): 663–82.

Aklin, Michaël, Chao yo Cheng, Johannes Urpelainen, Karthik Ganesan, and Abhishek Jain. 2016. "Factors Affecting Household Satisfaction with Electricity Supply in Rural India." *Nature Energy* 1: 161–70.

Aklin, Michaël, and Matto Mildenberger. 2020. "Prisoners of the Wrong Dilemma: Why Distributive Conflict, Not Collective Action, Characterizes the Politics of Climate Change." *Global Environmental Politics* 20 (4): 4–27.

Aklin, Michaël, and Johannes Urpelainen. 2014. "The Global Spread of Environmental Ministries: Domestic-International Interactions." *International Studies Quarterly* 58 (4): 764–80.

——. 2018. *Renewables: The Politics of a Global Energy Transition*. Cambridge, Mass.: MIT Press.

Aldy, Joseph E., and Robert N. Stavins. 2012. "Climate Negotiators Create an Opportunity For Scholars." *Science* 337 (6098): 1043–44.

Allan, Jen Iris, and Peter Dauvergne. 2013. "The Global South in Environmental Negotiations: The Politics of Coalitions In REDD+." *Third World Quarterly* 34 (8): 1307–22.

Allison, Graham T. 1972. *Essence of Decision*. Boston: Little, Brown.

Andonova, Liliana B., Michele M. Betsill, and Harriet Bulkeley. 2009. "Transnational Climate Governance." *Global Environmental Politics* 9 (2): 52–73.

Andrews, Matt, Lant Pritchett, and Michael Woolcock. 2017. *Building State Capability: Evidence, Analysis, Action*. New York: Oxford University Press.

Angelsen, Arild, ed. 2009. *Realising REDD+: National Strategy and Policy Options*. Bogor: CIFOR.

Austin, Kemen G, Amanda Schwantes, Yaofeng Gu, and Prasad S Kasibhatla. 2019. "What Causes Deforestation in Indonesia?" *Environmental Research Letters* 14 (2): 024007.

Ausubel, Jesse H., and David G. Victor. 1992. "Verification of International Environmental Agreements." *Annual Review of Energy and the Environment* 17: 1–43.

Axelrod, Robert, and Robert O. Keohane. 1985. "Achieving Cooperation Under Anarchy: Strategies and Institutions." *World Politics* 38 (1): 226–54.

Bäckstrand, Karin. 2006. "Democratizing Global Environmental Governance? Stakeholder Democracy After the World Summit on Sustainable Development." *European Journal of International Relations* 12 (4): 467–98.

Bardhan, Pranab. 2009. "India and China: Governance Issues and Development." *Journal of Asian Studies* 68 (2): 347–57.

Barrett, Scott. 1994a. "The Biodiversity Supergame." *Environmental and Resource Economics* 4 (1): 111–22.

——. 1994b. "Self-Enforcing International Environmental Agreements." *Oxford Economic Papers* 46 (Supplement): 878–94.

——. 1997. "The Strategy of Trade Sanctions in International Environmental Agreements." *Resource and Energy Economics* 19 (4): 345–61.

——. 2003. *Environment and Statecraft: The Strategy of Environmental Treaty-Making*. Oxford: Oxford University Press.

——. 2008. "Climate Treaties and the Imperative of Enforcement." *Oxford Review of Economic Policy* 24 (2): 239–58.

Baumol, William J., and Wallace E. Oates. 1988. *The Theory of Environmental Policy*. New York: Cambridge University Press.

Baviskar, Amita. 1995. *In the Belly of the River: Tribal Conflicts Over Development in the Narmada Valley*. New York: Oxford University Press.

Bayer, Patrick, Christopher Marcoux, and Johannes Urpelainen. 2014. "When International Organizations Bargain: Evidence from the Global Environment Facility." *Journal of Conflict Resolution* 59 (6): 1074–1100.

Bayer, Patrick, and Johannes Urpelainen. 2013a. "External Sources of Clean Technology: Evidence from the Clean Development Mechanism." *Review of International Organizations* 8 (1): 81–109.

——. 2013b. "Funding Global Public Goods: The Dark Side of Multilateralism." *Review of Policy Research* 30 (2): 160–89.

——. 2014. "Does It Pay to Play? How Bargaining Shapes Donor Participation in the Funding of Environmental Protection." *Strategic Behavior and the Environment* 4 (3): 263–90.

——. 2016. "It's All About Political Incentives: Democracy and the Renewable Feed-In Tariff." *Journal of Politics* 78 (2): 603–19.

Beckerman, Wilfred. 1992. "Economic Growth and the Environment: Whose Growth? Whose Environment?" *World Development* 20 (4): 481–96.

Benecke, Gudrun. 2009. "Varieties of Carbon Governance: Taking Stock of the Local Carbon Market in India." *Journal of Environment and Development* 18 (4): 346–70.

Benedick, Richard E. 1998. *Ozone Diplomacy: New Directions in Safeguarding the Planet.* Cambridge, Mass.: Harvard University Press.

Beresford, Melanie, and Lyn Fraser. 1992. "Political Economy of the Environment in Vietnam." *Journal of Contemporary Asia* 22 (1): 3–19.

Bernstein, Steven. 2012. *The Compromise of Liberal Environmentalism.* New York: Columbia University Press.

Besley, Timothy. 2005. "Political Selection." *Journal of Economic Perspectives* 19 (3): 43–60.

Besley, Timothy, and Torsten Persson. 2009. "The Origins of State Capacity: Property Rights, Taxation, and Politics." *American Economic Review* 99 (4): 1218–44.

Betsill, Michele M., and Harriet Bulkeley. 2004. "Transnational Networks and Global Environmental Governance: The Cities for Climate Protection Program." *International Studies Quarterly* 48 (2): 471–93.

Bhagwati, Jagdish, and Arvind Panagariya. 2013. *Why Growth Matters: How Economic Growth in India Reduced Poverty and the Lessons for Other Developing Countries.* New York: PublicAffairs.

Bhagwati, Jagdish N., ed. 1977. *The New International Economic Order: The North-South Debate.* Cambridge, Mass.: MIT Press.

Biermann, Frank. 2007. "'Earth System Governance' as a Crosscutting Theme of Global Change Research." *Global Environmental Change* 17 (3–4): 326–37.

Biermann, Frank, Philipp Pattberg, and Fariborz Zelli. 2010. *Global Climate Governance Beyond 2012: Architecture, Agency and Adaptation.* New York: Cambridge University Press.

Bloom, David E. 1995. "International Public Opinion on the Environment." Discussion Paper Series 732.

Bodansky, Daniel. 2010. "The Copenhagen Climate Change Conference: A Postmortem." *American Journal of International Law* 104 (2): 230–40.

BP. 2015. *BP Statistical Review of World Energy June 2015.* BP.

Broad, Robin. 1994. "The Poor and the Environment: Friends or Foes?" *World Development* 22 (6): 811–22.

Browder, John O., and Brian J. Godfrey. 1997. *Rainforest Cities: Urbanization, Development, and Globalization of the Brazilian Amazon.* New York: Columbia University Press.

Brown Weiss, Edith, and Harold K. Jacobson, eds. 1998. *Engaging Countries: Strengthening Compliance with International Environmental Accords.* Cambridge, Mass.: MIT Press.

Brulle, Robert J. 2010. "Politics and the Environment." In *Handbook of Politics*, ed. K. T. Leicht and J. C. Jenkins. New York: Springer.

Brulle, Robert J., and David N. Pellow. 2006. "Environmental Justice: Human Health and Environmental Inequalities." *Annual Review of Public Health* 27: 103–24.

Bryant, Raymond L. 1996. "The Greening of Burma: Political Rhetoric or Sustainable Development?" *Pacific Affairs* 69 (3): 341–59.

Bryant, Raymond L., and Sinead Bailey. 1997. *Third World Political Ecology*. New York: Routledge.

Bryant, Tannetje, and Brad Jessup. 2002. "The Status of International Environmental Treaties in Vietnam." *Asia Pacific Law Review* 10: 117–39.

Bueno de Mesquita, Bruce, Alastair Smith, Randolph M. Siverson, and James D. Morrow. 2003. *The Logic of Political Survival*. Cambridge, Mass.: MIT Press.

Bullard, Robert D. 1990. *Dumping in Dixie: Race, Class, and Environmental Quality*. Boulder, Colo.: Westview Press.

Buntaine, Mark T, and Lauren Prather. 2018. "Preferences for Domestic Action Over International Transfers in Global Climate Policy." *Journal of Experimental Political Science* 5 (2): 73–87.

Busby, Joshua W., and Sarang Shidore. 2017. "When Decarbonization Meets Development: The Sectoral Feasibility of Greenhouse Gas Mitigation in India." *Energy Research and Social Science* 23: 60–73.

Cameron, Colin, Shonali Pachauri, Narasimha D. Rao, David McCollum, Joeri Rogelj, and Keywan Riahi. 2016. "Policy Trade-offs Between Climate Mitigation and Clean Cook-Stove Access in South Asia." *Nature Energy* 1: 15010.

Cao, Xun, and Hugh Ward. 2015. "Winning Coalition Size, State Capacity, and Time Horizons: An Application of Modified Selectorate Theory to Environmental Public Goods Provision." *International Studies Quarterly* 59 (2): 264–79.

Capstick, Stuart, Lorraine Whitmarsh, Wouter Poortinga, Nick Pidgeon, and Paul Upham. 2014. "International Trends in Public Perceptions of Climate Change Over the Past Quarter Century." *Wiley Interdisciplinary Reviews: Climate Change* 6 (1): 35–61.

Carraro, Carlo, and Domenico Siniscalco. 1993. "Strategies for the International Protection of the Environment." *Journal of Public Economics* 52 (3): 309–28.

Carson, Rachel. 2002. *Silent Spring: 40th Anniversary Edition*. New York: Mariner Books. Originally published in 1962.

Carson, Richard T. 2010. "The Environmental Kuznets Curve: Seeking Empirical Regularity and Theoretical Structure." *Review of Environmental Economics and Policy* 4 (1): 3–23.

Carter, Neil T., and Arthur P. J. Mol. 2006. "China and the Environment: Domestic and Transnational Dynamics of a Future Hegemon." *Environmental Politics* 15 (02): 330–44.

Cashore, Benjamin. 2002. "Legitimacy and Privatization of Environmental Governance: How Non-State Market-Driven (NSMD) Governance Systems Gain Rule-Making Authority." *Governance* 15 (4): 503–29.

CAT. 2020. "Climate Action Tracker." https://climateactiontracker.org/, accessed January 7, 2021.

Cayford, Steven. 1996. "The Ogoni Uprising: Oil, Human Rights, and a Democratic Alternative in Nigeria." *Africa Today* 43 (2): 183–97.

Chakravorty, Ujjayant, Martino Pelli, and Beyza Ural Marchand. 2014. "Does the Quality of Electricity Matter? Evidence from Rural India." *Journal of Economic Behavior and Organization* 107: 228–47.

Chasek, Pamela S., David L. Downie, and Janet Welsh Brown. 2014. *Global Environmental Politics*. 6th ed. Boulder, Colo.: Westview Press.

Chaudhary, Ankur, Chetan Krishna, and Ambuj Sagar. 2015. "Policy Making for Renewable Energy in India: Lessons from Wind and Solar Power Sectors." *Climate Policy* 15 (1): 58–87.

Chayes, Abram, and Antonia Handler Chayes. 1995. *The New Sovereignty: Compliance with International Regulatory Agreements*. Cambridge, Mass.: Harvard University Press.

Cheibub, José Antonio. 1998. "Political Regimes and the Extractive Capacity of Governments: Taxation in Democracies and Dictatorships." *World Politics* 50 (3): 349–76.

China. 2012. "Full Text: China's Energy Policy 2012." Information Office of the State Council, People's Republic of China. http://www.gov.cn/english/official/2012-10/24/content_2250497.htm.

Chomitz, Kenneth M. 2007. *At Loggerheads? Agricultural Expansion, Poverty Reduction, and Environment in the Tropical Forests*. Washington, D.C.: World Bank.

Christoff, Peter. 2010. "Cold Climate in Copenhagen: China and the United States at COP15." *Environmental Politics* 19 (4): 637–56.

Ciplet, David, J. Timmons Roberts, and Mizan Khan. 2013. "The Politics of International Climate Adaptation Funding: Justice and Divisions in the Greenhouse." *Global Environmental Politics* 13 (1): 49–68.

——. 2015. *Power in a Warming World: The New Global Politics of Climate Change and the Remaking of Environmental Inequality*. Cambridge, Mass.: MIT Press.

Cisneros, Élias, Jorge Hargrave, and Krisztina Kis-Katos. 2013. "Unintended Consequences of Anti-corruption Strategies: Public Fiscal Audits and Deforestation in the Brazilian Amazon." Working Paper, Center for Development Research, Bonn.

Clapp, Jennifer. 1994. "The Toxic Waste Trade with Less-Industrialised Countries: Economic Linkages and Political Alliances." *Third World Quarterly* 15 (3): 505–18.

——. 2001. *Toxic Exports: The Transfer of Hazardous Wastes from Rich to Poor Countries*. Ithaca, N.Y.: Cornell University Press.

——. 2003. "Transnational Corporate Interests and Global Environmental Governance: Negotiating Rules for Agricultural Biotechnology and Chemicals." *Environmental Politics* 12 (4): 1–23.

Clapp, Jennifer, and Peter Dauvergne. 2011. *Paths to a Green World: The Political Economy of the Global Environment*. Cambridge, Mass.: MIT Press.

Clémençon, Raymond. 2006. "What Future for the Global Environment Facility?" *Journal of Environment and Development* 15 (1): 50–74.

Clemett, Alexandra. 2006. "A Review of Environmental Policy and Legislation in Bangladesh." Department for International Development, Country Report.

Çoban, Aykut. 2004. "Caught between State-Sovereign Rights and Property Rights: Regulating Biodiversity." *Review of International Political Economy* 11 (4): 736–62.

Conca, Ken. 2004. "Environmental Governance after Johannesburg: From Stalled Legalization to Environmental Human Rights." *Journal of International Law and International Relations* 1: 121.

Conca, Ken. 2015. *An Unfinished Foundation: The United Nations and Global Environmental Governance*. New York: Oxford University Press.

Dai, Xinyuan. 2005. "Why Comply? The Domestic Constituency Mechanism." *International Organization* 59 (2): 363–98.

Dalton, Russell J. 1994. *The Green Rainbow: Environmental Groups in Western Europe*. New Haven, Conn.: Yale University Press.

Dasgupta, Biplab. 1977. "India's Green Revolution." *Economic and Political Weekly* 12: 241–60.

Dasgupta, Susmita, Kirk Hamilton, Kiran D. Pandey, and David Wheeler. 2006. "Environment During Growth: Accounting for Governance and Vulnerability." *World Development* 34 (9): 1597–1611.

Dasgupta, Susmita, Benoit Laplante, Hua Wang, and David Wheeler. 2002. "Confronting the Environmental Kuznets Curve." *Journal of Economic Perspectives* 16 (1): 147–68.

Dauvergne, Peter. 1993. "The Politics of Deforestation in Indonesia." *Pacific Affairs* 66 (4): 497–518.

——. 2018. "Why Is the Global Governance of Plastic Failing the Oceans?" *Global Environmental Change* 51: 22–31.

Davenport, Deborah S. 2005. "An Alternative Explanation for the Failure of the UNCED Forest Negotiations." *Global Environmental Politics* 5 (1): 105–30.

Davis, Steven J., and Robert H. Socolow. 2014. "Commitment Accounting of CO2 Emissions." *Environmental Research Letters* 9 (8): 084018.

DeLong, J. Bradford. 2003. "India Since Independence: An Analytic Growth Narrative." In *In Search of Prosperity: Analytic Narratives on Economic Growth*, ed. Dani Rodrik. Princeton, N.J.: Princeton University Press.

DeSombre, Elizabeth R. 1995. "Baptists and Bootleggers for the Environment: The Origins of United States Unilateral Sanctions." *Journal of Environment and Development* 4 (1): 53–75.

——. 2000–2002. "The Experience of the Montreal Protocol: Particularly Remarkable, and Remarkably Particular." *UCLA Journal of Environmental Law and Policy* 19: 49–82.

Dickson, Barnabas. 2002. "International Conservation Treaties, Poverty and Development: The Case of CITES." *Natural Resource Perspectives* 74.

DiMaggio, Paul J., and Walter W. Powell. 1983. "The Iron Cage Revisited: Institutional Isomorphism and Collective Rationality in Organizational Fields." *American Sociological Review* 48 (2): 147–60.

Dimitrov, Radoslav S. 2005. "Hostage to Norms: States, Institutions and Global Forest Politics." *Global Environmental Politics* 5 (4): 1–24.

——. 2010. "Inside UN Climate Change Negotiations: The Copenhagen Conference." *Review of Policy Research* 27 (6): 795–821.

Dobermann, Tim. 2016. "Energy in Myanmar." International Growth Centre, London School of Economics.

Downie, Christian. 2015. "Global Energy Governance: Do the BRICS Have the Energy to Drive Reform?" *International Affairs* 91 (4): 799–812.

Downie, David L. 1999. "The Power to Destroy: Understanding Stratospheric Ozone Politics as a Common Pool Resource Problem." In *Anarchy and the Environment: The International*

Relations of Common Pool Resources, ed. J. Samuel Barkin and George Shambaugh. Albany: State University of New York Press.

Drezner, Daniel W. 2014. "The System Worked: Global Economic Governance during the Great Recession." *World Politics* 66 (1): 123–64.

Dubash, Navroz K. 2013. "The Politics of Climate Change in India: Narratives of Equity and Cobenefits." *Wiley Interdisciplinary Reviews: Climate Change* 4 (3): 191–201.

——. 2016. "Safeguarding Development and Limiting Vulnerability: India's Stakes in the Paris Agreement." *Wiley Interdisciplinary Reviews: Climate Change*. DOI:10.1002/wcc.444.

Dunlap, Riley E. 1991. "Trends in Public Opinion Toward Environmental Issues: 1965–1990." *Society and Natural Resources* 4 (3): 285–312.

Easterly, William. 2006. *The White Man's Burden: Why the West's Efforts to Aid the Rest Have Done So Much Ill and So Little Good*. New York: Penguin Press.

Eckersley, Robyn. 2007. "Ambushed: The Kyoto Protocol, the Bush Administration's Climate Policy and the Erosion of Legitimacy." *International Politics* 44 (2–3): 306–24.

Economy, Elizabeth C. 2011. *The River Runs Black: The Environmental Challenge to China's Future*. Ithaca, N.Y.: Cornell University Press.

Ehrlich, Paul R., and John P. Holdren. 1971. "Impact of Population Growth." *Science* 171 (3977): 1212–17.

ENB. 2005. "Summary of the Eleventh Conference of the Parties to the UN Framework Convention on Climate Change and First Conference of the Parties Serving as the Meeting of the Parties to the Kyoto Protocol." *Earth Negotiations Bulletin* 12/291. http://www.iisd.ca/download/pdf/enb12291e.pdf.

Ethiopia. 2011. "Ethiopia's Climate-Resilient Green Economy." Federal Democratic Republic of Ethiopia.

Falkner, Robert, Hannes Stephan, and John Vogler. 2010. "International Climate Policy After Copenhagen: Towards a 'Building Blocks' Approach." *Global Policy* 1 (3): 252–62.

Fearon, James D. 1998. "Bargaining, Enforcement, and International Cooperation." *International Organization* 52 (2): 269–305.

Fiorina, Morris P., and Samuel J. Abrams. 2008. "Political Polarization in the American Public." *Annual Review of Political Science* 11: 563–88.

Founex. 1971. "The Founex Report on Development and Environment." Report of Panel of Experts, Founex, June 1971.

Franzen, Axel, and Reto Meyer. 2010. "Environmental Attitudes in Cross-National Perspective: A Multilevel Analysis of the ISSP 1993 and 2000." *European Sociological Review* 26 (2): 219–34.

FSC. 2015. "Market Info Pack." Forest Stewardship Council. https://ic.fsc.org/preview.2015-fsc-market-info-pack.a-5067.pdf.

Gadgil, Madhav, and Ramachandra Guha. 1993. *This Fissured Land: An Ecological History of India*. Berkeley: University of California Press.

Gao, Xiang. 2013. "China as a 'Responsible Power': Altruistic, Ambitious or Ambiguous." *International Journal of China Studies* 4 (3 Supplement): 405–38.

Geddes, Barbara. 1994. *Politician's Dilemma: Building State Capacity in Latin America*. Berkeley: University of California Press.

Geist, Helmut J., and Eric F. Lambin. 2002. "Proximate Causes and Underlying Driving Forces of Tropical Deforestation." *BioScience* 52 (2): 143–50.

Genovese, Federica. 2014. "States' Interests at International Climate Negotiations: New Measures of Bargaining Positions." *Environmental Politics* 23 (4): 610–31.

Gerring, John. 2004. "What Is a Case Study and What Is It Good for?" *American Political Science Review* 98 (2): 341–54.

Ghosh, Arunabha, and Ngaire Woods. 2009. "Developing Country Concerns About Climate Finance Proposals: Priorities, Trust, and the Credible Donor Problem." In *Climate Finance: Regulatory and Funding Strategies for Climate Change and Global Development*. New York: New York University Press.

Giang, Amanda, Leah C. Stokes, David G. Streets, Elizabeth S. Corbitt, and Noelle E. Selin. 2015. "Impacts of the Minamata Convention on Mercury Emissions and Global Deposition from Coal-fired Power Generation in Asia." *Environmental Science & Technology* 49 (9): 5326–35.

Gilley, Bruce. 2008. "Legitimacy and Institutional Change: The Case of China." *Comparative Political Studies* 41 (3): 259–84.

——. 2012. "Authoritarian Environmentalism and China's Response to Climate Change." *Environmental Politics* 21 (2): 287–307.

GoB. 2009. *Bangladesh Climate Strategy and Action Plan*. Dhaka: Ministry for Environment and Forests, Government of the People's Republic of Bangladesh.

Green, Jessica F. 2014. *Rethinking Private Authority: Agents and Entrepreneurs in Global Environmental Governance*. Princeton, N.J.: Princeton University Press.

Grindle, Merilee S., and Mary E. Hilderbrand. 1995. "Building Sustainable Capacity in the Public Sector: What Can Be Done?" *Public Administration and Development* 15 (5): 441–63.

Grossman, Gene M., and Alan B. Krueger. 1995. "Economic Growth and the Environment." *Quarterly Journal of Economics* 110 (2): 353–77.

Gulbrandsen, Lars H. 2004. "Overlapping Public and Private Governance: Can Forest Certification Fill the Gaps in the Global Forest Regime?" *Global Environmental Politics* 4 (2): 75–99.

Guo, Gang. 2009. "China's Local Political Budget Cycles." *American Journal of Political Science* 53 (3): 621–32.

Gupta, Aarti, and Robert Falkner. 2006. "The Influence of the Cartagena Protocol on Biosafety: Comparing Mexico, China and South Africa." *Global Environmental Politics* 6 (4): 23–55.

Gupta, Joyeeta. 2010. "A History of International Climate Change Policy." *Wiley Interdisciplinary Reviews: Climate Change* 1 (5): 636–653.

Haas, Ernst B. 1980. "Why Collaborate? Issue-linkage and International Regimes." *World Politics* 32 (3): 357–405.

Haas, Peter M. 1989. "Do Regimes Matter? Epistemic Communities and Mediterranean Pollution Control." *International Organization* 43 (3): 377–403.

Hadden, Jennifer. 2015. *Networks in Contention: The Divisive Politics of Climate Change*. New York: Cambridge University Press.

Hale, Thomas N. 2011. "A Climate Coalition of the Willing." *Washington Quarterly* 34 (1): 89–102.

——. 2015. "Ratchet Up: Five Tools to Lift Climate Action After Paris." Policy memo, Oxford University.

Hale, Thomas, Chuyu Liu, and Johannes Urpelainen. 2020. "Belt & Road Decision-Making in China and Recipient Countries." Initiative for Sustainable Energy Policy, Blavatnik School of Government, and ClimateWorks Foundation.

Hansen, Matthew C., Peter V. Potapov, Rebecca Moore, Matt Hancher, S. A. Turubanova, Alexandra Tyukavina, David Thau, S. V. Stehman, S.J. Goetz, T. R. Loveland, et al. 2013. "High-Resolution Global Maps Of 21st-century Forest Cover Change." *Science* 342 (6160): 850–53.

Harrop, Stuart R., and Diana J. Pritchard. 2011. "A Hard Instrument Goes Soft: The Implications of the Convention on Biological Diversity's Current Trajectory." *Global Environmental Change* 21 (2): 474–80.

Heilmann, Sebastian, and Elizabeth J. Perry, eds. 2011. *Mao's Invisible Hand: The Political Foundations of Adaptive Governance in China*. Cambridge, Mass.: Harvard University Press.

Herbst, Jeffrey. 2000. *States and Power in Africa: Comparative Lessons in Authority and Control*. Princeton, N.J.: Princeton University Press.

Hicks, Robert L., Bradley C. Parks, J. Timmons Roberts, and Michael J. Tierney. 2008. *Greening Aid? Understanding the Environmental Impact of Development Assistance*. New York: Oxford University Press.

Hoben, Allan. 1995. "Paradigms and Politics: The Cultural Construction of Environmental Policy in Ethiopia." *World Development* 23 (6): 1007–21.

Hochstetler, Kathryn, and Margaret E. Keck. 2007. *Greening Brazil: Environmentalism in State and Society*. Durham, N.C.: Duke University Press.

Hochstetler, Kathryn, and Manjana Milkoreit. 2014. "Emerging Powers in the Climate Negotiations: Shifting Identity Conceptions." *Political Research Quarterly* 67 (1): 224–35.

Hochstetler, Kathryn, and Eduardo Viola. 2012. "Brazil and the Politics of Climate Change: Beyond the Global Commons." *Environmental Politics* 21 (5): 753–71.

Hoel, Michael. 1991. "Global Environmental Problems: The Effects of Unilateral Actions Taken by One Country." *Journal of Environmental Economics and Management* 20 (1): 55–70.

Hoel, Michael, and Aart de Zeeuw. 2010. "Can a Focus on Breakthrough Technologies Improve the Performance of International Environmental Agreements?" *Environmental and Resource Economics* 47 (3): 395–406.

Hoffmann, Matthew J. 2005. *Ozone Depletion and Climate Change: Constructing a Global Response*. Albany: State University of New York Press.

——. 2011. *Climate Governance at the Crossroads: Experimenting with a Global Response After Kyoto*. New York: Oxford University Press.

Hofman, Bert, and Kai Kaiser. 2006. "Decentralization, Democratic Transition, and Local Governance in Indonesia." In *Decentralization and Local Governance in Developing Countries: A Comparative Perspective*, ed. Pranab Bardhan, and Dilip Mookherjee. Cambridge, Mass.: MIT Press.

Honkonen, Tuula. 2009. "The Principle of Common but Differentiated Responsibility in Post-2012 Climate Negotiations." *Review of European, Comparative and International Environmental Law* 18 (3): 257–67.

Hovi, Jon, Tora Skodvin, and Steinar Andresen. 2003. "The Persistence of the Kyoto Protocol: Why Other Annex I Countries Move on Without the United States." *Global Environmental Politics* 3 (4): 1–23.

Hovi, Jon, Detlef F. Sprinz, and Arild Underdal. 2009. "Implementing Long-Term Climate Policy: Time Inconsistency, Domestic Politics, International Anarchy." *Global Environmental Politics* 9 (3): 20–39.

Hughes, Llewelyn, and Johannes Urpelainen. 2015. "Interests, Institutions, and Climate Policy: Explaining the Choice of Policy Instruments for the Energy Sector." *Environmental Science and Policy* 54: 52–53.

Humphreys, David. 1996. *Forest Politics: The Evolution of International Cooperation*. London: Earthscan.

——. 2006. *Logjam: Deforestation and the Crisis of Global Governance*. London: Earthscan.

Huq, Saleemul. 2001. "Climate Change and Bangladesh." *Science* 294 (5547): 1617–17.

Huq, Saleemul, Erin Roberts, and Adrian Fenton. 2013. "Loss and Damage." *Nature Climate Change* 3 (11): 947–49.

Hurrell, Andrew. 1991. "The Politics of Amazonian Deforestation." *Journal of Latin American Studies* 23 (1): 197–215.

——. 1994. "A Crisis of Ecological Viability? Global Environmental Change and the Nation State." *Political Studies* 42 (s1): 146–65.

Hurrell, Andrew, and Sandeep Sengupta. 2012. "Emerging Powers, North-South Relations and Global Climate Politics." *International Affairs* 88 (3): 463–84.

IEA. 2015. *India Energy Outlook*. Paris: International Energy Agency.

——. 2017. *World Energy Outlook*. Paris: International Energy Agency.

——. 2021. *India Energy Outlook*. Paris: International Energy Agency.

Ikenberry, G. John. 1986. "The Irony of State Strength: Comparative Responses to the Oil Shocks in the 1970s." *International Organization* 40 (1): 105–37.

Ivanova, Maria. 2007. "Designing the United Nations Environment Programme: A Story of Compromise and Confrontation." *International Environmental Agreements* 7 (4): 337–61.

——. 2013. "The Contested Legacy of Rio+20." *Global Environmental Politics* 13 (4): 1–11.

Ivashchenko, Yulia V., Phillip J. Clapham, and Robert L. Brownell, Jr. 2011. "Soviet Illegal Whaling: The Devil and the Details." *Marine Fisheries Review* 73 (3): 1–19.

Jacob, Thabit. 2017. "Competing Energy Narratives in Tanzania: Towards the Political Economy of Coal." *African Affairs* 116 (463): 341–53.

Jasanoff, Sheila. 1993. "India at the Crossroads in Global Environmental Policy." *Global Environmental Change* 3 (1): 32–52.

Jentleson, Bruce W. 2007. "America's Global Role After Bush." *Survival* 49 (3): 179–200.

Jin, Yana, Wei Peng, and Johannes Urpelainen. 2020. "An Ultra-Low Emission Coal Power Fleet for Cleaner but Not Hotter Air." *Environmental Research Letters*.

Johnson, Tana, and Johannes Urpelainen. 2012. "A Strategic Theory of Regime Integration and Separation." *International Organization* 66 (4): 645–77.

——. 2017. "The More Things Change, the More They Stay the Same: Developing Countries' Unity in International Politics." Working paper, Columbia University and Duke University.

Joseph, Kelli L. 2010. "The Politics of Power: Electricity Reform in India." *Energy Policy* 38 (1): 503–11.

Joshi, Shangrila. 2013. "Understanding India's Representation of North–South Climate Politics." *Global Environmental Politics* 13 (2): 128–47.

———. 2016. "North-South Relations: Colonialism, Empire and International Order." In *Routledge Handbook of Global Environmental Politics*, ed. Paul G. Harris, 272–283. New York: Routledge.

Keohane, Robert O. 1984. *After Hegemony: Cooperation and Discord in the World Political Economy*. Princeton, N.J.: Princeton University Press.

Keohane, Robert O., and David G. Victor. 2011. "The Regime Complex for Climate Change." *Perspectives on Politics* 9 (1): 7–23.

———. 2016. "Cooperation and Discord in Global Climate Policy." *Nature Climate Change* 6 (6): 570–75.

Kessie, Edwini. 2013. "The Future of the Doha Development Agenda." *European Yearbook of International Economic Law* 4: 481–94.

Killick, Tony. 1989. *A Reaction Too Far: Economic Theory and the Role of the State in Developing Countries*. London: Overseas Development Institute.

Kolbert, Elizabeth. 2014. *The Sixth Extinction: An Unnatural History*. New York: Holt.

Kostka, Genia, and Jonas Nahm. 2017. "Central-Local Relations: Recentralization and Environmental Governance in China." *China Quarterly* 231: 567–82.

Krasner, Stephen D. 1982. "Structural Causes and Regime Consequences: Regimes as Intervening Variables." *International Organization* 36 (2): 185–205.

———. 1985. *Structural Conflict: The Third World Against Global Liberalism*. Berkeley: University of California Press.

———. 1991. "Global Communications and National Power: Life on the Pareto Frontier." *World Politics* 43 (3): 336–66.

Kusumaningtyas, Retno, and Jan Willem van Gelder. 2017. *Towards Responsible and Inclusive Financing of the Palm Oil Sector*. Occasional paper 175. Bogor, Indonesia: CIFOR.

Lake, David A. 1987. "Power and the Third World: Toward a Realist Political Economy of North-South Relations." *International Studies Quarterly* 31 (2): 217–34.

Laurance, William F., Ana K. M. Albernaz, and Carlos Da Costa. 2001. "Is Deforestation Accelerating in the Brazilian Amazon?" *Environmental Conservation* 28 (4): 305–11.

Layman, Geoffrey C., Thomas M. Carsey, and Juliana Menasce Horowitz. 2006. "Party Polarization in American Politics: Characteristics, Causes, and Consequences." *Annual Review of Political Science* 9: 83–110.

Levin, Kelly, Benjamin Cashore, Steven Bernstein, and Graeme Auld. 2012. "Overcoming the Tragedy of Super Wicked Problems: Constraining Our Future Selves to Ameliorate Global Climate Change." *Policy Sciences* 45 (2): 123–52.

Levy, Brian. 2014. *Working with the Grain: Integrating Governance and Growth in Development Strategies*. New York: Oxford University Press.

Levy, Marc A. 1993. "European Acid Rain: The Power of Tote-Board Diplomacy." In *Institutions for the Earth: Sources of Effective International Environmental Protection*, ed. Peter M. Haas, Robert O. Keohane, and Marc A. Levy. Cambridge, Mass.: MIT Press.

Lieberthal, Kenneth, and Michel Oksenberg. 1988. *Policy Making in China: Leaders, Structures, and Processes*. Princeton, N.J.: Princeton University Press.

Lin, Justin Yifu, Fang Cai, and Zhou Li. 2003. *The China Miracle: Development Strategy and Economic Reform*. Hong Kong: Chinese University Press.

Litfin, Karen T. 1994. *Ozone Discourses: Science and Politics in Global Environmental Cooperation.* New York: Columbia University Press.

Liu, Jianguo, and Jared Diamond. 2005. "China's Environment in a Globalizing World." *Nature* 435 (7046): 1179–86.

Liu, Zhu, Dabo Guan, Douglas Crawford-Brown, Qiang Zhang, Kebin He, and Jianguo Liu. 2013. "Energy Policy: A Low-Carbon Road Map for China." *Nature* 500 (7461): 143–45.

Lorentzen, Peter, Pierre Landry, and John Yasuda. 2014. "Undermining Authoritarian Innovation: The Power of China's Industrial Giants." *Journal of Politics* 76 (1): 182–94.

Lukes, Stephen. 1974. *Power: A Radical View.* London: Macmillan.

Magallona, Merlin M., and Ben S. Malayang, III. 2001. "Environmental Governance in the Philippines." In *Environmental Governance in Asia: Synthesis Report on Country Studies.* Tokyo: Institute of Global Environmental Strategies.

Mani, Muthukumara, and David Wheeler. 1998. "In Search of Pollution Havens? Dirty Industry in the World Economy, 1960 to 1995." *Journal of Environment and Development* 7 (3): 215–47.

Marcoux, Christopher, and Johannes Urpelainen. 2012. "Capacity, Not Constraints: A Theory of North-South Regulatory Cooperation." *Review of International Organizations* 7 (4): 399–424.

——. 2013. "Non-Compliance by Design: Moribund Hard Law in International Institutions." *Review of International Organizations* 8 (2): 163–91.

——. 2014. "Profitable Participation: Technology Innovation as an Influence on the Ratification of Regulatory Treaties." *British Journal of Political Science* 44 (4): 903–36.

Maro, Paul S. 2008. "A Review of Current Tanzanian National Environmental Policy." *Geographical Journal* 174 (2): 150–54.

Martin, Pamela L. 2011. "Global Governance from the Amazon: Leaving Oil Underground in Yasuní National Park, Ecuador." *Global Environmental Politics* 11 (4): 22–42.

Martinez-Alier, Joan. 2002. *The Environmentalism of the Poor: A Study of Ecological Conflicts and Valuation.* Northampton, Mass.: Edward Elgar.

Matthews, G. V. T. 1993. *The Ramsar Convention on Wetlands: Its History and Development.* Gland, Switz.: Ramsar Convention Bureau.

Mayrhofer, Jan P., and Joyeeta Gupta. 2016. "The Science and Politics of Co-Benefits in Climate Policy." *Environmental Science and Policy* 57: 22–30.

McCright, Aaron M., and Riley E. Dunlap. 2011. "The Politicization of Climate Change and Polarization in the American Public's Views of Global Warming, 2001–2010." *Sociological Quarterly* 52 (2): 155–94.

McDermott, Constance L., Kelly Levin, and Benjamin Cashore. 2011. "Building the Forest-Climate Bandwagon: REDD+ and the Logic of Problem Amelioration." *Global Environmental Politics* 11 (3): 85–103.

McEvoy, David M., and John K. Stranlund. 2009. "Self-Enforcing International Environmental Agreements with Costly Monitoring for Compliance." *Environmental and Resource Economics* 42 (4): 491–508.

Meadows, Donella H., Dennis H. Meadows, Jorgen Randers, and William W. Behrens, III. 1972. *The Limits to Growth: A Report to the Club of Rome.* New York: Universe Books.

Mendy, Francisca Reyes. 2010. "Chilean Congressional Politics Under President Lagos: Environment and Politics in Chile 2000–2006." *Local Environment* 15 (2): 83–103.

Meyer, John W., John Boli, George M. Thomas, and Francisco O. Ramirez. 1997. "World Society and the Nation-State." *American Journal of Sociology* 103 (1): 144–81.

Meyer, John W., David John Frank, Ann Hironaka, Evan Schofer, and Nancy Brandon Tuma. 1997. "The Structuring of a World Environmental Regime, 1870–1990." *International Organization* 51 (4): 623–51.

Michaelowa, Axel, and Katharina Michaelowa. 2015. "Do Rapidly Developing Countries Take Up New Responsibilities for Climate Change Mitigation?" *Climatic Change* 133 (3): 499–510.

Michaelowa, Katharina, and Axel Michaelowa. 2012. "India as an Emerging Power in International Climate Negotiations." *Climate Policy* 12 (5): 575–90.

Mildenberger, Matto. 2015. "Fiddling While the World Burns: The Double Representation of Carbon Polluters in Comparative Climate Policymaking." Ph.D. dissertation, Yale University.

Miller, Marian A. 1995. *The Third World in Global Environmental Politics.* Boulder, Colo.: Lynne Rienner.

Mitchell, Ronald B. 1994. "Regime Design Matters: Intentional Oil Pollution and Treaty Compliance." *International Organization* 48 (3): 425–58.

——. 2006. "Problem Structure, Institutional Design, and the Relative Effectiveness of International Environmental Agreements." *Global Environmental Politics* 6 (3): 72–89.

——. 2010. *International Politics and the Environment.* Thousand Oaks, Calif.: Sage.

——. 2016. "International Environmental Agreements Database Project." Version1 2014.3. http://iea.uoregon.edu/.

Mitchell, Ronald B., and Patricia M. Keilbach. 2001. "Situation Structure and Institutional Design: Reciprocity, Coercion, and Exchange." *International Organization* 55 (4): 891–917.

Mol, Arthur P. J., and Neil T. Carter. 2006. "China's Environmental Governance in Transition." *Environmental Politics* 15 (02): 149–70.

Moran, Emilio F. 1993. "Deforestation and Land Use in the Brazilian Amazon." *Human Ecology* 21 (1): 1–21.

Mukherji, Aditi. 2006. "Political Ecology of Groundwater: The Contrasting Case of Water-Abundant West Bengal and the Water-Scarce Gujarat, India." *Hydrogeology Journal* 14 (3): 392–406.

Mwandosya, Mark J. 1999. *Survival Emissions: A Perspective from the South on Global Climate Change Negotiations.* Dar es Salaam: DUP(1996) LTD and CEEST-2000.

Myint, Tun. 2007. "Environmental Governance in the SPDC's Myanmar." In *Myanmar: The State, Community and the Environment,* ed. Monique Skidmore, and Trevor Wilson. Canberra: Asia Pacific Press.

Myllyvirta, Lauri, Xinyi Shen, and Harri Lammi. 2016. "Is China Doubling Down on Its Coal Power Bubble?" Greenpeace East Asia, updated version, February. http://www.greenpeace.org/eastasia/publications/reports/climate-energy/2016/coal-power-bubble-update/.

Nahm, Jonas, and Edward S. Steinfeld. 2014. "Scale-Up Nation: China's Specialization in Innovative Manufacturing." *World Development* 54: 288–300.

Najam, Adil. 2004. "Dynamics of the Southern Collective: Developing Countries in Desertification Negotiations." *Global Environmental Politics* 4 (3): 128–54.

——. 2005. "Developing Countries and Global Environmental Governance: From Contestation to Participation to Engagement." *International Environmental Agreements* 5 (3): 303–21.

Najam, Adil, Saleemul Huq, and Youba Sokona. 2003. "Climate Negotiations Beyond Kyoto: Developing Countries Concerns and Interests." *Climate Policy* 3 (2): 221–31.

Nandi, Paritosh, and Sujay Basu. 2008. "A Review of Energy Conservation Initiatives by the Government of India." *Renewable and Sustainable Energy Reviews* 12 (2): 518–30.

Narain, Sunita. 2016. *Why Should I Be Tolerant: On Environment and Environmmentalism in the 21st Century*. New Delhi: Centre for Science and Environment.

Narayanamoorthy, A. 2010. "India's Groundwater Irrigation Boom: Can It Be Sustained?" *Water Policy* 12 (4): 543–63.

Nash, John F. 1950. "The Bargaining Problem." *Econometrica* 18 (2): 155–62.

Nelson, Michael Byron. 2016. "Africa's Regional Powers and Climate Change Negotiations." *Global Environmental Politics* 16 (2): 110–29.

Nepstad, Daniel, David McGrath, Claudia Stickler, Ane Alencar, Andrea Azevedo, Briana Swette, Tathiana Bezerra, Maria DiGiano, João Shimada, Ronaldo Seroa da Motta, Eric Armijo, Leandro Castello, Paulo Brando, Matt C. Hansen, Max McGrath-Horn, Oswaldo Carvalho, and Laura Hess. 2014. "Slowing Amazon Deforestation Through Public Policy and Interventions in Beef and Soy Supply Chains." *Science* 344 (6188): 1118–23.

Nepstad, Daniel, Britaldo S. Soares-Filho, Frank Merry, André Lima, Paulo Moutinho, John Carter, Maria Bowman, Andrea Cattaneo, Hermann Rodrigues, Stephan Schwartzman, et al. 2009. "The End of Deforestation in the Brazilian Amazon." *Science* 326 (5958): 1350–51.

Newell, Peter. 2005. "Race, Class and the Global Politics of Environmental Inequality." *Global Environmental Politics* 5 (3): 70–94.

NITI-Ayog. 2017. "Draft National Energy Policy for Public Comments." Government of India, New Delhi. http://niti.gov.in/content/draft-national-energy-policy-public-comments.

North, Douglass C. 1990. *Institutions, Institutional Change and Economic Performance*. New York: Cambridge University Press.

Oberthür, Sebastian, and Florian Rabitz. 2014. "On the EU's Performance and Leadership In Global Environmental Governance: The Case of the Nagoya Protocol." *Journal of European Public Policy* 21 (1): 39–57.

Ockwell, David G., Ruediger Haum, Alexandra Mallett, and Jim Watson. 2010. "Intellectual Property Rights and Low Carbon Technology Transfer: Conflicting Discourses of Diffusion and Development." *Global Environmental Change* 20 (4): 729–39.

OECD. 2018. "Climate Finance from Developed to Developing Countries: Public Flows in 2013–17." OECD, Paris.

Olson, Mancur. 1965. *The Logic of Collective Action: Public Goods and the Theory of Groups*. Cambridge, Mass.: Harvard University Press.

——. 1993. "Dictatorship, Democracy, and Development." *American Political Science Review* 87 (3): 567–76.

O'Neill, Kate. 2000. *Waste Trading Among Rich Nations: Building a New Theory of Environmental Regulation*. Cambridge, Mass.: MIT Press.

——. 2009. *The Environment and International Relations*. New York: Cambridge University Press.

Ostrom, Elinor. 1990. *Governing the Commons: The Evolution of Institutions for Collective Action*. New York: Cambridge University Press.

Ostrom, Elinor, Marco A. Janssen, and John M. Anderies. 2007. "Going Beyond Panaceas." *Proceedings of the National Academy of Sciences* 104 (39): 15176–78.

Ovodenko, Alexander. 2016. "Governing Oligopolies: Global Regimes and Market Structure." *Global Environmental Politics* 16 (3): 106–26.

Oye, Kenneth A., and James H. Maxwell. 1994. "Self-Interest and Environmental Management." *Journal of Theoretical Politics* 6 (4): 593–624.

Palchak, David, Jaquelin Cochran, Ranjit Deshmukh, Ali Ehlen, Sushil Kumar Soonee, S. R. Narasimhan, Mohit Joshi, Brendan McBennett, Michael Milligan, Priya Sreedharan, et al. 2017. *Greening the Grid: Pathways to Integrate 175 Gigawatts of Renewable Energy into India's Electric Grid*. Berkeley: NREL.

Pallangyo, Daniel Mirisho. 2007. "Environmental Law in Tanzania: How Far Have We Gone?" *Law, Environment and Development Journal* 3 (1): 26–39.

Pallas, Christopher L., and Johannes Urpelainen. 2012. "NGO Monitoring and the Legitimacy of International Cooperation: A Strategic Analysis." *Review of International Organizations* 7 (1): 1–32.

Parson, Edward A. 2003. *Protecting the Ozone Layer: Science and Strategy*. New York: Oxford University Press.

Pasgaard, M., Z. Sun, D. Müller, and O. Mertz. 2016. "Challenges and Opportunities for REDD+: A Reality Check from Perspectives of Effectiveness, Efficiency and Equity." *Environmental Science and Policy* 63: 161–69.

Peng, Ren, Liu Chang, and Zhang Liwen. 2017. "China's Involvement in Coal-fired Power Projects Along the Belt and Road." Global Environmental Institute, Beijing.

Peng, Wei, Fabian Wagner, M. V. Ramana, Haibo Zhai, Mitchell J. Small, Carole Dalin, Xin Zhang, and Denise L Mauzerall. 2018. "Managing China's Coal Power Plants to Address Multiple Environmental Objectives." *Nature Sustainability* 1 (11): 693.

Peschard, Karine. 2017. "Seed Wars and Farmers' Rights: Comparative Perspectives from Brazil and India." *Journal of Peasant Studies* 44 (1): 144–68.

Pillai, Aditya Valiathan, and Navroz K. Dubash. 2021. "The Limits of Opportunism: The Uneven Emergence of Climate Institutions in India." *Environmental Politics*.

Porter, Gareth. 1999. "Trade Competition and Pollution Standards: 'Race to the Bottom' or 'Stuck at the Bottom.'" *Journal of Environment and Development* 8 (2): 133–51.

Prins, Gwyn, Isabel Galiana, Christopher Green, Reiner Grundmann, Mike Hulme, Atte Korhola, Frank Laird, Ted Nordhaus, Roger A. Pielke, Jr., Steve Rayner, Daniel Sarewitz, Nico Stehr, and Hiroyuki Tezuka. 2010. "The Hartwell Paper: A New Direction for Climate Policy After the Crash of 2009." University of Oxford and London School of Economics and Political Science.

Pritchett, Lant, Michael Woolcock, and Matt Andrews. 2010. "Capability Traps? The Mechanisms of Persistent Implementation Failure." Working paper, Harvard University.

Putnam, Robert D. 1988. "Diplomacy and Domestic Politics: The Logic of Two-Level Games." *International Organization* 44 (3): 427–60.

PWC. 2014. "Oil and Gas in Indonesia." PWC Investment and Taxation Guide, 6th ed. https://www.pwc.com/id/en/publications/assets/oil_and_gas_guide_2014.pdf.

Radelet, Steven. 2011. *Emerging Africa: How 17 Countries Are Leading the Way*. Washington, D.C.: Center for Global Development and Brookings.

Rajan, Mukund Govind. 1997. *Global Environmental Politics: India and the North-South Politics of Global Environmental Issues*. New Delhi: Oxford University Press.

Raustiala, Kal, and David G. Victor. 2004. "The Regime Complex for Plant Genetic Resources." *International Organization* 58 (2): 277–309.

Reeve, Rosalind. 2014. *Policing International Trade in Endangered Species: The CITES Treaty and Compliance*. New York: Routledge.

Reich, Michael R., and B. Bowonder. 1992. "Environmental Policy in India: Strategies for Better Implementation." *Policy Studies Journal* 20 (4): 643–61.

Rhinard, Mark, and Michael Kaeding. 2006. "The International Bargaining Power of the European Union in 'Mixed' Competence Negotiations: The Case of the 2000 Cartagena Protocol on Biosafety." *Journal of Common Market Studies* 44 (5): 1024–50.

Roberts, J. Timmons. 2011. "Multipolarity and the New World (Dis)order: US Hegemonic Decline and the Fragmentation of the Global Climate Regime." *Global Environmental Change* 21 (3): 776–84.

Roberts, J. Timmons, and Bradley C. Parks. 2007. *A Climate of Injustice: Global Inequality, North-South Politics, and Climate Policy*. Cambridge, Mass.: MIT Press.

Roberts, J. Timmons, and Romain Weikmans. 2017. "Postface: Fragmentation, Failing Trust and Enduring Tensions Over What Counts as Climate Finance." *International Environmental Agreements: Politics, Law and Economics* 17 (1): 129–37.

Rocha, Romero, Juliano Assunção, and Clarissa Gandou. 2014. "Amazon Monitoring and Deforestation Slowdown: The Priority Municipalities." Proceedings of the 41th Brazilian Economics Meeting.

Rockström, Johan, Will Steffen, Kevin Noone, Åsa Persson, F. Stuart Chapin, Eric F. Lambin, Timothy M. Lenton, Marten Scheffer, Carl Folke, Hans Joachim Schellnhuber, Björn Nykvist, Cynthia A. de Wit, Terry Hughes, Sander van der Leeuw, Henning Rodhe, Sverker Sörlin, Peter K. Snyder, Robert Costanza, Uno Svedin, Malin Falkenmark, Louise Karlberg, Robert W. Corell, Victoria J. Fabry, James Hansen, Brian Walker, Diana Liverman, Katherine Richardson, Paul Crutzen, and Jonathan A. Foley. 2009. "A Safe Operating Space for Humanity." *Nature* 461: 472–75.

Roger, Charles, and Satishkumar Belliethathan. 2016. "Africa in the Global Climate Change Negotiations." *International Environmental Agreements* 16 (1): 91–108.

Rosencranz, Armin, and Michael Jackson. 2003. "The Delhi Pollution Case: The Supreme Court of India and the Limits of Judicial Power." *Columbia Journal of Environmental Law* 28 (2): 223–54.

Ross, Michael L. 2012. *The Oil Curse: How Petroleum Wealth Shapes the Development of Nations*. Princeton, N.J.: Princeton University Press.

Ross, Rachel Posner. 2015. "Myanmar's Path to Electrification: The Role of Distributed Energy Systems." Center for Strategic and International Studies, Washington, D.C.

Rowland, Wade. 1973. *The Plot to Save the World: the Life and Times of the Stockholm Conference on the Human Environment*. Toronto: Clarke, Irwin.

Sagar, Ambuj D. 2000. "Capacity Development for the Environment: A View for the South, a View for the North." *Annual Review of Energy and the Environment* 25: 377–439.

Sagar, Ambuj D., and Stacy D. VanDeveer. 2005. "Capacity Development for the Environment: Broadening the Scope." *Global Environmental Politics* 5 (3): 14–22.

Saikawa, Eri. 2013. "Policy Diffusion of Emission Standards: Is There a Race to the Top?" *World Politics* 65 (1): 1–33.

Saxonberg, Steven. 2013. *Transitions and Non-Transitions from Communism: Regime Survival In China, Cuba, North Korea, and Vietnam.* New York: Cambridge University Press.

Saylor, Ryan. 2014. *State Building in Boom Times: Commodities and Coalitions in Latin America and Africa.* New York: Oxford University Press.

Schneider, Christina J., and Johannes Urpelainen. 2013. "Distributional Conflict Between Powerful States and International Treaty Ratification." *International Studies Quarterly* 57 (1): 13–27.

Schreurs, Miranda A. 2002. *Environmental Politics in Japan, Germany, and the United States.* New York: Cambridge University Press.

Selin, Henrik. 2010. *Global Governance of Hazardous Chemicals: Challenges of Multilevel Management.* Cambridge, Mass.: MIT Press.

——. 2014. "Global Environmental Law and Treaty-Making on Hazardous Substances: The Minamata Convention and Mercury Abatement." *Global Environmental Politics* 14 (1): 1–19.

Sell, Susan K. 1996. "North-South Environmental Bargaining: Ozone, Climate Change, and Biodiversity." *Global Governance* 2 (1): 97–118.

Shabecoff, Philip. 2003. *A Fierce Green Fire: The American Environmental Movement.* Washington, D.C.: Island Press.

Shah, Alpa. 2010. *In the Shadows of the State: Indigenous Politics, Environmentalism, and Insurgency in Jharkhand, India.* Durham, N.C.: Duke University Press.

Shah, Nihar, Max Wei, Virginie Letschert, and Amol Phadke. 2015. "Benefits of Leapfrogging to Superefficiency and Low Global Warming Potential Refrigerants in Room Air Conditioning." Lawrence Berkeley National Laboratory, LBNL-1003671.

Shah, Tushaar. 2009. *Taming the Anarchy: Groundwater Governance in South Asia.* Washington, D.C.: RFF Press.

Shapiro, Judith. 2001. *Mao's War Against Nature: Politics and the Environment in Revolutionary China.* New York: Cambridge University Press.

Sharma, Anju. 2017. "Precaution and Post-Caution in the Paris Agreement: Adaptation, Loss and Damage and Finance." *Climate Policy* 17 (1): 33–47.

Shearer, Christine, Nicole Ghio, Lauri Myllyvirta, Aiqun Yu, and Ted Nace. 2016. "Boom and Bust 2016: Tracking the Coal Plant Pipeline." Sierra Club, Greenpeace, CoalSwarm.

Shishlov, Igor, Romain Morel, and Valentin Bellassen. 2016. "Compliance of the Parties to the Kyoto Protocol in the First Commitment Period." *Climate Policy* 16 (6): 768–82.

Sims, Holly. 1999. "One-Fifth of the Sky: China's Environmental Stewardship." *World Development* 27 (7): 1227–45.

Sinha, Manisha. 2013. "An Evaluation of the WTO Committee on Trade and Environment." *Journal of World Trade* 47 (6): 1285–1322.

Skjaerseth, Jon Birger. 1992. "The 'Successful' Ozone-Layer Negotiations: Are There Any Lessons to Be Learned?" *Global Environmental Change* 2 (4): 292–300.

Sohn, Louis B. 1973. "The Stockholm Declaration on the Human Environment." *Harvard International Law Journal* 14: 423–515.

Solomon, Susan, Diane J. Ivy, Doug Kinnison, Michael J. Mills, Ryan R. Neely, and Anja Schmidt. 2016. "Emergence of Healing in the Antarctic Ozone Layer." *Science* 353 (6296): 269–74.

Sprinz, Detlef, and Tapani Vaahtoranta. 1994. "The Interest-Based Explanation of International Environmental Policy." *International Organization* 48 (1): 77–105.

Stern, David I. 2004. "The Rise and Fall of the Environmental Kuznets Curve." *World Development* 32 (8): 1419–39.

Stokes, Leah C., Amanda Giang, and Noelle E. Selin. 2016. "Splitting the South: Explaining China and India's Divergence in International Environmental Negotiations." *Global Environmental Politics*.

Streck, Charlotte. 2001. "The Global Environment Facility: A Role Model for International Governance?" *Global Environmental Politics* 1 (2): 71–94.

Streck, Charlotte, and Jolene Lin. 2008. "Making Markets Work: A Review of CDM Performance and the Need for Reform." *European Journal of International Law* 19 (2): 409–42.

Susskind, Lawrence E., and Saleem H. Ali. 2014. *Environmental Diplomacy: Negotiating More Effective Global Agreements.* New York: Oxford University Press.

Tacconi, Luca, Rafael J. Rodrigues, and Ahmad Maryudi. 2019. "Law Enforcement and Deforestation: Lessons for Indonesia from Brazil." *Forest Policy and Economics* 108: 101943.

Takao, Yasuo. 2016. *Japan's Environmental Politics and Governance: From Trading Nation to EcoNation.* New York: Routledge.

Tarannum, Roksana. 2015. "National Experiences in Environmental Governance: Bangladesh Perspective." Presentation, October 2015, Global Training Programme on Environmental Law and Policy, Nairobi, Kenya.

Tian, Huifang, and John Whalley. 2008. "China's Participation in Global Environmental Negotiations." NBER Working Paper 14460.

Tolba, Mostafa K., and Iwona Rummel-Bulska. 1998. *Global Environmental Diplomacy: Negotiating Environmental Agreements for the World, 1973–1992.* Cambridge, Mass.: MIT Press.

Tongia, Rahul. 2015. "The Indian Power Grid: If Renewables are the Answer, what was the Question?" In *Blowing Hard or Shining Bright? Making Renewable Power Sustainable in India,* ed. Rahul Tongia. New Delhi: Brookings India.

Trancik, Jessika E., Michael T. Chang, Christina Karapataki, and Leah C. Stokes. 2013. "Effectiveness of a Segmental Approach to Climate Policy." *Environmental Science and Technology* 48 (1): 27–35.

Urpelainen, Johannes. 2010a. "Enforcement and Capacity Building in International Cooperation." *International Theory* 2 (1): 32–49.

——. 2010b. "Regulation Under Economic Globalization." *International Studies Quarterly* 54 (4): 1099–1121.

——. 2012. "The Strategic Design of Technology Funds for Climate Cooperation: Generating Joint Gains." *Environmental Science and Policy* 15 (1): 92–105.

——. 2013. "A Model of Dynamic Climate Governance: Dream Big, Win Small." *International Environmental Agreements* 13 (2): 107–25.

——. 2014. "Sinking Costs to Increase Participation: Technology Deployment Agreements Enhance Climate Cooperation." *Environmental Economics and Policy Studies* 16 (3): 229–40.

Urpelainen, Johannes, and Thijs Van de Graaf. 2015. "Your Place or Mine? Institutional Capture and the Creation of Overlapping International Institutions." *British Journal of Political Science* 45 (4): 799–827.

Urpelainen, Johannes, and Antto Vihma. 2015. "Soft Cooperation in the Shadow of Distributional Conflict? A Model-Based Assessment of the Two-Level Game Between International Climate Change Negotiations and Domestic Politics." CEEPR WP-201-001, Massachusetts Institute of Technology.

USCC. 2017. *2017 Annual Report*. Washington, D.C.: U.S.-China Economic and Security Review Commission.

Vaishnav, Milan. 2017. *When Crime Pays: Money and Muscle in Indian Politics*. New Haven, Conn.: Yale University Press.

Van Arkadie, Brian, and Raymond Mallon. 2004. "The Introduction of Doi Moi." In *Viet Nam: A Transition Tiger?* Canberra: Asia Pacific Press, Australian National University.

VanDeveer, Stacy D., and Geoffrey D. Dabelko. 2001. "It's Capacity, Stupid: International Assistance and National Implementation." *Global Environmental Politics* 1 (2): 18–29.

Vatikiotis, Michael R. J. 1999. *Indonesian Politics Under Suharto: The Rise and Fall of the New Order*. New York: Routledge.

Victor, David G. 2008. "Climate Accession Deals: New Strategies for Taming Growth of Greenhouse Gases in Developing Countries." Harvard Project on International Climate Agreements Discussion Paper 08–18. December 2008.

——. 2009. "The Politics of Fossil-Fuel Subsidies." Global Subsidies Initiative, October 2009.

——. 2011. *Global Warming Gridlock: Creating More Effective Strategies for Protecting the Planet*. New York: Cambridge University Press.

Victor, David G., Joshua C. House, and Sarah Joy. 2005. "A Madisonian Approach to Climate Policy." *Science* 309: 1820–21.

Vihma, Antto. 2009. "Friendly Neighbor or Trojan Horse? Assessing the Interaction of Soft Law Initiatives and the UN Climate Regime." *International Environmental Agreements* 9 (3): 239–62.

Vihma, Antto. 2011. "India and the Global Climate Governance: Between Principles and Pragmatism." *Journal of Environment and Development* 20 (1): 69–94.

Vijay, Varsha, Stuart L. Pimm, Clinton N. Jenkins, and Sharon J. Smith. 2016. "The Impacts of Oil Palm on Recent Deforestation and Biodiversity Loss." *PloS One* 11 (7): e0159668.

Vogel, David. 1995. *Trading Up: Consumer and Environmental Regulation in a Global Economy*. Cambridge, Mass.: Harvard University Press.

——. 2003. "The Hare and the Tortoise Revisited: The New Politics of Consumer and Environmental Regulation in Europe." *British Journal of Political Science* 33 (4): 557–80.

Wade, Robert. 1985. "The Market for Public Office: Why the Indian State Is Not Better at Development." *World Development* 13 (4): 467–97.

——. 2000. *Governing the Market: Economic Theory and the Role of Government in East Asian Industrialization*. Princeton, N.J.: Princeton University Press.

Walsh, Sean, Huifang Tian, John Whalley, and Manmohan Agarwal. 2011. "China and India's Participation in Global Climate Negotiations." *International Environmental Agreements* 11 (3): 261–73.

Waltz, Kenneth N. 1979. *Theory of International Politics*. New York: McGraw-Hill.

Wara, Michael W., and David G. Victor. 2008. "A Realistic Policy on International Carbon Offsets." Stanford University, Program on Energy and Sustainable Development, Working Paper 74.

WB. 2006. "Nigeria: Rapid Country Environmental Analysis." World Bank, Nigeria Country Team.

———. 2014. *Strategic Assessment of the Ethiopian Mineral Sector*. Washington, D.C.: World Bank.

Weidner, Helmut, and Martin Jänicke, eds. 2002. *Capacity Building in National Environmental Policy: A Comparative Study of 17 Countries*. Berlin: Springer.

Williams, Marc. 2005. "The Third World and Global Environmental Negotiations: Interests, Institutions and Ideas." *Global Environmental Politics* 5 (3): 48–69.

Wolfram, Catherine, Orie Shelef, and Paul Gertler. 2012. "How Will Energy Demand Develop in the Developing World?" *Journal of Economic Perspectives* 26 (1): 119–38.

Woo-Cumings, Meredith, ed. 1999. *The Developmental State*. Ithaca, N.Y.: Cornell University Press.

World Commission on Environment and Development. 1987. *Our Common Future*. Oxford: Oxford University Press.

Yang, Dali L. 2003. "State Capacity on the Rebound." *Journal of Democracy* 14 (1): 43–50.

Young, Oran R. 1999. *The Effectiveness of International Environmental Regimes: Causal Connections and Behavioral Mechanisms*. Cambridge, Mass.: MIT Press.

———. 2002. *The Institutional Dimensions of Environmental Change: Fit, Interplay, and Scale*. Cambridge, Mass.: MIT Press.

Young, Zoe. 2002. *A New Green Order? The World Bank and the Politics of the Global Environment Facility*. London: Pluto Press.

Zhang, Chao, Lijin Zhong, and Jiao Wang. 2018. "Decoupling Between Water Use and Thermoelectric Power Generation Growth in China." *Nature Energy* 3 (9): 792–99.

Zhang, Wen, and Xun Pan. 2016. "Study on the Demand of Climate Finance for Developing Countries Based on Submitted INDC." *Advances in Climate Change Research* 7 (1–2): 99–104.

Zhang, Xuehua. 2017. "Implementation of Pollution Control Targets in China: Has a Centralized Enforcement Approach Worked?" *China Quarterly* 231: 749–74.

INDEX

Abacha, Sani, 214

abatement, 34–35

access and benefit sharing (ABS), 145–46

accession deal, 19, 48

activism, 195–96

adaptation, 97–98, 166, 243, 264

Africa, 2, 80, 104–5

Agarwal, Anil, 189–90

Agenda 21, 64

Agreement Respecting the Regulation of the Flow of Water, 59–60

Aichi Biodiversity Targets, 146

air conditioners, 3

Aklin, Michaël, 34, 39, 76

Aldy, Joseph E., 155

Ali, Saleem H., 96

Anderies, John M., 39

Andrews, Matt, 38

A.S. Bulk Handling, 127

authoritarianism, 183, 222; democracy and, 213; in Ethiopia, 242–45; Gilley proposing, 182; in Indonesia, 218

awareness, 36, 60–61, 62

Bali Action Plan, 158

Bali conference, 93

Bamako Convention, 129

ban, 128–29, 133, 138

Ban Amendment, 128–29, 138

Bangladesh, *106, 112, 209*, 210–11; development in, 234–35; history of, 235; INDC of, 237; India compared with, 234–35; institutional capacity of, 237; Myanmar and, 234–41; policy by, 235–37; population of, 235; poverty in, 234; protection in, 237–38

bargaining, 6; concessions in, 45; by developing countries, 162; by emerging economies, 152; by government, 13; with institutional capacity, 45–46

Barrett, Scott, 26, 78, 279n93

Basel Action Network, 129

Basel Convention, 41, 126–29, 137–38

BASIC. *See* Brazil, South Africa, India, China

Bayer, Patrick, 78, 98, 157

behavior, 11, 53–54, 128

Belliethathan, Satishkumar, 104

Beresford, Melanie, 222–23

Berlin Mandate: cooperation captured in, 58; Copenhagen Accord compared with, 87; in global environmental politics,

CPSIA information can be obtained
at www.ICGtesting.com
Printed in the USA
LVHW022120080622
720829LV00001B/99